PRINCESS ALICE

COUNTESS OF ATHLONE

THEO ARONSON

W0010546

THISTLE
PUBLISHING

This edition published in 2014 by:

Thistle Publishing
36 Great Smith Street
London
SW1P 3BU

www.thistlepublishing.co.uk

ISBN-13: 978-1-910198-13-1

To the memory of my Mother

CONTENTS

ILLUSTRATIONS

Princess Alice and the Earl of Athlone with their children, Lady May Cambridge and Viscount Trematon, in the early 1920s

Their Excellencies with their staff at the Opening of Parliament in Cape Town on 22 January 1926

Princess Alice with the Queen Mother of Swaziland in August 1925

Princess Alice working in her rock-garden at Brantridge Park, Sussex

Princess Alice in a tank during a visit to an armaments factory in wartime Canada

Mrs Roosevelt, Princess Alice and Mrs Churchill during the second Quebec Conference, September 1944

Princess Alice studying an Epstein head at an exhibition of children's portraits in December 1950

Princess Alice and her great-niece, Queen Elizabeth II, at the Windsor Horse Show

The nonagenarian Princess Alice, looking as alert and attractive as ever

AUTHOR'S NOTE

I first met H.R.H. Princess Alice, Countess of Athlone, early in 1974. This book is the result of many conversations with the Princess between that time and her death, almost exactly seven years later, in January 1981. It has been written with the help of Princess Alice's family, of various members of the Royal Family, of secretaries, ladies-in-waiting, aides-de-camp, friends and associates, and of the Royal Archives at Windsor.

My chief debt is to the late Princess Alice herself who, in the course of our many talks, gave me a great deal of the information used in this study. I am indebted, also, to Her Royal Highness's own book of memoirs, *For My Grandchildren*, for some of my source material. Permission to quote from this book has been granted by the Princess's daughter and son-in-law, Lady May and Sir Henry Abel Smith, and by the publishers, Evans Brothers. I have been granted full access to the Princess's scrap books and photograph albums and have been given permission to quote from various of Her Royal Highness's letters.

Lady May and Sir Henry Abel Smith have very kindly read my manuscript, made suggestions, answered all my questions and checked certain facts without, in any way, trying to influence or alter what I have written. All opinions expressed and conclusions drawn are my own. Their co-operation, advice and impartiality have been greatly appreciated.

I must thank Her Majesty Queen Elizabeth II by whose gracious permission certain extracts from the Journal of Princess Alice's grandmother, Queen Victoria, are here published for the first time. These extracts are indicated in the Notes on Sources. John Murray (Publishers) Ltd have allowed me to use quotations from *The Letters of Queen Victoria,* ed. G.E. Buckle, and the University of Toronto passages from *The Mackenzie King Records* by J.W. Pickersgill.

Members of the Royal Family who have very kindly received me in order to give me their impressions and memories of H.R.H. Princess Alice are Her Majesty Queen Elizabeth The Queen Mother; Princess Alice, Duchess of Gloucester, who also allowed me to see certain of her photograph albums; and the Rt Hon. the Earl of Harewood. I am deeply grateful for their help.

I am indebted also to the late Princess Alice's secretary, Miss Mary Goldie; her lady-in-waiting, Miss Joan Lascelles; and Lord Athlone's Secretary during his Canadian term of office, Sir Shuldham Redfern. Others whose assistance has proved especially valuable are the late Sir Kenneth Blackburne, formerly Governor and then Governor-General of Jamaica; Sir Philip Sherlock, one-time Vice-Chancellor of the University of the West Indies; Mr Neville Ussher, aide-de-camp to Lord Athlone in Canada; and Stella, Lady Bailey, of Cape Town, South Africa.

Then I must thank all those many people whose contributions, ranging from the slight to the considerable, have helped me to come to a fuller understanding of Princess Alice's life and work. They are, in alphabetical order, Mr David Arnott, Mr Harold J. Ashwell, Mrs M. Pierneef Bailey of the Marita Pierneef Collection, Cape, Mrs R. Barclay-Ross, Ms Anne Barlow of Canada House, London, Mrs E. Basson, Mrs J. A. Blackmore, Ms Deborah Boles of the Literary Department of the *Observer*, Mr Andre Bothner, Mrs W. Brodby, Mr Gordon Brown, Ms G. W. Brown, Transvaal Regional Secretary of the South African Red Cross Society, Mrs M. Ormond Brown, Mr F.F. Burrow, Mr R. Campbell-Ross, Mr Francis O. Cameron, Rev Canon K. Chaffey, Mrs S. Chaykowsky, Mrs G. Christiansen, Honorary Secretary of the Kensington Society, Mrs Peggy Clin,

Mrs Marcia Dalrymple, Rev G.F. Davies, Dr J. Elwyn
Davies, Mr R. Caradoc Davies, Mr D.C. De Kocks, Mr
Solomon de Souza, Ms Jean Devey of the Archives of
the Girl Guides of Canada, Mrs Emé de Villiers, Mrs
Isobel de Waal, Mrs F. Dickson, Mrs June Digby, Mrs
E.M. Dowling, Director of S.A. National Council for
Child and Family Welfare, Mrs Grace Doyle, Mrs Z.
Droskie, Director of S.A. Council for the Aged, Mr
L.F. Dunnett, Mrs Barbara Evans, Mrs M. Faiman,
Mrs Joyce Foord, Mrs Winifred Forrest, the Hon.
Mrs Margaret Fox, Major Anthony G.D. Gordon,
Mrs Joyce Grant, Mrs Cedryl Greenland, Mr Richard
Guy, Mr Brocas Harris, Mr W.A. Harrison, Principal
of the Claremont Fan Court School, Mrs Agnes
Harvey, Miss Norah Henshil-wood, Mrs V. Heyliger,
Mrs Lilian Hook, Mrs Margery Houghton, Mr Philip
Howard, Mr R.H. Hubbard, Cultural Adviser to the
Governor-General of Canada, Mrs Alma Inskip, Mr
C.E. Jackman, Registrar of the University of the
West Indies, Rev D.W. Jelleyman, Ms Bee Jordaan,
Mr Roy Kay, Mr Richard Kennett, Mr Stephen Kerr,
Mr Keith Killby, Ms Wyn Knowles of B.B.C. Woman's
Hour, Dr Julius H. Kretzmar, Mrs Agnes Lambe,
Mrs Jeannie Lascelles, Mrs Aileen Lee, Mrs Mary
Leeds, Mrs Cecile Lewis, Lady Longford, Mrs Julia
Ludwig, Mrs N. Lundy, Mrs E.A.L. Machanick, Dr L.
Marguerite Mackenzie, Mr and Mrs A. Mackenzie-
Elliot, Mr A.G. Mackie, Mrs Maisee Macnae, the late
Mr Arnold MacNaughton, Mrs A. Maddin, Bishop

William Manning, Miss C. Manthey, Dr Matthew Mellon C.B.E. and Mrs Mellon, Mr E.W. Mew, Miss W. Middlecote, Mrs Mary Miller, Mrs Gwen M. Mills, Mr R.C. Molk, Miss Kathleen Murray, Mr William Nash, Superintendent of Windsor Castle, Mrs Cecile Newberry, Mrs Dorothy L. Norrington, Mr E.J. Page, Dr Marian Parkinson, Mrs S.Y. Parkinson, Corps Commander W.T.S./F.A.N.Y., Miss D. Parsons, Mrs Z. Pearce, Mrs Ann A. Pike, Ms Phyllis Piper, Mrs Anne Raff, Mrs Mary Rapson, Mrs Fanella Richman, Mrs D. Roberts, Mr D.F. Robertson, Mr Kenneth Rose of the *Sunday Telegraph*, Mr Eric Rosenthal, Mrs Stella Ross, Mrs Pam Rothschild, Mrs A.M. Rutherford-Titus, Mrs E. Ryall, Headmistress of St Cyprian's School, Cape Town, Mrs Morar Ryton, Mr C.V. Sandiford, Mr A. Schapera, Mrs L.M. Sellery of the Archives of the Girl Guides of Canada, Mr Gerald Shaw of the *Cape Times*, South Africa, Mr Edwin G. Sinclair, Mrs Malcolm D. Smith, Mrs Dorothy Smuts, Mr H.M. Sparks, Mrs P.R. Standley, Mrs H.M. Starke, Director of the Child Welfare Society, Cape Town, Miss Ailsa Stephens, Mrs Hope Stewart, Mrs D. Stubbs, President of the Victoria League in South Africa, Mr William Tallon, Mrs E. Taylor, Mrs Lynda M. Tennant, Lady Mary Thelwell, Mrs Edna Theron, Mrs May Todd, Mrs Sheila Truscott, Mrs H.D. Tucker, Mr Stanley Uys, Mrs Kate Van Rensburg, Mrs M.C. Varty of the Londolozi Game Reserve, South Africa, Mr Hugo Vickers, Mrs Jean

Watkins, Mr R.I.B. Webster, Mr R.F.R. Wells, Ms Liz Westby-Nunn, Mrs Cynthia Wintringham White, Mrs Alpheus Gardner Williams, Dr W.W. Wilson, Senior Medical Officer of St Ann's Bay Hospital, Jamaica, Mr S.G. Wolhuter, Mrs Emily Wood, Miss Helen Woods, Mrs Kathleen York.

I am indebted also to Mr Clinton V. Black, the Government Archivist, Jamaica Archives; Miss Edith G. Firth of the Metropolitan Toronto Library; Mr K. E. Ingram, Librarian of the University of the West Indies; Miss L. Kennedy, City Librarian, Johannesburg Public Library; Ms Marie Lanouette, National Library of Canada; Mr Donald G. Mutch, Ottawa Public Library; Mr Gordon Phillips, Archivist and Researcher, London *Times;* Mr Koos Quinton, Chief Librarian, Parliamentary Library, Cape Town; Mr P.J. van der Walt, City Librarian, Bloemfontein Public Library; Mrs R. Wasserfall, State Archives, Pretoria. I am grateful to the staffs of the British Library, the Newspaper Library at Colindale, the library of the *Argus* newspaper, Cape Town; the Bath Reference Library, the Bristol Reference Library; and I should like to give a special word of thanks to Mrs S. Bane and the staff of Frome Library for their always efficient service.

I am grateful to my editor at Cassell, Miss Anne Carter, for her help and understanding; and above all, to Mr Brian Roberts, whose encouragement, help and expert advice have made the writing of this book possible.

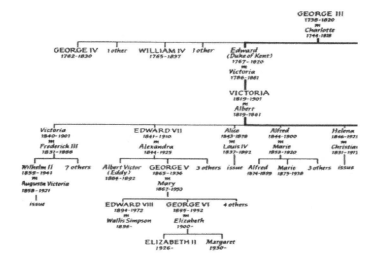

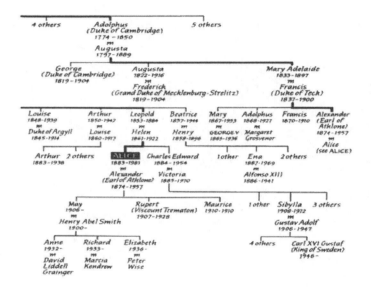

PART ONE
CLAREMONT HOUSE

CHAPTER ONE

1

'I can scarcely believe,' wrote Queen Victoria in her Journal one day in March 1883, 'that dear Leopold has got a child.'[1]

The Queen's incredulity is understandable. Her fourth son, Prince Leopold, Duke of Albany, had always been thought of as too 'delicate' to lead a normal life. That he had managed, not only to reach manhood but to achieve matrimony, had been surprising enough; that he had actually fathered a child seemed little short of miraculous.

But there it was. At half past six in the evening of Sunday 25 February 1883, the young Duchess of Albany gave birth to a daughter at Windsor Castle. Present at the bedside were three doctors, a bevy of nurses and the baby's two grandmothers – Queen Victoria and the Princess of Waldeck-Pyrmont.

From the very first moment, apparently, the infant Princess proved herself to be 'lively and cheerful'.[2] This, at least, was the impression gained by Sir

3

William Harcourt, the elephantine Home Secretary, who had been stationed in an adjoining room in order, as the Princess herself was later to put it, 'to make sure that I wasn't a fake.* In a subsequent letter to Prince Leopold, Sir William Harcourt expressed the gallant hope that the newly-born Princess would remain as lively and cheerful throughout her life. In this, Sir William's hope was to be fulfilled.

If, in the days ahead, the baby's cheerfulness was echoed by her immediate family, her liveliness was not. Her mother, understandably, was still confined to bed. But so, less expectedly, was her father. Poor Prince Leopold was going through one of his all-too-frequent bad patches. He was laid up with a sore knee. So, too, was his mother, Queen Victoria. A few days after the baby's birth, the Queen slipped on a step and sprained a leg. As a result, she could move only with difficulty.

Always more ready to see the funny side of things than most people imagined, Queen Victoria – on being wheeled in for yet another glimpse of her latest grandchild – was considerably amused at the spectacle of this mass invalidism. 'He was lying on the sofa, she on another and when I came in as a third helpless creature, it had quite a ludicrous effect,'⁴ she noted.

But for the small, mewling creature in the lacy bassinette, Queen Victoria had nothing but praise.

---

* The tradition of having the Home Secretary on hand to witness and verify every royal birth was only abolished in 1948 by King George VI before the birth of his first grandchild. Prince Charles

The baby might have been her twenty-seventh living grandchild, but the Queen's interest in her remained intense. 'Uncle Leopold's baby,' she announced to yet another of her many granddaughters, 'is a *beautiful* Child.'[5]

From Queen Victoria, this was high praise. In the ordinary way she was not very fond of babies and, if she thought them ugly, never hesitated to say so. She had once described the infant Prince Leopold as 'no beauty'[6] and on another occasion, when she was looking after some of her grandchildren while their mother was on holiday, she sent a telegram, *en clair,* to say, 'Children very well but poor little Louise very ugly.'[7]

The little Princess was christened on Easter Monday, 26 March 1883, in the Private Chapel at Windsor. Here again, an aura of invalidism was only too apparent. The Queen was in a wheelchair; Prince Leopold was on crutches. 'A sort of inclined plane had been arranged over the four steps into the Chapel and up these,' noted the Queen, 'I was rolled . . . I sat in my usual place near the altar, the Clergy and Sponsors coming in after me. Bertie[*] and Princess Waldeck stood next to me, the other Sponsors being represented. Two Hymns were sung. Mrs Brotherston, the monthly nurse, carried the Baby, and Mrs Moreton[†] handed it to me. Though

---

[*] Queen Victoria's eldest son, Albert Edward, Prince of Wales, afterwards King Edward VII (1841–1910).
[†] Jane Moreton, lady-in-waiting to the Duchess of Albany

I could not stand, I managed to hand the dear little Baby to the Archbishop, who named her: Alice, Mary, Victoria, Augusta, Pauline.'[8]

'Poor little mite!' sighed the watching Lady Knightly of Fawsley; one could only hope that God would bless the baby and make her 'grow up happy'.[9]

But there was really very little ground for Lady Knightly's apprehensions. The baby, after all, had been born into the grandest, most powerful, most firmly established royal family in the world. Among her sponsors were the Queen of England, the Prince of Wales, the German Empress, the German Crown Princess, the King of the Netherlands and the Grand Duke of Hesse. She was christened by no less a cleric than the Archbishop of Canterbury, Dr Edward Benson, and baptised with water from the River Jordan. That string of names, announced by the Queen in her 'usual clear, distinct'[10] voice, was rich in dynastic associations. Together, they had all the resonance of a royal fanfare.

In fact, far from being the poor little mite of Lady Knightly's imaginings, Princess Alice was a sturdy and spirited infant, on the threshold of a long, crowded and colourful life.

2

By the time of Princess Alice's birth, her father, Prince Leopold, had at last found a certain measure of contentment in life. Until then, or at least until his marriage the year before, his career had been a sadly frustrated one. It had been characterised, as Queen Victoria put it, by 'a restless longing for what he could not have'.[11]

The youngest of the Queen's sons, Prince Leopold was far and away the most interesting. When set against his bluff, extrovert, somewhat philistine brothers – the Prince of Wales, Prince Alfred and Prince Arthur – he was very much the odd-man-out. He even looked different. Slim and slight, with soulful eyes, a waxed moustache and a wispy imperial beard, Prince Leopold had a romantic, almost Byronic air. Except on his wedding day, he was never seen in uniform. To the public he was known as the Scholar Prince.

In some ways, Prince Leopold was not unlike his father, the late Prince Consort. The Queen, who was always on the look-out for even the palest reflection of the father's glory in the sons, at one stage declared that 'little Leo' had indeed inherited his father's brains. In this, perhaps, she was being too optimistic but Prince Leopold was certainly no fool. In an age when princes were usually little more than tailors' dummies, their lives given over to soldiering, shooting and high living, Prince Leopold was an intelligent, enquiring and conscientious young man, fond of the arts and keenly interested in politics. All in all, he came closest to the Prince Consort's dream of the perfect nineteenth-century prince: intellectual, enlightened, diligent.

7

In one respect, though, Prince Leopold fell sadly short of this ideal. He suffered from what was referred to, with deliberate vagueness, as 'very delicate' health.

Prince Leopold's delicateness had been apparent from the beginning. In the weeks following his birth, on 7 April 1853, he showed himself to be weaker than the Queen's other children had been. The birth itself had proved an exceptionally easy one for the mother. For the first time during an *accouchement.* Queen Victoria had been given chloroform. The result, as far as she was concerned, could hardly have been happier. The doctor, she noted ecstatically, 'gave that blessed Chloroform and the effect was soothing, quieting and delightful beyond measure'.[12]

At first the Queen was as happy with the baby as she was with the manner of its birth. He was 'a jolly fat little fellow'[13] she reported to her uncle, King Leopold of the Belgians. She had, in fact, named the infant after her 'dearest Uncle'. His full names were Leopold George Duncan Albert: George after the King of Hanover, Duncan 'as a compliment to dear Scotland'[14] and Albert, of course, after her adored husband.

But before long the baby had changed from that jolly fat little fellow into a thin and ailing one. Prince Leopold seemed fragile, he bruised easily, he bled profusely. 'Your poor little namesake is again laid up with a bad knee from a fall which appeared to be of no consequence . . .' wrote the Queen of her six-year-old son to King Leopold. 'This unfortunate defect has nothing to do with his general health . . . and no remedy or medicine does it any good.'[15]

For by now the puzzled parents had come to the realisation that their youngest son suffered from the dreaded bleeding disease: Prince Leopold was a haemophiliac.

Haemophilia is a strange and frightening disease. The blood of a haemophiliac lacks the qualities necessary to cause it to coagulate and so stop the flow: blood clotting takes place either slowly or not at all. Any wound suffered by a haemophiliac can be fatal. Even an apparently harmless bump, causing internal haemorrhage, often leads to death. This internal bleeding is sometimes accompanied by the most excruciating pain.

A peculiarity of the disease – medically termed 'sex-linked recessive inheritance' – is that it occurs exclusively in males. Men sufferers can pass it on to their children but it is more usually carried by females. However, every male in a family will not automatically suffer from it; nor will every female be a carrier. Not until a woman has had children will it be known whether or not she is a transmitter; not until a son first bleeds will it be known whether or not he has haemophilia.

Queen Victoria's anguish and bewilderment at the appearance of this mysterious disease in one of her sons is understandable. She could only protest that it did not come from her side – the Hanoverian side – of the family. But then there is no proof that it came from her husband's, Prince Albert's, side. No evidence of haemophilia existed in the Saxe-Coburg family before the marriage of Queen Victoria to Prince Albert. So perhaps, it did, after all, come from the Queen's side. There is a theory that the disease originated in Queen Victoria's father, the Duke of Kent, by way of a spontaneous mutation in his genes. The Queen, then, was a carrier. Through her, the disease was transmitted to her son Prince Leopold and to two of her daughters, Princess Alice and Princess Beatrice. They, in turn, transmitted it to their children and so carried it into the royal houses of Europe.

Of Queen Victoria's children, grandchildren and great-grandchildren, sixteen were definitely to be sufferers from, or transmitters of, the disease. Another twenty princesses might well have been carriers. As haemophilia spread, in time, through the royal families of Britain, Germany, Russia and Spain, so did it come to be known as 'the royal disease'. But it was in Prince Leopold that it first manifested itself.

Not unnaturally, Prince Leopold's entire life was coloured by this crippling affliction. With every cut or bump or nosebleed liable to prove fatal, he was kept under constant surveillance. Because of what Queen Victoria described as 'that sad propensity to bleeding', she could hardly bear to have him out of her sight; 'at least,' she wrote, 'no place which could not be reached within twenty-four hours.'[16] The result was that she became increasingly protective. The death of the Prince Consort in 1861, when

Prince Leopold was eight, considerably intensified this protectiveness. In her desolation, the Queen clung more and more desperately to her two youngest children – Prince Leopold and Princess Beatrice. She was determined that they, at least, should stay by her side for as long as possible.

Inevitably, Prince Leopold began to resent all this cosseting. As he grew up, so did he long to lead a more normal, active life. He realised, of course, that he could not indulge in those 'ordinary manly exercises' nor enter a branch of the armed services, but there must surely be some outlet for his naturally high spirits and his more than average intelligence? Even his tranquilly conducted education, at the hands of his private tutor, Canon Duckworth, was interrupted by long spells in bed.

'Our poor Leopold is just the same,' wrote Queen Victoria to her eldest daughter, the German Princess,* 'and as he dares not be moved till some days after the bleeding has entirely ceased, we may be kept here longer than next week. . . . It is a terrible anxiety for me and for all who take care of him.'[17]

And the more anxious, the more possessive she became. 'The Queen's attitude towards him,' according to her private secretary, Henry Ponsonby, 'was one of apparent solicitude in his constant ever-recurring illnesses, combined with thwarting and interfering with him when he was well.'[18]

---

* Princess Victoria (Vicky) afterwards Empress Frederick (1840–1901).

11

A spell at Christ Church, Oxford, sharpened Prince Leopold's natural appetite for study and increased his yearning to lead a more useful life. Quite clearly, he was more than just another spoilt princeling, idling away his university days. Encouraged by his tutor, the devoted and intelligent Robert Collins, Prince Leopold applied himself to his studies, cultivated a circle of interesting and intellectual friends, developed his literary and artistic tastes and immersed himself in the various social questions of the day. Always allowing for the sycophancy which colours the opinions of even the most incorruptible of men when writing of princes, Prince Leopold emerges from the letters of his contemporaries as a well-meaning, articulate and cultivated young man; a carbon-copy, even if a pale one, of his father the Prince Consort.

To return from the relative emancipation of his days at Oxford to the tedium, formality and predictability of his mother's way of life was not easy. Prince Leopold wanted to be treated as an independent adult; Queen Victoria wanted to treat him as a helpless child. And when she felt that her instructions were carrying no weight with her son, she would get others to issue them. Her private secretary, Henry Ponsonby, was always acutely embarrassed by having to acquaint the Prince with his mother's invariably dictatorial wishes.

'It is awkward talking to Leopold in the sense the Queen wishes as I do not in the least agree with her,'

Ponsonby once complained to his wife. 'She has laid down absolute rules for what he is to do, coming such a day and going such a day – never to dine out or to go to a club – to come to Osborne in July and leave it the day the Regatta begins, and all in that strain. I cannot support such a system and for one thing know it is useless to try it on. Will the Queen never find out that she will have ten times more influence on her children by treating them with kindness and not trying to rule them like a despot?'[19]

On the other hand, her possessiveness and exaggerated concern were understandable. Hardly three months went by without Prince Leopold suffering a severe attack of bleeding, often brought on by his own determination to lead as normal a life as anyone else.

'Leopold is of course quite laid up but free from pain and fever now,' wrote the exasperated Queen to her eldest daughter in December 1876 when Prince Leopold was twenty-three. 'His wilful neglect of the advice of all near him really prevents one pitying him, for if he could only be just a little prudent he might have so agreeable a life and one of use to others, but he throws all away and the result is this severe attack which he has now got and will, I am sure, weaken that leg which has had already five previous attacks within the year!'[20]

The Queen's exasperation boiled over some eighteen months later when Prince Leopold, bored to death with his mother's routine and particularly with those long, chilly, cheerless stays in Scotland, had the temerity to tell her of his 'intense aversion' to Balmoral. The Queen could hardly believe her ears. Dashing off letter after letter to her other children, she railed against that 'wayward, undutiful Leopold' and that 'strong-willed and wrong-headed boy'.[21] They were all, she instructed, to write to Prince Leopold, pointing out the base ingratitude of his ways.

But such storms blew over. At heart, the Queen was devoted to Prince Leopold. Although her third son, Prince Arthur, was her favourite, she was known to refer to Prince Leopold as 'the dearest of her dear sons'.[22] She appreciated Prince Leopold's particular qualities and even, in more reflective moments, sympathised with his predicament. And on every hand she heard him praised: for his intelligence, for his diligence and above all, for his prowess as a public speaker.

Gladstone, writing to Gerald Wellesley, Dean of Windsor, once pronounced as 'excellent' a speech made by the Prince on university education extension. The word 'excellent', wrote Gladstone in his ponderous fashion, 'will bear development. It applied to manner, voice, articulation, matter – keeping close to the subject, it was full of mind and it was difficult for anyone acquainted with the speeches of the Prince Consort not to recognise the father in the son.'[23]

And the Marquess of Lorne, writing to his wife, Prince Leopold's sister Princess Louise, congratulated

14

her on her brother's speeches. 'They have been very remarkable indeed – a quality about them which unmistakably reminds one of your Father's thoughtfulness and power of expression. They have attracted great notice and deservedly. I always knew that he was studious and reflective but I had no idea he had such powers as these speeches indicate and it is an immense satisfaction that when he is prevented by his health from doing so much that other young men do, he should have such resources in himself-and such fields of usefulness before him as these cannot fail to open up.'[24]

But what exactly were these fields of usefulness to be? And who was to open them up? Someone of consummate tact would be needed to talk the Queen into giving her son some more meaningful employment. And to talk Prince Leopold into accepting it. During the second half of the 1870s, when the Prince was in his mid-twenties, just such a person appeared on the scene. For six years, from February 1874 until 1880, Benjamin Disraeli was Prime Minister, and it took this pourer, *par excellence,* of oil on troubled royal waters, to bring some sense of purpose into Prince Leopold's frustrated life.

3

Over three-quarters of a century after the death of Prince Leopold, his only daughter, Princess Alice, came across a large, leather-bound book securely fastened by 'a strong brass clasp with an intricate lock'. Unable to find a key or to have the lock picked, she was forced to break the metal clasp from one of the covers. Inside was a treasure trove of letters, carefully pasted onto the pages of the book. These were letters from an extraordinary variety of people, ranging from statesmen, through cabinet ministers, professional men, writers, artists, musicians and casual university acquaintances to complete strangers. As such, reckoned his daughter rightly, the letters were of 'unique historical significance'.[25] And perhaps the most significant letter of all, as far as Prince Leopold's own career was concerned, was one from Disraeli.

Writing from his cluttered study at Hughenden Manor, on one of those hot summer days that he loved, Disraeli made an important proposal to Prince Leopold. The letter is dated 25 August 1876.

Sir and dear Prince,

I have not unfrequently recurred to the subject of our conversation at Osborne when you regretted your want of occupation: not having a profession like your royal brothers.

I think it is to be regretted that a young Prince, of your undoubted ability, and not inconsiderable acquirement, should be so circumstanced, and I should be happy, if any suggestion of mine might assist you in this particular.

The Prime Minister then went on to suggest that Prince Leopold assume the cloak, or one of the cloaks, that his illustrious father, the Prince Consort, had once worn: that he become Queen Victoria's assistant and adviser in her dealings with foreign affairs. He could read official despatches, correspondence with ambassadors and ministers, and letters to and from the Queen's fellow sovereigns. He could make *précis,* draw up memoranda and, in time, find himself in a position to wield considerable influence.

In this manner [continued Disraeli] you would, in due course, obtain such a knowledge and command of affairs, as to find great interest and excitement in life, and critical occasions might even occur, when your talents and acquirements might be appealed to for the public service of the nation.[26]

Prince Leopold's reaction to this mellifluously phrased proposal must have been mixed. What he was after was a cutting of his mother's apron-strings, not a strengthening of them. Working so closely with his masterful parent could only increase his feelings of subordination and frustration. On the other hand, Prince Leopold would have felt flattered by the fact that both his mother (with whom the Prime Minister would have discussed the plan beforehand) and Disraeli himself considered him capable of handling the job. And with his haemophilia denying him any more active and responsible position (he would dearly have loved some colonial governor-general-ship) Prince Leopold felt obliged to agree to the scheme.

For the following three or four years then, Prince Leopold attempted to fill – as far as he was allowed to – the late Prince Consort's shoes, becoming part personal assistant, part confidential secretary, part adviser and part go-between to Queen Victoria. Just how valuable he proved himself to be is difficult to say. Ministers, and particularly the Prime Minister, Disraeli, were careful to consult him, to include him and to make use of his services. And the Queen seemed well enough pleased.

'Prince Leopold has been working very steadily,' she reported to Henry Ponsonby one day in February 1877. 'The Queen will send boxes down and General Ponsonby will select what is of interest for Leopold to read and make abstracts of. He is getting much quicker at it.'[27]

But Ponsonby was not entirely happy with the arrangement. Although admitting that Prince Leopold took an intelligent interest in foreign affairs, he complained that he 'had no powers of concentration or of mastering any subject'.[28] He also thought that Prince Leopold interfered too much; he considered his political advice to be 'mischievous'. Once, when complaining about the fact that his mother had still not created him a Royal Duke, Prince Leopold threatened to stand for Parliament.

'In which interest?' asked his equerry. 'Extreme Radical,' answered Prince Leopold.[29]

But the Prince's advice to the Queen – and this was Ponsonby's complaint – was far from being Extreme Radical: it was Extreme Conservative. Instead of encouraging the Queen to tread an impartial, strictly constitutional path (as the Prince Consort would have done) Prince Leopold backed her up in her growing conservatism; or rather, in her conviction that the shining liberal mantle of the Prince Consort's day had now fallen squarely on the shoulders of the Conservatives. He even sanctioned her in her occasional blatantly unconstitutional behaviour, such as allowing himself to be used as a go-between when she continued, secretly, to consult Disraeli long after Gladstone had replaced him as Prime Minister. Any letters sent through Prince Leopold, the Queen assured Disraeli, would be 'QUITE SAFE'.

It was no wonder that Disraeli could describe Prince Leopold as 'a Prince in whose career I ever feel an interest and whose intelligence I have from the first recognised'.[30]

But it was not, by any means, all work and no play for Prince Leopold. Although he did very little of what Queen Victoria called 'running up to London' (by which she meant emulating his worldly brother, the Prince of Wales) he led as active a social life as his health, and his mother, would allow. His circle was Bohemian rather than smart; women found him 'gay and amusing'. 'With us girls . . .' testified one of them, 'the Prince was ever the best of company.'[31*]

Passionately interested in music, he sang, he composed, attended concerts and the opera, and was friendly with people like Gounod and Sullivan. Often he would pay unannounced calls on Gustave Doré at his studio. ('Je regrette infiniment,' wrote Dore on one occasion, 'de ne pas avoir eu le bonheur de vous rencontrer cette seconde fois . . . à mon atelier . . .')[32] Sarah Bernhardt once painted a picture for him and he kept a photograph of her – in daring satin trousers – actually busy at the easel. He counted Ruskin and Lewis Carroll among his friends. The irrepressible Ouida once sent him one of her novels. And there is an apocryphal story that on one occasion an outraged Queen Victoria clambered up onto a chair to take down the portrait of Lillie Langtry which Prince Leopold had hanging above his bed.

When he felt up to it, he travelled. The Prince visited France, he visited Germany, he visited Italy. In 1880, when he was twenty-seven, he travelled to Canada (where his brother-in-law, the Marquess of Lorne, was Governor-General) and the United States. When he arrived with his sister, Princess Louise, in New York, one newspaper welcomed these two children of Queen Victoria under the banner headline: VIC'S CHICKS. It happened that Prince Leopold owned a terrier bitch

---

* There is a story that, at Oxford, Prince Leopold had been in love with Alice Liddell, daughter of Dean Liddell, the Vice-Chancellor of Christ Church, and one of Lewis Carroll's little girl friends

named Vic, so that when the Queen saw the article, she quite misunderstood the headline.

'How odd of them,' she observed, 'to mention your dog.'[33]

It was while Prince Leopold was in Chicago that his appearance was tellingly observed by some local reporter. 'He is a young man, seven-and-twenty years of age, rather small in stature, not more than five feet six inches in height, very slender, and animated in his movements, with a slight stoop forward when he walks. He looks eminently like an Englishman, and bears the marks of gentility in his face and manners. His eye is blue, his moustache diminutive and blond, and his features are little like those of the rest of his family, his nose being slightly aquiline, and his mouth small. . . . Prince Leopold is as far removed as possible from what is known as the English cad or snob. He is not even a swell. He has nothing about his dress whatever of the loud style which young England affects. H.R.H certainly employs a good tailor, for the fit of his garments was perfect.'[34]

It was with considerable unease that Queen Victoria followed the course of Prince Leopold's travels; or what she considered to be manifestations of his 'restlessness'. Every now and then she would put her foot down. Once, when it was tentatively suggested that Prince Leopold visit Australia to open an exhibition, the Queen would not hear of it.

'The Queen wishes to say . . .' she wrote to Disraeli, 'that she *cannot* consent to send Leopold to Australia . . . she cannot bring herself to consent to send her very delicate son, who has been *four or five times at death's door,* who is *never* hardly a *few* months without being laid up, to a great *distance,* to a climate to which he is a stranger, and to expose him to dangers which he may not be able to avert. . . . So she must ask Lord Beaconsfield to look *elsewhere* for someone to represent her at this great Exhibition in Australia.'[35]

It was exactly this sort of dashed hope, this yearning for the impossible, that brought home to Prince Leopold the futility of his life. On one occasion, during a discussion with a group of friends on the attainment of the ideal life, one of them suggested that the Prince himself, who enjoyed the pleasures and privileges of royalty without the responsibility of kingship, probably led as satisfying a life as could be hoped for. Prince Leopold turned those limpid melancholy eyes on the speaker. 'You forget,' he said, 'I am worst off of all. I want the chief thing. It is health – health – health.'[38]

There was only one way, reckoned Queen Victoria, to bring some peace to her son's unquiet soul: he must get married. With characteristic thoroughness, she decided to do something about it.

4

The celebrated Frances (Daisy) Countess of Warwick, the aristocratic heiress who was afterwards converted to Socialism, always claimed that she was Queen Victoria's first choice of a bride for Prince Leopold.

It was Disraeli, she says, who suggested to the Queen that she – the seventeen-year-old Daisy Maynard, owner of Easton Lodge and worth £30,000 a year – would make an eminently suitable wife for the Queen's youngest son. To Windsor, then, with her mother and her step-father, Lord Rosslyn, the lovely young Daisy Maynard was summoned. They were to 'dine and sleep'.

Lady Warwick, as she afterwards became, had a sharp eye and she has left a vivid account of that evening at Windsor Castle.

Before dinner, which was to be at eight-thirty, we all assembled in a draughty corridor – it was long before the days of central heating – and there waited for three-quarters of an hour talking in low voices. Suddenly the doors were thrown open, and a very little old lady ran in, bowed with grace right and left to the whole company, while we stood at attention, and then sped into the dining-room with Princess Beatrice hurrying after her. When we took our places, the Queen as usual had Princess Beatrice on her right. Lord Beaconsfield sat next to the Princess, and my step-father sat at the Queen's left. We were a small and intimate party, and I seemed to feel the Queen's eyes on me all the time. She whispered a great deal to Princess Beatrice, and talked much in a low and pretty voice to

Lord Rosslyn, who amused her immensely. My stepfather, indeed, talked as usual, and kept both the royal ladies laughing, but the rest of us spoke in undertones and did not dare to laugh. . . .

Dinner was served in hot haste. In half an hour, the Queen got up as abruptly as she had arrived, and seemed to run from the room, so rapid was her walk, followed as before by Princess Beatrice. Now we streamed into the corridor in her wake, and the Queen went from one to another, talking intimately to each in turn. . . . Suddenly the Queen came over to talk to me. How did I like the idea of coming out? Was I fond of music or of drawing? Each interrogation was softened by gleams of her rare smile. I was agonisingly shy and over-awed in the presence of this mysterious Queen who lived alone and secluded at Windsor and never came to London. But self-consciousness was my usual state of mind in those early days. I had no idea of how good-looking I was, and I certainly believed that I was anything but clever. Perhaps the worst agony of mind I used to suffer was when I felt that a man was going to propose to me and I wanted to put him off.[37]

Well, Daisy Maynard was spared any such agony of mind on this occasion. Prince Leopold did not

24

propose. He had already, she says, 'lost his heart to someone else, whom he took great care not to name', while she had lost hers to his equerry, Lord Brooke. So, instead of asking Daisy to marry him, Prince Leopold arranged for her to marry Lord Brooke, afterwards fifth Earl of Warwick. 'Under a large umbrella, on the muddy road between Claremont and Esher,' writes Lady Warwick, '[Lord Brooke] proposed to me, and I accepted.'[38]

If Lady Warwick had not been able to win the heart of one of Queen Victoria's sons, she would one day win the heart of another. In the years ahead she was to become the mistress of the Prince of Wales: his 'Darling Daisy', his 'little Daisy wife'. What Queen Victoria had to say about that, one does not know.

With that particular plan having fallen through (and perhaps there was never as much to it as Lady Warwick claimed) another had to be thought up. Although the Queen was anxious enough for Prince Leopold to find a wife, she was never one for forcing a marriage. She had no sympathy whatsoever with the way in which her eldest daughter, the German Crown Princess, would pick a bride or groom from the pages of the *Almanach de Gotha* and open negotiations before the young couple had so much as laid eyes on one another.

'Moretta has expressed a strong wish *not* to marry now,' she once wrote to the Crown Princess about her daughter Princess Victoria, known in the family as Moretta, 'and I own – I think you should let it alone for the present. Let her *see* people–*but pray don't* force it on, for *if* she has no inclination, if she don't like anyone, it would *never* do . . . *don't force* or *press* her to marry for *marrying's sake,* that is dreadful.'[39]

But if the Queen was against forced marriages, she was equally against sitting back and doing nothing. Very circuitously, she made approaches towards two or three likely candidates. The offers were refused. Not every girl was prepared to take on a haemophilic husband. The Queen found these refusals 'very painful'.[40] But painful or not, the course had to be pursued.

Then, in the autumn of 1880, when Prince Leopold was twenty-seven, the Queen had another idea. 'It suddenly struck me,' she wrote to the Crown Princess, that Prince Leopold should 'go and look at Princess Helen of Waldeck'.[41]

Prince Leopold crossed to Germany to look and, liking what he saw, indicated to his mother that if the Princess in question would have him, he was prepared to marry her.

With the negotiations for Princess Helen's hand under way, the Queen agreed to the long-delayed bestowal of a dukedom on her son. Once again, and with a blithe disregard for accepted constitutional practice, the Queen ignored her new Prime Minister, Gladstone, and consulted her old Prime Minister, Disraeli, on the subject. She would agree to Prince Leopold being granted a peerage (and with it, of course, the right to take his seat in the House of Lords) only on condition that he promised not to use his new status as an excuse for running up to London. Disraeli advised her against pressing for any such undertaking. He would hold himself responsible, he said, for Prince Leopold's behaviour.

The matter happily settled between the Queen, the Prince and the ex-Prime Minister, the correct constitutional procedure was once more adopted. The Queen's private secretary wrote to Gladstone for his acceptance of the Queen's wish to grant a peerage on her son. On 24 May 1881, Prince Leopold was raised to the peerage under the style of Baron Arklow, Earl of Clarence, and Duke of Albany. But the Queen still had one proviso. Her son would continue to be called Prince Leopold under her roof: 'I always say,' she explained robustly, 'that not everyone can be a Prince, but anyone can be a duke.'[42]

It was as the Duke of Albany, then, that Prince Leopold once more crossed the Channel late that autumn to take yet another look at Princess Helen of Waldeck. Previously they had met at a little spa near Darmstadt, seat of Prince Leopold's brother-in-law, the Grand-Duke of Hesse.* This time the couple met at Frankfurt. On 18 November 1881 Prince Leopold asked Princess Helen to marry him.

'Very shortly after ten,' noted Queen Victoria in her Journal that evening, 'received a telegram in cypher from Leopold saying: "I have proposed to

* Ludwig IV, Grand Duke of Hesse and by the Rhine (1837–92), husband of Queen Victoria's daughter. Princess Alice (1843–78).

27

Princess Helen of Waldeck, and been accepted. May I receive your consent to the engagement?" This was hardly a surprise to me, as since last autumn, when he had met the young lady, I knew he had taken a liking to her, and now they had met again at Frankfurt. But the news rather upset me, and I can't help feeling as if I were losing dear Leopold, but as Hélène Waldeck is said to be so good and nice, it may be a blessing to us all.'[43]

5

'She is rather,' wrote *The Graphic* of Princess Helen of Waldeck-Pyrmont, 'like a Princess out of a fairy-tale who has hitherto lived in a simple and patriarchal style at the tiny capital of her father's tiny Principality, the total population of which is about that of one of the sub-divisions of a tiny London parish.'[44]

The picture, up to a point, was accurate. Waldeck was a small, pretty, hilly, pine-forested principality lying at the very heart of the western half of the German Empire. Surrounded entirely by Prussia, it still enjoyed the limited independence of most of that galaxy of German states which had been unified to form the Second German Reich in 1871. Ruling – if in a somewhat emasculated fashion – over this little domain was His Serene Highness Prince George Victor of Waldeck-Pyrmont. His principal home was at Arolsen, a grandiose, formally planned, impressively pillared and pedimented *Schloss* set on a plateau with sweeping views across the undulating countryside to a line of distant blue mountains. Beyond the palace walls clustered the little town of Arolsen; the nearest railway station was eighteen miles away.

It was at Arolsen, or sometimes at his more modest home at Pyrmont (although its bridge, with its parapet-crowned statues, gave Pyrmont a certain elegance), that Prince George held what Carlyle affectionately called his 'pumpernickel court'.[45] With his luxuriant beard and his cat's-whisker moustaches, the Prince of Waldeck-Pyrmont was a distinguished-looking man, but it was his wife, born Princess Hélène of Nassau,* who was the more forceful personality. Richly typical of so many nineteenth-century matrons, the Princess of Waldeck was a hypochondriac with a will of iron.

'With all her gifts,' claimed one of her granddaughters, 'Grandmother would certainly have been suited to a greater task in larger surroundings. She showed devotion and imagination in fulfilling her duties towards her people in Waldeck. While her health permitted, her active interest was felt in everything.'[46]

The Princess's latter days were spent on a couch in a hushed and darkened room; 'bemoaning,' as her granddaughter Princess Alice was afterwards to say, 'her frail health, and demanding exorbitant attention, service and sympathy from everyone around

---

*Princess Hélène (1831–88) was the daughter of Wilhelm, Duke of Nassau.

29

her.[17] Yet her mind was lively enough to fascinate a man like Carlyle and ambitious enough to ensure that her daughters made brilliant marriages. There was nothing like the appearance of an important royal suitor on the market to get the Princess of Waldeck off her couch, out of her unbecoming velvet invalid's cap and into the scramble to secure the prize for one of her daughters.

Her triumphs, to date, had been the marriage of her eldest surviving daughter, Princess Pauline, to the Hereditary Prince of Bentheim; her second daughter, Princess Marie, to Prince Wilhelm, afterwards King Wilhelm II, of Württemberg; and, most gratifyingly, if most cynically of all, her third daughter, the 20-year-old Princess Emma, to the fat, dissolute, 62-year-old widower, King Wilhelm III of the Netherlands. It is not altogether surprising then, that when the chance came for her fourth daughter, Princess Hélène, to marry Queen Victoria's son, the Princess of Waldeck, haemophilia notwithstanding, grabbed it.

Princess Hélène Friederike Auguste had been born at Arolsen on 7 February 1861. At the time of her engagement to Prince Leopold, in November 1881, she was twenty years old. In a way, Princess Hélène's looks belied her personality. A certain doll-like prettiness masked a bold, intelligent, almost masculine mind. Strictly brought up by her astute mother and that indispensable adjunct of all nineteenth-century European courts, the English nanny, Princess Hélène was a capable, conscientious young woman, as far a cry from the average pampered princess as her husband-to-be was from the usual sporting, swashbuckling princeling. She was relatively widely travelled, having visited, besides several German cities and spas, Paris, Florence, Venice, Copenhagen and Stockholm. Six winters had been spent on the Riviera. She had even, some ten years before, stayed for several weeks in Torquay, a visit marked by the death of her eldest sister, the 15-year-old Princess Sophie.

None of this is to say that Princess Hélène struck strangers or even acquaintances (and, in truth, Prince Leopold was hardly more than that at the time of their engagement) as anything other than a shy, pretty, well-bred young woman. The Prince described her as 'very lovable'; 'I *can't* tell you how happy I am,'[48] he enthused. Only in the months following the engagement (and he spent much of the period either at Arolsen or with his Hesse relations at nearby Darmstadt) did Prince Leopold come to an appreciation of her more worthwhile qualities.

As yet, Queen Victoria had not set eyes on her future daughter-in-law. 'I hope,' she commanded one of her granddaughters, then visiting Waldeck, 'you will write to me about Arolsen and Helen. I fear Uncle Leopold will be (as everyone is under these circumstances) very tiresome if he is absorbed with his bride.'[49]

Not until Prince Leopold brought Princess Hélène to England, towards the end of February 1882, was the Queen able to satisfy her curiosity.

Faced with the short, squat, awe-inspiring old lady in the white widow's cap, Princess Hélène obviously acquitted herself very well. 'Though the idea of [Leopold] marrying makes me anxious,' confided the Queen to her Journal, 'still, as he has found a girl, so charming, ready to accept and love him, in spite of his ailments, I hope he may be happy and carefully watched over.'[50]

6

The couple were married, in St George's Chapel, Windsor, on 27 April 1882. The ceremonial was brilliant but not without its hitches. It appears that Prince Leopold had commissioned his friend Charles Gounod to compose a 'Marche Nuptiale' especially for the occasion. Gounod happily complied with a stirring composition to be rendered, ran his stipulation, 'à Grand Orchestre et Orgue'. So far, so good. But then someone (the Queen herself, possibly) decided that not only was the 'Marche Nuptiale' too long but that it should be played on the organ only, without the orchestral accompaniment. Would M. Gounod, wrote an apprehensive Prince Leopold, please attend to this?

Gounod was furious. 'Cette Marche Nuptiale,' he answered indignantly, 'dure *exactement* le temps indiqué par vos renseignements, c.a.d. cinq minutes.'[51] As for its being rendered by organ only, that was impossible. He would rather regard his masterpiece as 'un travail perdu' (although only lost, he hastened to make clear, to this particular ceremony) and compose another, shorter, simpler and, by implication, lesser piece to be played on the organ only.

It was to Gounod's re-written wedding march, then, that Princess Hélène – or Helen, as she was from now on to be known – entered St George's Chapel that spring morning in 1882. For a girl from the relatively humble court of Waldeck, the magnificence of the scene must have been almost overwhelming. Here, beneath the soaring, vaulted, banner-hung ceiling of St George's Chapel were gathered some of the most important, the most powerful and the most decorative people on earth.

Queen Victoria, standing in front of her crimson and gold chair, was in a dress and train of black satin, her ample bosom crowded with jewels and orders, a diamond crown glittering on her head. All around her stood the members of her vast family: the men splendidly uniformed and bemedalled; the women kaleidoscopic in their satins and brocades and diamonds. At the altar stood Prince Leopold, the swagger of his scarlet and gold uniform belied by the fact that he had to support himself on a cane. 'There was on his set lips the cruel wrench of pain every time he put his foot to the ground,'[52] wrote one observer. On one side of him stood his brother, the Prince of Wales, in his Field Marshal's uniform; on the other stood his brother-in-law, the Grand-Duke of Hesse. And all about waited those other, no less gorgeously

33

dressed actors in this royal pageant – the clergy in their embroidered copes, the ministers of state in their crimson Windsor uniforms, the Bearers of the Gold Stick and of the Silver Stick, the Gentlemen-at-Arms, the Yeomen of the Guard, the equerries, the heralds, the pages.

But, inevitably, it was the bride who drew all eyes. Her dress, far from being something run up by a provincial German seamstress, had been made in Paris, the gift of her sister Queen Emma of the Netherlands. It was of white satin, lavishly decorated with orange blossom and myrtle, and trimmed with point d'Alençon lace. Her long train was embroidered with silver, her floating lace veil held by a crown of orange blossom and myrtle. She was supported by her father, the Prince of Waldeck-Pyrmont, and her brother-in-law, the King of the Netherlands. She was attended by eight bridesmaids, 'the unmarried daughters of Dukes, Marquesses and Earls'. The marriage service was conducted by the Archbishop of Canterbury and, as it was a day of bright spring sunshine, 'the sunlight shone in through the gorgeous stained-glass windows, filling the Chapel with beautiful colour'.[53]

The ceremony over, the register was signed in the Green Drawing-room of the Castle and, after the wedding luncheon (the 'Royal Personages' in the dining-room; the lesser guests in the Waterloo Gallery) the newly-married pair drove away in an open carriage, drawn by four horses with outriders and a jangling escort of Life Guards. The Queen stood waving her handkerchief until the little procession had disappeared from view.

That night, in the lamplit quiet of her drawing-room, Queen Victoria settled down to her Journal. 'This exciting day is all over, and past, like a dream, and the last, but one,[*] of my children is married and has left the paternal home. . . . It was very trying to see the dear boy, on this important day of his life, still lame and shaky, but I am thankful it is well over. I feel so much for dear Helen, but she showed unmistakably how devoted she is to him. It is a great blessing. God bless them both.'[54]

---

[*] Queen Victoria's youngest daughter, Princess Beatrice (1857–1944).

CHAPTER TWO

1

'We congratulate ourselves,' said Prince Leopold to a crowd of welcoming local dignitaries crammed into a specially erected 'floral pavilion' in the village of Esher, Surrey, 'on possessing Claremont as a residence, and we hopefully anticipate spending the greater portion of our days here.'[1]

The newly-married couple had every reason to be pleased with their home. Claremont House was an elegant, Palladian-style mansion set above wide sloping lawns in a vast, leafy park. The property had once belonged to Thomas Pelham, the Earl of Clare, afterwards Duke of Newcastle, but it had been sold by his widow to Lord Clive – the famous Clive of India. Out of the spoils, it was said, of his Indian conquests Clive had spent £100,000 on building this great house. The mansion had been designed and the grounds laid out by Capability Brown; the large drawing-room had been especially planned to accommodate the huge carpet which Clive had brought with him from India.[*]

After Clive's death, the property passed through various hands, first becoming a royal residence on the marriage of Princess Charlotte, daughter of the future King George IV, to Prince Leopold of Saxe-Coburg. On Princess Charlotte's death, in childbirth, in 1817, Prince Leopold lived on in the house until, fourteen years later, he was invited to ascend the Belgian throne as King Leopold I.

With a grant for its upkeep provided by the British Government, King Leopold was able to retain Claremont (all prudent continental sovereigns kept a bolt-hole, and King Leopold was more prudent than most) so that when his father-in-law, Louis Philippe, King of the French, was thrown out of France, King Leopold was able to offer him Claremont as a home for his exile. The ex-King of the French lived there until his death.

King Leopold's own death, in 1865, meant that Claremont passed into the hands of his niece, Queen Victoria. The Queen, with her penchant for scenes of melancholy, loved the house and would often drive over from Windsor to trail through its rooms. Occasionally she would allow a member of her vast

---

[*] This carpet was later installed by Prince Leopold's only son, Prince Charles Edward, in a castle in Austria. It was looted by the Russian troops at the end of the Second World War and is now, presumably, somewhere in Russia.

family to honeymoon there. In 1881, the year before his marriage, she presented it to Prince Leopold.

Pleased enough to have a home of his own, Prince Leopold could have wished for one with more cheerful associations. When his friend, the celebrated Monckton Milnes, visited the Prince at Claremont, Milnes told his host that the house had once belonged to his grandfather and that his mother had been born there. 'I am very glad to hear of anyone being born here,' answered Prince Leopold wryly. 'The place is haunted with death; there is a tragedy in every room.'[2]

But he quickly adapted himself to his new setting. Not long after moving in, Prince Leopold built a second lodge gate at the north-east entrance and planted an avenue of chestnut trees. In anticipation of his marriage, he converted a smaller drawing-room into a bedroom and bathroom for his bride and arranged a combined library and study for his own use. 'The house,' noted one visitor, 'is really very pretty and Prince Leopold had taste, or employed those who had, in the things he bought.'[3]

To enable the Prince to keep up his more lavish way of life, Parliament voted an additional grant of £10,000; together with the £15,000 voted to him on attaining his majority, Prince Leopold now had an annual income of £25,000. In the event of his death, his widow would be granted £6,000 a year.*

* In 1977, almost a century later, his daughter Princess Alice received an annual grant of exactly the same sum — £6000.

Princess Helen, now Duchess of Albany, did not have long to wait before she was given an indication of the immensity of the task she had undertaken in marrying Prince Leopold. Within a couple of months of his wedding he was laid up. Hardly had he recovered than he 'began at once to do too much' and had a relapse. 'Poor Aunt Helen is most devoted,' reported the Queen to one of her granddaughters, 'and we can hardly get her to leave him to get out.'[4]

In addition to the young Duchess of Albany's apparent devotion to her son, Queen Victoria was gradually becoming aware of another of her daughter-in-law's characteristics: her frankness. The Duchess of Albany was not cowed by the Queen. Alone of all Queen Victoria's daughters-in-law (or sons, daughters and sons-in-law for that matter) the Duchess spoke up for herself. She flatly refused to contact the Queen by letter or through an intermediary when she had a complaint. She insisted on confronting her mother-in-law 'face to face'.[5] On one occasion, apparently, the interview between the two of them was so stormy that the Duchess refused to dine with the Queen; she ate alone with Prince Leopold.

At first astonished by this show of spirit, Queen Victoria soon came to respect her daughter-in-law for it. She realised that the young Duchess of Albany was not being insolent; merely honest. She appreciated, too, that her life was not going to be an easy one. In any case, such tiffs were quickly forgotten and forgiven in the general euphoria surrounding the birth, ten months after marriage, of the Duchess's first child, Princess Alice.

'Such an intense relief, and that all is going well,' wrote the Queen in her Journal on the night of the baby's birth, 25 February 1883. 'The child is fine and large, with a quantity of dark hair.'[6]

2

'All I can remember of [my father],' wrote Princess Alice in her old age, 'is a faint impression of a man sitting by his writing table, wearing light-grey trousers to which I clung unsteadily and was picked up in his arms, but I have no remembrance of a face.'[7]

Princess Alice was often in Prince Leopold's arms for he was, by all accounts, devoted to his little daughter. Almost every day – health and weather permitting – he would settle her and her nurse into his light, low-slung dog cart and go spinning through Capability Brown's park or into the little village of Esher. Assuming the role of a country squire rather than that of Prince, this small, dapper young man would nod cheerfully to passers-by or stop the pony to have a chat with some village tradesman. His most frequent calls were on the popular sculptor, F.J. Williamson. Not only did Prince Leopold dearly love the atmosphere of an artist's studio but he had commissioned Williamson to model a figure of the infant Princess Alice. 'Nothing,' claims one observer, 'pleased him more than to nurse the child whilst the sculptor was engaged in reproducing its features in the clay.'[8]

Another member of the Prince's artistic circle was John Ruskin.

I got here all right yesterday afternoon [reported Ruskin to his cousin Joan Severn in October 1883, when Princess Alice was eight months old], and found Duke and Duchess and baby and nobody else. Baby hadn't expected me and took some time to consider me: after which deliberation she took my hand, and then my head, into favour – and I was very glad my hair was long enough for her to pull, to her much contentment.

The Duchess does not at present seem to care much for anything else; but seemed to like standing to turn her husband's music for him in the evening. Baby came down to breakfast – and sate quiet and happy, playing with a silver spoon, chained to her mother's finger to save the trouble of picking up. . . .

I wish I could have a photograph of the scene in the hall after tea yesterday. They have a lovely piano organ for baby, like one of the Italian street ones. The Duke ground it – mama sate upon the stairs with baby on her lap – and I danced to it – to its evident interest – not to say admiration.[9]

41

Prince Leopold was involved in other, less domestic, activities as well. He continued his work as chairman of various philanthropic and cultural committees. Together with his Duchess, he visited a Fine Art Exhibition and opened a park in Huddersfield; he distributed prizes to school pupils in Liverpool; he had a degree conferred on him by Durham University; he paid a visit to Seaham Harbour. He even, on 15 February 1884, took part in an amateur concert in Esher in aid of school funds, where he sang, with great verve, 'The Sands of Dee'.

Such activities were all very well in their way but for a man of Prince Leopold's intelligence and ambition they were hardly enough. He still yearned for some more demanding work. Neither the undoubted delights of marriage and fatherhood nor the more doubtful advantages of his chief employment – acting as his mother's assistant – could compensate for the meaninglessness of his life. So, less than three months after the birth of his daughter, Prince Leopold wrote a letter to the Queen. He would like, he said, to be considered as a successor to his brother-in-law, Lord Lorne, the retiring Governor-General of Canada.

His bombshell caused an explosion of official activity. The Queen's private secretary, Sir Henry Ponsonby, passed the request on to the Colonial Secretary, Lord Derby. Lord Derby passed it on to the Prime Minister, W.E. Gladstone. But Gladstone already knew about it. Prince Leopold had written to him as well. With neither Gladstone nor Derby wanting to be the one to turn down the Prince's request – or rather, to be the one to put the Queen's turning down of the request into words – each penned an evasive letter and left it to a third party to try and dissuade the Prince.

This was the celebrated Professor Goldwin Smith, former lecturer in history at Oxford who had since settled in Canada. In a letter to Prince Leopold's ex-tutor and close companion, Robert Collins, the Professor advised the Prince not to think of coming to Canada at the present time. The Fenians, warned the Professor, were very active in the dominion just then; the presence of Queen Victoria's son would be the very thing to cause these 'desperadoes' to 'run amuck'. And in any case, he continued doggedly, the unscrupulousness of Canadian politicians was such that 'the soul of any man of spirit would rebel'.

That Prince Leopold was taken in by any of these protestations was highly unlikely. He must have known, his daughter afterwards said, 'that Canadians have an expression for this sort of stuff which compared it to the by-product of a bull'.[10]

Canada refused, the Prince tried Australia. In January 1884 he applied for the vacant post of Governor of the state of Victoria. Again his request brought forth a flurry of tactfully worded refusals. All applauded his patriotism, his dedication and his loyalty in wishing to serve the Crown in distant lands. All made clear that it was 'Her Majesty's maternal reluctance to a severance at the present moment'[11] that prevented them from acceding to his wishes.

Perhaps it was this latest dashing of his hopes, or perhaps it was the belief that a warmer climate would do him some good, that decided Prince Leopold to set out for Cannes late in February 1884. Even so, the timing seemed odd. The Duchess of Albany was again pregnant, and with his daughter less than a year old, she could hardly have thought of accompanying her husband. 'I think it rather a pity,' noted a disapproving Queen Victoria, 'that he should leave her.'[12]

In Cannes, Prince Leopold was the guest of his former equerry, Captain Perceval, at the Villa Nevada – a small, ornate, châlet-like cottage set in a garden of palms and flowering shrubs high above the glittering Mediterranean. The change to this relaxed and balmy atmosphere obviously did Prince Leopold good: within a few weeks he was said to be in 'buoyant spirits'.[13] So buoyant, in fact, were his spirits, that on 25 March he attended the Bachelors' Ball in nearby Nice where he danced until almost dawn. Back in Cannes, two days later, he was an enraptured spectator at the 'Battle of Flowers'.

It was on that same day, Thursday 27 March, that while climbing the stairs of a local club, the Cercle Nautique, Prince Leopold slipped and bumped his knee. It was the right knee, the one which had always given him trouble. Dr Royle, who was with the Prince in Cannes, immediately applied splints and bandages and arranged for him to be driven back to the Villa

Nevada. Here Prince Leopold was put to bed. But as the pain was not particularly severe, he was able to read the newspapers and to chat, in his animated fashion, to his companions. At nine that night he had a light supper and after some more reading, went to sleep.

At about three o'clock the following morning Dr Royle, who was sleeping in the same room, was woken by the sound of the Prince's heavy breathing. Realising at once that something was seriously wrong, the doctor called Captain Perceval. Helplessly, Prince Leopold's two companions stood beside the narrow iron bed. There was nothing they could do. The Prince died at half past three in the morning of 28 February. He would have turned thirty-one in ten days' time.

The news was broken to the Duchess of Albany by her sister-in-law, Princess Christian.* She was 'greatly overcome, but quite quiet and natural', reported Princess Christian. 'It was piteous to see her, for she was so good and patient.'[14]

On the following day the Queen drove over to Claremont. 'Went at once to Helen's sitting-room,' she afterwards wrote. 'She got up to meet me, in tears, but so gentle, and so sweet and touching. Was much overcome, for it is quite overwhelming to see her deep, unmurmuring grief. She laid her hand on my shoulder, and kept saying: "Poor mother", and

---

* Princess Helena (1846–1923), who married Prince Christian of Schleswig-Holstein.

looked so sweet, young and touching. She is so good and patient, and thankful that there had been so little suffering. . . . It was piteous to look at her poor young face.'

But most poignant of all was the sight of the 13-month-old Princess Alice. She was brought into the room, with its two doleful, weeping, black-clad widows, looking as 'merry and lively' as ever.

'She looks very well,' noted the Queen, 'and stands at a chair quite alone, and pushes it about.'[15]

3

In less than two years after his marriage ceremony, and again on a day of brilliant spring sunshine – 5 April 1884 – the funeral service of Prince Leopold, Duke of Albany, was held in St George's Chapel at Windsor.

The Prince of Wales, on hearing of his brother's death, had immediately offered to travel to Cannes to fetch the body. This mournful mission had taken a full week to accomplish. Having crossed the Channel and travelled to the South of France by train, the Prince had had to endure the long, solemn journey back. He had seen the massive, flower-piled coffin carried, by hearse, from the Villa Nevada to the railway station at Cannes, where it had been put into a special, black-draped funeral van, which was then hitched to the Nice-Paris express. The Prince had travelled with it to Cherbourg, where the coffin was carried aboard the royal yacht *Osborne* and laid in a specially arranged *chapelle ardente*.

Towards evening on 3 April the *Osborne* reached Portsmouth. Not until the following day, to the mournful tolling of bells and the solemn thud of the minute guns, were the remains carried ashore to be laid in yet another funeral van and taken by train to Windsor.

At Windsor station the funeral train was met by Queen Victoria with her daughters Princess Christian and Princess Beatrice. The Duchess of Albany, now over five months pregnant, was not with them. But she attended the short service in the Albert Memorial Chapel in which the coffin was to remain until the funeral the following day. She came again the next morning for her last look at her husband's remains. The funeral service itself she did not attend.

The Duchess had the consolation, though, of knowing that she had seen her husband's last wish carried out. For, after Prince Leopold's death, his wife had found a letter addressed to her, in which he expressed a wish to be buried in the royal vault beneath St George's Chapel, and not, as the Queen would have preferred, in the mausoleum which she had had built to house Prince Albert's, and in time her own, remains. Prince Leopold chose St George's Chapel because 'he had been married there, and because there would always be singing over him'.[16]

There was a further consolation just over three months later, on 19 July, when the Duchess of Albany gave birth to a son. Queen Victoria announced him to be a 'pretty, healthy-looking baby – very like dear Uncle Leopold – his eyes quite remarkably so'.[17] The Duchess, again carrying out her late husband's wishes, gave him the names of Charles Edward.[*] Characteristically, Prince Leopold had always been drawn to the bitter-sweet saga of the Stuarts and he had wanted his heir to be named after Charles Edward Stuart, the 'Young Pretender' or 'Bonnie Prince Charlie'.

'The christening at Claremont was very *touching . . .*' reported the Queen to her granddaughter, Princess Victoria of Hesse. 'Poor dear Aunt Helen was greatly tried but behaved so courageously though she was nearly breaking down often, but she bore up till it was all over. Little Charlie is quite a fine, big boy and very like dear Uncle Leopold.'[18]

For 'little Charlie', Prince Charles Edward, born Duke of Albany, fate had a very strange future in store.

---

[*] His full names were Charles Edward George Albert.

CHAPTER THREE

1

Throughout her long life, Princess Alice always retained the happiest memories of her childhood home at Claremont. As she grew up so did that aura of melancholy, of which Prince Leopold had been so aware, gradually disappear from the house. It was as though she had broken the spell. Too young to mourn the death of her father, or to notice the grief of her mother, or to understand the Duchess of Albany's suddenly straitened circumstances,* Princess Alice flung herself, with a gusto that was to be one of her chief characteristics, into the enjoyment of living.

The Duchess's poverty, of course, was relative. Six thousand pounds, in the last decade of the nineteenth century, was still a considerable sum of money:

---

* Prince Leopold's annual grant of £25,000, due on 1 April 1884, was withheld because he had died four days earlier. His widow was from then on obliged to manage on less than a quarter of that sum

worth at least ten times the amount a century later. So the Duchess of Albany was able to live in some style. Her household, in addition to her lady-in-waiting, comptroller and the children's governess and nurses, boasted a full complement of servants – ranging from Mr Long, the butler, through the under-butler, the housekeeper, the footmen, the nursery footmen, the lady's maids, the head housemaid, the housemaids, the cooks, the kitchenmaids, the scullery maids, the coachmen, the stable boys and the gardeners. Even so, a member of Queen Victoria's household bemoaned the fact that Claremont could not be 'thoroughly lived in by the Duchess with her present means'.[1]

This same sense of abundance characterised the decor of the house. The pillared and pedimented chasteness of the exterior of Claremont was certainly not echoed within. The rooms were the customary high ictorian clutter; the atmosphere-like the atmosphere within most of the royal homes – was *gemütlich.*

It was in this cosy, comfortable, well-ordered household that Princess Alice grew up. 'I firmly believe,' she said in later life, 'that our characters are moulded by circumstances and early training more than by any other factors.'[2] In her case, the circumstances could hardly have been more favourable or the training more thorough. She grew up, she once claimed, 'in a wonderfully *loving* atmosphere'.[3]

In common with most children of her time and class, she saw her mother at set periods only. This was usually in the late afternoon, when the Princess and her little brother (they were separated by some eighteen months) had their supper at a little table in their mother's sitting-room. The Duchess was 'marvellous with children; any children,'[4] said Princess Alice. The little girl always remembered the day that her mother first put aside mourning and appeared in a pale grey summer dress: she thought her quite beautiful. When the children had finished their supper, they would stay with their mother until bedtime.

There, in the flaring gaslight they would sit, this little family group, the Duchess's pretty head (always crowned by a lace cap) bent over a book as she read aloud, while the children worked at their knitting or sewing or painting. Even little Prince Charles Edward, or Charlie, learnt to knit. By way of an incentive, the Duchess would wind a little bronze animal in a great ball of wool (a *Wunder Knäuel*) which the children could only claim on finishing the wool. They kept these bronze animals in tins decorated with pictures from *Alice in Wonderland*, which had been given to them by Lewis Carroll himself.

Lewis Carroll was very friendly with the Albany family. On first meeting them, he had found the Duchess to be 'very pleasant indeed'; Prince Charlie to be 'entirely fascinating: a perfect little Prince and the picture of good humour'; but Princess Alice, although 'a sweet little girl', he considered to be far too high-spirited and unruly. This might have been because the six-year-old Princess Alice, on listening to a story being told by Lewis Carroll – who stammered badly – asked in a loud, clear voice, 'Why does he waggle his mouth like that?'[5] She was whisked away by an anguished lady-in-waiting.

Within a couple of years, though, Lewis Carroll's opinion of Princess Alice had changed. 'Little Alice is improved, I think, not being so unruly as she was two years ago,' he wrote. He taught her, and her brother Charles, to make paper pistols, to 'blot their names on creased paper'[8] and promised to give Princess Alice a copy of *The Fairies* by William Allingham. When he sent her a decorated tin, his accompanying note read, 'Whenever Charlie is *very* naughty, you can just pop him in and shut the lid! Then he'll *soon* be good. I'm sending one for him as well; so now you know what will happen when *you're* naughty!'[7]

Another time when the children would be with their mother was on Saturdays, when she would accompany them on their walk. The Duchess of Albany was an accomplished story-teller and she would hold the children enthralled with her latest episode of a story that would last for many weeks. On Sundays, before the children went to church, she would give them their Sunday School lesson. Raised a Lutheran, the Duchess of Albany had adopted the Anglican faith on her marriage and throughout her life she remained a devout, if some-what straitlaced Christian.

There was something of this same severity in her dealings with her children. The Duchess of Albany might have been loving but she was never lax. She saw to it that her children were brought up strictly; she tried to instil into them some of her own vigorous sense of duty. On the lively, independent, outgoing little Princess Alice the results of this firmness were all beneficial, but on the more highly-strung Prince Charles Edward the effects were less happy. He tended to be afraid of his mother, to submit too easily to the will and domination of others. The children's first nurse, Nanna Creak, who doted on Princess Alice, simply could not handle the 'delicate, nervous and tiresome'[8] Prince Charles Edward; after four years she left. Queen Victoria, who had chosen her, was very put out by this.

Princess Alice's nursery was on the first floor of the house. Here, during her early years, Nanna Creak presided. Hers was the typical, late nineteenth-century nursery: a small, self-contained world of early-to-rise, porridge for breakfast, vigorous hair-brushings, buttoned boots, holland pinafores, pick-a-back rides, stories, squabbles, tears, treats and punishments, bland nursery meals, walks to the lake to feed the wild ducks with squares of dry bread ('these I particularly enjoyed eating myself',[9] remembered Princess Alice), little covered baskets holding soup or jelly or junket for the sick, pony rides in the park, baths filled with hot water from highly polished copper cans, firelight, lamplight, warming-pans, good-night prayers, nightlights.

From the very earliest nursery days Princess Alice revealed a trait that was to become very characteristic of her: an almost obsessional neatness of person. Even as a baby she would hold out her hands to be wiped if they were dirty; if she was ever splattered with mud she would be highly indignant. As the years went by, so did this passion for cleanliness, combined with a highly developed fashion sense, ensure that Princess Alice never looked anything less than immaculately groomed and stylishly dressed.

> I remember one summer day [writes Lady Byng, whose mother had been the Duchess of Albany's lady-in-waiting, Jane Moreton] when we all went for a solemn drive in an open landau and the Duchess said to us, 'Don't take any notice of Alice's new gloves.' Away we went and then began a comedy which photographed itself vividly on my mind. The small hands, in a pair of new gloves, were very much in evidence, spread out on the child's knees, while she shot surreptitious glances from one to the other to see if they had been noticed. But we all stared into the distance or talked of the weather, the scenery, and any subject which had no reference to gloves. Up and down, sideways, backwards and forwards went the small hands, till gradually the face grew angry in its expression, and at the end of the drive an outraged little figure clambered up the long steps to the portico of Claremont, her head defiantly high, though I think tears

were not far off had she allowed herself to give way to her mortification.

It was a comic incident, but I think the Duchess might have given the child the small happiness of getting those treasured gloves admired — or at least noticed. How my mother would have rejoiced had I, at the age of six, been clothes-conscious enough to act as the Princess did that afternoon![10]

With the staff at Claremont, the little Princess was always on the best of terms. The servants, she says, 'considered themselves part of the family and were always accepted as such'.[11] Mrs Lawley the housekeeper, with her old-fashioned ringlets, would give her treats of sugar candy on long strings and Mr Long, the butler, would carry her upstairs, always stopping to explain to his insistent little charge the intricacies of the famous Franco-Prussian War print, 'La Dernière Cartouche'. She was delighted when Jo, the wall-eyed footman, married Kitty, the buxom nursemaid. 'All these people played a great part in our young lives and all were devoted,'[12] says the Princess.

Occasionally, the reassuring routine of these nursery days would be broken by some exciting incident. On one occasion the Princess was woken before dawn to be shown the glittering tail of a comet as it streaked across the night sky. For over seventy years, until some pedant put her right, the Princess stoutly maintained that she had seen Halley's Comet that morning.

On another occasion, she was woken for a less romantic reason: three burglars were busily clambering through her bedroom window. The nursemaid's screams, as she entered the room to investigate the noise, woke the entire household and sent the three men scrambling out of the window again. The Duchess of Albany, in an effort to soothe her daughter, explained that it had been a somewhat unseasonable visit from Father Christmas. (Why then, wondered the little Princess not unreasonably, had her nursemaid screamed?) The *Daily News* took the Father Christmas story a stage further. The Princess, it said, had been overjoyed to have had two visits from Father Christmas in one year. Others, even more fancifully, claimed that she had asked one of the burglars why he was not wearing his white beard and red coat and why he had come through the window instead of down the chimney.

The version which the Princess herself preferred was the nursemaid's: only by waking the household with her screams, claimed the girl excitedly, had she been saved from death by strangulation. 'Of course,' says the Princess, 'I swallowed every word of all this and was flattered and proud of having been the central figure in such an adventure.'[13]

2

Far and away the most important member of the Claremont household was the Duchess of Albany's

Comptroller, Sir Robert Collins. Born in 1841, the son of a country parson, and educated at Marlborough and Lincoln College, Oxford, Robert Hawthorn Collins had been appointed tutor to the late Prince Leopold in 1867. With the completion of the Prince's education, Collins had become Comptroller of his household. In 1876 he had married Mary Wightwick; in 1884 he had been knighted; and on Prince Leopold's death he had stayed on as Comptroller to the Duchess of Albany.

In many ways, Sir Robert Collins was an exceptional man. In his early forties at the time of Prince Leopold's death, he was a slight, spare, athletic figure, a famous runner and boxer in earlier days and still a man of extraordinary vigour and agility. Yet his manner was anything but hearty. Sir Robert, like so many of those who occupy important positions in royal households, was a quiet, tactful, discreet, patient and self-effacing man possessing, as a friend has put it, 'the old knightly virtues of courage, chivalry, purity and honour'.[14] And just as his athleticism had never coarsened into heartiness, so did his devotion to duty never degenerate into obsequiousness or pomposity. For, above all, Sir Robert Collins was a wry, humorous, sharp-witted man, of strong artistic and intellectual tastes. His conversation was 'shrewd, entertaining and stimulating'.[15]

Among the members of the Claremont household, Sir Robert was extremely popular. To the young, widowed and inexperienced Duchess of

Albany he was like a rock; to her children he was the most delightful companion, part-father, part-friend. Little Princess Alice adored him. For over forty years, from the time that he first became tutor to the young Prince Leopold until his death in 1908, Sir Robert Collins was to be intimately associated with the fortunes of the Albany family. 'He was everyone's confidant,' says Princess Alice, 'and knew everything good or bad that happened in our family.'[16]

When Princess Alice was seven, another important person entered her life. This was her governess, Miss Jane Potts. Inevitably, the governess's surname gave rise to ribald remarks, particularly from the Princess's Uncle Bertie, the Prince of Wales. In his chaffing way, he always referred to her as 'Mademoiselle Vase'; 'very inappropriate,' commented Princess Alice briskly in later life, 'as she was not the sort of person who could easily be sat upon.'[17] But the Princess and her brother had their own, only slightly less ribald, name for Miss Potts: because of the way the governess wound her plaited hair into a flat bun at the back of her head, they called her 'Cow Pat'.

Yet the young Princess Alice was devoted to Miss Potts. The governess was one of those tall, gaunt, no-nonsense but sympathetic women who know how to hold a child's interest. The bedroom which had once belonged to the unfortunate Princess Charlotte of Wales was converted into a schoolroom and there Miss Potts set about educating her young charges. Her greatest success, apparently, was with history. By allowing the children to act various historical characters, she imbued them with a deep and lasting interest in the subject. Her achievements, in both history and literature, were augmented by the Duchess of Albany: each evening, before dinner, the Duchess would read to her children. In this way they came to appreciate, and be fascinated by, the novels of Charles Dickens, Robert Louis Stevenson, Sir Walter Scott, Charles Kingsley, Charlotte Yonge and G.A. Henty.

Miss Potts broadened their horizons in other ways as well. She weaned them from their cosseted, slightly prissy nursery ways: she taught them to climb fences, to munch apples picked up from the ground, to go for long healthy walks. It was Miss Potts; with her love of the outdoors, who first kindled in Princess Alice her life-long passion for walking.

She kindled in her another passion as well: her interest in people beyond the restricted royal circle. In a way, it was a case of needs-must. Of Queen Victoria's granddaughters, Princess Alice was alone in having a brother only. All her cousins belonged to families of three, four, five or even six children. 'You are so many of yourselves,' as Queen Victoria once put it, 'that you *want no one* else.'[18] And because of the Princess's lack of sisters or cousins of her own age at Claremont, the sensible Miss Potts encouraged her to make friends among neighbourhood girls.

This was not always easy. Queen Victoria had very strong views on the dangers of girlhood friendships: 'girls' friendships and intimacies are very bad and often

59

lead to great mischief. . .'[19] she warned darkly. And then there was always the vexed question of class. Only among daughters of the aristocracy could Princess Alice really hope to make friends. Professional people might be invited, very occasionally, for a meal; businessmen almost never; the rest, if they were respectable enough, were simply herded into the annual garden party. So the field for making outside contacts was limited. But Miss Potts saw to it that her pupil made friends with at least two fairly ordinary little girls: Kitty Wightwick, a relation who had been adopted by Sir Robert and Lady Collins, and Muriel Hone, the local rector's daughter. 'Funny little girls we were . . .'[20] mused Princess Alice many years later.

But these outside friends, for all their value, could not compensate for the gap in the schoolroom when little Prince Charles Edward was packed off to become a pupil at nearby Sandroyd School. From there he went on to prep school at Lyndhurst. This left Princess Alice alone with her governess. And for the following ten years Miss Potts would be there; to instruct, interest and encourage her pupil. Only much later in life did Princess Alice come to appreciate the thanklessness of a governess's duties. 'Poor Miss Potts had a very dull and lonely time, I fear . . .'[21] she afterwards wrote.

But whether she did or not, Miss Potts certainly allowed no dullness or loneliness to affect her relationship with her pupil. To Princess Alice she seemed always 'wise and kind and understanding'.[22]

In one's mind's eye, and down the vista of over ninety years, one can still see the two of them sitting there in the sun-shafted schoolroom at Claremont: the tall angular Miss Potts with her 'cow-pat' pinned firmly in place, and the pretty little Princess Alice of Albany with her brown eyes, her long golden-brown hair, her full-skirted dress and her alert, vivacious and enquiring air.

3

A large picture, painted to commemorate Queen Victoria's Golden Jubilee in 1887, hangs in Buckingham Palace. It is the work of the Danish artist Lauritz Tuxen. The painting depicts the Queen, seated in the Green Drawing-room at Windsor Castle, surrounded by the members of her enormous family. It is a sumptuous, swaggering, crowded canvas. Between bearded princes and elaborately coiffured princesses in bustles peep the children – little kilted or sailor-suited princes and little princesses in frilled skirts with satin sashes. Forming the focal point of the picture are two figures: the one is the 68-year-old Queen Victoria in her black dress and snowy cap, the other is Princess Alice of Albany in a short, full-skirted white dress. The Queen is reaching out to take a posy from her granddaughter. *

---

* Some eighty-five years later, when Princess Alice was discussing a reproduction of the painting used on the jacket of my book *Grandmama of Europe,* she pointed to the posy-clutching little figure and said cheerily, 'That's me. All the others are dead now. I remember posing for the picture, and I kept that little dress for years.'

Nothing could better capture the flavour of the influential, interrelated and cosmopolitan family to which Princess Alice belonged than this Jubilee painting. To each other, these impressive-looking figures might be known by such arch nicknames as Ducky or Mossie or Sossie, but among the group were a host of future kings, queens, emperors and empresses. In time, these direct descendants of Queen Victoria would sit on no less than ten European thrones. With good reason was the old Queen known as the 'Grandmama of Europe'. And in an age when it was still widely believed that monarchs were as important as they looked, it would be only natural for a little British princess to assume that she was a member of the most powerful clan on earth. After all, did Queen Victoria not blithely claim that hers was 'the greatest position there is'?[23]

Her grandchildren certainly believed it. To them Grandmama Queen or 'Gan-Gan' was the sun around which their young lives revolved. And little Princess Alice's life revolved round it more often than most for she lived, after all, not far from her grandmother. Whereas some of her cousins might live in Berlin or Darmstadt or Malta or even faraway India, the Albanys were just a carriage drive away from the Queen's principal home, Windsor Castle. In Princess Alice's life, Queen Victoria played a very dominant part indeed.

Whenever they were summoned to spend a few days at Windsor, the Albany family would travel there by train. To have gone by carriage would have been a much simpler operation but, for some obscure reason, they always took the train.

'There is something indescribable about Windsor Castle,' remembered Princess Alice. 'The moment we entered the door of the "Sovereigns' Entrance" there was a special Windsor Castle smell – a smell like nowhere else – old furniture kept very clean, flowers and, altogether, a special delicious and welcoming smell that only now is fading away. There was an *aura* about the whole place – the dignified page who helped us, the housekeeper in black silk and a lace cap at the door, and, of course, the equerry-in-waiting; then the beauty and richness of the wide corridor with all its treasures which one accepted yet never noticed.'[24]

It seemed, to Queen Victoria's young grandchildren, that they were obliged to walk for miles along wide, silent and deeply carpeted corridors before reaching the Queen's apartments. Soundlessly, one after another, double doors would be opened by low-bowing, liveried footmen. Like a flock of 'well-behaved little geese'[25] the children would be driven on by their anxious nurses. Everyone spoke in hushed voices. Even reprimands were delivered in whispers. 'Mind you curtsey at the door and kiss Grandmama's hand and don't make a noise and mind you are good'[26] would run the scarcely audible instructions. 'The hush around Grandmama's door was awe-inspiring,' wrote one of these grandchildren.

'It was like approaching the mystery of some sanctuary.'[27] The final doors were opened and there, sitting at her writing-table in an old-fashioned black silk dress and her white widow's cap and veil, would be Queen Victoria.

To the children, her rooms were a treasure store. Although crammed with furniture and ornaments, they were never stuffy or gloomy. The Queen always insisted on open windows and the air in the rooms would be sweet with the scent of orange blossom. There was so much to look at: Grandpapa – the late Prince Consort – who featured in innumerable paintings, photographs, prints, busts and statuettes; Landseer's wonderful pictures of dogs and deer and horses; silver-framed photographs of people long since dead; a glass ball shimmering with different colours; 'all sorts of delicious queer little objects made of Scotch granite and cairngorm'.[28]

In the middle of this Aladdin's cave would be the Queen: 'Not idol-like at all, not a bit frightening, smiling a kind little smile, almost as shy as us children, so that conversation was not very fluent on either side'.[29] A quick, nervous laugh always preceded the Queen's opening remarks. Conversation was made up, for the most part, of questions about the children's behaviour. Any report of naughtiness would be met with exclamations of mock-horror on the part of the Queen. Her voice was sweet and silvery; her air was tranquil.

The halting conversation over, the Queen would allow her grandchildren to play on the carpet at her feet. They would use her despatch boxes for building walls and little Princess Alice was especially fond of working the spinning-wheel. 'This invariably brought a rebuke from Grandmama.'[30] Sometimes, the fascinated Princess would watch one of the dressers gently massage the Queen's legs from knee to heel. Equally fascinating was to see her grandmother's famous tulle cap removed to reveal her fine silver hair done up in a tiny bun.

On occasions, a cabinet minister would be ushered in. 'Say how do you do to Lord Salisbury,'[31] the Queen would command and once the diminutive Princess had greeted the huge, bearded Prime Minister, her grandmother would dismiss her. She would hurry out to the little room next door where the maids sat waiting. Here things were much more relaxed. In defiance of Nanny's rules, the Princess would be given freshly made lemonade and delicious biscuits.

Upstairs, in the nurseries, things were more relaxed still. There would be riotous games with her Connaught or Battenberg relations and hilarious pick-a-back rides on the bustles of her grown-up girl cousins. In fact, by the late 1880s, bustles jutted out so far that there was room for both Princess Alice and Prince Charles Edward to ride behind their mother.

On hot summer days at Windsor the Queen would work out of doors, often with one or more of her grandchildren nearby. 'It's a glorious day,' wrote her granddaughter Princess Victoria of Prussia to her mother one day in 1889, 'but rather too hot for Grandmama's and my taste, so walking is an impossibility. Grandmama wrote in the garden this morning and I sat not far off to be in readiness, lest she might want anything. The flowers and grass smell so sweet, the whole is perfumed and the birds sing beautifully as if their little throats were going to burst. . . . Today is a great day at Eton – the 4th of June is *the* day for all the boys – every sort of thing takes place – boating, games, teas, lunches etc and we are all going down tonight to see the boys row! Aunt Helen [the Duchess of Albany] is looking well and bright and the little ones have grown, Alice is so like Uncle [Leopold] now, even Grandmama says so . . .'[32]

Grandmama had other opinions of Princess Alice as well. She pronounced her to be 'a charming child';[33] and on another occasion wrote that 'Alice and Charlie were here, both very merry, good and obedient children – the former *very* pretty'.[34] Only once, claims Princess Alice, was she given a really serious telling-off by her grandmother. She was never to forget the quiet but none the less 'devastating' way in which Queen Victoria said, 'You are a very naughty little girl.'[35]

As Princess Alice grew older, she would be allowed to attend some of the evening entertainments at Windsor. The Queen loved the theatre. In the Waterloo Chamber, surrounded by her family and household, she would enjoy concerts, plays and operas. *Lohengrin,* says Princess Alice, was one of her grandmother's favourites. There were less sophisticated amusements as well. After much rehearsing, often in the presence of the Queen, her children and grandchildren would take part in plays and tableaux. These the Queen enjoyed immensely.

'It is extraordinary how pleased Grandmama is with such small things,' wrote her grandson, Prince Eddy,* to his brother, Prince George * on one occasion about some 'tiresome' theatrical performance, 'for she is quite childish in some ways about them.'[36] One of her gentlemen, Alec Yorke, was a gifted and enthusiastic amateur performer: at his hilarious sketches, the Queen 'laughed until she was red in the face'.[37]

The evenings could become more amusing still after the Queen had gone to bed. One of her ladies, Marie Mallet, notes that the Duchess of Albany was always ready to prolong the entertainment. The Duchess ('such a dear and so un-stiff')[38] might get someone to sing and was even known to turn the handle of the mechanical piano while the others danced.

But by the time these scenes of relative impropriety were taking place the Queen – and Princess Alice—would be sound asleep upstairs.

4

---

* Prince Albert Victor (1864–92).
* Afterwards King George V (1865–1936).

Another setting for these family gatherings was Osborne House on the Isle of Wight. This vast, Italianate pile, part-seaside villa, part-palace, had been designed by the Prince Consort. Here the Queen would spend most of the winter months of December and January and the summer months of July and August. During both these seasons but more often at Christmas time, the Albany family would stay with the Queen. Osborne too, recalls Princess Alice, 'had its own wonderful smell which I can always bring to mind even now.'[39]

At Osborne, in the summer, the Princess would usually see her grandmother out of doors. Sometimes she would be allowed to breakfast with her. Instead of the deep pile carpets of Windsor, here the marvellously smooth, springy green lawns would muffle any foot-falls. The Queen would be seated under a large écru tent, lined and fringed with green. All about, in nervous attendance, stood turbaned Indians, kilted Highlanders, footmen and ladies-in-waiting. Dogs – collies, pomeranians, Scotch or Skye terriers – sprawled on the grass. The air would be pungent with the smell of coffee and of certain curly biscuits, imported from Germany, which the Queen might, or might not, offer to her grandchildren. The children, says Princess Alice, always squabbled over these biscuits. 'Modulate your voice, Alice,'[40] the Queen once said firmly to Princess Alice at table when her naturally high spirits seemed to be getting out of hand. The minute breakfast was over, the children would be packed off, the table cleared and the despatch boxes brought out.

For the rest of these summer days Princess Alice and her cousins would enjoy themselves in the park: scrambling about the buildings erected by the Prince Consort for the delight, and edification, of the previous generation – the beautifully equipped Swiss Cottage and the miniature fort. Or else they would play on the beach, beside the glittering Solent. 'I took a long walk . . .' wrote Princess Alice's Aunt Vicky* from Osborne in 1893, 'through the woods and down by the sea. The water was gently rippling – with a little lazy splash on the beach – and the birds were singing. . . . I am never tired of going down to the beach – and wandering in the woods – and listening to the Birds!'[41]

Innumerable photographs capture the atmosphere of these summer days of Princess Alice's childhood at Osborne: the princesses dressed like little adults in their straw boaters and leg-o'-mutton sleeves, the princes sporting kilts or Eton suits, the miniature carriages, the ponies, the dogs, the gravelled pathways and, behind, the massive, dark-leaved trees.

But it was Christmas at Osborne that Princess Alice enjoyed most of all. The famous Indian Room, with its exotic white, wedding-cake decor, would be rendered more exotic still by the lavish Christmas

---

* The Empress Frederick, formerly the Princess Royal.

decorations. Tables, covered in long white cloths, would be stacked, not only with presents, but with 'piles of delicious German cakes'.[42] Towering over the row of other Christmas trees would be the Prince Consort's tree, 'an enchanting one . . . that played Christmas tunes as it rotated round and round'.[43]

Although the climate of the Isle of Wight was comparatively mild, it was certainly never as mild as Queen Victoria claimed it to be. The Queen was impervious to cold and an aspect of life in her grand-mother's homes which Princess Alice would after-wards recall with amusement was the iciness of the rooms.[†] The grates were often empty, the windows almost never closed. The Queen demanded the wear-ing of full evening dress – a low neckline and short sleeves – at dinner, and a low bodice, coupled with the Queen's insistence on open windows, could have disastrous results.

One evening during a dinner party, at Osborne, one of the ladies fainted at table. 'You see, Beatrice,' cried the Queen, rounding triumphantly on her youngest daughter, 'you will keep the rooms so warm!'[44] So, in spite of the fact that a chill wind was already blowing across the lady's bare shoulders, more windows were flung open and the company was subjected to a further drop in temperature.

[†] This iciness was not confined to the Queen's houses. 'She refused to allow my mother to install central heating at Claremont,' Princess Alice once told me.

There were limits, though, says Princess Alice, to the lowness of the neckline allowed at the Queen's table. On one occasion, as the royal party was about to process into dinner, Queen Victoria pointed her fan towards the décolletage of her granddaughter, Princess Helena Victoria, and instructed, 'A little rose in front, dear child, because of the footmen.'[45]

5

It was the annual holiday at Queen Victoria's favourite home, Balmoral, that Princess Alice preferred to all the others. 'Here,' she says, 'we spent some of the happiest days of our lives.'[46] The Queen would lend the Duchess of Albany Birkhall, a shooting lodge near Ballater, some ten miles from Balmoral. To Princess Alice and Prince Charles Edward it was like paradise: the comfortable home with its garden full of fruit and flowers, the chain bridge swaying above the rushing River Muick, the enormous teas of cakes and scones and jam, the visits to the village shop kept by the two Misses Simons ('inveterate robbers,'[47] says Princess Alice), the long walks across the heather-covered hillsides, the drives to Crathie church on Sundays, the expeditions through the magnificent Highland scenery, the vast family picnics.

Then there would be the visits to Balmoral itself. In this aggressively Scottish setting – the exterior, designed by the Prince Consort, was all granite and turrets and crenellations, the interior was a riot of tartan walls, curtains and chair-covers – Queen Victoria would be at her most content. At Balmoral, too, her parasol tent would be pitched in the garden until, but not until, 'the snow drove her in'.[48] Then she would work in her library.

But no matter what the weather, the Queen enjoyed nothing more than driving out to picnic in some lonely glen. Princess Alice remembered one occasion when, in pelting rain, her grandmother arrived in an open landau for a picnic tea in the Ballochbhui wood. A fire was lit so that the young people could dry their sopping coats and luckily, by the time the tea board was laid across the Queen's carriage and the tea poured, the rain had stopped. 'But even if it had not done so,' claimed Princess Alice, 'we should have still gone on with our picnic'

On another occasion it was not only raining but snowing when the Queen announced that she was ready for her morning drive. Understandably (to everyone, that is, other than the Queen herself) no one was prepared to accompany her in her open pony carriage. So the little Princess Alice – to her 'intense joy and pride' – was chosen to accompany her grandmother. 'Out we went,' remembers the Princess, 'sleet pouring down on us, nothing daunted.'[49]

Although, by the time the Princess was growing up, the Queen was no longer astonishing her family and household by the vigour with which she danced at the annual Gillies Ball, she still attended and enjoyed them. Always so awkward in, and disapproving of,

London Society, the Queen felt thoroughly at ease among the simple Highlanders as they roistered their way through the ball that marked the end of her stay in Balmoral.

For Princess Alice, these balls were 'the greatest fun'.[50] She tells the story of the doleful old Miss Campbell of the Glassalt Shiel on Loch Muick, who explained to the Duchess of Albany that she would not be attending the ball because she had recently had all her teeth extracted. But there, on the night, was a beaming Miss Campbell. She had managed, she confided happily, to borrow a set of false teeth from her friend, Miss Cameron of Altna-Giuthasach Shiel.

'I often recall with nostalgia these early days at Balmoral,' wrote Princess Alice in her old age. 'Our expeditions and our picnics and how we used to take tea with different keepers in their nice granite homes. We were just like one big family. . . .'[51]

6

A more exotic setting for these meetings with Queen Victoria would be the South of France. During the last decade of the nineteenth century Queen Victoria went, each spring, to Cimiez, above Nice. At the same time the Albanys would go to Cannes, to the Villa Nevada in which Prince Leopold had died. By now, the villa had been given to the Duchess of Albany 'as a memento'. Queen Victoria, who had visited the villa on several occasions, had lost no time in erecting a memorial to her dead son. It was, says Princess Alice irreverently, 'a large and singularly repulsive marble bench seat surmounted by the inscription, "Not lost but gone before" '. [52]

At the Villa Nevada, as at Claremont, the aura of melancholy had been dispelled by the presence of the two Albany children. In any case, melancholy was not easy to sustain in such sparkling sunshine, amid such sweet-scented flowers and with such glorious views. The children chased butterflies, collected botanical specimens and sailed their little boats along the canal which brought the drinking water from Grasse to Cannes. At least once or twice each season the Queen, attended by the faithful Princess Beatrice and her ladies, would drive over to the Villa Nevada, or else the Duchess of Albany would take the children to luncheon with their grandmama in her palm-filled dining-room at the Grand Hotel Excelsior Regina at Cimiez.

7

These regular visits to Queen Victoria at Windsor, Osborne, Balmoral and the Riviera were to be an almost uninterrupted feature of the first eighteen years of Princess Alice's life. They gave her, in this most formative period, a wonderful sense of security. There was something infinitely reassuring about the old Queen's unchanging pattern of life; only for the most drastic reasons (and then with a very bad grace) would Queen Victoria change her annual routine. To grow to adulthood against a background of such continuity, of such predictability and of such stability was of inestimable value to Princess Alice.

Her close association with Queen Victoria gave her something else as well: an appreciation of her grandmother's true character. It was a character very different from the popular conception of the Widow of Windsor. Princess Alice was always to maintain that Queen Victoria was a greatly misunderstood and mis-represented person. She was by no means the dour, disapproving, narrow-minded ogre that she was made out to be. On the contrary, the Princess always found her tolerant, sympathetic and far from prudish. 'She was a wonderfully *kind* person,'[53] she would say.

The truth was, that by the time Princess Alice was growing up, the Queen had emerged from her long period of mourning for Prince Albert. Coaxed back into an enjoyment of life by the support of John Brown, the attentions of Disraeli, and the *joie de vivre* of her son-in-law (her daughter Princess Beatrice's husband, Prince Henry of Batten-berg*) Queen Victoria was once more allowing her true, robust, down-to-earth nature to emerge. This meant that to her grandchildren, she was a warmer, much less frightening person than she had been to her own children. They found her approachable, amenable, easily amused.

---

* Prince Henry (1858–96) was the third son of Prince Alexander of Hesse, who had made a morganatic marriage.

'I once asked Queen Victoria,' Princess Alice would say in later life, 'if she ever said "We are not amused", and she said no, she hadn't. She never said it.'[54]

On the contrary, the Queen's capacity for laughing uproariously at some funny story was noted time and again by her grandchildren. 'She used to open her mouth and roar with laughter, showing all her gums,'[55] claims Princess Alice. She tells a story of her grandmother hiding her face in her hands when, in Crathie church one Sunday, the preacher earnestly prayed that the Queen might 'skip like a he-goat upon the mountains'.[56]

And Princess Alice's cousin, the prince who was to become Kaiser Wilhelm II, used to tell about a certain hilarious conversation which once took place at Osborne.

A sailing frigate, *Eurydice,* having sunk off Portsmouth, had been salvaged and towed in. As the Queen was very interested in the incident, she invited Admiral Foley to luncheon to tell her more about it. 'After she had exhausted this melancholy subject,' said Prince Wilhelm, 'my grandmother, in order to give the conversation a more cheerful turn, inquired after his sister, whom she knew well, whereupon the Admiral, who was hard of hearing and still pursuing his train of thought about the *Eurydice,* replied in his stentorian voice: "Well, Ma'am, I am going to have her turned over and take a good look at her bottom and have it well scraped."

'My grandmother put down her knife and fork, hid her face in her handkerchief and shook and heaved with laughter until the tears rolled down her face.'[57]

CHAPTER FOUR

1

Queen Victoria's claim that her grandchildren needed *'no one* else' when it came to finding companions was certainly true. By the time that Princess Alice turned ten, in 1893, she had no less than thirty-one cousins from Queen Victoria's side of the family alone. They ranged from the 34-year-old Kaiser Wilhelm II to the 2-year-old Prince Maurice of Battenberg. No one could deny that the Queen had played her part in swelling what she used to describe as 'the Royal Mob'.[1]

However, not all these cousins were always to hand. Over half of them had grown up, or were growing up, in Germany: some in Berlin, some in Darmstadt and some in Coburg. Marriage had carried some of the Princess's girl cousins further afield still: to Greece, to Romania and to Russia. This meant that in England there lived only the families of her Uncle Bertie, Prince of Wales; of her Aunt Lenchen, Princess Christian of Schleswig-Holstein; of her

Uncle Arthur, the Duke of Connaught; and of her Aunt Beatrice, Princess Henry of Battenberg.

With her Wales cousins, Princess Alice did not have a great deal to do. Even the youngest of them, Princess Maud, was fourteen years older than she was. To the young Princess Alice, the Prince of Wales was a big, bluff, blustering figure, difficult to talk to and much given to teasing: that 'odious chaffing mood'[2] his daughter-in-law used to call the Prince of Wales's embarrassing brand of *bonhomie*. But underneath the banter the Prince of Wales was a magnanimous man. The Duchess of Albany was always grateful to her brother-in-law for showing no resentment of the fact that Queen Victoria had shown a confidence in the late Prince Leopold which she had never been prepared to extend to him, her heir. On the contrary, the Prince of Wales was always kindness itself to the Duchess and her two children.

In turn, the outspoken Duchess of Albany always took the Prince's part in his frequent misunderstandings with the Queen. 'I have always admired and respected your mother,'[3] the Prince once confided to Princess Alice.

The Princess was always to remember one incident connected with a visit to the Wales family at Sandringham. Four years old at the time, she had been lifted up onto a writing table for inspection by her Uncle Bertie. 'I shall never forget the look of consternation on Mother's face when, losing control of myself from excitement, a pool suddenly appeared on the table!'[4]

Equally kind, in her *distrait* way, was Aunt Alix, the Princess of Wales. Beautiful, elegant, apparently ageless ('there was about Aunt Alix, something invincible, something exquisite and flower-like',[5] wrote one of Princess Alice's cousins), the Princess of Wales would drift in and out of Princess Alice's life, always trailing her three identically-dressed and strangely negative daughters, 'the Whispering Wales girls' – Princess Louise, Princess Victoria and Princess Maud. With these women of the Wales family, young Princess Alice would have felt completely at ease; the Princess of Wales might have been socially accomplished and flawlessly groomed but she shared her daughters' unsophisticated tastes and knockabout brand of humour. At times, they seemed hardly more grown-up than Princess Alice herself.

This air of permanent adolescence characterised the two Wales princes as well. The elder, Prince Albert Victor, known to the family as Eddy, was a listless, apathetic, slow-witted creature, immature to an alarming degree. As Prince Eddy sported extra high collars and long cuffs in a misguided attempt to minimise the length of his neck and his arms, his father would insist on Princess Alice referring to him as 'Collar and Cuffs'. Of this the Duchess of Albany strongly disapproved. The younger brother, Prince George, was a much livelier, more disciplined personality, but even he seemed to suffer from arrested development.

Unsuspected by Princess Alice at the time, a drama was being played out in the Wales family that would affect her future position considerably. In December 1891 Prince Eddy had become engaged to be married. The engagement had been engineered by the Prince's despairing family in the hope that marriage to a sensible and dependable wife would help give some sort of shape to his amorphous personality. As his future bride, they had chosen Princess May of Teck.

Princess May was the only daughter of the Duke and Duchess of Teck. The Duke of Teck was the son, by a morganatic marriage, of Duke Alexander of Württemberg, while the Duchess was Queen Victoria's first cousin: like the Queen, the Duchess of Teck (who had been Princess Mary Adelaide of Cambridge) was a granddaughter of King George III. The Tecks were thus members, but only fringe members, of the British royal family. Indeed, the *Almanach de Gotha* had recently demoted the Tecks: they were now relegated to Part Two where they were obliged to rub shoulders with non-royal company. ('We are *furious and indignant* beyond words',[6] spluttered Queen Victoria on hearing the news.) All this meant that Princess May of Teck's engagement to the heir presumptive was due more to her dependability of character than to any spectacular social position.

The engagement lasted less than six weeks. On 14 January 1892 Prince Eddy died of pneumonia.

Hardly had he been laid to rest in the vault of St George's Chapel at Windsor than his family began to think in terms of marrying Princess May to her late fiancé's only surviving brother, Prince George, who had now, in turn, become heir presumptive. He, hardly less than his brother, was in need of an intelligent, capable and conscientious wife. And so, on 6 July 1893, eighteen months after Prince Eddy's death, Prince George married Princess May.

The Duke and Duchess of Teck were delighted. Their relatively obscure daughter would one day be Queen of England and their own importance had increased enormously. For the 10-year-old Princess Alice, this shift in the Teck fortunes was one day to have considerable significance.

At the time, though, the marriage of Princess Alice's cousin Georgie was significant to her in one respect only: it brought her a bitter disappointment. She was holidaying at her grandfather's home, Arolsen in Waldeck, when the engagement was announced, and not long after this she was asked to be one of Princess May's bridesmaids. Princess Alice was ecstatic. For one thing she longed to be a bridesmaid: for another, both she and the faithful Miss Potts were anxious to get back home. But it was not to be. Another telegram arrived to tell her that she need not bother to come back: Princess Alice of Battenberg* had been chosen to take her place.

She was a 'much prettier girl anyhow', conceded Princess Alice gallantly, 'but I never got over the disappointment."

---

* Princess Alice (1885–1969) was the eldest daughter of Prince Louis of Battenberg (afterwards created Marquess of Milford Haven) and future mother of Prince Philip, Duke of Edinburgh.

Like her Wales cousins, Princess Alice's Schleswig-Holstein cousins – the four children of her Aunt Lenchen or Princess Christian – were too old to be playmates. Some ten years separated the youngest of these Schleswig-Holstein princesses from Princess Alice.* But with the remaining cousins, the Connaughts and the Battenbergs, the Albany children were very close. These last nine grandchildren of Queen Victoria had been born in the nine years between 1882 and 1891, which meant that during her visits to Windsor, Osborne and Balmoral, Princess Alice never lacked friends of her own generation.

Although the three Connaught children-Princess Margaret, Prince Arthur and Princess Patricia – were closest to Princess Alice in age, she tended to see more of the Battenberg children – Prince Alexander, Princess Victoria Eugenie (known as Ena), Prince Leopold and Prince Maurice. This was because they lived with Queen Victoria. Their mother, the Queen's youngest daughter, the shy Princess Beatrice, had been allowed to marry the swashbuckling Prince Henry of Battenberg only on the condition that he made his home with the Queen. This, with a fairly good grace, he did. The result was that the four Battenberg children grew up very much under the wing of their grandmother. When Prince Henry died, somewhat unheroically, in 1896 of fever while on his

---

* The Schleswig-Holstein children were Prince Christian Victor (1867–1900), Prince Albert (1869–1931), Princess Helena Victoria (1870–1948) and Princess Marie Louise (1872–1956).

way out to serve in the Ashanti campaign (he had finally to get away, it seems, from his mother-in-law's overwhelming presence), the Battenberg children were tucked even more tightly under the Queen's wing.

It was almost inevitable then that the young Battenbergs should become closely associated with their other fatherless cousins – the Albanys. With Princess Ena, Princess Alice developed an especially close friendship; one which was to last all their lives. Princess Alice admired Princess Ena's 'gaiety and pretty looks'[8] and shared her taste for the open air – for rowing, for riding, for bicycling. Both girls had a certain open, honest-to-goodness quality; both glowed with apparent good health. Both, despite the strongly Germanic strains in their ancestry, came to epitomise everyone's idea of a British princess: fair-skinned, rosy-cheeked, high-spirited, sensible, conscientious, unaffected and as honest as the day was long.

2

But Princess Alice belonged to another world as well. Through her mother she was related to various smaller, humbler but invariably stiffer continental courts. She had Bentheim relations at Schloss Burgsteinfurt in the Rhineland, Württemberg relations at the Royal Palace in Stuttgart, Orange-Nassau relations at the Royal Palace in The Hague and, of course, her Waldeck-Pyrmont relations at Schloss Arolsen.

To these continental courts and to various other European cities, the Duchess of Albany and her children would pay frequent and prolonged visits. There were holidays in such elegant cities as Prague, Dresden and Vienna. There were weddings where hordes of German relations would sit down to gargantuan banquets at splendidly decorated tables. There were overnight journeys in plush-upholstered saloon carriages; meetings with first or second cousins in the *Kursaal* of some spa; outings – complete with ladies-in-waiting, equerries and liveried footmen – to gaze at spectacular views, romantic ruins or shimmering lakes. It was all a wonderfully privileged, cushioned and secure-seeming way of life. Few of those who were fortunate enough to enjoy it could have guessed how soon it was to be swept away.

To a British-born princess like Princess Alice, these continental courts had a formal, old-fashioned, almost comic-opera air. The rooms of the various palaces were often depressingly musty, the furniture uncomfortably shabby, the gardens inhibitingly formal. Dinner would be an enormous meal, eaten early in the afternoon, at which full evening dress would be worn. It was a world of rigid protocol, of stilted conversation, of close chaperonage, of narrow-minded attitudes, of obsessive interest in such things as quarterings, ancestry and the purity of blood lines. A morganatic marriage was considered hardly less shameful than a mortal sin.

To her credit Queen Victoria would have no truck with such bigotry. When, on sanctioning the marriage of not only one, but two morganatic Battenberg princes into her own family, the Prussian royal family wrote to express their reservations, the Queen was furious. How *dare* they address her in that tone? How *could* they refer to the Battenbergs as not being *Geblüt* – pure bred – as though they were animals!

None of this is to say that Princess Alice's close relatives shared this blinkered outlook. On the contrary, the Waldeck family was surprisingly progressive. The court at Arolsen 'could certainly be called enlightened,' noted one of Princess Alice's continental cousins, 'particularly when one considers the fact that the small German courts were half a century or more behind the rest of society. This home was in advance of its time.'9

But, even so, Princess Alice was always conscious of the punctilious, old-world atmosphere at Arolsen. Her visits there brought her into contact with a way of life that was fast disappearing; it reminded her that she was rooted, not only in Queen Victoria's England, but in the old Germany – that assortment of kingdoms and principalities and free cities which had only comparatively recently been unified into a single state. She could still have found traces of Germany as it had been before its transformation into the showy, swaggering, Prussian-dominated militarism of the Second Reich. At Arolsen there remained something of the grace and culture and tranquillity of pre-Wilhelmine days. For Princess Alice, it must have been like stepping back into the eighteenth century. Life in the rococo palace of Arolsen, for all its comparative enlightenment, was certainly a far cry from the free-and-easy ways of Claremont.

Once every two years the Albany family would travel to Waldeck to take part in a great family reunion. The journey from Claremont would be a mammoth operation. The huge party – the Duchess, her two children, her comptroller, her lady-in-waiting, the children's governess, their nursemaid and several other servants – would make the nightmarish ten-hour crossing to Flushing. There, together with their wardrobe trunks, their cabin trunks, their suitcases, their hampers, their rugs, their coats and the children's toys, they would transfer to the waiting train. The train journey always seemed interminable. Princess Alice and Prince Charles Edward would be obliged to sit still, playing with their toys or reading their books; the only relief would be the unpacking and eating of luncheon, the washing up of the dishes in the lavatory between the two compartments and their midday sleep. And when they arrived, hours later, tired and fretful at Warburg station, they still had to face an eighteen-mile carriage drive to Arolsen.

The Princess's Waldeck grandmother, that intelligent and iron-willed invalid, had died in 1888 when Princess Alice was five, and her grandfather had married, as his second wife, the 30-year-old Princess Louise, daughter of the Duke of Schleswig-Holstein. The Princess has dismissed this step-grandmother as 'a first cousin and an ugly likeness of Queen Alexandra'.[10]

Little Princess Alice was much more taken, apparently, with the wife of her Uncle Fritz – her mother's eldest brother Friedrich – who succeeded to the title of Prince of Waldeck-Pyrmont on the death of his father in 1893. Two years after his succession, he married Princess Bathildis of Schaumburg-Lippe. Princess Alice always remembered the triumphal return of her Uncle Fritz and his bride to Arolsen after their wedding in Bohemia. As she and her brother Prince Charles Edward (watched over by the ubiquitous Miss Potts) stepped forward to present a bouquet to the beautiful and vivacious young bride in her pale lilac dress, Princess Alice warmed to her immediately.

'She took Charlie and me to her heart for ever after and we spent many happy days visiting her and Uncle Fritz and their charming children until the First World War separated us completely and changed our relationship with the dear old people we had known so well'.[11]

Far and away the most important of Princess Alice's maternal relations to attend these family gatherings at Arolsen was the daughter of her Aunt Emma – her mother's sister who had married King William III of the Netherlands. The old King had died in 1890 and as all three sons of his first marriage had predeceased him, his crown went to his only child by his second marriage: his daughter

Princess Wilhelmina. As Princess Wilhelmina was only ten at the time of her father's death her mother, Queen Emma, had to act as Regent until her daughter's coming of age in 1898. (How gratified Princess Alice's ambitious grandmother, the Princess of Waldeck-Pyrmont, would have been to know that three of her descendants – Wilhelmina, Juliana and Beatrix – would all in turn be Queens Regnant of the Netherlands.)

Like her cousin Princess Alice, young Queen Wilhemina adored these family reunions at Arolsen. 'It was always a wonderful experience for me to play as an equal among my cousins,' wrote this only child. 'There we fought over our toys, as children will do. Only very rarely did I have a chance to practise my fighting at home, when the cousins came to stay with us.'[12]

'Arolsen,' she wrote on another occasion, 'the castle and-its surroundings, have a charm all their own, and the same can be said of Waldeck with its fields and deep forests, its ravines, mountains and hills and its bracing climate'.[13] It was very different, in short, from the flat, featureless landscape of the Netherlands.

Princess Alice was equally appreciative of the delights of the countryside around Arolsen. Chattering happily away in German, she and her cousins would go walking or driving through the picture-postcard landscape. She loved the walks through the dense pine forests, the drives through the villages with their narrow streets and leaning, timbered houses, the views of the

89

gently rolling fields with the plough being hauled, if the farmer were poor, by his wife.

Sometimes the Princess's continental cousins might visit her in England. In the spring of 1895, for instance, when Princess Alice was twelve, Queen Emma and the 14-year-old Queen Wilhelmina came to stay with the Duchess of Albany at Claremont. On 2 May they made the obligatory visit to Queen Victoria at Windsor. 'Shortly before two,' noted the Queen in her Journal that evening, 'went downstairs to receive the Queen Regent of the Netherlands and her daughter, the young Queen Wilhelmina. Beatrice had been to meet them at the station, and Helen came with them. The young Queen, who will be fifteen in August, has her hair still hanging down. She is very slight and graceful, has fine features, and seems to be very intelligent and a charming child. She speaks English extremely well, and has very pretty manners.'[14]

Quite obviously, Princess Alice was very impressed by the fact that her cousin was a Queen. Queen Victoria's lady-in-waiting, Marie Mallet, was highly amused at Princess Alice's views on her Dutch cousin's future. The 16-year-old Queen, explained young Princess Alice to Marie Mallet at tea one day, was to have two years of complete 'liberty and amusement' before taking up the reins of office at eighteen.

'Why,' asked Marie Mallet, 'what would she do? Give balls and parties?'

'No,' replied the Princess solemnly. 'She only likes dancing by herself, twirling round on one leg or in a "valse", but when she is really Queen she means to visit her *own* Indies and she is learning the language out of lesson time.'

But surely, argued Marie Mallet, her mother, Queen Emma, would not allow her to leave the country?

'Oh, she has thought of that,' answered the Princess, 'she will leave her mother as Regent; Grandmama goes abroad, why should not she?'

It was on Queen Victoria, in fact, that the young Queen Wilhelmina was planning to model herself.

'When I grow up I shall not be a Queen like you,' Queen Wilhelmina once assured her mother, 'but a *real* Queen like the Queen of England.'[15]

3

When Princess Alice was fourteen she took part in what she has described as 'the most unforgettable event in my life'.[16] This was Queen Victoria's Diamond Jubilee procession. It opened her eyes, for the first time, to the full splendour of the position occupied by the royal House to which she belonged.*

---

* Princess Alice had memories of the Queen's Golden Jubilee, in 1887, as well. She would have been four years old at the time. In old age the Princess would describe how her nurse had hurried her away from the luncheon table (it had been her favourite, fish, she said) on to the balcony at Buckingham Palace so that she could see the return of Queen Victoria's carriage procession from Westminster Abbey.

The Diamond Jubilee differed from the Golden Jubilee, ten years before, in that it was a manifestation of British imperial power rather than a gathering of European royalties. No crowned heads were invited. The thought of all those kings and emperors crowding into Buckingham Palace was more than the 78-year-old Queen could bear. Nevertheless, there was no shortage of lesser royals. Princes and princesses from every court in Europe came swarming into London: Buckingham Palace, reported the Empress Frederick to one of her daughters, was like a beehive. It was so crammed that the visiting members of the royal family hardly saw anything of each other.

But it was as the ruler of a mighty Empire rather than as the doyenne of Europe's sovereigns or the head of a great dynasty that Queen Victoria was being fêted on Jubilee Day – 22 June 1897. The 3-hour-long drive through the streets of London, with a pause for a thanksgiving service outside St Paul's Cathedral, was designed as a grand imperial gesture – a display of the diversity, unity, might and magnificence of the British Empire.

For Princess Alice, then in her most impressionable years, it was a day of unforgettable brilliance. The weather had been cloudy to begin with but as the guns began to thunder out in Hyde Park and as, one after another, the carriages carrying the members of the Queen's family began to leave Buckingham Palace, the sun burst forth. In an instant, the whole kaleidoscopic scene was set alight. With Princess Alice in her carriage were her two Battenberg cousins. Princess Ena and Princess Alice and, to keep an eye on the three of them, the Mistress of the Robes, the Duchess of Buccleuch.

In the carriage behind rode Princess Alice's brother, Prince Charles Edward, with several of his cousins. 'The gravity with which the tiny Princes and Princesses acknowledged the greetings of the spectators occasioned great delight among the people', noted one observer, 'and the military salutes of the young Duke of Albany and Prince Arthur of Connaught were signals for fresh outbursts of applause.'[17]

But it was not military salutes all the way for Prince Charles Edward. Because he had spent so much time on the palace roof, watching the start of the great procession, he had had to bolt his breakfast just before scrambling into the carriage. The combination of the hot sun, the rocking carriage and the general excitement soon proved too much for him: an ambulance was summoned and the queasy Prince relieved of his meal.

As Princess Alice drove in procession through the crowded, clamorous, brightly decorated streets so, ahead of her, stretched a vast river of troops. The colonial contingent was led by the jaunty, diminutive Lord Roberts and was made up of soldiers from every corner of the earth: 'white men, yellow men, brown men, black men', Zaptiehs from Cyprus in fezzes,

Australians in slouch hats, Sikhs in turbans, Malays, Dyaks, Chinese, 'grinning Hausas so dead black that they shone like silver in the sun'.[18] The royal procession proper was led by the 6ft. 8in. Captain Oswald Ames, the tallest (and, says Princess Alice, the stupidest) man in the British Army. Now the pageant became more colourful still. Plumes waving, breastplates gleaming, swords thudding, accoutrements all a-jingle, came Life Guards, Hussars, Lancers and Batteries of the Royal Horse Artillery.

And all the while, as Princess Alice drove along in this spectacular cortege, she could hear the even more vociferous cheering behind her as the crowd greeted the Queen. Preceded by an escort of Household Cavalry and escorted by a troop of princes, the old Queen passed by in her open landau. It was drawn by eight cream-coloured horses, complete with mounted postillions and liveried footmen. With the Queen sat the Princess of Wales and Princess Christian. As always, Princess Alexandra, in a mauve dress and mauve flowered toque, looked flawlessly elegant, while the Queen looked hardly different from her everyday self. Her dress was of black moiré silk embroidered with silver roses, shamrocks and thistles; her cape was of black and white lace. Her black lace bonnet was trimmed with jet, white acacia, ostrich feathers and a diamond aigrette. To shield herself from the blazing sun, she carried a Chantilly lace parasol, presented to her by the House of Commons.

'Almost pathetic, if you will,' wrote an observer, 'that small, black figure in the middle of these shining cavaliers, this great army, this roaring multitude; but also very glorious.'[19] So moved, so gratified, so elated was the old Queen by her reception that tears sometimes rolled down her cheeks. When they did, the Princess of Wales would gently press her hand.

On and on – up Constitution Hill, along Piccadilly, down St James's Street, along Pall Mall and the Strand – rolled the procession. Princess Alice had eyes for everything: for the spectators crowding the rooftops (the Queen had sent anxious messages to the Home Office to ensure that the roofs and balconies would not be overloaded), for the Fijian troops with their hair teased heavenwards and dyed red, for the Lord Mayor valiantly mounting his mettlesome horse in full robes of office, for the motionless soldiers and sailors lining the entire route, for the 'richly clad rajahs and picturesque oriental dignitaries'.[20]

At the steps of St Paul's Cathedral the procession halted and, with the lame old Queen remaining firmly in her carriage, a short thanksgiving service was conducted in the open air. 'No,' exclaimed the Queen's cousin, the British-born Grand Duchess of Mecklenburg-Strelitz, on first hearing of the plan, 'that out-of-doors service before St Paul's! Has one ever heard of such a thing! after sixty years' reign, to thank God in the street!!!'[21]

But thanked in the street God duly was. And the unusual proceedings in no way detracted from the memorability of the occasion. 'The cheering which greeted Grandmama as she arrived and drove away was stupendous and deafening,'[22] says Princess Alice.

On then, by way of the Mansion House, across the Thames to the poorer districts of the South Bank, back over Westminster Bridge and home to Buckingham Palace. It had all been a brilliant success. 'Grandmama,' remembered Princess Alice, 'was radiant throughout and did not seem in the least tired – probably owing to the stimulating effect of the demonstrations, the excitement of the experience and her gratitude for the devotion of her people.'[23]

Nothing, Princess Alice would claim in later life, not even the four coronations which she attended, ever equalled the impressiveness of Queen Victoria's Diamond Jubilee procession.[*]

4

But hand in hand with the glory went the responsibility. Very early on Princess Alice had learnt that there was more to being a national life. None of them escaped the royal round of speech-making, foundation stone-laying, tree-planting, hospital-visiting, bazaar-opening, prize-giving, exhibition attending and charity concert-going. And there were other, less noticeable public duties as well: the committee work, the organisation and the patronage of various public

---

[*] To mark the occasion, Princess Alice was awarded the V. A. (Lady of the Order of Victoria and Albert) in 1898.

charities. Driven on by a highly developed sense of duty and responsibility, the members of the British royal family fulfilled their manifold tasks to the best of their abilities.

Whether any of them had any real appreciation of the shameful social injustices of the time is doubtful. In common with the vast majority of the members of the Victorian upper classes, they simply accepted things as they were: they never reflected on the causes of the poverty and misery and inequality of their day. Their attitudes were those of Lady Bountiful. Kindhearted, generous, concerned, they tried to alleviate whatever hardships were brought to their attention by acts of charity. Their contacts with the lower classes were mainly with their servants (and, goodness knows, they seemed happy enough); poverty was personified by the cap-doffing crofter in the Highlands or the ruddy-cheeked farmhand on various royal and aristocratic estates. Of the grinding penury and seething discontent in the great industrial cities they knew very little and understood even less.

Princess Alice's reflections on the order of things during her girlhood is typical of these well-intentioned, if uncomprehending, attitudes.

Class distinctions permeated the whole social structure and could be as rigid in the servants' hall and in the village as they were in the castle. These distinctions were, however, tempered by gracious manners and, in general, a courteous consideration for others, alas so rare today, governed the relationships between all ranks of society. Servants considered themselves part of the family and were always accepted as such. Their children worked under them in the house and were appointed to vacancies as these occurred or as they grew up. We were trained from childhood to help the needy and care for the sick living in our neighbourhood. Tuberculosis was a scourge in those days and a regular duty of ours was to take soup, jelly and other invalid diets to the homes of those afflicted with it. Discipline at home and familiarity with the troubles of others, with illness and with death, cultivated in us a sense of responsibility, poise and self-control.[24]

The Duchess of Albany, in fact, had a rather more highly developed social conscience than most. On the Duchess's marriage to Prince Leopold, Queen Victoria had been afraid that, like many German-born princesses, she would not be prepared to adopt the British royal tradition of visiting the poor and the sick. She was very relieved to find that the Duchess liked 'to go among the people'.[25] The Duchess went among them, in truth, with a will that sometimes startled her less energetic relations. She lent her name, her time and her talents to numberless humanitarian causes: the Hospitals Joint Appeal, the Waterloo

Hospital for Women and Children, the Hospital for Epilepsy, the Needlework Guild.

Her most celebrated charitable achievement was the Deptford Fund. On hearing that young girls were being employed at the Deptford Cattle Market, at shamefully low wages, to clean out the guts of the slaughtered cattle, the Duchess made her way through the blood and slime of the market to see conditions for herself. What she saw appalled her. Immediately she tackled the Home Secretary who, on her insistence, put a stop to the revolting practice. This meant, though, that the girls were now out of work and, in order to relieve their plight, the Duchess founded the Deptford Fund. This organisation provided either money or alternative work for the girls. The Duchess was actively concerned with the Fund for the rest of her life.

With such a mother as an example, it is no wonder that Princess Alice was involved in charity work from a very early age. 'Almost from infancy,' she says, 'we were trained to work for, and take part in, charitable movements. These disciplines applied to every walk of life, but I think they were more strictly enforced in royal families.'[26] Throughout her life, the Princess was more than merely conventionally associated with countless charities.

Equally important, for a young princess, as the development of a sense of service, was the development of social graces. She had to learn to paint, to sing, to recite, to play the piano, to dance, to carry

99

herself properly and above all, to talk. 'Nothing,' Princess Alice's Aunt Marie, Duchess of Edinburgh, used to say, 'is more hopeless than a princess who never opens her mouth.'[27] This was all very well but when they were girls the princesses were expected to keep their mouths closed unless addressed directly. 'In our day,' as Queen Mary once said, 'children were brought up to be seen and not heard. There's something in it: we learned a lot by listening to our elders – only when we went out into company it was supposed that hey presto! we should at once scintillate in sparkling conversation.'[28]

She was right. Queen Victoria certainly expected her grown-up granddaughters, if not exactly to scintillate, at least to hold their own in conversation. Even when they were not fully grown she expected it. When Princess Alice's cousin, Princess Marie Louise of Schleswig-Holstein, was only fifteen, she once found herself seated at dinner beside the Lord Chancellor. Overcome by shyness, she sat mum. Mum, that is, until she heard a message being whispered in her ear. 'The Queen wishes the young princesses to remember that their duty is to entertain their neighbours at table.'[29]

In many ways Princess Alice was more fortunate than most of her girl cousins. As she grew up, so did the Duchess of Albany arrange for her to go up to London for extra classes: in science, in literature, in drawing and in dancing. She was the first royal pupil at Madame Vacani's famous dancing school. All this brought her into contact with a great variety of people; it opened her eyes to different ways of life; it encouraged her to make conversation.

But where Princess Alice was most fortunate was in not being cursed with the shyness that has plagued so many members of Queen Victoria's family from the old Queen down to the present generation. The Princess was naturally vivacious, naturally gregarious, naturally curious, naturally outgoing. Such shyness as she occasionally experienced was simply the charming bashfulness of youth; it was not that frightening, inhibiting, unconquerable shyness that has turned the life of so many a royal person into a form of torture.

Another step on the road to adulthood came when Princess Alice was fifteen. She was confirmed. The confirmation took place in the South of France, while the Albanys were holidaying at the Villa Nevada. The ceremony, on a spring day in 1898, was held in the little Albany Chapel (a memorial chapel to the late Prince Leopold) and conducted by the Bishop of Winchester.* Both Queen Victoria and the Prince of Wales drove over from Nice for the occasion.

'I cannot ever be thankful enough to my dear mother,' says Princess Alice, 'for her splendid religious faith which she instilled into both my brother and myself.'[30] This 'splendid', sincere, unquestioning Anglican faith remained with the Princess throughout

---

* Randall Davidson, afterwards Archbishop of Canterbury.

101

her life. Of a Laudian, if broad-minded variety, it was reinforced by regular church-going. There must have been very few Sundays during her lifetime that Princess Alice did not attend Divine Service. Even in her eighties and nineties, in some far-flung corner of the world – the north coast of Jamaica, the Cape Peninsula of South Africa – the small, elegant figure, in a pale summer dress, hat and gloves was to be seen tripping up the steps of some tiny Anglican church to join the local congregation in worship.

Chapter Five

1

On 6 February 1899, when Princess Alice was not quite sixteen, her cousin Prince Alfred, only son of her Uncle Alfred, Duke of Edinburgh, died of consumption at the age of twenty-four. His death brought a dramatic change in the life of the Duchess of Albany and her children. The change was linked with the fortunes of the dukedom of Saxe-Coburg and Gotha.

Of all the territories of continental Europe none was more precious to Queen Victoria than the Duchy of Coburg. She regarded it as the cradle of her dynasty. From this small, picturesque German state had sprung that extraordinary family which in two or three generations was to wear most of the crowns of Europe. In time, the Coburgs and their offshoots would people the thrones of Great Britain, Germany, Russia, Spain, Portugal, Norway, Sweden, Denmark, Bulgaria, Romania, Yugoslavia and Greece. They would marry into the ruling families of Austria,

France and Italy. One of them was even, for a short, dramatic period, an Empress of Mexico.

Not for nothing would Prince Bismarck refer to Coburg as 'the stud farm of Europe', or a disgruntled Hapsburg archduke complain that 'the Coburgs gain throne after throne and spread their growing power abroad over the whole earth'.[1]

Queen Victoria's closest links with the Duchy of Coburg were through her mother – Princess Victoria of Saxe-Coburg – and through her husband – Prince Albert of Saxe-Coburg. So determined, in fact, was Queen Victoria to be identified with the House that had given her her adored husband, that she insisted that the British royal House from now on be known, as she once forcefully put it, as 'the *Coburg* line, like formerly the Plantagenet, the Tudor . . . the Stewart and the Bruns-wicks. . . .'[2]

It was for this reason, then, that Queen Victoria took such an active interest in the affairs of the little Duchy of Coburg. For the greater part of her reign, the Duchy had been ruled over by her brother-in-law, Prince Albert's brother, Duke Ernst II of Saxe-Coburg and Gotha. Known in the family as 'terrible old Uncle Ernest',[3] Duke Ernst could hardly have differed more from his brother, the high-minded Prince Consort. An ugly, uncouth and licentious old roué, Duke Ernst's later years had been largely given over to the seducing of young women. His wife, the Duchess Alexandrina, *

---

* Alexandrina, Duchess of Saxe-Coburg and Gotha (1820–1904), eldest daughter of Leopold, Grand Duke of Baden.

was a sad, faded creature who was never known to complain about her husband's infidelities. On the contrary, she always referred to him as 'Der Lieber, Gute Ernst'.[4]

Only occasionally did the dear, good Ernst have to pull himself together. This was whenever his formidable sister-in-law, Queen Victoria, arrived on one of her periodic visits to the scenes of her late husband's happy childhood. She would stay either at Rosenau, the mock-Gothic, ochre-coloured Schloss so beloved of the Prince Consort, or at the official ducal residence, Ehrenburg, on the Schlossplatz in Coburg.

As the Queen's apartments at Ehrenburg boasted no flush lavatory, she once summoned the Works Superintendent of the palace and ordered him to install one. 'She concluded her lengthy and detailed instructions,' says Princess Alice, 'with a final admonition "and mind you test it and sit on it to make sure it is the right height".'[5]

Although 'Der Lieber, Gute Ernst' had had children by almost every willing, or even not so willing, wench in Coburg, he had had none by his wife. This meant that on his death, in 1893, the right of succession passed to his nearest legitimate relation: the eldest son of his late brother, Prince Albert. But as it had long ago been decided to keep the British Crown free of any territorial entanglements on the Continent, the Prince of Wales (as the future King of Great Britain) waived his right of succession to the dukedom in favour of his younger brother, Alfred, Duke of Edinburgh.

So in 1893 the Duke of Edinburgh (who, together with his family had been sitting waiting in Schloss Rosenau for terrible old Uncle Ernest to die) succeeded to the dukedom of Saxe-Coburg and Gotha. 'Of course,' wrote Queen Victoria at the time, 'my interest in dear old Coburg is *very great now* that Uncle Affie is Duke.'[6]

But Uncle Affie's reign was not, quite frankly, much of an improvement on Uncle Ernest's. A bluff, handsome, uncomplicated man who, in younger days, had made a considerable success of his career in the Navy, Prince Alfred had never really fulfilled his early promise. It seems that what his family tactfully referred to as 'intemperance' had been his undoing. In short, drink rather than women was Prince Alfred's trouble. According to his niece, Princess Alice, her uncle's after-dinner conviviality, combined with his uncertain skill on the violin, diverted many a guest at Schloss Coburg. 'Full of confidence and old vintage,' she says, 'Uncle Alfred would . . . oblige with a few of his favourite selections.'[7] Those who were drunk applauded exuberantly at the wrong moments; those who were sober heard him out in embarrassed silence.

Prince Alfred's wife, the Duchess of Edinburgh, was made of altogether sterner stuff. She had been born the Grand Duchess Marie Alexandrovna, the only daughter of Tsar Alexander II of Russia. The Duchess of Edinburgh's plump figure and softly pretty face belied her strength of character: she was an energetic, proud, autocratic and masterful woman, spartan in her way of life, fanatically religious and devoted to her native Russia. With its combination of simplicity and formality, life at Coburg suited the Duchess of Edinburgh (or the Duchess of Coburg as she now was) to perfection. She was able to live, as one of her daughters put it, 'entirely according to her desires, uncontrolled by Grandmama Queen and uncriticised by those who were inclined to find her ways foreign and out of keeping with British traditions'.[8]

The couple had five children – a son and four daughters.* Although Princess Alice had not seen a great deal of these princesses (their father's career had kept them out of England for long periods) she 'adored' her somewhat exotic Edinburgh cousins. Their only brother, Prince Alfred, she did not know well. For one thing, he was nine years her senior; for another, he had been brought up in Germany in preparation for the day when he would succeed his father as Duke of Coburg.

'My memories of Alfred,' wrote one of his sisters, 'are of a stripling, eager, blundering, a little swaggering, always getting into trouble, always being scolded.' He was gay but easily offended, had keen intelligence but want of balance.[9] On completing his education, Prince Alfred had joined the Prussian Guard.

---

* The Edinburgh children were Prince Alfred (1874–99), Princess Marie (1875–1938), Princess Victoria (1876–1936), Princess Alexandra (1878–1942) and Princess Beatrice (1884–1966).

The death of this young Prince, in 1899, revived the whole vexed question of the Coburg succession. By rights the new heir to the dukedom should have been the next in order of birth of the Prince Consort's sons – this was the Duke of Edinburgh's brother, Prince Arthur, Duke of Connaught and, after him, his 15-year-old son, also named Prince Arthur.

On this assumption, the Duke of Connaught's name was submitted to the diets of the duchies of Saxe-Coburg and Gotha for their approval. But Kaiser Wilhelm II was having none of it. Whatever the legal niceties of the position might be, Coburg was part of the German Empire and the Kaiser felt that he should have been consulted on the matter. Furious at this slight, he threatened his grandmother, Queen Victoria, and her Prime Minister, Lord Salisbury, with a veto of the Reichstag.

The Duke of Connaught was not sorry to withdraw. Promptly renouncing his candidature, he suggested that his son Prince Arthur became the next heir. But now it was the young Prince Arthur's turn to dig in his heels. He had not the slightest intention, he said, of leaving Eton in order to finish his education in Germany; and even if he were forced to do so, he would simply renounce his rights to the Duchy when he turned twenty-one. He then, so runs the story, sought out his younger cousin, Prince Charles Edward, Duke of Albany, 'and threatened him with a thrashing if he did not at once offer himself as a candidate'.[10]

For, with the Connaughts, father and son, out of the running, it would indeed be the 14-year-old Duke of Albany to come next in line of succession. But the Duke of Connaught was still not reconciled to his son's refusal of the position. 'The whole family,' sighed the bewildered old Queen Victoria, 'is united in thinking it must be Charlie. But Uncle Arthur has got [it] into his head it must be young Arthur. I will not here dwell on the almost, if not *quite* insuperable difficulties of that, and all the advantages of the other, arrangement.'[11]

But, in time, the Duke of Connaught was talked round and 'the other arrangement' – the choice of Prince Charles Edward, Duke of Albany, as the heir apparent – finalised. It was agreed that the Duchess of Albany and her family would leave England to make their home in Germany so that her son could complete his education there.

Understandably, the Duchess of Albany was very upset. By now she had lived at Claremont for some seventeen years. Yet the thought of remaining there and of allowing her son to go to Germany alone was something she never seriously contemplated. 'Poor Helen,' as Queen Victoria put it, 'has been greatly agitated in the settling of the details, but the principal thing is that she need not be separated from her son.'[12]

However, it was not only the thought of leaving England that was upsetting the Duchess of Albany. What Princess Alice has described as her mother's 'great heart-break'[13] was due mainly to the fact that her small, blue-eyed, exceptionally handsome and highly strung young son was about to be transformed into a foreign princeling. 'I have always tried to bring Charlie up as a good Englishman,' she sighed, 'and now I have to turn him into a good German.'[14]

For Princess Alice, though, there seem to have been no lasting regrets. 'I was now sixteen,' she says, 'and realized that I had reached that turning point in life when I had ceased to be a child and had become more interested in adult activities.'[15] What better time, then, for a change of scene and for starting out on a new, different and possibly more exciting way of life?

2

The Duchy of Coburg, in the last years of the nineteenth century, was a charming place. Mountainous, forested, dotted with ancient villages and massive, steep-roofed castles, it seemed to epitomise the Germany of an earlier, more romantic age. Coburg, its little capital, is described by Prince Alfred's daughter Princess Marie (who afterwards became the highly theatrical Queen Marie of Romania) as 'a wee town with picturesque old parts and an ancient fortress looking down upon it from a hill which could be seen for miles around. . . . There was an old-world simplicity about Coburg; it had the ways, habits, tastes of most wee German capitals, little centres of importance that did much for the prosperity of Germany as a whole. Looking back, I understand how cosy it all was. . . .'[16]

For the newly-arrived Albany family, however, it was not quite so cosy. Things got off to a bad start. The Duchess and her children presented themselves at Schloss Reinhardsbrunn – a hunting seat in the magnificent Thuringian Forest – to find Prince Alfred in an uncooperative mood. Resolutely quaffing champagne while the others were drinking more decorous tea, he announced that not only was he not prepared to offer the Duchess a permanent home in Coburg but that he wanted to adopt Prince Charles Edward and have him live with him and his family.

The Duchess of Albany would not hear of it. So, packing up once more, they left Coburg to take advantage of the offer made by King Wilhelm II of Württemberg (the husband of the Duchess of Albany's late sister, Princess Marie of Waldeck-Pyrmont) of a suite of rooms in his palace at Stuttgart. Here, while Princess Alice attended a finishing school, Prince Charles Edward knuckled down to work with a German tutor.

This gave the Duchess a little breathing space in which to settle the question of her son's future education. There was no dearth of suggestions, helpful and unhelpful. Prince Alfred, still determined to have the boy under his wing, wanted him to attend a 'horrid, scruffy place' near Reinhardsbrunn. Princess Alice's Aunt Vicky, the enlightened but busy-bodying German Empress Frederick, insisted that he be sent to a new progressive school at Frankfurt, not far from her own home at Kronberg. But in spite of these family pressures, the Duchess of Albany held firm; 'in her quiet and unobtrusive way', says Princess Alice, her mother 'showed herself very determined'.[17] In the end she agreed to Kaiser Wilhelm's suggestion that her son attend the famous Leichterfelde military cadet school at Potsdam.

In one of those lengthy telegrams, so beloved of nineteenth-century royalty, Kaiser Wilhelm II thanked his grandmother, Queen Victoria, for approving his plan for Prince Charles Edward's education. 'Sincerest thanks,' he cabled to Windsor, 'for your kind message, approving the arrangement I suggested to Helen for the boy, modelled on the education of our eldest boy; as the scheme has so well answered with him, it will doubtless be the same with little Albany. He passed a good examination, and my General *à la suite* von Seckendorff has chosen eight well-behaved boys to form a class for him. He is a pretty and very sweet boy, and reminded me of his dear father, with whose memory so many sunny hours of my boyhood in Windsor and Osborne are linked.'[18]

The Kaiser's gushing sentiments might well have ed some smiles among the members of Queen ria's family. The most vivid memory by which Kaiser was linked to his late Uncle Leopold was e occasion, at the Prince of Wales's wedding in when little Prince Wilhelm bit his kilted – and ophilic – young uncle in the leg.

112

So the Albany family settled down in the garrison town of Potsdam to prepare for the day when Prince Charles Edward would come into his inheritance. They did not have long to wait. On 30 July 1900 Prince Alfred died of cancer of the throat, at the age of fifty-five. This meant that Charles Edward, Duke of Albany, now became Karl Eduard, Duke of Saxe-Coburg and Gotha. But as, at sixteen, the new Duke was clearly too young to become the ruler of his Duchy, it was decided that Prince Ernst of Hohenlohe-Langenburg – husband of the late Prince Alfred's second daughter, Princess Alexandra – would act as Regent until the Duke turned twenty-one.

The young Duke of Coburg was therefore able to remain at Leichterfelde and, after passing out from there, to join the famous First Regiment of Guards. During the next few years he was to be steeped in the atmosphere of brash, boastful, self-confident militarism that characterised the Second Reich.

3

Princess Alice claims to have spent some of the happiest days of her life at Potsdam. Less than half an hour by train from Berlin, Potsdam was the summer seat of the Hohenzollerns – the German imperial family. With the River Havel widening into several lakes and its low, wooded hills, Potsdam made an ideal setting for several splendid palaces: the Potsdam Palace, Sanssouci, the Neues Palais, the

Marble Palace, Babelsberg. Disraeli once described this imperial centre as 'a Paradise of Rococo'.[19] The town itself, with its tree-lined canals, its Italianate façades and its many foreign embassies, had an elegant, cosmopolitan flavour. Its over-riding atmosphere, though, was military. The streets swarmed with spectacularly uniformed soldiers; hardly a day went by without some swaggering parade. It was a place of triumphal arches, heroic monuments, processional ways and vast, many-windowed barracks. The Garrison Church, housing the tomb of Frederick the Great, was regarded as the very symbol of Prussian military might. In many ways Potsdam was the heart of the German Empire.

But the place had its gentler aspect as well. 'Potsdam will remain in my mind to the end of my life', wrote a member of the British Embassy staff at the time, 'associated with memories of fresh breezes and bellying sails; of placid lakes and swift-gliding keels responding to the straining muscles of back and legs; a place of verdant hills dipping into clear waters; of limbs joyously cleaving those clear waters with all the exultation of the swimmer; a place of rest and peace, with every fibre in one's being rejoicing in being away, for the time being, from crowded cities and stifling streets, in the free air amidst woods, waters, gently-swelling, tree-clad heights.'[20]

This is the aspect of Potsdam that would have appealed to the athletic, open-air loving Princess Alice.

The Kaiser had lent the Duchess of Albany the Villa Ingenheim, an undistinguished house with a garden that sloped down to the River Havel. By Claremont standards, the Duchess's household was a modest one: besides the Comptroller, Sir Robert Collins, her ladies-in-waiting and Miss Potts, there were a dozen or so servants, some of them from Claremont, others engaged locally and paid for by Coburg. Princess Alice's most vivid memories of this Potsdam staff were, not surprisingly, of the housemaid who tried to drown herself in the Havel and of the housekeeper who went mad.

At Potsdam the Princess was able to fling herself into those outdoor activities that she loved; rowing on the lakes in a boat that had been sent over from Claremont, skating on the frozen Havel, riding along the sandy pathways through pine woods, playing energetic games of hockey and tennis. When her brother brought his fellow cadets home from Leichterfelde she would delight in making 'stiff young lieutenants and princelings run in their tight undress uniforms'.[21]

But things were not always so informal. A great deal of the Princess's time was spent in the company of her Prussian relations – the Kaiser Wilhelm II and his family.

Even through the eyes of a young girl, Kaiser Wilhelm II emerges as a complex, puzzling, double-sided personality. On the one hand there was the restless, bombastic, brilliantly-uniformed monarch who seemed to delight in impressing his young cousin;

on the other there was the kindly, genial, generous man who was always ready for a game of tennis or a chat. For all the militarism of his appearance – the fiercely-waxed moustaches, the towering helmets, the showy uniforms – Kaiser Wilhelm II's presentation of himself as a warrior monarch was somewhat less than perfect. Acutely conscious of his undersized left arm, damaged at birth, he was careful to keep it bent; embarrassed by his shortness, he always sat on a cushion. Apparently never happier than when astride a rearing charger, acknowledging the cheers of the crowd at some *Fahnenparade,* he was just as ready to devote his time to the choosing of his Empress's hats which he would put on display so that all might appreciate the excellence of his taste.

Neurotically jealous of the might of the British Empire, the Kaiser none the less once sent Queen Victoria a letter – which the Queen opened in the presence of the visiting Princess Alice – in which he explained to his grandmother exactly how Britain could achieve victory over the Boers. 'This piece of presumption', says Princess Alice, 'aroused her most violent indignation'.[22]

Notoriously touchy, the Kaiser was yet quite capable of telling a joke against himself. One Sunday morning, says Princess Alice, aboard his yacht *Hohenzollern,* the Kaiser delivered one of his wordy and didactic sermons to the crew. During the inspection that followed, he asked a young Bavarian sailor whether he had listened attentively to the sermon.

'Yes, Majesty,' answered the Bavarian.

'Well,' asked the Kaiser, 'who are the "inner" and the "outer" enemies?'

'The "outer enemy" is the French,' answered the lad.

'That is correct; and who are the "inner enemies"?'

The Bavarian sailor did not hesitate. 'The Prussians,' he answered.

By this, the Prussian Kaiser was highly amused and would often repeat the story.[23]

'It was not easy to understand everything William did,' claims Princess Alice, 'because he was flamboyantly vain and temperamentally unstable. Without being blind to the consequences of his actions, he seemed unable to resist an opportunity of throwing his weight about if it helped to magnify his importance and the might of the empire whose destiny, with God's connivance, it was his duty to shape. Invariably he regretted his impetuosity and tried, not often successfully, to repair the harm done by his rashness.'[24]

The Empress Augusta Victoria* (known to the family as Dona) was quite different. Tall, good-looking and always beautifully dressed, she was a submissive creature whose life was entirely dedicated to her husband. 'For a woman in that position,' wrote the sharp-tongued Princess Daisy of Pless, 'I have never met *anyone* so devoid of any individual thought or agility of brain and understanding. She is just like a

---

* The German Empress (1858–1921) was the eldest daughter of Friedrich, Duke of Schlcswig-Holstein-Sonderburg-Augustenburg.

good, quiet, soft cow that has calves and eats grass slowly and ruminates. I looked right into her eyes to see if I could see anything behind them, even pleasure or sadness, but they might have been glass.'[25]

In the Empress's adoring, if glass-like, eyes, the Kaiser's increasing eccentricities were simply manifestations of his genius; her role in life was to see that nothing was ever allowed to anger or upset him.

Princess Alice always found the Empress Dona to be 'affable and kind'. She was intrigued by the Empress's tight corseting which gave her, she says, a permanently flushed face and which made sitting in an easy chair all but impossible.

The Empress had borne her husband seven children – six boys and a girl.[†] At the time of Princess Alice's arrival in Potsdam, these second cousins ranged from eight to eighteen years. The eldest, Crown Prince Wilhelm (whom the Princess considered conceited and who was to be known to his English relations as Silly Willy) was just a year older than Princess Alice. The second son, Prince Eitel, was exactly her age. The Princess saw a great deal of these young Prussian relations; they played tennis together, they rode together, they danced together. Not a week passed, during these Potsdam summers, without a visit to the cousins at the Neues Palais.

[†] Prinee Wilhelm (1882–1951), Prince Eitel (1883–1942), Prince Adalbert (1884–1948), Prince August Wilhelm (1887–1949), Prince Oskar (1888–1958), Prince Joachim (1890–1920) and Princess Viktoria Luise (1892–1980).

Indeed, Princess Alice and Prince Charles Edward became 'like another brother and sister to them'.[26]

4

In the winter, life moved to Berlin. At the beginning of each winter season, the Duchess of Albany and her daughter would put up at the elegant Potsdam Hotel, close to the Wilhelmstrasse. From here they would play their part in the brilliant season. This would be a seemingly endless round of drawing-rooms, receptions, dinners, banquets and balls. After the simplicity and restraint of Queen Victoria's court, the court of Kaiser Wilhelm II struck Princess Alice as being almost overwhelming in its opulence, almost Byzantine in its splendour. The palaces were sumptuously appointed; the footmen resplendent in powdered wigs, knee-breeches, silk stockings and buckled shoes; the palace guards in uniforms copied from the days of Frederick the Great. The rooms of the Kaiser's principal palace, the Old Palace, were said to be among the most magnificent in Europe. The flamboyantly decorated Throne Room, with its painted ceiling, its glittering chandeliers, its tapestried panels and its wealth of rococo detail was claimed to be without equal in the world.

'The whole of the wall surface was gilded – carvings, mouldings and pilasters forming one unbroken sheet of gold . . .' enthused one witness. 'When the Throne Room was lighted up at night, the glowing colours of the Gobelin tapestry and the sheen of the great expanses of gold and silver produced an effect of immense splendour.'[27]

The magnificence of the scene would be matched by its formality. 'The protocol at the Prussian Court was quite overpowering,' said Princess Alice. 'In comparison, Grandmama's "drawing rooms" would seem like an informal private party.' The huge, gilt-edged invitation to each function would carry precise instructions regarding dress; the functions themselves would be planned with 'iron precision'.[28] Guests were rigidly classified according to rank: royal high-nesses in one salon, lesser royalty in another, mere nobility in a third. Princess Alice's cousin Pauline, the daughter of her Uncle Willy, King Wilhelm II of Württemberg, once found herself parted from her husband on the grounds that she was a *royal,* and he merely a *serene,* highness. Court chamberlains moved about with long lists, making quite certain that no persons of lesser rank made their obeisance to the Kaiser before being entitled to do so.

This same rigidity permeated every facet of social life in Berlin. Princess Alice, fresh from enlightened England, was frequently astonished at the rules governing social behaviour. The daughters of the Kaiser's Hofmarshall were forbidden to play tennis for fear that they might see young men in shirt sleeves. Once married, young women were not supposed to dance; to ignore this convention was to be considered 'fast'. Chaperonage was unbelievably strict. The Princess was once severely reprimanded for having driven through the streets with a girl cousin but no lady-in-waiting. 'That,' she remarked wryly, 'was Berlin at the turn of the century.'[29]

But with her rapidly developing sense of humour, the Princess found these conventions amusing rather than irritating. In any case, she was far too busy enjoying herself to be annoyed by any petty restrictions. Once the British Ambassador, Sir Frank Lascelles, had given her her coming-out ball, she was free to indulge one of her greatest passions: her passion for dancing. Five nights a week, she says, while her 'angelic' mother sat watching with the other mothers, she would dance until one in the morning, when it would be time for the officers to catch the last train back to Potsdam. Her first dance would always have to be with an ambassador or 'one of the bigwigs' but from then on she would be waltzed, almost non-stop, round the floor by 'tall young men in lovely uniforms who danced divinely'.[30] With much heel-clicking and head-bowing the girls would be escorted back to their mothers from where, without a pause, they would be whisked away for the next dance. There would not even be time for talking, let alone flirting.

The purpose of several of these balls, given by various Berlin hostesses, was to allow the young people to perfect dances such as the lancers, minuets and quadrilles which they would then be expected to perform at court balls. These court balls were the most gorgeous occasions of all. They took place

121

in the famous White Hall of the Old Palace. Here, in contrast to the kaleidoscopic brilliance of the Throne Room, the decoration was entirely white and silver, and served as an excellent foil for the dresses and uniforms of the dancers. The sight of the imperial *cortège* entering the ballroom was claimed to be 'one of the finest spectacles in the world'.[31] Only one thing was likely to mar the majesty of the occasion. An inlay, in the shape of a crowned Prussian eagle, decorated the centre of the dance floor and was kept in a state of high polish. It was consequently as slippery as ice. If, in his exuberance, an officer set foot on it and crashed to the floor, he would be banned from all court balls for a year.

But the most nerve-racking moment of all came when the long rows of dancers – the men in their wasp-waisted uniforms, the girls in their puffed sleeves and pastel colours – were obliged to perform the minuet while the Kaiser, standing like 'a drill sergeant'[32] on the steps of his gold and crimson throne, fixed them with his level, piercing, unblinking stare.

5

The glamour and formality of Princess Alice's life in Berlin would be relieved by visits from various members of her family. There would be Bentheim cousins ('loutish and trying'); the Prince and Princess of Waldeck-Pyrmont ('beloved Aunt Tilly and Uncle Fritz'); pretty and favourite Princess Ena of

Battenberg who, at the Berlin Zoo, missed by inches the 'rude behaviour of a lion' who squirted a 'veritable jet' over an unfortunate couple beside her; nice, plump, bespectacled Aunt Emma – whose Regency of the Netherlands had ended in 1898 – and her daughter, Queen Wilhelmina, who had just become engaged to Henry, Duke of Mecklenburg-Schwerin.

The choice of fiancé had astonished the rest of the family. Princess Alice had sometimes come across him in Potsdam where he was an officer in the Guard Jäger. Interested in little other than hunting, he had adorned the walls of his Potsdam villa with elephants' heads – souvenirs of a tour through India. The Princess dismissed him as a 'very dull, thick young man'. Nothing on earth, she assured Queen Victoria, would have induced *her* to marry him. 'However,' she added philosophically, 'Wilhelmina was blissful!'[33]

The bliss did not last long. The best that Queen Wilhelmina, in later life, could find to say about her Consort was that 'simplicity was his chief characteristic. He was simple in his manner, in his tastes, in his character'.[34]

The engagement of Princess Alice's cousin emphasised a lack in her own, otherwise busy life: at eighteen she seems to have formed no attachment, however slight or fleeting, with a young man of her own age. 'We were growing up', writes one of her Edinburgh cousins, 'and our hearts were expanding together with the lengthening of our limbs, expanding in such a way that they felt empty unless at least partly filled by some sentimental interest. . . .'[35] But Princess Alice seems to have had very little opportunity for developing any such sentimental interest. Her relationships with her Prussian cousins and her brother's fellow cadets seem to have been of a tomboyish, knock-about variety; if ever she paused, even for a moment, 'to exchange a few words and a laugh'[36] with one of her dashingly uniformed dancing partners, her strait-laced mother would accuse her of flirting.

As a result, there were times when Princess Alice felt lonely, restless, unfulfilled. The departure of her beloved Miss Potts, after ten years of faithful service, robbed her of one of her most sympathetic companions. In the wave of anti-British sentiment engendered by the Boer War she suffered from a certain feeling of isolation: she felt the need of a familiar, undemanding, understanding presence. In short, her undefined, late adolescent yearnings sought an outlet.

So the Princess found herself being drawn, as so many princesses in so many royal homes have been drawn, to an older man in the household: her mother's Comptroller, Sir Robert Collins. There was, of course, no time in her life when Sir Robert had not been there: this quiet, charming, humorous, worldly courtier had shared the family's every joy and sorrow. Now in his late fifties, he was still an exceptionally slim, agile and athletic man, certainly fit enough to join the Princess in her rides and her walks and her games of tennis. He was also unspoiled enough to share her sense of fun: 'we had tremendous jokes together',[37] she says. But, above all, he was interesting enough to fire her adolescent imagination: there was so much that he could tell her and, at the same time, there seemed to be so much that he wanted her to tell him.

Sir Robert Collins had the ability, claims a friend, 'to draw out [his companions'] best qualities by his frank interest and sympathetic recognition . . . he possessed, to a singular degree, the power of winning and retaining the affection and confidence of all with whom he came in contact.'[38] As the two of them – the sparkling Princess and the sage courtier – jogged along those sandy bridle paths at Potsdam, reciting poetry to each other, Princess Alice must have felt that she could not have wished for a more interesting, amusing or sympathetic male companion.

None of this is to say that Princess Alice was in love with Sir Robert Collins. Theirs was simply one of those touching, blameless yet curiously romantic relationships between an unsophisticated young girl and a worldly-wise older man. At the time, and for a year or two, Sir Robert Collins was Princess Alice's closest male companion, 'best friend' and perfect, gentle knight.

'I loved him,' she admitted to her grandchildren many years later, 'more than any other man till Grandpa came along.'[39]

6

Princess Alice was to remain in Germany for just over three years. She would come back to Claremont in 1903 when the Duchess of Albany felt that the young Duke of Coburg could manage without her. The Princess paid several visits to England during that period but twice she returned to play her part in important state ceremonies: the first was the funeral of Queen Victoria in February 1901, the second was the Coronation of King Edward VII in August 1902.

The Queen had died, on 22 January 1901, in her great bed at Osborne House. At the moment of her death, her pillows were being supported by a touchingly solicitous and uncharacteristically mute Kaiser Wilhelm II. The Queen's body had been taken from Osborne, first in the royal yacht *Alberta* to Gosport and then by train to Victoria station. Her coffin was put on a gun-carriage, covered with the Royal Standard and borne, in solemn procession, through the streets of London to Paddington Station.

Behind the gun-carriage rode the new King, Edward VII, with his nephew Kaiser Wilhelm II on his right and his only surviving brother, the Duke of Connaught, on his left. Among the galaxy of brightly uniformed kings and princes that followed was Princess Alice's brother, the 16-year-old Duke of Coburg. The Princess herself drove, with the other princesses of the British and continental royal families, in the carriage procession. At Windsor Station the horses that were to draw the gun-carriage reared and snapped their traces; but someone had the happy inspiration of replacing them by a company of sailors, who dragged the gun-carriage up to St George's Chapel. After a short service (the one thing she admired most in a sermon, the Queen had once remarked, was brevity) the body was removed to the Albert Memorial Chapel. On 4 February, the Queen was finally laid to rest beside the long-dead Prince Albert in the flamboyant mausoleum that she had had specially constructed.

On the young Princess Alice, the death of Queen Victoria had a profound effect. She could hardly believe that this hitherto omnipotent presence had simply disappeared. 'I had come to regard her,' she says, 'as permanent and indestructible – like England and Windsor Castle.'[40] Her grandmother's death became one of the watersheds of her life. It seemed to mark the end of her youth; from this time on, claims Princess Alice, she entered adulthood.

It was as an adult, then, that Princess Alice came from Germany to attend her Uncle Bertie's Coronation, eighteen months later, in the high summer of 1902. It was the first of many coronations that she was to attend during her long lifetime and she admits to being 'quite sick with the excitement of it all'.[41] As King Edward VII, unlike his mother, was a royal showman *par excellence,* his Coronation was a magnificently stage-managed affair.

Princess Alice drove to Westminster Abbey, through the acclaiming, lavishly decorated streets, sitting beside that grand old man of the British royal family, Uncle George Cambridge. Now eighty-two years of age, George, Duke of Cambridge, was Queen Victoria's first cousin. Until his recent, reluctant retirement, he had held the post of Commander-in-Chief of the British Army for almost forty years. Sitting side by side, these two members of the reigning House made a touching picture: the bluff, bulky, bewhiskered old soldier, in his field marshal's uniform and ducal robes, and the young and beautiful princess. He was nearing the end of his long life of service to the Crown; she was at the start of hers.

The old Duke of Cambridge was not the only member of his family to be impressed by the beauty and sparkle of Princess Alice on Coronation Day. On several occasions during the day's long, moving, and triumphant ceremonial, she appears to have caught the eye of one of the old Duke's nephews: the dark, handsome, 28-year-old Prince Alexander of Teck.

CHAPTER SIX

1

The court to which Princess Alice returned, as a young woman of twenty in 1903, was very different from the one which she had left in 1899. Her word for the court of her Uncle Bertie, now King Edward VII, was 'glamorous'.[1] It was certainly that. The new King had lost very little time in sweeping away all traces of his mother's dowdy regime. In its place he had created the most opulent, the most self-confident and the most sophisticated court in Europe.

Everything bore the mark of the new King's highly-developed sense of style. The ceremonial aspect of the monarchy was not only restored but expanded. Parliament was once more opened with great pageantry, spectacular state visits were exchanged, glittering courts, balls and receptions were held at Buckingham Palace. There was a drastic reorganisation of all household departments. The sedate afternoon 'Drawing-rooms' were replaced by brilliant evening 'Presentation Courts'. Osborne House was given to the Navy (on the understanding that the central part would be preserved as a family shrine), Balmoral Castle was centrally heated and the famous tartan stripped from the walls, Windsor Castle was modernised and redecorated, and Buckingham Palace transformed into one of the most splendidly appointed royal houses in Europe. The King ordered its façade and its setting to be redesigned. Its galleries and staircases were recarpeted. Its chandeliers were electrified. Its reception rooms were regilded, refurnished and fitted with enormous looking-glasses; on state occasions they were filled with pyramids of roses, carnations and hydrangeas.

No capital in Europe – not the barbaric splendour of St Petersburg nor the showy militarism of Berlin – could match the assured magnificence of King Edward VII's court. With the decorative and perennially youthful Queen Alexandra by his side, King Edward restored to the British monarchy a lustre that it had not known since the days of the Stuarts.

Although the Albanys were now considered members of the 'old' royal family, they still played their part in all this lavish ceremonial. Princess Alice, with her abundant brown hair piled on top of her head, her figure moulded into the fashionable S-shape, and her skirts trailing behind her, was certainly one of the prettiest, freshest and most extrovert of the princesses surrounding this splendid throne. She was also one of the most natural. 'As she is not in the least *blasé,*' wrote one contemporary, 'she is not afraid of showing her happiness in a way that is at once simple and fascinating.'[2]

But life at the Edwardian court was not, as Princess Alice once briskly remarked, 'comparable to the pampered lot of the queen bee'.[3] Patiently she would stand with the other princesses on the left of Queen Alexandra on the dais at Presentation Courts; she would sit on the rock-hard, special gold and white chairs waiting to dance with some fat and ugly princeling at court balls; she would have to force conversation with ambassadors and cabinet ministers at state banquets; she would have to join house parties at Windsor or Sandringham to help entertain visiting royalty.

Yet, characteristically, it was the odd humorous incident rather than the grinding ordeal of these occasions that the Princess remembered best. The presence of Queen Elena of Italy, for instance, was made memorable for her by the fact that the Duke of Connaught, out on a specially organised shooting party, very narrowly missed bringing down the wrong bird: the huge, brightly plumaged fowl decorating the Queen's elaborate hat.

With the new monarch, her Uncle Bertie, even the normally vivacious Princess Alice felt no more at ease now than she had ever done. But then, there were very few people who could relax in the company of this restless, mercurial, easily bored sovereign. When sitting beside him at table, the Princess would be disconcerted by his habit of fiddling with the cutlery; she would find it quite impossible to keep up a consecutive conversation.

'Don't worry about that,' advised the King's current mistress, 'we all experience that trouble. He likes to join in general conversation, injecting remarks at intervals, but he prefers to listen to others rather than to talk himself. . . .'[4]

But even if King Edward VII did not spend much time talking to his niece, she was certainly on his mind. 'The prettiest minx of a princess in Europe today,'[5] he would call her and, as such, the King had high hopes for her future. With an eye ever open to any opportunity of enhancing the power and prestige of the British monarchy, the King was thinking in terms of some grand matrimonial alliance for Princess Alice. It was during his reign, after all, that his House enjoyed its most spectacular flowering. His nephew Wilhelm was German Emperor; his niece Alix was Empress of Russia; his niece Sophie was to become the Queen of the Hellenes; his niece Marie was to become Queen of Romania; his niece Ena was to become Queen of Spain; his niece Daisy of Connaught was to marry the future King of Sweden; his daughter Maud was to become Queen of Norway. It was no wonder, then, that the King was hoping for his niece Alice to marry, if not some future king, at least some important foreign prince.

But it was not to be. Although, from time to time, there were rumours that she was about to become engaged ('I do hope it isn't true that pretty Princess Alice is to marry the Duke of Saxe-Weimar,' wrote one observer. 'We are satiated with semi-Royal German marriages, whether we send our English princesses to Germany or, what is worse, have German princelings quartered on us here.'[6]) she kept clear of any possible foreign alliances.

The Princess was not, of course, impervious to masculine attention. Now that she was back in England there were plenty of handsome young officers only too willing to dance attendance on this radiant Princess. 'Our lives,' she says, 'were not devoid of romance. We had our own decorous methods of conducting a flirtation or attracting masculine attention . . . eloquent messages can be conveyed by downcast eyes, embarrassed blushes, a graceful curtsey, a slim waistline, a turn of soft shoulders or the discreet glimpse of a beautiful bosom. . . .'[7]

But it was in distinctly more robust circumstances that Princess Alice conducted her romance with a young officer in the 7th Hussars. He was that distant relation whose eye she had caught at King Edward VII's Coronation: Prince Alexander of Teck. As his regiment was stationed at Hampton Court, a mere three miles from Claremont, Prince Alexander could very easily visit the Duchess of Albany and her daughter. He had, says Princess Alice, a very good excuse for these visits. Soon after her return to Claremont, Princess Alice had acquired a new horse. As the horse shied whenever she tried to mount the side-saddle,

Prince Alexander offered to have it trained at the regimental riding school at Hampton Court. This gave him plenty of opportunity for visiting Claremont; and not only for visiting it but for helping the Princess into the saddle and for accompanying her on her rides.

'It does not require the exercise of much imagination,' writes the Princess, 'to visualize how our friendship developed and his courtship followed.'[8]

2

His Serene Highness Prince Alexander Augustus Frederick William Alfred George of Teck, born on 14 April 1874, was the youngest of the four children of the Duke and Duchess of Teck.

The Tecks were a colourful couple. Among the generally sedate and four-square members of the British royal family, the Duke and Duchess of Teck struck a distinctly outré note. Born in 1837, the Duke of Teck had had his entire career and personality blighted by the fact that he was the son of a morganatic marriage. Had his father, Duke Alexander of Württemberg, not married the beautiful Hungarian, Countess Rhedey of Kis-Redé, the Duke of Teck would one day have become the King of Württemberg. But with his father's romantic alliance having cost his branch of the family their right of succession, the Duke of Teck (or Prince Teck as he was known at that stage) was obliged to make his own way in the world.

There was only one method by which a disinherited, penniless but handsome prince (*der schöne Uhlan* they had called this young officer in Vienna) could secure his future, and this was by marriage. But this was easier said than done. Prince Teck was too conscious of his royal, if 'tainted', blood to want to marry anyone other than a princess, while most continental princesses were too conscious of that very taint to want to marry him. Only at the court of Queen Victoria, it seemed, was there no prejudice about morganatic marriages. And, as luck would have it, there was one British princess who was more than ready to give herself in marriage to this romantic misfit. This was Princess Mary Adelaide of Cambridge.

The Cambridges were a younger branch of the British royal family: the descendants of King George III's seventh son Adolphus, Duke of Cambridge, who had died in 1850. The late Duke of Cambridge's three children were therefore first cousins to Queen Victoria. These three Cambridges were Prince George, the second Duke of Cambridge (that grand old man who would one day drive beside Princess Alice to King Edward VII's Coronation), Princess Augusta of Cambridge who had married the heir to the Grand Duke of Mecklenburg-Strelitz and gone to live in Germany, and Princess Mary Adelaide of Cambridge who was about to marry Prince Teck.

In George, Duke of Cambridge, all the immoralities and idiosyncrasies of Queen Victoria's 'wicked uncles', which both she and the Prince Consort had tried so hard to live down, were cheerfully revived. Born in 1819, the Duke of Cambridge was a gruff, blustering, quick-tempered but kind-hearted man who in his thirty-nine years as Commander-in-Chief of the British Army stoutly resisted almost every attempt at reform or modernisation. A great man for the ladies ('in or out of Society'[9] as Princess Alice so graphically puts it) he contracted, in 1847, a private marriage with an actress named Louisa Fairbrother. The couple had three sons who bore the surname of Fitz-George. To these three stalwart Fitz-George second cousins, Queen Victoria always turned a resolutely blind eye.

As he grew older, so did the Duke of Cambridge become more and more eccentric. The family was full of stories about Uncle George's quirks. On one occasion, when Princess Alice had been invited to go sailing with King Edward VII, she found herself sitting on deck between her Uncle Bertie and her Uncle George Cambridge. A passing steam barge, which had been somewhat slow in giving way to the royal yacht, so incensed the Duke of Cambridge that he worked himself up into a state of almost apoplectic outrage. Steam ships, he thundered, should not be allowed on the Solent at the same time as sailing ships. And to emphasise each impassioned remark, he would thump poor Princess Alice on the leg. By the time he had calmed down, she could hardly walk.

On another occasion, when the Duke was staying with Princess Christian at Cumberland Lodge, he embarrassed the family at Sunday church service by answering the chaplain's injunction, 'Let us pray', with a stentorian 'By all means!' But there was worse to come. When the chaplain offered up a special prayer for the relief of the prolonged drought, Uncle George, in that same carrying voice, exclaimed, 'Oh God! My dear man, how can you expect rain with the wind in the east?'[10]

Something of this same strong individuality marked the Duke's two sisters. His sister Princess Augusta was an outspoken woman of decided views (it was she who was so appalled at the idea of Queen Victoria, at her Diamond Jubilee, thanking 'God in the street'), while his younger sister, Princess Mary Adelaide was, in every sense of the phrase, larger than life.

For Princess Mary Adelaide of Cambridge was huge. A conservative estimate of her weight, says Princess Alice, was seventeen stone. Plump-cheeked, double-chinned, big-breasted, huge-hipped, Princess Mary Adelaide looked, in the crinolines of her young womanhood, like a mountain. The springs groaned as she entered a carriage; the not one, but two, chairs that were needed to accommodate her bulk creaked as she lowered herself onto them; she had only to turn too energetically on the dance floor for anyone in her way to be knocked flying. Yet Princess Mary Adelaide was not without a certain grace. She was tall, she carried herself well, she dressed with great panache, she moved nimbly and with ease. Had she not been so grossly fat, Princess Mary Adelaide would have been quite beautiful. With the Princess's generosity of girth went a generosity of heart. Princess Mary Adelaide was an ebullient, extravagant, impulsive, unpunctual, compassionate, fun-loving woman, the darling of the London crowds. 'There goes fat Mary,'[11] they would shout as, with moon face tilted and hand waving joyously, the beaming Princess Mary Adelaide passed by in her carriage.

The whole world, it seemed, was ready to love her but no man was ready to marry her. One after another various continental suitors arrived to take one look at this billowing Princess and to return home without having proposed. 'Alas!' declared the Foreign Secretary, Lord Clarendon, 'no German Prince will venture on *so vast an undertaking*.'[12] And until Princess Mary Adelaide had reached the almost unmarriageable age of thirty-two it seemed as though no one would.

This was why, when Prince Teck arrived on a reconnoitring expedition in the spring of 1866, the Cambridge family welcomed him with open arms. The circumstances seemed perfect. Prince Teck was on the look-out for an undeniably royal bride; Princess Mary Adelaide was on the look-out for a presentable royal husband. If he would overlook her vast bulk (and the fact that she was four years older than he was) she could overlook his morganatic blood. After what Princess Mary Adelaide's sharp-tongued sister, the Grand Duchess of Mecklenberg-Strelitz, called an 'incredibly short'[13] acquaintanceship, Prince Teck proposed and Princess Mary Adelaide accepted. They were married on 12 June 1866.

Marriage to a member of the British royal family and a home (granted to them by Queen Victoria) in Kensington Palace by no means meant the end of Prince Teck's search for recognition. On the contrary, he became increasingly obsessed with matters of rank, position and precedence. Not even his elevation to a dukedom five years after his marriage could still his sense of being slighted. He felt that his cousin, King Carl of Württemberg, should have made him Duke of Württemberg and not merely Duke of Teck. Denied not only what he felt to be his proper status but any worthwhile occupation, the Duke of Teck became steadily more moody and irascible. In time, he was to become as well known for his dark and violent rages as was his wife for her generosity and spontaneity.

Between the years 1867 and 1874, the Tecks had four children: a daughter and three sons. As was the way in most royal families, they were each known by slight variants of their given names. The eldest, Princess Victoria Mary, was called May. The second, Prince Adolphus, was called Dolly. The third, Prince Francis, was called Frank. The fourth, Prince Alexander, born in 1874, was called Alge, pronounced Algy.

The birth of their fourth child, four years after the birth of the last son, was generally regarded as yet another, rather regrettable, example of Princess Mary Adelaide's tendency to overdo things. 'I really hope this charming Trio will suffice,' her sister had written on the birth of the Princess's third child. Now, on the birth of the fourth, Queen Victoria reported to her daughter, the German Crown Princess, that 'May Teck was safely confined yesterday, with another and *still* bigger boy! That seems hardly possible.'[14]

But it was possible. Prince Alge – the name was a contraction of his first and last names, Alexander and George – was a splendidly big baby. 'The infant Prince is the finest child you ever saw, finer than either of his brothers,' reported his proud nurse, 'with a quantity of very dark hair, and I fancy a little like the Duke, his father.'[15]

One of the most popular royal photographs of the year, taken by the celebrated Downey of Ebury Street, was of the massive and handsome head of the Duchess of Teck tilted over the cradle in which her dark-haired and dark-eyed baby son lay happily smiling.

3

'The boys,' wrote the Duchess of Teck proudly to a friend in 1875, 'are said to be as handsome as ever, and No 3, I think, bids fair to surpass his brothers! He has splendid dark brown eyes, and is wonderfully like his father, and such a pet! So merry and full of fun and mischief, and *all over* dimples. He is a very large child for sixteen months. . . .'[16]

The early years of this big, dark, good-natured boy were to be largely coloured by his parents' improvident way of life. The Duchess of Teck's slap-happy attitude to money ensured that both at Kensington Palace and at White Lodge in Richmond (which the Duchess had managed to wheedle out of Queen Victoria as a country seat) life was lived on the most lavish scale. While the unpaid bills steadily mounted, the Duchess of Teck established herself as a superlative hostess and an open-handed benefactor. About her precarious financial position she knew very little and cared even less. Once, on opening a new church hall in Kensington, largely paid for by the Kensington grocer, John Barker, to whom the Duchess was deeply in debt, the Duchess of Teck delighted the crowd by turning to him with a gracious smile to say, all unwittingly, 'and now I must propose a special vote of thanks to Mr Barker, to whom we all owe so much'.[17]

Yet, for all her apparent giddiness, the Duchess was a conscientious parent. 'A child has quite enough to do . . .' she once said of her daughter to a friend, 'to learn obedience, and attend to her lessons, and to *grow*, without many parties and late hours, which take the freshness of childhood away, and the brightness and beauty from girlhood – and then children become intolerable. There are far too many grownup children in the present day.'[18]

So the Tecks raised their four children kindly but strictly; with his sons, the Duke of Teck was something of a martinet. Those who imagined that the Teck children might be over-indulged were always pleasantly surprised by their charm, intelligence and good manners. Queen Victoria admitted that 'Mary's boys are splendid'[19] and the Duchess of Edinburgh once wrote to the Duchess of Teck to say that 'The boys are too splendid, I would not believe their age . . . they had tea in my room and we held long conversations; they were particularly interested in the description of the Russian winter and I had to relate about it while they were having their tea with great appetites. They are now romping with my children and making a tremendous noise. Thank you for having sent them, they are so very charming and so well-behaved.'[20]

Like his brothers, Prince Alge was educated partly at a local 'morning school' and partly by tutors at home. The parents encouraged their children's study of languages by insisting that they speak only French at certain meals and only German at others. In May 1882, Prince Dolly and Prince Frank went off to boarding school, leaving only the 14-year-old Princess May and the 8-year-old Prince Alge .with their parents at White Lodge. They did not remain there long. With the creditors becoming more and more insistent and with the Tecks finding it utterly impossible to cut down, their royal relations decided that they must leave England for a few years in order to try and live more cheaply on the Continent. So in 1883 the Tecks crossed the Channel to settle down, eventually, in a villa near Florence.

It was during these years in exile in Florence that Princess May and Prince Alge established the close companionship that was to last all their lives. To look at, they were very different. Princess May was fair and slender; Prince Alge was dark and fat. Both had already been affected by the Duchess of Teck's exuberant personality. Having a mother who was so voluble, the children tended to say very little; having suffered the humiliation of financial ruin, they were learning the lesson that one should always live within one's means.

If the British royal family had imagined that by being forced to withdraw to the Continent the Tecks would be leading a somewhat chastened existence, they were soon proved wrong. The Duchess of Teck remained as sociable and as hospitable as ever. Prince Alge soon found that the routine of his days with his tutor, Mr Campbell, was being broken by exciting visits to various continental spas and to various continental relations. Less welcome, sometimes, would be the arrival of his two older brothers, for by now these two maturing youngsters ('Dolly's voice is completely changed, he speaks in deep gruff voice. So funny!'[21] reported Princess May) felt infinitely superior to this fat little boy. Their attitude upset their mother considerably.

'The one thing that distressed and worried me,' she wrote to her two elder sons on their return to school on one occasion, 'was your unkindness to poor Alge and intolerance of his, I must admit, trying

143

ways, always forgetting that he is, after all, but a child and requires humouring a little and being treated as such, instead of only knocks and pinches and bruises and hard words – and perpetual teasing, which in itself must irritate beyond measure a nature like his. It is *unmanly* and unworthy of you and is a fault you must especially guard against.'[22]

The Tecks spent just under two years in Florence. When they were allowed to return home, in the spring of 1885, Prince Alge, by now almost twelve years old, was packed off, first to the Reverend A.H. Morton's school at Farnborough and then, at the beginning of the Lent term of 1889, to Eton.

'What,' asked a disapproving friend of the Duchess of Teck, 'can Eton possibly teach your son that selected tutors cannot?'

'It will teach him to cook his own breakfasts and teas,' was the Duchess's robust answer. 'Every good soldier should know how to cook.'[23]

For already Prince Alge had decided that, like his two older brothers, he would become a soldier. And whatever else he might have learned at Eton, he did learn how to cook: the sizzling of bacon and eggs, he assured his parents, made him 'glad to be an Englishman'.[24]

Quickly shedding his puppy fat, Prince Alge developed into a popular and conscientious schoolboy, with a talent for mimicry that delighted his friends. In his second year he moved into the Army Class, with its specialised studies, to prepare him for the entrance examination for the Royal Military College at Sandhurst. This he passed in the summer of 1892, when he was eighteen.

On passing out of Sandhurst, two years later, Prince Alge was commissioned second lieutenant in the 7th Hussars, at that stage stationed at Mhow, in Central India. 'Alas,' wrote the Duchess of Teck to a friend in December 1894, 'early in the coming year we have to part with our much-loved youngest son, Alexander, who has to join his Regiment, the 7th Hussars, in India. I dread the long separation; for next autumn the 7th are probably to be moved to the Cape, and it may be three years before he returns to England. It is an *awful wrench* and I scarcely dare trust myself to think of it.'[25]

But for the tall and jauntily moustached Prince Alge, looking 'too handsome',[26] as Princess Alice wrote later, in his frogged, braided and epauletted Hussar uniform, it was all a great adventure.

4

By the time that Prince Alge sailed to India, in January 1895, the fortunes of the Teck family had undergone a dramatic change. This was due, almost entirely, to the marriage, in 1893, of Princess May of Teck to Prince George, heir presumptive to the British throne. This brilliant match made up for all those years of battling against an inadequate income and an equivocal social position. In fact, the Duke of Teck, highly elated by the coup, now hoped that his eldest son, Prince Adolphus or Dolly, would make an equally advantageous match. He saw no reason why the handsome and popular Prince Dolly, now an officer in the 17th Lancers, should not marry one of the daughters of the Prince of Wales, or at least Princess Pauline, the daughter of King Wilhelm II of Württemberg.

But Prince Dolly had other ideas. On 12 December 1894, he married Lady Margaret Grosvenor, daughter of the first Duke of Westminster, one of the richest men in the world. If the Duchess of Teck was highly gratified by this financially advantageous match, the Duke was not. He could not bring himself to approve of the non-royal Lady Margaret Grosvenor. 'If the girl had been an ugly German princess,' wrote Princess May's knowing ex-governess to Prince Alge, 'your father would have found her charming.'[27]

So the Duke's hopes were switched to the second Teck son. Prince Francis or Frank. Prince Frank, who turned twenty-five in 1895, was very much his mother's son: flamboyant, improvident, affectionate. The Tecks' careful upbringing, which had turned Princess May, Prince Dolly and Prince Alge into such disciplined and conscientious personalities, had been wasted on Prince Frank. He drifted, he gambled, he ran up enormous debts. At one stage, having lost a £10,000 bet in Ireland (where, reported his mother to Prince Alge, he was 'surrounded by a dangerous set, who flatter him and turn his weak head,'[28]) he

146

was packed off to India. Much as he hated his exile there, he learned nothing from it. His amusing letters home revealed him to be as feckless, as extravagant and as unrepentant as ever.

Yet a glittering matrimonial prize was within Prince Frank's grasp. Princess Maud, the youngest daughter of the Prince and Princess of Wales, was in love with him. Known, in the chaffing way of her family, as 'Harry', Princess Maud was a cheerful, tomboyish and sweet-natured creature. That this unsophisticated young Princess should be attracted to so exotic a *beau* as Prince Frank was understandable. It was also unfortunate, for Prince Frank hardly gave her a thought. He certainly never bothered to answer her letters. The truth was that his affections were otherwise engaged. Prince Frank had by now embarked on a liaison with a married woman much older, and more resolute, than himself. So, in spite of his parents' desperate hopes, Prince Frank was not prepared to waste any time on the immature and love-lorn Princess Maud.

Rebuffed, Princess Maud followed her parents' promptings and married her cousin, Prince Charles of Denmark, instead. In time, Prince Charles was to mount the newly-created Norwegian throne as King Haakon VII.

It was with considerable relief, then, that the Duke and Duchess of Teck could follow the progress of their youngest son. Prince Alexander. A dedicated and impressive-looking soldier, Prince Alge played his part in all those military adventures and royal ceremonies that marked the closing years of the nineteenth century. From India, where he enjoyed a 'very thorough course of training, varied by a good deal of pig-sticking and polo',[29] his regiment sailed to South Africa to take part in the Matabele War of 1896.

This was Prince Alge's first personal contact with a country with which both he and his future wife, Princess Alice, were to be very closely associated. In Matabeleland – afterwards part of Southern Rhodesia, now Zimbabwe – the Prince was involved in what Colonel Baden-Powell described as 'a brilliant and most opportune action'.[30] As a result of his resource and bravery during an attack on the stronghold of Chief Wedza, the Prince was mentioned in despatches.

In May 1897, the Prince was granted temporary leave of absence to take part in Queen Victoria's Diamond Jubilee celebrations. This was the last occasion on which his mother, the irrepressible Duchess of Teck, was able to enjoy a great royal occasion. She had undergone an operation earlier that year and although she recovered sufficiently to evoke the usual enthusiasm of the crowds as she drove in the carriage procession, the Duchess of Teck had a relapse. On 27 October she died. Prince Alge, together with his father and his sister, was with her at the end.

'It seems impossible to realise that darling Mama,' wrote the heart-broken Princess May, 'of all people in the world, so full of life and happiness, should have left us, it is awful, awful, and I dread to think of how we can live without her – For Papa it is cruel and his sad state makes it so much worse, he was so dependent on Mama for everything and now God knows what he will do.'[31]

For by now the Duke of Teck, whose mental state had been deteriorating badly over the years, was almost helpless. 'Dear Mama has left us at a very trying time,' wrote Prince Alge about his father, 'and just now her advice and kindness would indeed have been a boon.'[32] In fact, the Duke of Teck did not long survive his wife. He died, a confused and broken man, in January 1900. This time only Princess May was near at hand. Her three brothers were all in South Africa, fighting in the Anglo-Boer War.

On the outbreak of the war, in October 1899, Prince Alge – realising that the 7th Hussars were unlikely to be engaged – transferred to the Inniskilling Dragoons and sailed to the Cape. With his regiment he took part in the various engagements which marked the turn of the tide in that muddled campaign: the operations round Colesburg, the surrender of General Cronje, the relief of Kimberley and the march to Bloemfontein. During the much-vaunted relief of Mafeking, the Prince, by now a captain, acted as aide-de-camp to Colonel Mahon. He was mentioned in despatches as 'a very promising Cavalry officer, quick and always cool and collected'.[33]

In the weeks that followed the relief of Mafeking, Prince Alge was actively engaged in what were regarded – somewhat optimistically – as mopping-up operations; and, in the widespread but mistaken belief that the war was almost over, Prince Alexander returned to England. Frequently mentioned in despatches, he was awarded the D.S.O. in 1901.

'How pleased poor Mama and Papa would have been . . .'[34] sighed his sister Princess May.

5

Hardly had Prince Alexander returned home than he was obliged to embark on a different sort of imperial venture. He joined his sister and brother-in-law (at this stage still Duke and Duchess of York) on their tour of the Empire in the liner *Ophir*.

Sailing from Portsmouth on 16 March 1901, the royal party was away for almost eight months. They visited Gibraltar, Malta, Port Said, Ceylon, Singapore, Australia, New Zealand, Mauritius, South Africa and Canada. It was the most extensive tour ever undertaken by members of the royal family. At the end of the voyage Prince George, in his methodical fashion, noted that they had travelled 45,000 miles (33,000 by sea and 12,000 by land), laid 21 foundation stones, received 544 addresses, presented 4,329 medals and shaken hands, officially, with 24,855 people. It was, in fact, the first of those great royal tours that were to become such a feature of the Empire and Commonwealth in the century that lay ahead.

Throughout this mammoth journey Prince Alge was everywhere: standing stiffly for group photographs, riding in procession through bizarre triumphal arches, listening to interminable speeches, encouraging his naturally reserved sister ('May reminding me of Mama and I felt quite proud of her,'[35] he once reported), shooting duck with his brother-in-law at Poplar Point, Manitoba. During it all he remained affable and approachable, only occasionally giving way to the quick and violent temper that he had inherited from his father. Those who had dealings with Prince Alge found him to be a practical, sensible and dependable young man; and one whose bluff, soldierly manner marked both a shrewd common sense and an extremely kind heart.

This voyage of the *Ophir* must have brought home to Prince Alexander, in the most vivid way, something of the size and nature and complexity of the Empire with which his family was so closely associated. At that stage, the Empire was undergoing great changes. Whereas, until then, the British monarch had reigned over a collection of British dependencies, of colonies of British people who looked to Britain as home, Prince Alge's brother-in-law, the future King George V, would one day reign over a commonwealth of separate nations. Slowly a British family of independent states was evolving; states with a dual loyalty – first to their own nation, and then to the mother country. No longer were these simply Englishmen living abroad; they were beginning to think of themselves as Australians or New Zealanders or Canadians or South Africans – different from Englishmen and different from each other.

And the symbolic link between these rapidly expanding nations and the country from which they sprung was the Crown. The people in the colonies knew little and cared increasingly less about British party politics. As Prince Alexander could see for himself, colonial governments managed their own affairs; men born in the colonies ran their own countries. What these diverse people cared about was the imperial ideal, embodied in the person of the monarch. Not only did trade, defence and shared traditions bind these increasingly self-sufficient countries to Britain; more important was their joint allegiance to a common sovereign.

And this great journey of the heir to the throne, at a time when royal tours were a rarity, seemed to crystallise this still-fluid situation; to prove that the Crown was indeed the bond that linked these countries, not only to Britain but to each other.

Although it is doubtful that Prince Alexander, at the age of twenty-seven, would have grasped the full significance of this imperial development, the voyage of the *Ophir* must certainly have given him a fuller understanding of the structure of the Empire. He was to remain a convinced, and enlightened, imperialist throughout his life and, supported by his wife, Princess Alice, was to be one of the great pro-consuls of the British Empire.

6

Princess Alice of Albany and Prince Alexander of Teck were married on 10 February 1904 in St George's Chapel at Windsor. The ceremony, admits Princess Alice, was 'a spectacular affair'.[36] King Edward VII, having forgiven his niece for not having married some future king, flung himself with customary gusto into the arrangements. "This marriage gave him scope for his powers of organisation,' says his Assistant Private Secretary, Frederick Ponsonby, 'and everything went without a hitch.'[37]

But not quite everything. Among the constellation of continental royals invited to the wedding – Württembergs, Weids, Waldeck-Pyrmonts, Schaumburg-Lippes, Erbach-Schönbergs, Bentheim-Steinfurts – were, as the most important guests, Queen Wilhelmina and her mother, Queen Emma, of the Netherlands. Now King Edward VII enjoyed few things more than greeting fellow sovereigns in state. And nothing infuriated him more than arrangements that went wrong. Dressed with customary splendour and precision, the King made ready to drive from Windsor Castle to Windsor station to welcome the two Queens, but although the Household Cavalry was there to escort him, he was infuriated to discover that the Palace Guard had not turned out. And on his arrival, still seething, at the station, he found that the guard of honour had not yet turned up. Exploding with rage, the King sent for Lieut.-Col. Bouverie, the officer in charge of the military arrangements. He was told that Colonel Bouverie was not available: he was away hunting. Matters had been left in the hands of his second-in-command, Major Granville-Smith. Only the steaming in of the royal train prevented poor Major Granville-Smith from being subjected to his sovereign's full and frightening wrath.

The only other muddle was in St George's Chapel itself. As there had been only one wedding in the Chapel since the marriage of Princess Alice's parents, over twenty years before,* the ushering arrangements were not all they might have been. As the assembled royal guests – the women in their elaborate dresses and long trains, the men in their skin-tight uniforms with jutting swords – edged along the narrow gangways in the choir, there was considerable confusion. 'An error made is often very difficult to rectify,' notes one long-suffering usher that day. 'Royal personages have usually a good idea of their own rank and of their appointed seats, but they still required some careful steering, for one or two were noted for their absence of mind and their proclivity to take a wrong place. It is very easy to get flustered. . . .'[38]

But everyone was happily settled by the time the silver trumpets rang out to herald the arrival of the royal processions. First came the princes and

---

* This was the short-lived marriage of Princess Marie Louise of Schleswig-Holstein (1872–1956), daughter of Princess Christian, who married Prince Aribert of Anhalt on 6 July 1891.

princesses of the British royal family; then the bride-groom, Prince Alexander of Teck, handsome in his Hussar uniform and supported by his brothers, Prince Dolly (now Duke of Teck) and Prince Frank. They were followed by King Edward VII and Queen Alexandra.

'One great feature of the royal garments,' wrote the watching Lady Violet Greville, 'was the magnificent ermine cloaks worn by Queen Alexandra and the Princess [May] of Wales. Ermine is essentially majestic in its association, and lends itself to beautiful dressing in the daytime. For the rest, the show of jewels was superb; crowns and tiaras and *rivières* of diamonds, now coming back into fashion, were visible on all sides.'[39]

The fourth and final fanfare announced the arrival of the bride with the Duchess of Albany, the Duke of Coburg and the five bridesmaids. These were Princess Alice's Connaught cousins, Princess Margaret and Princess Patricia; her Waldeck cousin, Princess Helen, the 3-year-old daughter of her Uncle Fritz, Prince of Waldeck-Pyrmont; and two of the bridegroom's nieces – Princess Mary, only daughter of the Prince and Princess of Wales, and Princess Mary of Teck, daughter of the Duke and Duchess of Teck. They were all in pale blue silk.

Princess Alice is said to have looked charming. Her dress was a lavish Edwardian confection of ivory-coloured *satin charmeuse,* flounced, fringed, embroidered, tucked, swathed and garlanded, and with a long, sweeping train. The whole effect was soft, girlish, romantic. On her high-piled hair she wore a tiara of diamond wheat-ears, a gift from her bridegroom. Her Honiton lace veil had been worn by her late mother-in-law, the Duchess of Teck, by her sister-in-law, Princess May, and by the present Duchess of Teck, the wife of Prince Dolly.

On the arm of her brother, the Duke of Coburg, the bride was escorted to the altar, where King Edward VII waited to give her away. The couple were married by the Archbishop of Canterbury, Randall Davidson, who had confirmed Princess Alice six years before in Cannes. The hymn, 'O Perfect Peace' was sung before the Blessing and to the triumphant strains of the Wedding March and through an avenue formed by men of the 7th Hussars, the couple made their way out of the Chapel.

'The Royal Wedding', ran Lady Violet Greville's summing-up of the ceremony, 'took place with all the stateliness and dignity to which the King has accustomed us in court ceremonies.

'Unlike most royal brides,' she continued, 'this bride looked "the picture of happiness".'[40]

PART TWO
WINDSOR CASTLE

CHAPTER SEVEN

1

It was as Her Royal Highness Princess Alexander of Teck that Princess Alice started her married life. The qualification of 'Highness' (without the prefix 'Royal') granted to the Duke of Teck by Queen Victoria in 1887 could not be passed on to his sons, so Prince Alexander remained simply a Serene Highness. The couple were to be known by these titles and qualifications for the next thirteen years.

The first part of the honeymoon was spent at Brocket Hall, near Hatfield, an impressive house lent to the couple by Lord Mount Stephen. After that they moved to the Villa Nevada at Cannes for a few weeks. Their first real home – and they were to live in it for nineteen years – was in the Henry III Tower at Windsor Castle. This was given to them by King Edward VII in recompense for the King's insistence that Prince Alge transfer from the 7th Hussars – who were due to go abroad – to the Royal Horse Guards.

This regiment of the Royal Horse Guards (the Blues) was then stationed at Windsor.

For the newly-married Princess Alice, settling into the Henry III Tower was rather like coming home. She had been born in Windsor Castle, she had spent many days and weeks of her girlhood there, she had been married there. To her, the massive grey pile with its great central keep, its deep moat, its soaring walls and its indefinable aura of majesty, had always been steeped in romance. With the death of Queen Victoria, she had wondered if she would ever be as closely associated with Windsor again. Now, on her return, she fancied that the spirit of the old Queen still pervaded the place: that it had 'returned to animate the halls and rooms that had known her footsteps for over sixty years'.[1]

The Henry III Tower was a fascinating, if highly inconvenient, structure: a massive, four-storied stone tower rising above the walls, courts and jumbled rooftops of the castle buildings. From a central spiral staircase, rooms of varying shapes and sizes led off at different levels. Some of the main rooms were exceedingly handsome, with high ceilings, deep-embrasured windows and views across the lawns towards the Great Park; others were hardly more than large cupboards.

To help run this warren-like establishment the couple employed a considerable staff: a butler, a footman, a lady's maid, a cook,* a scullery maid, two housemaids, a nurse, a nursery maid and eventually a

---

* It had always been her regret, the Princess once said in her old age, that the only thing she had ever learned to cook was toffee.

governess. Yet the Tecks were far from wealthy. It was simply that, with an average wage of something like £2 a month, plus free board, lodging and uniforms, they could well afford to employ so many.

According to Princess Alice, these servants were perfectly content with their lot. Many years afterwards, she would receive letters from a former scullery maid who had married a wealthy Australian during the First World War, remembering, with nostalgia, the happy times spent in the Henry III Tower. 'Those were the days,' she would write: for all the world, says the Princess, 'as though she were an exiled Russian Princess reminiscing about the times she had spent in the Imperial Palace at St Petersburg . . . instead of an ex-scullery maid dreaming about the luxuries she had enjoyed on £16 a year!'[2]

The greater part of Prince Alge's time was taken up with his military duties. When his regiment was not training and parading in the Great Park at Windsor it would be in London, where it was stationed either at Knightsbridge Barracks or the Albany Street Barracks, near Regent's Park. The couple would then take a house in the capital. For recreation they rode and walked in Windsor Great Park; Prince Alge played a great deal of polo; Princess Alice kept up her music and her drawing (for which she had considerable talent); they both tried, unsuccessfully, to master golf.

Their wedding present from Lord Shrewsbury had been a 1903 Talbot car. It looked, said the Princess, not unlike a four-poster bedstead with curtains to draw when it rained, and they were 'inordinately proud' of it. One of their first journeys in this vehicle was to visit Prince Alge's uncle, the die-hard old Duke of Cambridge, in his great house on the corner of Park Lane and Piccadilly. 'Uncle George's disgust when he saw the car beggars description,' said Princess Alice. His reaction to this 'damned fool contraption' was extreme. They thought that he was about to have an apoplectic fit.

One can only hope that the old Duke's death, at the age of eighty-five, a month later, was not entirely due to his chagrin at the sight of this 'noisy, smelly mechanical monster'.[3]

Although Prince Alge shared so many of his wife's interests, he did not share her passion for dancing. In fact, he did not dance at all. Yet this was a period celebrated for the magnificence of its balls; 'it was quite a usual occurrence,' wrote Princess Alice's cousin, Princess Marie Louise, 'to go to more than one ball in the same night'.[4] Night after night during the season, in all the great London houses there would be balls and receptions of almost breathtaking splendour. None, says Princess Alice, could compare with those given at Stafford House by the Duke and Duchess of Sutherland. 'To watch the beautiful Duchess Millicent standing at the head of that impressive staircase, dressed superbly and covered with family jewels as she received her guests . . . was a sight which once seen could never be forgotten.'[5]

In deference to her husband, Princess Alice would agree to leave the party at one o'clock; 'but I always danced madly until then'.[6] Equally enjoyable to her, for she was never *blasé*, were the less formal regimental dances. On these occasions, the one o'clock ruling did not apply. 'We danced practically the whole night through, ending up with a wild rollicking set of lancers during which we ladies were swung off our feet horizontally by hefty officers, sergeants and corporals.'[7]

Another form of entertainment, richly typical of the period, was the Friday-to-Monday country house party. Not only at Windsor and Sandringham, but in great houses throughout the land, Prince and Princess Alexander of Teck would take part in that luxurious weekend ritual: the countless changes of clothes, the gargantuan meals, the shooting, the croquet, the tennis, the bridge. On the hardly less typical ritual of late-night country house activities, the Princess has her own story to tell.

Among the comforts provided by one's host would be a blazing fire in the bedroom and a bed heated by a copper warming-pan. If the housemaid was too lazy to prepare the warming-pan, she would often heat the bed with her own body, scrambling out of it just before the arrival of the guest.

'A story is told,' says Princess Alice, 'about a Scottish widower who gave parties for his men friends and was especially proud of the hospitality he provided for his guests. The scene of the story is the corridor when the host and a distinguished visitor were saying goodnight outside their respective rooms, each holding a silver candlestick. The guest, primed with good wine, discovered on entering the room that a maid who had been warming his sheets with her body had fallen asleep and was still in his bed. He doubled back into the corridor and called to his host, "Aye, mon, the victuals were delicious, the liquor stimulating, the cigar fragrant – but (winking and pointing towards his bedroom) mon, ah, mon, yon's the height of hospitality!'[8]

This story illustrates yet another facet of Princess Alice's personality: she was never prissy. Provided a story were funny, she never minded if it were slightly *risqué*. Even in extreme old age, she delighted in a 'naughty' story.

Another of her anecdotes, dating from this period, concerns the absent-minded Dean and his blue-stocking wife. This wife had just achieved a double success: she had had a book published at the same time as giving birth to her first child. On being congratulated on the latter event by one of his canons, the Dean replied, 'Yes indeed, my wife has accomplished her life's work with little or no assistance on my part, but with the occasional collaboration of the Sub-Dean'.[9]

2

Part of the pattern of Princess Alice's life at this stage would be regular visits to the Continent; particularly to her brother, the Duke of Coburg. On turning twenty-one, on 19 July 1905, the Duke had finally assumed control of the administration of his little Duchy. A spell at Bonn University and a course in law in Berlin had helped prepare him for this task. Prince Alge, who visited Coburg for his brother-in-law's accession celebrations, had his own amusing story to tell about the visit. Although there had been so many changes in the reigning family recently, it was only a dozen or so years since the death of that old reprobate, Duke Ernst. On strolling one day through the streets of the little capital with the Duke of Connaught, Prince Alge was astonished by the familiarity with which dozens of townsfolk greeted the two visiting princes.

Who, asked Prince Alge, were all those people? 'Oh,' answered the Duke of Connaught, 'they're just a few of Der Lieber, Gute Ernst's illegitimates!'[10]

Three months after his accession, the Duke of Coburg married the 20-year-old Princess Victoria Adelaide, eldest daughter of the Duke of Schleswig-Holstein, and a niece of the German Empress Dona. It was a highly successful marriage and, in time, the couple had five children. Having grown to maturity in an atmosphere of strident Prussian militarism (he was to become a general in the 1st Regiment of Prussian Guards and in the 1st Saxon Hussars), the Duke of Coburg was none the less a cultivated young man, fond of music and the theatre, interested in history and architecture. It was due, very largely, to his enthusiasm that the Coburg Theatre could survive and that the great fortress dominating the town was restored and converted into a museum.

By selling off a great deal of the property acquired by Duke Ernst in earlier, more ambitious days, the Duke of Coburg was able to bring some order into his own, previously mismanaged, inheritance. He retained, though, the castle of Greinburg in Austria and another at Hinterris in the Austrian Tyrol. It was here, and at the picturesque Reinhardsbrunn Castle near Gotha, that Princess Alice and Prince Alexander (sometimes sporting national dress) would join their Coburg relations for shooting parties: Reinhardsbrunn for deer stalking; Hinterris for chamois; Greinburg for roe deer. The couple were both enthusiastic and skilful shots. And when they were not shooting, they would be sightseeing; for Coburg was within easy reach of all those romantic, medieval German towns such as Bamberg, Nuremberg and Rothenburg.

On one occasion the couple travelled north to the flat, sandy wasteland of Mecklenburg-Strelitz to visit Prince Alge's redoubtable old Aunt Augusta, Grand Duchess of Mecklenburg-Strelitz. By then in her eighty-eighth year, the Grand Duchess was a small, sharp-eyed, bird-like figure, every bit as reactionary as her late brother, the Duke of Cambridge, and every bit as voluble as her late sister, the Duchess of Teck. For almost forty-five years the Grand Duchess Augusta had presided over the stiff, old-fashioned little court at Neu Strelitz. Only since 1904, on the death of her husband, Grand Duke Frederick, and the accession of her only son, Adolphus Frederick V, had the Grand Duchess withdrawn from public life.

But she remained as trenchant, as outspoken and as critical as she had ever been. And as mean. Refusing to have rubber tyres fitted to her carriage wheels, she would go rattling over the cobblestones on iron rims. Whenever she visited London, said Princess Alice, the old Grand Duchess would economise by doing her own shopping. Alighting from her carriage some distance away, so that she would be seen walking and not driving to the shop, the Grand Duchess would give the name of the charwoman at her London home – Mecklenburg House – in the hope that she would be charged less for her purchases.

But for all her thrifty and old-fashioned ways, the Grand Duchess Augusta was an intelligent woman; doomed, she used to sigh, to live out her life in this provincial backwater. She missed her native Britain terribly. 'One feels so far away from life and interest and commotion of the *mind*,'[11] she would complain. Politics were her passion, although by the time that Princess Alice came to know her, the old lady's political views were firmly embedded in the nineteenth century: Disraeli remained her god and Gladstone her devil.

She was astute enough, though, to realise the dangers of the Prussian-inspired militarism that was sweeping through Germany during these early years of the twentieth century. 'Strelitz, that never was a

Military State,' she grumbled to her niece, Prince Alge's sister Princess May, 'suddenly is all drums and fifes, such a pity, such a bad imitation of Schwerin and the small German Courts, while we *were* a Gentlemanlike *Civilian* Court.'[12]

Always conscious of the fact that she was a British princess in a foreign land (on her deathbed, during the First World War, she sent a message to King George V to say that 'it is a stout old English heart that is ceasing to beat')[13] the Grand Duchess lived to the age of ninety-four. Her record, as the longest-lived member of the British royal family, was to be broken by the small and pretty young Princess now visiting her at Neu Strelitz – Princess Alice.

3

Another of the Tecks' continental journeys took them into an infinitely more colourful atmosphere. This was an official visit to Spain, in May 1906, for the marriage of Princess Alice's cousin, the pretty Princess Ena of Battenberg, to the young King Alfonso XIII.* The two princesses had always been close and Princess Alice was delighted to be invited to attend the succession of lavish ceremonies in Madrid.

For formality, no court in Europe – not even the court of Kaiser Wilhelm II – could match the Spanish. From the moment that Princess Alice

---

* King Alfonso XIII (1886–1941) was the posthumous son of King Alfonso XII and Queen Maria Cristina.

and Prince Alexander (she in powder blue with an osprey-trimmed hat, he in his Royal Horse Guards uniform) arrived in Madrid, after a hot, crowded and seemingly endless train journey, they were plunged into the stiff and brilliant ceremonial for which the Spanish court was renowned.

For someone of Princess Alice's relatively relaxed upbringing, the formality of life in the Palacio Real was almost overwhelming. Each day yet another *marquesa* or *condesa* would be assigned to look after her; every noblewoman in Spain, apparently, was anxious to be associated with a princess. Whenever she wanted a bath a uniformed halberdier, complete with beribboned pike, would arrive to escort her to the bathroom. As Prince and Princess Alexander left their apartments to make their way along the vast, colonnaded corridors, an official would clap his hands and halberdiers, presenting arms, would cry out, one after another, the echoing salutation, *'Arriba Princesa! Arriba Principe!'*[14]

But the wedding day itself was remarkable for more than this customary ceremonial. After the three-hour-long marriage ceremony in the Church of San Jeronimo the carriage procession wound its way back through the clamorous streets to the Palacio Real. Prince and Princess Alexander of Teck, with Princess Frederick of Hanover and Prince Henry of Prussia, were in the eighth carriage from the end. In the last carriage drove the newly-married King Alfonso XIII and Queen Ena. The Tecks had already arrived at the

Palace and were waiting with the other royal guests on the grand staircase when they heard what they thought was 'a salute of guns'. Only on the arrival of Queen Maria Cristina (the King's mother) and of the bride's mother, Princess Beatrice, who had been travelling in the third-to-last coach, did they learn the truth.

'Someone threw a bomb,' exclaimed Queen Maria Cristina, 'but they are both alive.'

When the bridal couple finally arrived in the *coche de respeto* – the empty coach which traditionally, and fortuitously, preceded the royal carriage – they alighted, it is said, 'with quiet dignity'. With a great many people and some of their own horses having been killed or wounded by an anarchist's bomb, the King and Queen had been obliged to make their way through scenes of carnage to the *coche de respeto*: Queen Ena's satin shoes and the train of her dress were splattered with blood. Behind them, in the street, they had left twelve dead and over a hundred wounded.

'In indescribable excitement we rushed upstairs behind them,' writes one of the guests, 'and accompanied them to their rooms. Ena was incredibly self-controlled, in spite of the deadly shock, and the terrible things she had seen, but she kept on repeating, "I saw a man without any legs" '.[15]

But bomb or no bomb, the day's ceremonial had to continue. The State Luncheon which followed was an anything but convivial occasion. Princess Alice's cousin George, the Prince of Wales, had the unenviable task of proposing the health of the bride and groom. Nor was the already overwrought atmosphere improved by Princess Alice's Aunt Marie, the Russian-born Duchess of Coburg, assuring everyone that she was 'so accustomed to this sort of thing'.[16] She was indeed, having had both her father and her brother blown to bits by anarchists.*

To the assembled royalty, the day's tragedy was yet another chilling reminder of the risks of their calling. As Princess Alice's sister-in-law, Princess May, so matter-of-factly put it to her Aunt Augusta, 'we have been through a most unpleasant experience and we can only thank God that the anarchist did not get into the church, in which case we must all have been blown up!'[17]

4

Between the years 1906 and 1910, Prince Alexander and Princess Alice had three children. Their daughter, Princess May Helen Emma, was born on 23 January 1906. Their first son, Prince Rupert Alexander George Augustus, was born on 24 August 1907. Their second son, Prince Maurice Francis George, was born on 29 March 1910. All three children were delivered under the watchful eye of their grandmother, the Duchess of Albany, at Claremont

---

* Tsar Alexander II (1818–81) and his fifth son Grand Duke Serge (1857–1905).

House. The younger son, Prince Maurice, baptized in Esher church by the Bishop of Peterborough with water from the River Jordan, lived for less than six months. He died at Reinhardsbrunn while his parents were visiting the Duke of Coburg, and was buried there.

By the time that the parents were struck by what the Princess has called this 'great sorrow',[18] they were already having to bear another. For by now they knew that their elder son. Prince Rupert, was a haemophiliac. Like her cousins – Princess Alix of Hesse who had become the Empress Alexandra of Russia, Princess Ena of Battenberg who had become Queen of Spain, and Princess Irene of Hesse who was the wife of Kaiser Wilhelm II's brother, Prince Henry of Prussia – Princess Alice had proved to be a carrier of haemophilia.

'I do *wish,*' Queen Victoria had written enviously to her daughter, the Crown Princess of Prussia, at the time of Princess Mary Adelaide's engagement to Prince Teck, 'we could find more black-eyed Princes and Princesses for *our* Children! I can't help thinking what dear Papa said – that it was in fact a blessing when there was some little *imperfection* in the *pure Royal* descent and that some fresh blood was infused. In Prince Teck's case this is a very good thing . . . for this constant fair hair and blue eyes makes the blood so lymphatic . . . it is *not* as *trivial* as you may think, for darling Papa – *often* with vehemence said: We *must* have some strong dark blood.'[19]

172

Alas, the infusion of this *strong dark blood* into Queen Victoria's family – by the marriage of Princess Alice to Prince Alexander of Teck – had made no difference. Prince Rupert might have inherited his father's and his grandfather's dark colouring but from his mother came that less welcome legacy. For the parents it was a terrible blow. But with, one suspects, less self-pity and less self-dramatisation than her cousins, Princess Alice learnt to live with the realisation that her son might die at any time. Naturally self-controlled, inherently optimistic, and never one for wearing her heart on her sleeve, Princess Alice kept her fears and her anguish to herself.

There must have been times, though, as she watched her handsome, high-spirited son growing up, when she felt almost overwhelmed by this blow from a capricious fate. She could only have agreed with Queen Victoria who had once cried out that, 'Our poor family seems persecuted by this awful disease, the worst I know.'[20]

It was, perhaps, because of her determination not to allow her son's inherited illness to warp his, or her, life, that Princess Alice gradually developed her own attitude towards all forms of ill-health. As far as possible, she refused to recognise or rather, to give in to it. In this, her approach was to be not unlike that of a Christian Scientist. Although she might not have considered all forms of ill-health to be illusory, she did believe in a sensible, spartan, unsentimental approach to illness. Her attitude was greatly helped by the fact that her own constitution was exceptionally robust.

This was one of the terrible ironies of haemophilia: that so healthy a mother should transmit so deadly a disease to her son.

5

Deaths, for Prince Alge and Princess Alice, came thick and fast during these first few years of their marriage.

On 2 November 1908 Princess Alice's 'beloved Bob' – her mother's Comptroller and her mentor, Sir Robert Collins – died after an operation for peritonitis at the age of sixty-seven. Since Princess Alice's marriage, and with typical generosity of spirit, Sir Robert had done his best to train Prince Alge as his successor by initiating him into the complexities of running Claremont House. Lithe and athletic almost to the end, he had leapt over a tennis net earlier in the very year in which he died. His funeral, in the church at Esher, was notable, it is said, for 'a remarkable demonstration of public sympathy'.[21] Of all the wreaths, sent by such leading figures as King Edward VII and Queen Alexandra, the Queen Mother of the Netherlands, Princess Henry of Battenberg and the Duke and Duchess of Coburg, none carried a more touching message than that from Princess Alice: 'In token of love and gratitude to him who was both father and truest of friends'.[22]

Less than two years later, on 22 October 1910, Prince Alge's brother, the profligate Prince Francis of Teck, died at the age of thirty-nine. The passing years had done very little towards improving Prince Frank's gay, reckless and irresponsible character. Although, in recent years, he had done some charitable work for the Middlesex Hospital, the greater part of his life had still been given over to high living. Never married, Prince Frank would delight his little nephews and nieces by whisking them about London in his elegant motor-car and by buying them expensive presents at shops at which he first made sure their parents had accounts.

In the summer of 1910 he had had a minor nasal operation. While still recovering from this he had developed pleurisy, was operated on, and died. His brothers, Prince Dolly and Prince Alge, and his sister Princess May, who had so often been exasperated by his fecklessness, were nevertheless heartbroken by his sudden death. They felt, perhaps, that in losing him they were losing the last echo of the Duchess of Teck's gay insouciance. At his funeral, in St George's Chapel, Windsor, his normally self-controlled sister, by now the Queen of England, broke down and wept.

Queen Mary was not quite so overcome, however, as not to be able to attend to one unfinished bit of business. Several years before, on the Duchess of Teck's death, Prince Frank had shocked his sister by giving to his elderly lady-love his mother's famous emeralds. No sooner had Prince Frank been buried than Queen Mary, much to the amusement of her brothers Prince Dolly and Prince Alge, despatched one of the gentlemen of her household to demand the return of the jewels.

'The mission,' reports the no less amused Princess Alice, 'was successful and the gems were peacefully surrendered by Frank's heart-broken *chère amie*'.[23]

The most internationally significant death, however, had taken place earlier that year: King Edward VII had died on 6 May 1910. His funeral, says Princess Alice, 'was the most magnificent, if doleful, pageantry I have ever witnessed.' Indeed, of the many cavalcades which had marked King Edward VII's reign, this final one was the most spectacular. The weather was glorious; the crowds were enormous; the ceremonial was superb. Most impressive of all was the famous parade of kings, heirs apparent, imperial, royal and serene highnesses who rode, three by three, behind the gun-carriage bearing the flag-draped coffin. 'How Uncle Bertie, who loved display, would have enjoyed it!' says the Princess.

One touch of humour, among the day's overwhelming solemnity, was supplied by Princess May, the 4-year-old daughter of Princess Alice and Prince Alge, who had been allowed to watch the cortège from the roof of the Henry III Tower. 'What!' she piped loudly as the coffin went trundling by on its gun-carriage, 'Uncle Bertie in a box?'[24]

6

The new reign, of King George V, brought Princess Alice even closer to the throne. For she was doubly related to the new sovereigns: King George V was her first cousin, Queen Mary was her sister-in-law. The relationship between the two couples had always been close. During the reign of King Edward VII, when Prince George and Princess May had been Prince and Princess of Wales, Princess Alice and Prince Alge had often been to stay with them at York Cottage, Sandringham.

Here, in this cramped and hideous house, looking for all the world like a large suburban villa, the future King and Queen had spent much of the first seventeen years of their married life. The drawing-room, says Princess Alice, was small enough when two adults were sitting in it; when the Wales's five children crowded into it after tea, 'it became a veritable bedlam'.[25] Yet Prince George adored it. His years in the Navy had given him the taste for small, cabin-like rooms. In his library, a room housing his treasured collection of guns rather than any treasured collection of books, he was at his happiest; or rather, he was almost as happy as when he was out shooting.

Although Queen Mary was some sixteen years older than Princess Alice, the two women were very compatible. The Queen, as the Princess of Wales, had been delighted at her brother's marriage to Princess Alice. 'I am in a great state of excitement over It . . .' she had admitted to her Aunt Augusta, 'for I seem always to have "bemothered" Alge all my life, he being seven years younger than me – The two

177

ought to suit very well, as she has been well and sensibly brought up and I have always been fond of her.'[26]

For her part, Princess Alice always admired her sister-in-law for her calm, her dignity and her impressive bearing. And, with the years, she came to appreciate other traits of Queen Mary's character, not always apparent to those who did not know her well: behind that rigid façade was a woman of great kindness and sympathy. And they shared an unshakable sense of royal vocation.

As a tribute to his wife, King George V conferred the Grand Cross of the Order of the Bath on Prince Adolphus and Prince Alexander. He was also anxious to promote Prince Dolly from a 'Serene' to a 'Royal' Highness. Very prudently, Prince Dolly refused the honour. Not wishing to benefit unduly from his sister's new status, he let the King know that he would be content with a simple 'Highness'. His father, who would have given almost anything to be known as a Royal Highness, must have turned in his grave.

Another of the new King's moves to affect his brothers-in-law was his insistence that Prince Alge transfer from the Horse Guards to the 2nd Life Guards. The King was anxious for the 2nd Life Guards to be strengthened by the addition of some more experienced officers and much to his disappointment, for he was devoted to his regiment, Prince Alge was one of the first to have to make the move. Whether, mused Princess Alice, his presence 'contributed any notable improvement in the tone and efficiency of the 2nd Life Guards is open to question',[27] but Prince Alge was soon as happy with his new regiment as he had been with his old.

Together with these family changes, there were changes at court. There was a distinct alteration in its tone. King George V was a very different man from his worldly father, and his court became more decorous, more sedate, less dazzling. It was still magnificent but it was more sober.

> Nothing [wrote one of Princess Alice's continental cousins of his new régime] is more irreproachably perfect in every detail than the King of England's court and household, a sort of staid luxury without ostentation, a placid, aristocratic ease and opulence which has nothing showy about it. Everything is run on silent wheels that have been perfectly greased; everything fits in, there are no spaces between, no false note. From the polite, handsome and superlatively groomed gentleman-in-waiting who receives you in the hall, to the magnificently solemn and yet welcoming footman who walks before you down the corridor, everything pleases the eye, satisfies one's fastidiousness. When I call up before my eye the royal English abodes I always have a vision of softly carpeted, picture-hung corridors, with a silent-footed footman walking ahead of you, discreetly impersonal and yet

belonging to the whole; I have the feeling of mounting shallow-stepped stairs leading towards rooms as perfectly 'groomed' as were the horses of the royal carriage which brought you to the front door, as perfectly groomed also as the tall sentry presenting arms before the gates. . . .[28]

This same blend of magnificence and perfection marked King George V's Coronation on 22 June 1911. And of all the princesses present in Westminster Abbey that day, it was generally agreed that none looked lovelier than the 28-year-old Princess Alice. Walking up the aisle beside her tall, handsome husband (having been part of the Sovereign's mounted escort, Prince Alexander had had to scramble into his velvet mantle in order to join the royal procession) Princess Alice was said to have looked the epitome of grace, elegance and beauty. On her luxuriously piled brown hair flashed her tiara of diamond wheat-ears; around her throat and cascading down her bosom were rows of pearls; an elaborate stomacher of diamonds and sapphires, which had once belonged to the Duchess of Teck, glittered on her breast; her dress was a simple, high-waisted, stylishly-fashioned creation of white brocade; on her shoulder were clustered her various orders; behind her trailed her long, ermine-lined mantle.

If, at King Edward VII's Coronation, ten years earlier, Princess Alice had been regarded as a fresh and pretty girl, she now stood revealed as a woman of considerable style and presence, capable of playing an important role in the affairs of the court, the country and the Empire.

7

'Throughout my life,' wrote Princess Alice in her old age, 'I have always been a traveller.'[29] Until the year 1911 her travels, although extensive, had been confined to the Continent of Europe. Now, in Coronation year, she accompanied Prince Alexander to the East: to the Coronation of King Vajiravudh of Siam. The journey, which was to take her to Ceylon, Malaya and Siam, gave her a taste for sunny, exotic and colourful places. It was a taste which she was never to lose.

Though constantly courted and occasionally bullied by the various Great Powers during the hey-day of European imperialism, the kingdom of Siam* had managed to retain its independence. This made the rivalry between the nations of Europe – particularly between Britain, France and Germany – for the goodwill of the Siamese monarch all the more intense. With the new King, who had succeeded his father in 1910, Britain was at something of an advantage: King Vajiravudh had been educated at Oxford and had undergone his military training at Sandhurst. None the less, when King George V heard that

---

* Now Thailand.

Kaiser Wilhelm II was sending his brother, Prince Henry of Prussia, as his representative, the British monarch decided that his brother-in-law, Prince Alexander of Teck, would have to represent him. Accompanying the Prince on his mission would be Sir Stanley Colville, General Sir James Grierson and Sir Beilby Alston. Princess Alice, though, was not to be included: no wives had been invited.

Never one for sitting meekly at home if there was an opportunity for adventure, the Princess worked out a plan by which she could take advantage of her husband's journey. As his passage was being paid for by the Government, he could afford, she reckoned, to buy a passage for her; while he went to Bangkok to attend the Coronation, she would go to Java and await his return. With Java then being part of the Dutch East Indies, Princess Alice – as Queen Wilhelmina's cousin – would be sure of a comfortable stay on the island. Prince Alge agreed to the plan. And as Sir Stanley Colville would be accompanying the Prince on his mission, his wife, Lady Colville, could accompany the Princess as her lady-in-waiting.

There remained the children. But it was not really much of a problem. Both the 5-year-old Princess May and the 4-year-old Prince Rupert were in the care of the excellent Nanny Kemence. All that was needed was for Nanny Kemence to move with her charges from Windsor Castle to Claremont House, where the Duchess of Albany was only too happy to look after them. And as to the children's own feelings on the matter, a stay at Claremont, says their mother, 'was always a high-light in their lives'.[30]

Prince and Princess Alexander set out on 27 October 1911. They travelled first by train to Brindisi, then by ship to Port Said, and so by the P. and O. liner *Mongolia* to Colombo in Ceylon. During their short stay in Colombo they received a message from the King of Siam. Having heard that the Princess and her lady-in-waiting were accompanying their husbands, the King invited them both to continue on to Bangkok to attend the Coronation.

Princess Alice was delighted. The only drawback was that she had brought no dress or jewellery suitable for such an occasion. But Sir Hugh Clifford, about to become Acting Governor of Ceylon, assured her that when she reached Singapore she would find a Chinese tailor capable of running up anything she might want in a very short time. And Lady Clifford (she had been Elizabeth de la Pasture, the novelist) would lend her a tiara. So with that organised, and with cabled permission from King George V, Princess Alice felt able to accept the King of Siam's invitation.

Leaving Ceylon in the S.S. *Assaye,* the party sailed to Penang in Malaya. From here they travelled south, overland down the Malaysian peninsula, to Singapore. For Princess Alice, this tour through Malaya was all enchantment: the balmy air, the lush scenery, the elephant rides, the waterfalls, the vast rubber plantations, the airy Government Houses, the friendly, honey-coloured people.

Having arrived in Singapore at the end of the tour, the Princess's first concern was for her dress. She was astonished to find not only a suitable dressmaker, but one who had formerly worked for a couturier in Grosvenor Place, London, and had made clothes for the Princess's late mother-in-law, the Duchess of Teck. The Princess showed her a photograph of herself in the dress that she had worn to King George V's Coronation and in a surprisingly short time the dressmaker had converted a length of Chinese brocade into an excellent copy. With this dress, with Lady Clifford's tiara and with a necklace hired from a Singapore jeweller, Princess Alice felt ready to attend the Coronation.

During her stay in Singapore the Princess, with typical verve, sampled whatever diversions the city had to offer: a visit to the Stock Exchange where a welcoming sprinkling of attar of roses helped offset the smell of so many fat, naked and profusely sweating torsos; a Chinese theatre which seemed to be given over mainly to the sensuous swaying of the actresses and the insistent beating of brass gongs; a 'European' theatre where the performance resembled nothing she had ever seen in Europe; tea houses remarkable for their rowdiness and opium dens for their tranquillity. As the British held sway in Singapore there was the inevitable regimental football match. (One British diplomat simply could not understand why, when the British kept themselves so busy with sport, the French 'mope indoors complaining of the heat'.[31] The Germans, he said, were better.) For the watching Princess Alice, this football match was made memorable by the fact that the splattering mud ruined her white tropical dress and that the ball landed squarely on her white *broderie anglaise* hat.

From Singapore, while Prince Alge and his delegation sailed north to Bangkok in H.M.S. *Astrea* (a rumour that Prince Henry of Prussia would be arriving in a battleship stirred the British Government into providing their mission with a battleship as well), the Princess, Lady Colville, and the various other royal representatives travelled in the King of Siam's yacht. 'It was,' says Princess Alice, 'the second roughest sea voyage I have ever endured – the roughest being the return journey in the same yacht!'[32] Her most vivid memory of it was of a brilliantly dressed little page – one of the innumerable sons of the late King of Siam – holding out an ornamental basin for her to be sick in.

Siam, like Malaya, left Princess Alice with a kaleidoscope of happy memories: the gondola-like state barge, with its scores of oarsmen, gliding up the river between the cluttered sampans; the dazzling firework displays; the flamboyant temples; the royal mausoleum with the dead kings in golden caskets; the elaborate entertainments ('Nothing is too extravagant in this line,' grumbled one Englishman, *en poste* in Bangkok, 'but it does not occur to the Siamese to spend sixpence to mend a road or make a drain')[33]; the gigantic statues of Buddha; the actors in their shimmering costumes and towering, tinkling head-dresses; and, of course, the Coronation itself, with all its ritual and its splendour and its mystique.

Through all this activity – through the enervating heat, the exhausting travelling, the often boring ceremonial, the sometimes uncomfortable accommodation, the frequently inedible meals, the terrifying sea voyages – Princess Alice remained cheerful, adaptable, uncomplaining. Never once did her sense of humour desert her. Her eye was on the look-out for the amusing and the ridiculous just as often as it was for the interesting and the picturesque. In Colombo she remarked on the Governor, so determined to walk ahead of her, and she as determined to keep up, that at a luncheon party they astonished the assembled guests by bursting through the door 'at a trot'.[34]

In Bangkok, she says, a certain breakfast party on board the official launches was enlivened by a Hungarian count, amorous on champagne, making persistent advances to Lady Colville. In an effort to shake him off, the desperate Lady Colville was forced to leap from one rocking launch to the next, always followed by her tipsily leering 'satyr'. Only by hitching up her skirts and taking a flying leap across an alarmingly wide stretch of water to yet another launch could she finally shake off her pursuer.

But it is about the Queen Mother of Siam that Princess Alice is at her most amusing. 'As her royal partner had been dead for some months and court mourning was over,' says the Princess, '[the Queen Mother] began to miss the masculine company he had so generously provided. She was the Chief Queen and had four children, but, like Solomon, he had had many other wives, and, to judge from the number of children he left behind him, his attentions must have been as constant and satisfying as they were productive. Like the famous Empress of China, she decided that her Master of the Horse and Court Chamberlain was adequately equipped to carry on worthily those of the late King's duties which most intimately concerned herself. This was an open secret and the Master of the Horse, who was quite good-looking, was carried up to her apartments by uniformed attendants every evening in a washing basket and reverently decanted on her divan.'[35]

8

Not all the official duties of Prince and Princess Alexander of Teck carried the excitement and glamour of their journey to Siam. As much as any other members of the royal family, the couple worked for numberless worthy causes and carried out numberless public tasks. Prince Alge was chairman of the Middlesex Hospital; he was involved with the League of Mercy; he was actively concerned with various youth movements – the Church Lads' Brigade, the Boy Scouts, the British Boys' Training Corps. Princess Alice organised fêtes, presented prizes, laid foundation stones, planted trees. Together the couple toured docks, inspected mines, attended civic luncheons. Prince Alexander went to The Hague to confer the Order of the Bath on Queen Wilhelmina's consort, Prince Henry of the Netherlands; he travelled to Athens to represent King George V at the funeral of the assassinated King George I of the Hellenes. And wherever the couple appeared – he so tall and she so small – they were noted for their good looks, their ease of manner, their apparently unfeigned interest and their undeniably regal aura.

Official recognition of these exceptional qualities came early in 1914. Prince Alexander was chosen to succeed the Duke of Connaught (Queen Victoria's third and only surviving son) as Governor-General of Canada. For the 39-year-old Prince Alexander this was a notable achievement. Not only was the Governor-Generalship of Canada one of the most important imperial posts but it was known to be an extremely difficult one. 'It is no easy thing to be a governor-general of Canada,' complained the Marquess of Lorne, husband of Queen Victoria's fourth daughter, Princess Louise, who had been the Governor-General of Canada from 1878 to 1883; 'You must have the patience of a saint, the smile of a cherub, the generosity of an Indian prince, and the back of a camel.'[36]

Prince Alexander may or may not have had all these qualities but his appointment, which was made official in May 1914, met with widespread approval. In its leading article of 8 May 1914, *The Times* gave its opinion of his qualifications for the task.

Prince Alexander of Teck is to succeed the Duke of Connaught as Governor-General of Canada. His work will not be easy; but we have no doubt that its difficulties are for him more than balanced by the splendour of the opportunity which it offers. The work which lies before him is *royal* in the fullest sense of a word that has grown to have a wider meaning for the people of the British Dominions during recent years. . . .

His appointment will, we are sure, be warmly welcomed in Canada. In every way he is qualified to carry on the tradition of broad sympathy and simplicity of character which has enabled the Duke of Connaught to win the affectionate respect of the Canadian people.[37]

Prince Alexander and Princess Alice were to take up their new post in October 1914.

CHAPTER EIGHT

1

For Princess Alice the First World War brought, with all its other anguish, the anguish of a family feud. The outbreak of hostilities found her relations in firmly opposed camps. Germany, headed by her cousin Kaiser Wilhelm II, was chock-a-block with members of her family: not only her brother, the Duke of Coburg, but many of her late father's relatives and most of her mother's relations were on the German side. So, too, were Prince Alexander's family, the Württembergs. Against them were ranged the families of her British cousin, King George V, and of her Russian cousin, the Empress Alexandra. Still neutral at the outbreak of war were the countries in which lived yet more of her cousins: Queen Ena of Spain, Queen Maud of Norway, Queen Sophie of the Hellenes and Crown Princess Marie of Romania. Overnight, close, dearly-loved relatives had to be treated as enemies; princes who had grown up together now faced each other across the firing line.

In. fact, the outbreak of the First World War proved, if proof had been necessary, the irrelevance of these family ties between the various royal houses of Europe. That the majority of European sovereigns were so closely related made not the slightest difference to the course of events. Although, during the hectic days before the fighting began, telegrams flew between the cousins who reigned in Germany, Russia and Great Britain – Willy, Nicky and Georgie – their urgent phrases affected the outcome not at all.

Yet Kaiser Wilhelm II, ever prone to over-estimate the powers of reigning sovereigns, simply could not admit that the war had been caused by anything other than the duplicity of his relations. He accused King George V of conspiring with Tsar Nicholas II to complete the nefarious policy of encirclement begun by King Edward VII. To think, he exclaimed, that Georgie and Nicky should have played him false. If his grandmother, Queen Victoria, had been alive, she would never have allowed it.

Although Princess Alice was always to maintain that the well-known antagonism between her Uncle Bertie and her Cousin Willy had more to do with Anglo-German rivalry than was afterwards believed, she never made the mistake of accusing Kaiser Wilhelm II of wanting war. Bumptious, braggardly and aggressive he might have been, but she appreciated that he was a sabre-rattler, not a warmonger. His belligerence was a pose and nothing more. And she fully understood his ambivalent attitude towards

Britain. Neurotically envious of Great Britain's power, 'deep down he loved England and English customs'.[1]

One day, soon after the outbreak of war, Princess Alice and Prince Alge went to call on the Empress Eugenie at her home at Farnborough Hill. For almost fifty years, since her husband the Emperor Napoleon III had lost his throne during the Franco-Prussian War, the Empress had lived in exile in England. As much as anyone, the old Empress had reason to resent German militancy. Yet she told her guests that she did not think that Kaiser Wilhelm II, for all his truculence, was responsible for the war. He was simply the victim of circumstances. 'When a river reaches the waterfall,' she said, 'no earthly power can stop it.'[2]

This was an accurate summing-up of the situation in 1914. One of the chief reasons for the great conflict of 1914–18 was that Europe had developed into a series of rival power blocs, all competing with each other, all striving to be larger, stronger, more magnificent than each other. Germany was probably no worse than the rest of them. It was simply that her diplomats had isolated her in a hostile world and that, like her Kaiser, she had become too self-confident, too boastful and too militant. Sooner or later she would have to prove herself. Princess Alice's contention that it was the German generals, and not the Kaiser, who wanted war was correct.

For few members of a royal family were the divided loyalties of this great struggle worse than for

Princess Alice's brother, the Duke of Coburg. Born an Englishman, partly educated in England, and with a mother and sister living in England, he found himself in an agonising position. On the one hand he took pride in his rank as a Prussian general in Germany's spectacularly burgeoning army; on the other he could not bear the thought of taking up arms against his native land. In the years before the war, while his sister and brother-in-law stood by in embarrassment, the Duke would join in lusty toastings to *der Tag;* yet he would feel obliged to warn Prince Alexander that Admiral von Tirpitz had predicted that Germany would declare war on the completion of the Kiel Canal in 1915. By nature intense, emotional and irresolute, the Duke of Coburg was the very worst person to be trapped in this particular dilemma.

When the news of the assassination of Archduke Franz Ferdinand of Austria was announced in July 1914, the Duke of Coburg happened to be visiting Princess Alice at Windsor. Realising its implications, he returned at once to Coburg. It was possibly on this occasion that he admitted to his sister that had it not been for his wife and children, he would have returned to fight for England. This, of course, was impossible: he was a general in the German Army. All that the Duke of Coburg could do was to ask to be sent to the Russian Front so that he need not fight against his countrymen.

'The outbreak of the war between England and Germany in 1914 shattered his life,' says Princess

Alice, 'he was denounced in Germany for being English and in England for being German.'[3]

At the end of the war, the Duke of Coburg was to be accused of being a 'Traitor Peer' for 'having adhered to the King's enemies'.[4] By order of the King in Council, his titles were removed from the Roll of Peers.

2

While the Duke of Coburg was battling with his dilemma, Princess Alice and Prince Alexander were battling with theirs: whether or not, because of the outbreak of war, they should accept the Canadian appointment. It was, admits Princess Alice, 'the most painful decision in our lives'.[5] Now that Prince Alge was second in command of the 2nd Life Guards he felt that this was not the time to leave it. On discussing the matter with the King, Prince Alexander argued that whereas the Duke of Connaught, by now too old for active service, would be more useful staying on in Canada, he would be more useful at the Front. The King agreed. King George V would have been sorry, for both his own sake and that of the Queen, not to have this stalwart member of his family nearer at hand during the ominous days that lay ahead.

So instead of going to Ottawa, Prince Alexander went to Windmill Hill, Ludgershall, to join a composite brigade made up of the 1st and 2nd Life Guards and the Royal Horse Guards, known as the

7th Cavalry Brigade. On 7 October 1914, they sailed for Belgium. During the following weeks the 7th Brigade was actively engaged in Flanders, covering themselves with glory at a desperately fought action at Zillebeke. In the action Prince Alge lost some of his closest comrades.

At home, in the Henry III Tower, Princess Alice was deeply involved in various wartime activities. She was Chairman of the Sailors' and Soldiers' Families Association – an organisation concerned with servicemen's families suffering from the sudden loss of the household's normal, peacetime income. Half a century later she could still remember her weekly programme: on Mondays it was War Pensions, on Tuesday the Munitions Canteen, on Wednesdays the Beaver Hut in the Strand where she waited on Canadian soldiers, on Thursdays the Munitions Canteen again and on Fridays a tea party for wounded overseas soldiers at Windsor Castle. For years afterwards, old Canadian or Australian or South African soldiers would recall their lively and comforting conversations with the Princess and treasure the inscribed photographs which she had given them.

Princess Alice devoted Saturdays and Sundays to her children. In the year that war broke out, Princess May turned eight and Prince Rupert seven. Their governess was 'the delightful and very cultured'[6] Mademoiselle Stroh, from Alsace, but by now young Prince Rupert had already passed out of her hands and was attending a preparatory school for the boys of the choir of St George's Chapel at Windsor. In time, Princess May would attend St Paul's School for Girls.

It was during these war years that Princess Alice, accompanied by the young Prince Rupert, went to congratulate an old Miss Baily on reaching her hundredth birthday. The royal visitors, having presented their presents, stayed on to tea with Miss Baily and, on leaving the cottage, Prince Rupert turned to his mother to say, 'Fancy, mummy – a hundred years old – and not married yet!'[7]

There were times, as year followed year, when even the normally resilient Princess Alice felt sick at heart by the dragging on of a conflict which so many had imagined would be over in a matter of months. 'One hardly has the heart to enjoy anything much at present,' she confided to a friend during the second winter of the war. 'However, the good news of our successes in France and Flanders makes one see that there is, and can be, an end to this terrible war.'[8]

3

Yet for Princess Alice the war had its lighter, or at least more interesting moments. Late in October 1914, Prince Alexander was appointed to the British Mission with the Belgian Army of which King Albert of the Belgians was Commander-in-Chief. As the Prince was to remain with the Mission until the end of the war, Princess Alice was able to pay several visits to her husband at Belgian Headquarters. These were centred on La Panne, in the far western corner of the otherwise enemy-occupied country. The Princess's visits to La Panne allowed her to experience something of the dangerous yet strangely unreal world of life behind the trenches and brought her into contact with two exceptional fellow royals: King Albert and Queen Elisabeth of the Belgians.

After a desperate defence of the country against the invading Germans the Belgian troops had fallen back beyond the River Yser. By ordering the sluice gates to be opened, and thereby flooding the valley of the Yser, King Albert had been able to ensure that the last twenty square miles of Belgian soil remained free. His army now formed the extreme left wing of the Allied line stretching from Switzerland to the North Sea. After the great battle of Ypres, of which the Belgian defence of the Yser was a stirring episode, the war bogged down, quite literally, in the trenches. Except for the gain of a few hundreds yards here and the loss of a few hundred yards somewhere else – always at the cost of thousands and often tens of thousands of lives – the Western Front remained static for four long years. The combatants dug themselves in and life immediately behind the lines took on a semblance of normality.

It was at the little seaside resort of La Panne, some eight miles from the front and a stone's throw from the French border, that King Albert and Queen Elisabeth of the Belgians had established themselves.

Their home was a solid, red-brick villa, situated at the far end of the sea-front. The house was tastelessly furnished, the bedrooms were without heating, there was no hot water. From the windows, when the swirling winter mists allowed one to see out of them, was a view of the flat grey sea. More often than not it was raining. The dunes, with their salt grasses swaying in the wet wind, spread to the very steps of the villa.

It was here, in this doleful house, that Princess Alice would visit the Belgian sovereigns on her periodic trips to see her husband. How, asked Princess Alice of the Belgian Queen, could she possibly bear to live in such bleak surroundings? To make the house more attractive, answered the Queen, would be to accept it as a home. She would simply not allow herself to believe that she would go on living here much longer.

King Albert and Queen Elisabeth were an extraordinarily interesting couple. As a Coburg – the grandson of Queen Victoria's Uncle Leopold, first King of the Belgians, after whom Princess Alice's father had been named – King Albert was related to Princess Alice. Normally shy, gauche and diffident, the King had emerged from his country's time of trial as a man of immense stature: brave, resolute, realistic. Few monarchs in Europe could match his quiet courage, his unfeigned modesty or his self-deprecating humour. A solemn, preoccupied man in public, King Albert could be very witty in private. He would keep Princess Alice highly amused with his wryly-told anecdotes:

about his uncle, the notoriously lecherous old King Leopold II, or about his donnish father and short-sighted mother, the Count and Countess of Flanders. His patience, says Princess Alice, was inexhaustible; his speech, with its long pauses between each word, unbelievably slow. When the Princess once asked him how he could possibly put up with the maddening behaviour of the visiting Margot Asquith, his reply was characteristically dry. 'Well . . .', he drawled, 'one . . . must . . . be . . . polite . . . to . . . the . . . wife . . . of . . . the . . . Prime . . . Minister . . . of . . . England.'[9]

Queen Elisabeth was quite different. Born a Wittelsbach, this small, sharp-witted, animated woman was possessed of great personal charm. Her reputation, too, had been considerably enhanced by her behaviour during the dark days of the war. By her tireless nursing of the wounded, her unfailing cheerfulness and her unconquerable spirit, Queen Elisabeth had become an object of veneration to the troops. Her calm in the face of danger was astonishing. The almost daily enemy shelling seemed to bother her not at all. Princess Alice would sometimes accompany the Queen on her daily visits to the hospitals or the troops and she never knew Queen Elisabeth to flinch when the shells landed nearby.

Once, when a hospital was struck and set ablaze, the Queen refused to be hustled away to safety. She worked tirelessly, helping the nurses get the patients out of the burning building. When the raid was over and the wounded had to be accommodated elsewhere, the doctor in charge complimented her on her courage. In what way, answered the Queen with a wry smile, had *her* courage differed from that of the nurses?

But Queen Elisabeth had another side as well: a romantic, theatrical, bohemian side. She was, after all, a member of the eccentric and artistic Wittelsbach family. She loved, says Princess Alice, to entertain 'artistic people from the regiments'.[10] In the grounds of her sombre villa, the Queen had had a movable wooden bungalow erected. Its interior, said one of those 'artistic' visitors, the French writer Pierre Loti, was entirely hung with pale blue Persian silk, relieved with a touch of rose-pink and decorated with a large design representing the portico of a mosque. Its furniture consisted solely of divans, piled high with brightly patterned cushions. The conversation, said the admiring Loti, was confined almost entirely to the religions of the East.

If, with Pierre Loti, the Queen was content to discuss religion, with more robust men she could reveal a distinctly flirtatious side. Princess Alice often spoke of the Queen's tendency to flirt. Even Prince Alge would sometimes be the object of her arch banter. Once, when the Queen and Princess Alice were going to dine at the Headquarters of the Guards Division, the two of them went up to General Gathorne-Hardy's room to tidy up after their drive. Before leaving the room, the Queen slipped one of Hardy's hair-brushes between the sheets of his bed. The next day a despatch rider arrived at Belgian Headquarters with a note for the Queen.

'Petit attaque de nuit sur le point d'appui',[11] ran General Gathorne-Hardy's straight-faced message.

Princess Alice and Prince Alexander were once present at a simple but moving ceremony at which the heir to the Belgian throne, the thirteen-year-old Prince Leopold,* was accepted into his regiment. As soon as the collapse of the Belgian resistance seemed imminent, the Queen had taken advantage of Lord Curzon's offer to look after her three children – Prince Leopold, Prince Charles and Princess Marie-José, and they had gone to live at Hackwood, Lord Curzon's country home. Even though the boys' clothes were considered somewhat bizarre (Margot Asquith was astonished that their necks should be so décolleté and their legs so naked) the children soon settled down to life in England. It was just before going to Eton that Prince Leopold joined the Belgian Army.

On 8 April 1915, with the 12th Regiment of the Line standing in square formation on the windswept shore, King Albert introduced his son, looking slight and vulnerable in his private's uniform, to the Troops.

'Soldiers,' he said, 'Princes must be brought up in the school of duty, and no school is better than his own army, which represents the nation's heroism. My

---

* Afterwards the controversial King Leopold III (1901–)

201

son has claimed the honour of wearing the uniform of our valiant soldiers. He will be particularly proud to belong to a regiment which, by its deeds of courage and patriotic devotion, deserves to be remembered in our national history.'[11]

From then on, during his school holidays, young Prince Leopold would serve with his regiment.

With Prince Alexander spending some four years with the British Mission to Belgium, Princess Alice was able to make firm friends with the Belgian sovereigns. They were exactly the sort of people she liked: informal, unpretentious, yet utterly devoted to their royal calling. Their air of optimism, and their lightly-worn fortitude, echoed her own. Even in the dreariest or most dangerous days of their four-year-long wait, the King and Queen of the Belgians never doubted that they would one day return home. When the war ended, they promised Princess Alice, they would invite her to Brussels to see them make their triumphant entry.

Yet there must have been times, as the four royals sat talking in the dreary house on the sand dunes at La Panne, when it seemed as though that day would never come.

4

In the third year of the war King George V decided that in the face of the criticism of his family's German origin and connections those branches of the British royal family still bearing German names and titles must change them for English ones. Queen Victoria's dream, that her dynasty would be kown as the Coburg line, was to be short-lived. After rejecting various suggestions, it was agreed that the King would change his surname from the compromisingly German one of Wettin to the unequivocally British one of Windsor.

Other branches of the family to be affected by the ruling were the Battenbergs and the Tecks. The King's two cousins, Prince Louis of Battenberg and Prince Alexander of Battenberg,* became respectively Marquess of Milford Haven and Marquess of Carisbrooke, with the family name of Mountbatten. And the King's two brothers-in-law, the Duke of Teck (Prince Dolly) and Prince Alexander of Teck, became respectively Marquess of Cambridge and Earl of Athlone, taking their late mother's family name of Cambridge.

The Royal Warrant concerning Prince Alexander's change of name and title was published on 14 July 1917.

The King has been graciously pleased, by Warrant under His Majesty's Royal Sign Manual, to give and grant unto His Serene Highness Prince Alexander Augustus

---

* Prince Louis of Battenberg (1854–1921) was the husband of King George V's cousin, Princess Victoria of Hesse (1863–1950); Prince Alexander of Battenberg was the son of Queen Victoria's daughter, Princess Beatrice.

Frederick William Alfred George of Teck, Knight Grand Cross of the Most Honourable Order of the Bath, Knight Grand Cross of the Royal Victorian Order, Companion of the Distinguished Service Order, Brevet Lieutenant-Colonel and Temporary Brigadier-General in the Army, His Licence and Authority that he and his issue may relinquish the use of the styles, dignities, titles and attributes of 'Serene Highness' and of 'Prince' and all other states, degrees, dignities, titles, honours or appellations in the Kingdom of Württemberg or German Empire to him or to them belonging, and the designation of 'Teck', that he may take and use the surname of Cambridge, and that such surname may be taken and used by his issue: Provided that the said Royal Concession and Declaration be recorded in His Majesty's College of Arms, otherwise the said Royal Licence and Permission to be void and of no effect.

And to command that the said Royal Concession and Declaration be recorded in His Majesty's College of Arms.

This resounding declaration was followed, some time later, by another to the effect that the former Prince Alexander of Teck, 'and the heirs male of his body lawfully begotten' would be known by 'the names, styles, and titles of Viscount Trematon in the County of Cambridge, and Earl of Athlone'.[13]

His Serene Highness Prince Alexander of Teck now became the Right Honourable the Earl of Athlone; his wife remained Her Royal Highness Princess Alice but with the title of Countess of Athlone; their daughter ceased to be a princess and became Lady May Cambridge and their son, Prince Rupert, became Viscount Trematon.

Her husband, says Princess Alice, was furious about the change: 'he thought that kind of camouflage stupid and petty'.[14]

Others took it more philosophically. Prince Louis of Battenberg, having lost his family name, seems to have retained his family sense of humour. Arriving to spend a few days at the home of his eldest son two days before the change, and leaving it as the Marquess of Milford Haven three days later, wrote in the visitors' book, 'arrived Prince Jekyll . . . departed Lord Hyde.'

But perhaps Kaiser Wilhelm II's comment was the wittiest. When next a certain Shakespeare play was performed in Berlin, he scoffed, it would be called 'The Merry Wives of Saxe-Coburg-Gotha'.

5

Whether Prince Alexander liked it or not, it was as Lord Athlone that he joined the Allied advance in the autumn of 1918. The long wait was over. On 26 October, when King Albert and his family entered

Bruges, the Earl of Athlone rode with them through the acclaiming streets. But it was the royal entry into Brussels, on 22 November, that was to be such a memorable occasion.

True to their word, the King and Queen of the Belgians had invited Princess Alice to witness their return to the capital. Accompanied by Lady Byng, the wife of General Viscount Byng and daughter of Jane Moreton, who had been the Duchess of Albany's lady-in-waiting, Princess Alice sailed to Dunkirk in a destroyer. There they were met by Lord Athlone, who drove them along the slithery, shell-pitted roads to Brussels. From the windows of the sadly delapidated Foreign Office the Princess was able to watch the triumphant entry of the royal family.

They say that no one who was in Brussels that day ever forgot this homecoming. Every rooftop, every window, every inch of pavement was packed with people. Flags fluttered, handkerchiefs waved, cheer upon tumultuous cheer broke out as the procession passed by. Throats were hoarse, arms were limp, faces wet with tears. Dressed in khaki, with a steel helmet topping his lined and weather-beaten face, King Albert rode slowly through the streets. Beside him, mounted on a huge white charger and wearing a faded grey riding habit, rode Queen Elisabeth. Behind, the one in khaki and the other in the blue of a midshipman, came Prince Leopold and Prince Charles. Among the horsemen who followed after were Britain's Prince Albert – the future King George VI – and his uncle, the Earl of Athlone.

For Princess Alice, as she stood looking down on the scene from the windows of the Foreign Office, it proved to be 'one of the most unforgettable moments of our lives'.[15] And for the rest of his days the Earl of Athlone treasured the photograph of the Queen of the Belgians which bore the inscription. 'To my dear Alge. In affectionate remembrance of four years in Flanders. Elisabeth. 1914–18.'[16]

CHAPTER NINE

1

'That's been my life,' Princess Alice once said smilingly in old age, 'opening things and closing things.'[1] Certainly, in the five years following the end of the First World War, the Princess opened, closed, organised, presided over, attended meetings of, took part in, appeared at and worked for countless things. Sometimes alone, sometimes with Lord Athlone, she carried out an extraordinary variety of royal duties, ranging from the judging of the Windsor Baby Show to her work as President of the Women's Section of the British Legion. She was at the first meeting of, and was afterwards closely associated with, the British Israel World Federation; as President of the National Children's Adoption Association she inaugurated the Woman's Hour programme at the B.B.C.'s new studio at Savoy Hill; she was involved in the Soldiers' and Sailors' Pension Fund; she raised money for the 6th North London (Princess Alice's Own) Troop of Boy Scouts; she launched an appeal for funds for an extension of the Nurses' Home at the Middlesex Hospital. She presented prizes, she opened hospital wards, she sat through concerts, she unveiled memorials, she attended dedication ceremonies, committee meetings and memorial services.

If, to the general public, Princess Alice was simply a small, smiling, always stylishly dressed member of the royal family who did her job with grace and ease, to those who were more closely associated with her she was known as a woman of considerable ability. Not at all shy, she could create a relaxed and uninhibited atmosphere. She was an accomplished public speaker. 'I was rather surprised to find,' she said disarmingly of her first public speech made early in married life, 'I was not very nervous and imagined that I had performed the opening ceremony with such aplomb that nobody could have suspected that I was a novice.'[2]

Those who worked on committees with her found her orderly, well-organised, conscientious and energetic. Without being in the least officious, she was very thorough: she always insisted on being kept fully informed on whatever was happening; she never shirked her responsibilities.

In her late thirties, Princess Alice had by the early 1920s developed the personality and characteristics that were to be hers for the rest of her life. Although no intellectual, she had a lively, intelligent, enquiring mind. Having inherited something of her late father's taste for the arts, she was especially interested in painting. She read widely and, in her letters, expressed herself naturally and vividly. But the Princess was probably happiest out of doors; she loved all open air sports and activities. Walking was almost an obsession. She was an enthusiastic traveller: she loved change, movement, adventure. Her energy, and her curiosity, were almost insatiable. She was extrovert, friendly, gregarious, with a keen sense of humour and of fun. Her nature was buoyant, optimistic, not easily cast down. She had a great lust for life.

Yet for all her breeziness and heartiness, Princess Alice remained intensely feminine. With her flawless complexion and her pale colouring she had all the beauty and delicacy of fine china; very interested in clothes, she dressed with a soft, romantic elegance, her charm was undeniably feminine. She had a eye for beautiful things; she loved flowers.

But perhaps Princess Alice's most important trait was the least immediately apparent one: her great strength of character. Self-disciplined and self-controlled, she had an inner steeliness that was to support her through the various changes and vicissitudes of her long life.

And, with it all, Princess Alice remained essential royal. She was dignified, gracious, one-stage-removed; very aware, not so much of her rank and status, as of herself as a representative of the monarchy. 'Whatever we did,' she once explained in old age, 'we did for the King, or the Queen, or whatever the case was.'[3] Even in her most relaxed moments, Princess Alice could never be mistaken for anything other than a princess.

Her marriage was very happy. She and Lord Athlone suited each other very well although she, as the years went by, emerged as the stronger personality. Her husband was, she says, 'the kindest of men and had a generally amiable disposition, but he had inherited from his father (though to nothing like the same extent) a tendency towards sudden bursts of temper on rare occasions.'[4] Forty-five at the end of the First World War, the Earl of Athlone was an impressive-looking man: tall, balding, with an upright, soldierly bearing and a distinguished public manner. Like his sister Queen Mary – although not to the same degree – he suffered from a certain shyness in public. His lack of small talk he compensated for by asking innumerable questions; he was, in fact, extremely interested in people and places. His manner of speaking was hearty, soldierly, staccato. Even less of an intellectual than his wife, Lord Athlone was possessed of a great deal of sound common sense; by his practical, no-nonsense approach, he often showed a surer grasp of affairs than did his more erudite colleagues. Above all, he was a transparently honest man: 'a model of integrity,'[5] says one of his close associates.

Until 17 April 1919 Lord Athlone had remained with the Belgian Mission, but not long after his return to Britain he retired from active service in the Army.

Permitted to retain the rank of Honorary Brigadier-General, he was appointed Personal Aide-de-camp to his brother-in-law, King George V. No less than Princess Alice, Lord Athlone was involved in numberless royal duties. His chief concern was with health. To his longstanding chairmanship of the Middlesex Hospital were now added his duties as Chairman of the Athlone Committee – a body of eminent doctors and surgeons set up to investigate the long-term needs of the medical profession. He was associated with the British Empire League, the Windsor and Eton Royal Albert Institute, the Weavers' Company, the Vintners' Company, Dr Barnado's Homes, the League of Mercy, the Philanthropic Society. He was awarded decorations, honorary degrees and the freedom of boroughs.

So the Earl of Athlone would have had every sympathy with his nephew, the Prince of Wales and future King Edward VIII, who, on once being accused of being a member of the idle rich, snapped back to the effect that although he might be rich, he was certainly never idle. And Lord Athlone did not even have the compensation of being very rich.

But there were, of course, breaks in this gruelling royal treadmill. There would be visits to Scotland, as the guests of the King and Queen, either at Balmoral or Abergeldie. There were holidays at the Villa Nevada in Cannes. The couple visited King Albert and Queen Elisabeth in Brussels where they were enthusiastically greeted by the crowds who appreciated Lord

Athlone's wartime association with their country. They visited Lord Athlone's niece, Princess Mary, and her husband, Viscount Lascelles, who were holidaying in Florence. One year they ventured further afield. Sailing from Cannes to Oran in s.s. *Gibel Sarsar,* they toured Southern Algeria, spending a week at the Oasis of Figuig, in the heart of the desert.

In August 1921 the couple spent a holiday with King Alfonso XIII and Queen Ena at Santander on the north coast of Spain. The Athlones particularly enjoyed this holiday. Away from the overwhelming formality, splendour and clericalism of the Palacio Real in Madrid, the Spanish sovereigns were revealed, says Princess Alice, as 'excellent company'.[6] The ebullient, athletic King Alfonso and the elegant, unpretentious Queen Ena, both in their thirties, shared their guests' taste for informal living and outdoor activities. Like Princess Alice, Queen Ena always retained something of the frank, unaffected quality of a princess raised at Queen Victoria's court. The Spanish Queen could be extremely amusing about the, to her, ridiculous stiffness of the Palacio Real, and as both she and Princess Alice were 'great gigglers', they enjoyed each other's company enormously. They were more like sisters,'[7] it is said.

It was during this Spanish holiday that Princess Alice attended her 'first and only bull-fight'.[8] One may be certain that the Princess shared with Queen Ena the usual British disapproval of this Spanish national sport. Few of Queen Ena's subjects realised that the binoculars through which their Queen followed the gory progress of a bull-fight were fitted with opaque glass: she could see nothing.

These two granddaughters of Queen Victoria, who had shared such happy girlhood days at Windsor, Osborne and Balmoral, shared something less happy. Both were carriers of haemophilia. Two of Queen Ena's four sons – the heir, Prince Alfonso, and her youngest son, Prince Gonzalo – were haemophiliacs. Her second son, Prince Jaime, was a deaf mute. So, of her four sons, only the third, Prince Juan, was bodily sound. Poor Queen Ena's sense of failure and disappointment, in a country where such store was set on masculine virility, was acute. And while all Spain seethed with rumours of the nature of the illness within the royal family, the King felt incapable of taking his people into his confidence. Living as he did, under a constant threat of assassination, it was important that the succession be made to appear secure.

The presence of the honest-to-goodness Princess Alice, who would have understood her position so well, must have been of considerable comfort to Queen Ena that summer. The children of both families were together at Santander; there can be little doubt that the two mothers discussed their shared predicament. Queen Ena's was the harder to bear, for whereas Princess Alice had the support of a devoted and sympathetic husband, Queen Ena did not. King Alfonso XIII had many good qualities, but constancy, patience and tenderness were not among them. Where he, as the years passed, would remain virile, high-spirited, perennially boyish, Queen Ena, weighed down by the knowledge of her sons' illness and her husband's philanderings, would gradually become sadder, quieter, more fatalistic. In the tragic times that lay ahead Princess Alice could always count on the love of her husband: Queen Ena could not.

2

For some thirty-five years, ever since she had first arrived as a bride from Waldeck, the Duchess of Albany had lived at Claremont House. Now in her late fifties, the Duchess had developed into a plump, comfortable-looking matron, always with an old-fashioned lace cap on her head. There was some-thing reassuringly old-fashioned about her values and attitudes as well. For all her natural warmth of heart, the Duchess of Albany remained austere, rig-idly conscientious and, says Princess Alice, 'a bit of a Covenanter'.' Devoted to her grandchildren, she treated them with a quiet firmness.

The Duchess's position, during the war, had been an extremely difficult one. German by birth, with a son fighting in the German Army, she was regarded with a certain amount of suspicion. 'Some people,' wrote one of her champions, 'were prejudiced against her because she was German. She was German by birth, but she was English by marriage, by adoption, and by affection. She was never a Prussian. She was devoted to the British cause. She detested the Prussian policy and the Prussian Government. No one who knew her could doubt the intensity of her feeling, that of genuine British loyalty, in the great struggle. It must have been a sore trial to her that her son became of necessity the enemy of this country during the war . . .'[10]

It was indeed. But hiding her heartache, the Duchess of Albany had thrown herself, with her usual briskness and efficiency, into war work. Part of Claremont House was converted into a convalescent home for officers; she worked regularly at Princess Beatrice's War Hospital Supply Depot in Cavendish Square; she actively supported the Professional Classes War Fund; and at one stage she sold a necklace of 258 large pearls, left to her by Queen Victoria, in aid of the Deptford Fund, which she had founded many years before.

When the expense of running Claremont became too much the Duchess moved to Clock House, Kensington Palace, which had been offered to her by King George V. For all its red-brick elegance and convenience, the Duchess's Kensington Palace apartment was a far cry from the grandeur of Claremont House and the spaciousness of its park. After the war, with Claremont let to a girls' school, Leatherhead Court, the Duchess of Albany went to live in a much smaller house, Loseberry, in nearby Claygate. By now she realised that her son, regarded as an enemy alien and stripped of his British style and titles, would never be able to inherit the house. In fact, after her death, Claremont was to be confiscated and sold by the Public Trustee.

Not until two years after the end of the war, in February 1921, was the Duchess reunited with the 37-year-old Duke of Coburg, in the South of France. Princess Alice and Lord Athlone were there as well. By now, with the wholesale collapse of German principalities after the First World War and the declaration of a republic, the Duke no longer reigned in Coburg. He had to content himself with the life of a politically powerless, if wealthy, land-owner. 'It was a sad time for us all,'[11] says the Princess simply.

The next year mother and son met again; this time in August, at the Duke of Coburg's castle at Hinterris in the Austrian Tyrol. And it was here on 1 September 1922 that the Duchess died, quite suddenly, of a heart attack at the age of sixty-one. The Athlones were staying at Abergeldie when they heard the news and, as the Duchess was to be buried in the Tyrol, they set out at once. Present at the funeral on 8 September, in addition to the Athlones, were two of the Duchess of Albany's sisters – Queen Emma of the Netherlands and Princess Erbach-Schönberg – and her brother, the Prince of Waldeck-Pyrmont.

Anxious to perpetuate her mother's memory by some practical gesture, Princess Alice decided on the endowment of a hospital ward for children, as the Duchess had always been deeply concerned with the welfare of young people. The Princess organised a Christmas Market Fair at Claridges which she opened on 12 December 1922, and the funds raised on this occasion went towards the endowment of a new children's wing at the Waterloo Hospital.

In many ways, the Duchess of Albany had been a remarkable woman. Transplanted from a pastoral, provincial little state to the leading court in Europe, widowed after only twenty-two months of marriage, and torn, during the First World War, by cruelly divided loyalties, she never faltered. She never gave way to despair, she never indulged in self-pity.

'She triumphed over all this,' says the admiring Princess Alice, 'because . . . she had a tremendous personality and was full of courage and intelligence.'[12]

3

In the summer of 1923, the Athlones finally left the Henry III Tower at Windsor Castle. For nineteen years they had lived in these rambling and romantic surroundings; now they felt the need of a more conventional and convenient country home, set in its own grounds. So they moved to Brantridge Park, near Balcombe in Sussex – a large, spreading, creeper-covered mansion set in a huge estate some forty miles from London. As a town house they had the use of the late Duchess of Albany's apartments in Clock House, Kensington Palace.

The official leave-taking from Windsor, on 11 July 1923, was an emotional occasion. The Mayor of Windsor, Sir Frederick Dyson, made a moving farewell speech and presented the couple with gifts subscribed to by the townspeople. The Princess received, among other things, a diamond and platinum wristwatch.

Any plans for the redecorating of Brantridge Park or for the landscaping of its grounds were still-born. Not only did the Athlones have their customary royal round to carry out – including the opening, after an appallingly rough Channel crossing, of the British Seamen's Institute in Dunkirk, and the annual September visit to Scotland – but, during the course of that Scottish holiday, King George V offered his brother-in-law a new appointment. He was asked to succeed Prince Arthur of Connaught as Governor-General of South Africa.

The idea, says Princess Alice, had been born earlier that summer. The Athlones had attended an official dinner at the Home Office and the Princess had been placed beside General Jan Christian Smuts, then Prime Minister of the Union of South Africa, who was in London for the Imperial Conference. The one-time Boer General, who had fought against the British in the Anglo-Boer War of 1899–1901, was by now a dedicated champion of the Imperial ideal. He was also an ardent – indeed some of his many political enemies said a sycophantic – monarchist. Smuts had considerable faith, not only in the efficiency of royalty in carrying out their ceremonial duties, but in their power to influence public opinion. So, on finding himself seated beside this animated and attractive Princess, Smuts was at his most winning.

Sitting opposite the happily chatting couple was the South African Minister of Justice, Senator N.J. de Wet. 'Why,' asked de Wet of Smuts, 'are you keeping that charming lady all to yourself?'[13] He joined in their conversation and, during the course of it, asked the Prime Minister if he did not think that the Athlones should succeed the Connaughts in the Governor-Generalship. Smuts was non-committal, but the idea had obviously taken root. The General had met the Earl of Athlone during the war and had seen a great deal of him during his visits to the Western Front. 'The personal relationship we had then and our later acquaintance made a great impression on my mind,'[14] he afterwards said. A few months later, on the advice of General Smuts, the King offered Lord Athlone the appointment.

The Athlones accepted it with very mixed feelings. Although they would be able to take their daughter, the 17-year-old Lady May Cambridge, with them, it would mean leaving their delicate son, Viscount Trematon, at Eton. It would also mean leaving their other relations, their many friends, their various official commitments and their newly-acquired home, Brantridge Park.

But at no stage would the couple ever seriously have considered refusing the appointment. Imbued with an unshakable sense of royal obligation, the Athlones simply accepted it as a job to be done.

Besides, the post was a prestigious and responsible one; the couple felt proud and honoured at having been offered it. Knowing something of South African politics, they would have realised that, at the time, the post of Governor-General of South Africa was one of the most difficult in the Empire.

Lord Athlone's appointment as Governor-General, Commander-in-Chief and British High Commissioner of the Union of South Africa was announced on 27 October 1923. As General Smuts was anxious for them to open the new parliamentary session at the end of January 1924, it was decided that they would leave early in the New Year. There were countless arrangements to be made. On the advice of Lady Buxton, wife of a previous South African Governor-General, it was decided that young Rupert would accompany his parents in order to spend a few weeks with them in South Africa. In that way, and even though it meant his missing the spring term at Eton, he would be able to obtain a mental picture of his parents' new home, life and activities. As a result, he would not feel quite so cut off from them when he returned to school.

Their staff was chosen with great care. Major Ulick Alexander was appointed Comptroller; Capt. Reginald Hargreaves was Private Secretary; the aides-de-camp were Lieut. G.A.V. Hawkins, Capt. the Lord Bingham and Capt. the Hon. C.G.W. Weld-Forester. On the advice of General Smuts, Lord Athlone retained the services of Capt. the Hon. Bede Clifford,

Official Secretary to the outgoing Governor-General, Prince Arthur of Connaught. As lady-in-waiting, the Princess chose the pretty Miss Kaitilin Dawson.*

The month of December 1923, the Athlones' last clear month before sailing, was packed with public and private engagements. There were luncheons with the Upper Bailiffs of the Weavers' Company, with the Royal Colonial Institute, with the South African Luncheon Club (at which Princess Alice was presented with a superb ostrich feather cloak); a ball at Grosvenor House in aid of Toe H; a festival dinner in aid of the Royal Earlswood Institution for Mental Defectives; a radio appeal by Lord Athlone for the British Empire Cancer Campaign; and the presentation of a farewell gift, by the Middlesex Hospital, in gratitude for all the work done by the Earl of Athlone for the hospital since 1910.

Their Excellencies could not have been sorry to set sail, on the *Windsor Castle*, on 4 January 1924.

'I have got you a jewel of a Governor-General . . .' exclaimed General Smuts to reporters on his return to South Africa from the Imperial Conference late in 1923. 'He is certain to be a great success and with him I associate Princess Alice. South Africans will find them perfectly charming, and the Earl of Athlone has a great personal knowledge of South Africa.'[15]

---

* Changes during the Athlones' South African term of office were: Capt. H.T. Birch-Reynardson as Secretary; Capt. J.N.P. Lascelles, Capt. G. Fielden, Lieut. E. Edmonstone, Capt. H. Abel Smith, Capt. A.G.H. Heber-Percy, and the South Africans Capt. L Beyers and Capt. P. de Waal as aides-de-camp.

As the *Windsor Castle* sailed out of the dense, delaying January fog into the shimmering sunlit Atlantic Ocean, so did the passengers' spirits lift. The Athlones joined wholeheartedly in all the ship's activities: they played deck games, attended concerts, distributed prizes, walked energetically around the slowly-heaving decks. By mixing freely with the passengers, they soon established the fact that they were a friendly, approachable couple, interested in everything. From Madeira Lord Athlone wrote to his brother Adolphus, now Marquess of Cambridge, bemoaning the fact that the Governor of the island would be coming on board to pay his respects; he would far rather be getting some exercise ashore. 'The honour of being great already staggers me!'[16] he admitted.

Their Excellencies landed in Cape Town on 21 January 1924. The scene which greeted them was exhilarating. Under a cloudless sky and against the great blue bastion of Table Mountain, the city sparkled in the hot sunshine. The docks and the brightly beflagged streets were packed with people. On the quayside stood General Smuts, the members of his Cabinet and an assortment of civil and military dignitaries.

When the anthem had been played, the formal introductions made and the guard inspected, the Athlones climbed into the open landau that was to carry them through the jubilant streets to yet another official welcome at the City Hall. Bowing and smiling what she hoped was a gracious smile of farewell to the assembled dignitaries, Princess Alice took her seat, but like a jack-in-the-box she shot up again. The landau had been waiting for hours in the scorching sun and the leather seat, as she sat down on it, was like fire. Not until someone had brought a couple of cushions could the Princess resume her seat. She had had, the Princess afterwards remarked wryly, 'a most warm welcome'[17] to South Africa.

But South Africa was to make a less immediate impression on Princess Alice as well. Her arrival in Cape Town marked the start of a long love affair with a colourful, complex and, although she might not have thought so, sadly benighted land.

PART THREE
GOVERNMENT HOUSE

CHAPTER TEN

1

The Athlones were to spend seven years in South Africa. These were to be some of the stormiest years in the country's always turbulent history.

Of all the territories that made up the British Empire, none was more complex than the Union of South Africa. Its racial groupings alone presented a daunting variety. Of its population of some seven million, over five million were Africans belonging to various tribes; about one-and-a-half million were of European descent but divided, mainly, into those of British and those of Dutch ancestry; two smaller but far from insignificant peoples were the descendants of the Indians who had been imported to work on the sugar plantations in Natal, and the Coloured, or mixed-race group, made up of various elements – including a strong contingent of Malays — who lived mainly in the Cape. This multi-racial population ranged from the most highly sophisticated Europeans to the most primitive Bushmen.

All political power rested firmly in the hands of the country's white population. The conquered and emasculated African tribes were subject peoples: the colonists of colonists. The Indian and the Coloured peoples lived in a sort of racial and political no-man's-land. Yet even the whites were split into various factions, and it was the conflict between the two main white groups that seemed, at the time of Lord Athlone's assumption of office, to be the most important political question.

The conflict was a bitter one. Less than a quarter of a century had passed since Great Britain, supported by the English-speaking population in the South African colonies of the Cape and Natal, had conquered the two Boer republics of the Transvaal and the Orange Free State. Magnanimous in victory, Britain had lost little time in granting responsible government to the two vanquished Boer republics, and in 1910 the four South African territories – the Cape Colony, Natal, the Transvaal and the Orange Free State – had been welded together to form the Union of South Africa. In November 1910, Princess Alice's Uncle Arthur, the Duke of Connaught, had opened the first Union Parliament.

This welding together had proved to be only a matter of geography; it by no means put an end to the country's political and racial divisions. At the time of Union, it had seemed as though it might. Two one-time Boer generals, Louis Botha and Jan Smuts, brought together into one political party – the

South African Party – moderate English-speaking and Afrikaans-speaking white South Africans. Their party won the first election and General Louis Botha became Prime Minister.

But any hope that, in time, the majority of Boers, or Afrikaners, would follow the lead of the two generals, was short-lived. The fact that the South African Party professed loyalty to the British Empire proved too much for more nationally minded Afrikaners. Led by yet another general, J. B. M. Hertzog, they formed a party of their own: the National Party. It was not, explained Hertzog, that he was anti-British. He simply saw no reason why the interests of the British Empire should be placed above those of South Africa. 'South Africa first' was his rallying cry. What he wanted was a South Africa free from British interference. But what the majority of his followers wanted was an independent republic outside the Empire.

On the death of Botha in 1919, Smuts became Prime Minister. His term of office was to see more fundamental changes still. Not only was he faced with the various political and racial divisions among the whites (there was a rabidly pro-British Unionist Party, a predominantly English-speaking Labour Party, his own South African Party and the National Party) but industrialisation was beginning to affect the blacks.

Until now the Africans, their power broken and their territories annexed, had lived pastoral lives under fairly benevolent white control. Now, with increased economic expansion, they were flocking to the towns and cities. Here they came up against the white working-man who had likewise come crowding into the urban areas in search of better financial rewards. Fearing the competition from cheap black labour the white workers, mainly mine-workers represented by the Labour Party, were determined that there should be no economic integration between black and white.

Here, in a nutshell, was the great South African dilemma. Without economic integration there could be no real industrial expansion; but with economic integration would come demands for social and political integration.

Determined to retain the colour bar in industry, the white mine-workers on the Witwatersrand – the gold-mining area around Johannesburg – struck in the summer of 1922. 'Workers of the world, fight and unite for a White South Africa!'[1] read what must have been one of the most extraordinary slogans in the history of a labour movement. The Rand Strike, which came dangerously close to being a revolt, was ruthlessly crushed by Smuts.

Yet, in the long run, it achieved its aims. The Strike of 1922 brought the Afrikaans-speaking National Party and the English-speaking Labour Party together. The National Party, many of whose followers also belonged to the urban working-class, saw in this labour unrest the chance of gaining power. By combining forces with Labour, they hoped to defeat the pro-British, pro-Capitalist Smuts; together, they would make South Africa safe for the white man. The next election would tell.

This, then, was the political state of affairs when the Earl of Athlone arrived in Cape Town to open the 1924 session of the Union Parliament. At this stage, the Governor-General of South Africa was still in a position of considerable influence. Not only was he the personal representative of the British sovereign but he was the personal representative of the British Government. Only some years later would it be decreed that, in South Africa, the King could act only on the advice of his South African ministers. In theory, the British Government, through the Governor-General, still had formal control over the Union of South Africa.

What, in fact, was the new Governor-General's view of the South African political situation? A dedicated imperialist, Lord Athlone would have been in full accord with that champion of the imperial connection – the Prime Minister, General Smuts. With him, he would have considered the Boer-British, or Afrikaans-English, or National-South African Party rivalry to be the most important South African political question. To him as to Smuts, and as to the majority of the whites, the 'non-European' problems – such as the dawning political awareness of the Africans, the seething discontent of the Indians, the equivocal position of the Coloured people – would have been of secondary importance. Lord Athlone's mission was to uphold and strengthen the British connection, to keep South Africa in the great family of British nations. And Smuts saw things from this same international, or rather imperial, angle. Part-visionary, part-realist, the South African Prime Minister was far happier trying to solve the problems of the great world than in coping with what he considered to be the 'little troubles'[2] of his own country.

General Smuts, wrote an admiring Lord Athlone to King George V after the ceremonial opening of Parliament on 25 January 1924, was 'too big a man for his own people'.[3]

2

From the very first, Princess Alice was enchanted by the Cape. This south-western corner of South Africa, with its sparkling seas (the meeting-place of the Indian and Atlantic oceans), its white beaches, its blue mountains, its profusion of wild flowers, its vineyards, its white-washed houses, its oaks and its pines, is one of the loveliest places on earth. Cape Town in the 1920s was a small, gracious, still largely Georgian and Victorian city, crowded between Table Mountain and the sea and full of the vitality and colour that comes from the mingling of different cultures.

Government House was a sprawling, white-washed, veranda'd building set in a large garden in the heart of the city. Built as a garden 'Pleasure Lodge' over two centuries before, the house had been much altered and added to since serving as a home for first the Dutch and then the British governors. The South African politician, John X. Merriman, used to describe Government House as 'the only gentleman's residence in South Africa'.[4] On one side of the house rose the red-brick, impressively-porticoed Houses of Parliament; almost opposite was the Anglican Cathedral. Beside the house an oak-lined avenue led up from the city's main thorough-fare to the suburbs on the slopes of the mountain. In fact the huge, steeply-sided, flat-topped, mauve-blue mountain, often with its tablecloth of cloud, formed an ever-present backdrop: 'it seemed to rise abruptly from our very doors,'[5] says the Princess.

Half-an-hour's drive around the flank of Table Mountain brought them to their summer, or country home, Westbrooke. This was one of the two houses on the Groote Schuur estate, the property which that great imperial visionary, Cecil John Rhodes, had bought and developed during the last years of the nineteenth century. The Dutch word *schuur* meant barn, and in the days when the Dutch East India Company controlled the Cape, it had built three barns for the storing of grain. Rhodes had chosen the largest of these, the already converted Groote Schuur, as his home: he had remodelled it and, after a fire, rebuilt it. A massive, masculine, gabled homestead in the Cape Dutch style, Groote Schuur was at this time the home of South Africa's prime – ministers.

The original Onder Schuur, now Westbrooke, lay below Groote Schuur. With its porte-cochere and its airy rooms and its french windows opening out onto terraced lawns, it had the atmosphere of a Victorian colonial country house. It was Princess Alice's favourite South African home. For the Athlones, the chief joys of Westbrooke were its spacious, tree-shaded grounds and its closeness to the mountainside, with its walks and bridle paths. "The wild flowers on the mountain slopes are beautiful beyond description',[6] enthused Princess Alice. The couple enjoyed few things more than walking in the cool, resin-scented shade of the pine trees that crowded the mountain slopes.

Within days of arrival the couple were already exploring the Cape Peninsula. They drove to Muizenberg, a resort on the warm Indian Ocean, to lunch with Sir Abe Bailey, the South African mining magnate, at Rust-en-Vrede, his home overlooking the rolling surf.* Sir Abe had a huge farm near Colesburg in the interior of the Cape Colony where he bred ostriches. He presented his guests with some splendid feathers and it was arranged that young Lord Trematon, on his way back from a visit to the Victoria Falls, should stay at the farm to shoot springbok. For, in spite of his haemophilia, Lord Trematon was a high-spirited and adventurous youngster. 'He seemed like a perfectly normal boy', claims Princess Alice, Duchess of Gloucester, who remembers him

---

* Half a century later, Princess Alice would spend several weeks each year in yet another Cape Dutch-styled mansion, standing on Muizenberg beach, within sight of Rust-en-Vrede.

joining in riotous – and, for him, dangerous – family games of 'billiard fives'.[7]

Lord Athlone knew the Colesburg area well as he had seen active service there during the Anglo-Boer War. He also knew Muizenberg. During the war he and his brother, Prince Adolphus – also serving in the British Army – had stayed at a hotel in Muizenberg. 'How little we thought,' he now wrote to his brother, 'when we ragged at old Muizenberg that I should now drive through a crowded seaside resort in *my* motor cars with a family and be addressed by the inhabitants "glad to see you, Your Excellency"!'[8]

The Athlones had hardly time to accustom themselves to the Cape before they were obliged to move to Pretoria in the Transvaal. One of the more difficult problems facing the National Convention that had met to bring about the union of the four self-governing colonies in 1910 had been the choice of a capital for the new, unified country. Each of the principal cities in the four colonies – Cape Town in the Cape Colony, Pretoria in the Transvaal, Bloemfontein in the Orange Free State and Durban in Natal – had harboured hopes of becoming the new capital. But with Durban being considered too exclusively British and with Bloemfontein having little other than its central position to commend it, the real choice lay between Cape Town, which was South Africa's Mother City, and Pretoria, which had been the old Boer capital of the Transvaal.

A judgement of Solomon prevailed. Cape Town was made the legislative capital, the seat of parliament, while Pretoria was made the administrative capital, the seat of government. Bloemfontein became the seat of justice. Having two capitals entailed an annual one-thousand mile move – of personnel, officials and documents – between Cape Town and Pretoria, with parliament sitting for roughly the first six months of every year in Cape Town, and the business of government then being transferred to the majestic Union Buildings which overlooked Pretoria.

For the Athlones, this meant dividing their time between two main centres: Government House and Westbrooke in Cape Town, and Government House in Pretoria.

Pretoria was very different from Cape Town. Less than a century old, it was a small, four-square, neatly planned and not inelegant city set between hills in the spacious, ochre-coloured landscape of the Transvaal Highveld. Lacking the mellow charm, leafiness and variety of Cape Town, Pretoria none the less had a certain open, honest-to-goodness quality that was to grow on the Athlones. Like so many people who spend any time in South Africa, the couple gradually developed a taste for the wide-open spaces and limitless horizons that characterise so much of the interior of the country.

Government House, Pretoria, which had been designed by Rhodes's favourite architect, that darling of the South African *fin-de-siècle,* Herbert Baker, was a beautiful home, standing high on a hillside in superbly landscaped grounds. Built, and largely furnished, in what can only be described as Edwardian Cape-Dutch, Government House was a comfortable, spacious and convenient home. With its swimming-pool, its tennis courts, its shady loggias and its wide views, the house was greatly loved by the Athlones.* Often, at night, the sentries would be diverted by the sounds of an old-fashioned singsong as His Excellency led the household in full-throated renderings of Negro spirituals or English carols.

There was no official residence in Bloemfontein during the Athlones' term of office. On their visits to this little city, the couple stayed in their comfortably appointed White Train. An impressive local house was offered to them but it was considered more convenient to remain on the train. 'A caravan on the outskirts of town," was how the Princess laughingly referred to their Bloemfontein accommodation.

The Athlones paid their first visit to Bloemfontein in September 1924. Like Pretoria, Bloemfontein had been laid out in the mid-nineteenth century and had the same tranquil, neatly-planned atmosphere of a Boer capital. This was Their Excellencies' first experience of an entirely Boer-, or Afrikaner- dominated society, as even Pretoria had become somewhat anglicised since the end of the Anglo-Boer War in 1902. Expecting a certain amount of hostility, the couple were surprised by the warmth of their reception and by the lack of bitterness between the two white

---

* The Government House succulent rock-garden, started by Princess Alice, has since become renowned.

races. It was, perhaps, their first taste of Afrikaner hospitality and decorum. Lord Athlone was soon happily reminiscing with Anglo-Boer War veterans and particularly enjoyed his conversations with F.W. Reitz, former President of the Orange Free State. There was something about the Governor-General's self-confident, down-to-earth quality that appealed to the Boer War veterans. One young aide-de-camp admits to being so bored at the dinner table by His Excellency's re-living (with much shifting about of salt cellars and cutlery) of the Anglo-Boer War campaigns with his Boer companions that he fell asleep; he woke, hours later, still in his chair in the dark and deserted dining-room.

The Athlones came away from Bloemfontein with the not entirely accurate impression that the Boers 'all admired the royal family and did not mind being under a king, but would like him to act in local matters on the "advice of his South African Ministers" '.[10]

Durban, where the Governor-General spent several weeks each winter, was very different. Lush, sub-tropical, exotic, its streets thronged with Indian women in colourful saris and with gleaming, half-naked Zulu, its buildings a riot of Victorian renaissance architecture, Durban was like some British provincial city set down beside the Indian Ocean. Its citizens – or at least its white citizens – were imperialists to a man. No hearts, as the Athlones were soon to discover, beat more loyal and true for the British Empire. From King's House, their elegant home set on a ridge above the palm-studded city and the busy port, Princess Alice wrote an ecstatic letter to Queen Mary. 'I just love Durban,' she enthused, 'it is so completely English.'[11]

It was during these first months in South Africa that the Athlones came to know something more of Mrs Isie Smuts, the Prime Minister's wife, who was generally known as Ouma – Grandma – Smuts. In many ways a remarkable woman, astute, intelligent and highly educated, Ouma Smuts played very little part in her husband's official life. Where he adored the limelight, she shunned it. Only very rarely did she appear beside him in public. A woman of simple tastes, she much preferred life on their farm at Doornkloof, near Pretoria, where, on the stoep of their unpretentious wood and iron homestead, she would entertain whatever illustrious guests her world-famous and highly regarded husband cared to bring home.

The Athlones had had their first meeting with this exceptional woman soon after their arrival in the country. The Prime Minister had given a garden party for the Athlones at Groote Schuur and, on finding out that it had been Lady May Cambridge's birthday that day, Ouma Smuts had baked her a magnificent cake. To keep her own children from eating it, she confided to Princess Alice, she had had to hide it under her bed. 'With the pots,'[12] Lord Athlone would always add on repeating the story.

On another occasion, when the Athlones were visiting the Smuts family in what Lord Athlone called their 'shanty' at Doornkloof, one of their dogs dirtied his hands while he was playing with it. He asked if he could wash them before having tea. 'Santa,' called Ouma Smuts to her daughter, 'you had better take the hot-water jug from the tea table for His Excellency to wash his hands.'[13] This, apparently, was the only jug available.

In contrast to her spruce, always immaculately-dressed husband, Ouma Smuts wore the simplest clothes in the drabbest colours. 'She keeps one black dress for best,' reported Lord Athlone to his brother, the Marquess of Cambridge, 'and turns down the neck of an evening.'[14] Once, after completing one of those long trips through the veld which she so adored, the fastidious Princess Alice admitted to Ouma Smuts that there was only one drawback to these safaris: it was always so difficult to organise the washing of one's underclothes.

'You must do what I do, my dear,' answered Ouma Smuts confidentially. 'Always wear black underwear. It never shows the dirt.'[15]

3

Jan Christian Smuts, whose reputation stood so high in the councils of the world, was not anything like so highly regarded in his own country. By his imperialist, 'pro-British' policies he had estranged a good half of Afrikanerdom, and by his pro-capitalist policies he had estranged English-speaking South African Labour. Although he was hardly more sympathetic to the nation's black population than were his opponents, these opponents felt that Smuts had not done enough to protect the white working-man from black competition.

In April 1924, just over two months after the arrival of the Athlones, there was a by-election in a Transvaal constituency. No less a candidate than the ex-Administrator of the province fought the seat for the Smuts Government. To general surprise he lost it. Bitterly disappointed, Smuts decided to call a General Election. On 24 April 1924 he asked the Governor-General to dissolve Parliament.

The election, held in June, was a great victory for Smuts's opponents. Between them, the Nationalists and Labour, who had formed an election pact, won 81 seats, as opposed to the 53 won by Smuts's South African Party. Even Smuts lost his seat. There was nothing for him but to resign. Lord Athlone was obliged to call on the Nationalist Leader, General Hertzog, to form a Government.

For the newly-arrived Governor-General it was a challenging situation. General Hertzog himself might not have been rabidly anti-British but a great many of his followers were. There had been much talk, during the tumult of the election, about the severing of ties with Britain and about the establishment of a republic. Several die-hard Nationalists, with a long history of anti-British oratory and activity, were among the members of Hertzog's cabinet. The swearing-in of his new ministry, says Princess Alice, was for her husband 'an interesting but not entirely agreeable ceremony, as he had to shake hands with . . . more than one rebel. . . ."[16]

Almost equally disconcerting were the Labour members. One of Her Excellency's stiff-backed English footmen was considerably affronted during an official luncheon on being addressed by the Labour Minister, the cocky Thomas Boydell, as 'mate'.[17] And there was to be many a time when Their Excellencies' butler would find himself being heartily shaken by the hand by some backveld backbencher under the misapprehension that he was the Governor-General.

Smuts's South African Party, smarting from its defeat at the hands of this 'unholy alliance' between the National and Labour parties, predicted that such a Government could not possibly last. Before long, they said, this 'government of amateurs'[18] would collapse. It did not. On the contrary, the Pact Government lasted for almost ten years. Throughout Lord Athlone's term of office, it was with Hertzog's National Government that he had to deal.

That there was not, in spite of all predictions, an open break between South Africa and Britain during the Nationalists' term of office was due, in no small measure, to the tact, friendliness and skill of the Earl of Athlone and Princess Alice.

4

It was during these seven years in South Africa that Princess Alice came into her own. At home, in Britain, she had been merely one of several members of the royal family busily carrying out their routine, and often tedious, duties. When set against such personalities as Queen Mary, Queen Alexandra, Princess Mary and the Duchess of York, she had not even ranked especially high. But now, with her husband representing the British monarch, she was the undoubted first lady of the land. Holding the centre of the stage, Princess Alice was able to realise her full potential. She was at last being granted the opportunity to make use of all her considerable talent. The Princess, who had celebrated her forty-first birthday soon after her arrival, was in her prime. During the following seven years she was to build up the reputation — for elegance, charm, taste, friendliness, vivacity, professionalism and spirit – that was to remain a legend in South Africa.

In an era when so many women looked gauche and frumpish, Princess Alice always looked chic. Her small, slender figure and slim, shapely legs suited the low-waisted, increasingly short-skirted fashions of the 1920s to perfection. She even managed to carry off those deep-crowned, head-hugging hats. Whenever possible, she wore pale colours; her dresses were simply styled; she always looked cool, immaculate, romantic. Time and again, in remembering her during those days, people fall back on the cliche of a 'fairy princess'. Cliche it might be, but there was many a princess at the time who would not, by any stretch of the imagination, have qualified for this description.

'I remember very well . . .', claimed one Girl Guide in later life, 'being completely enchanted by the beauty and grace of Princess Alice. Even the unbecoming cocked hat of a Guider, the military uniform and the four-square shoes couldn't dim her radiance.'[19] To little girls like this, she seemed almost to have come from another world.

Her opinion was echoed by a young Belgian diplomat, then stationed in South Africa. 'Dances were given at Government House,' he remembers, 'where Princess Alice, beautiful and fragile as Dresden china, received her guests with smiles that were gracious, yet somehow a little distant, as though she were a fairy whose thoughts were lingering in fairyland.'[20]

But, of course, there was nothing ethereal about Princess Alice's personality. Guests at Government House were usually more struck by her down-to-earth qualities – her naturalness and her practicality. 'Princess Alice has been a very domesticated and practical Governor-General's wife,' claimed one observer at the end of the Athlones' term of office. 'She supervised her household like any other woman and daily had consultations with her housekeeper and cook, and took the greatest interest in the upkeep of Westbrooke's furnishings.'[21]

Sir Abe Bailey's future daughter-in-law, the lively and lovely Stella Chiappini, a member of Cape Town's young 'Government House set', quotes countless examples of Princess Alice's brisk informality. Unlike many later, South-African born Governor-General's

244

wives, the Princess always referred to Lord Athlone as H. E. or Alge. 'As Lord Athlone was rather shy,' says Stella Chiappini, 'she was the one who made everyone feel at home.'[22]

On one occasion, the Princess organised a ball in the Cape Town City Hall in aid of the King Edward VII District Nursing Association. She planned the black and white decor and sketched the costumes to be worn by the couples chosen to dance the Lancers. Just before setting out for the ball from Westbrooke, Stella Chiappini's white satin costume was spoiled by having a cup of coffee spilt over it. The Princess rushed her upstairs, pulled off her dress, flung a shawl over her shoulders (Lord Athlone was in the room), plunged the stained part of the dress into hot water, hurried a maid into ironing it dry, bundled Stella back into the dress and whisked the party off to the City Hall. Not until, in the Royal Bay at the ball, Stella was squeezed between Lady May Cambridge and the visiting Auntie B – Queen Victoria's youngest daughter Princess Beatrice – did the combined heat of their bodies finally dry the dress.

Once, as part of a parlour game at Government House, one of the young A.D.C.s inveigled Princess Alice into clambering onto a table and holding up a long stick at the end of which a glass of water was balanced against the ceiling. He then made some excuse and disappeared, leaving her alone in the room. After a few agonising minutes, she was forced to lower her arm and allow the glass to come crashing onto the floor. 'He told me,' remembers one of his friends, 'how very well on the whole she had taken this.'[23]

The Princess could be equally informal beyond her intimate circle. On their walks through the woods on the mountainside or on their regular morning rides near the Cape Town suburbs of Pinelands, Their Excellencies would always greet or talk to whomever they happened to meet. On occasions, visiting outlying farms during their many journeys through the *platteland* – the interior of the country – the Princess would immediately establish a rapport with the often shy country people by asking to borrow a pair of tennis shoes in order to go walking or a bathing costume to swim in. The little daughter of the Mayor of Johannesburg was never to forget how, after the formal festivities of the local Rose Day, the Princess borrowed the Mayoress's bathing costume and, changing out of her silvery dress and feathered hat, went for a dip in the swimming-pool.

She was never stuffy. The three young Dalrymples, sons of Sir William and Lady Dalrymple in whose home in Johannesburg the Athlones would often stay during their visits to that bustling city, thought her full of fun. Hugh, the most mischievous, was her particular favourite. 'She found it hilarious when he indulged in some of his nonsense, such as putting gadgets under cushions which gave off rude noises when sat upon . . .'[24] recalls one member of the family.

'Thank God,' exclaimed the Princess robustly to someone who suggested that she might like to visit the cloakroom after a long drive up from Durban to inspect a sugar estate. 'Thank God there's someone who knows that I'm a human being.'[25]

There were times, though, when the Princess's informality was mirrored in others. On one occasion, Their Excellencies were visiting the little town of Montagu, in the Western Cape Province. An official luncheon was underway at the local hotel when the rough-and-ready Portuguese proprietor, wandering round the tables to see that all was well, gave the Princess a hearty slap on the back and cried out, 'Eat up, my girl, enjoy yourself!'

'Thank you,' answered the highly amused Princess, 'I shall.'[26]

The Athlones particularly enjoyed visiting the farms which lay in the beautiful mountain valleys within a hour or two's drive of Cape Town. Here they made many friends. One of the homes they would visit was Neethlingshof, a large wine farm five miles from the pretty town of Stellenbosch, belonging to two brothers, Tinnie and Koos Louw. Accompanied by Lady May Cambridge and, if he were in South Africa on holiday, Lord Trematon, Their Excellencies would tour the wine cellars, taking a deep interest in everything they saw, chatting casually to the Coloured labourers and asking endless questions. The Princess loved the sweet, amber-coloured Hanepoot grapes and Lord Athlone gratefully accepted the bottles of wine and sherry with which he was always presented. The Louws grew Turkish tobacco as well, and Princess

Alice would stroll through the great sheds, talking to the Coloured women who worked there, smiling at the babies and handing out sweets to the youngsters.

If the Athlones stayed for the midday meal, a party of at least fourteen adults would sit down to a spread of roast mutton or roast pork, roast chicken and, whenever possible, roast baby pigeon. This would be followed by home-canned fruit and fresh fruit – watermelons, sweet-melons, peaches and plums. And, of course, always wine and liqueurs.

On some afternoons, the Princess might arrive at Neethlingshof alone and unannounced. On one occasion she surprised Mrs Louw and her servants sitting on the back stoep peeling yellow cling-peaches for canning. She immediately offered to help, and sat happily peeling peaches with the rest of them.

Princess Alice played a significant part in the cultural life of the country as well. She was very interested in the history and architecture of South Africa, particularly in the period when it had been ruled by the Dutch East India Company. She found its past 'absolutely fascinating'[27] and developed a great feeling for the old Cape Dutch homesteads with their white-washed walls, high stoeps, shuttered windows, thatched roofs and huge, muscular gables. For years afterwards, she would always be on the look-out for pieces of china bearing the V.O.C. monogram of the Dutch East India Company.

The Athlones regularly attended concerts and, with her interest in painting, the Princess was always taking official guests to see the Michaelis Collection in Cape Town and the Art Gallery in Johannesburg. She did a great deal to encourage local artists. She was especially impressed by the work of Jacob Hendrik Pierneef and of Gwelo Goodman. Very friendly with the Pierneef family, she became Patron of the Marita Pierneef Collection of paintings. And of Gwelo Goodman's work, the Princess said, 'No artist . . . had so captured the atmosphere of the country, the deep blues in the shadows of the mountains, the golden reflections of sunlight on their slopes and the style of the old Dutch homesteads. . . . .'[28]

The Princess not only bought several of Goodman's paintings, including eleven especially commissioned ones which later hung in her drawing-room at Kensington Palace, but she befriended the artist, often visiting him at his home in the Cape Town suburb of Newlands. A few weeks before finally leaving South Africa, the Princess was to take a last walk on Table Mountain and, having picked a bunch of wild flowers, was to ask Gwelo Goodman to paint a picture of them for her. His painting of the Cape Dutch homestead, *La Provence,* she gave as a gift to Queen Mary.

To the ceremonial and official aspects of her duties, the Princess brought all her accustomed dedication, energy and panache. Within days of their arrival, the Athlones had learned enough Afrikaans to allow them to say at least a few words to the Afrikaans-speaking members of the community.* Within days, too, the Princess was employing her celebrated tact. 'Princess Alice', wrote one observer, 'has tact in such a remarkable degree that to say the plain truth about this gift of hers might seem fulsome flattery. It is not flattery. All South Africans who have met her know; and this is the secret of her universal popularity.

'She can get behind the reserve of a shy person with unerring speed She knows instinctively how to set about the job, and to see her at work with a succession of strangers, each of whom melts in turn from embarrassment into delighted pleasure is to see a feat of genius, done as though it was the simplest thing in the world.'[29]

The Princess was tireless in her work for various causes: for hospitals, for the aged, for children, for the poor. Late at night, accompanied by the redoubtable Dr Zerilda Steyn, she toured the Cape Town slums in search of first-hand knowledge of the living conditions among the poor of the Coloured community. As President of the South African Council for Child Welfare she quickly established a reputation for being practical, innovative and deeply concerned. It was on her suggestion that one day a year was set aside as 'Our Children's Day'; 'an occasion when, throughout the Union, everyone shall unite in an attempt to remember and assist the children of South Africa.'[30]

---

* In old age, the Princess would always take leave of South Africans visiting her at Kensington Palace with a cheerful ' *Tot Siens*' – until we meet again.

She sat on committees, she addressed meetings, she launched appeals, she was patron of many societies. There were Princess Alice homes and Princess Alice hospitals and Princess Alice funds and Princess Alice halls and Princess Alice regiments. On remote, treeless mission stations in the Northern Transvaal she unveiled memorial tablets; among the lush green foliage of Natal she graced garden parties; by the barren shore of Walvis Bay she opened a new wharf; through the clamorous streets of Johannesburg she drove to present awards or cut ribbons or lay wreaths. For the rest of their lives hundreds upon hundreds of little girls would remember the day that they had presented a bouquet to Princess Alice.

No South African Governor-General's lady, before or since, has worked so hard or left so lasting an impression. One commentator, in the jargon of the period, described her list of official activities as 'shudder-making'. They were also, he says, 'record-making for any Government House regime since Union began.'[31]

Princess Alice, claimed one newspaper editor lyrically, 'was the darling of every heart as soon as she came among us.'[32]

5

During their term in South Africa the Athlones were able to play host to several of their relations. When the 67-year-old Princess Beatrice, 'Auntie B\ came out in November 1924 for several months, they took her by train along the spectacular 'Garden Route' – a stretch of coastline between Cape Town and Port Elizabeth. At Oudtshoorn, in the heart of the ostrich-farming area, an old Afrikaans woman showed Lord Athlone a letter, dated 30 March 1900, which had been written to him by Queen Mary – at that stage still Duchess of York – but which had been intercepted by the Boers. It had been given to the woman for safe-keeping and now, twenty-five years later, she was able to deliver it. Lord Athlone allowed the delighted woman to keep it.

Queen Victoria's youngest son, Prince Leopold,
Duke of Albany, at the time of his engagement

Princess Alice's mother, Princess Helen of
Waldeck-Pyrmont, in her wedding dress

The young Princess Alice of Albany, in angelic pose

The dashingly uniformed Prince Charles Edward,
by now Duke of Saxe-Coburg and Gotha

The marriage on 10 February 1904 of Princess
Alice of Albany to Prince Alexander of Teck

Princess Alice in her robes for the Coronation of King George V

Princes Alice opening the door of the new British
Seamen's Institute in Dunkirk in July 1923

Princess Alice and the Earl of Athlone with their children, Lady
May Cambridge and Viscount Trematon, an the early 1920s

Their Excellencies with their staff at the Opening of
Parliament in Cape Town on 22 January 1926

Princess Alice with the Queen Mother
of Swaziland in August 1925

Princess Alice working in her rock-garden at Brantridge Park, Sussex

Princess Alice in a tank during a visit to an armaments factory in wartime Canada

Mrs Roosevelt, Princess Alice and Mrs Churchill during the second Quebec Conference, September 1944

Princess Alice studying an Epstein head at an exhibition of children's portraits in December 1950

Princess Alice and her great-niece, Queen
Elizabeth II, at the Windsor Horse Show

The nonagenarian Princess Alice,
looking as alert and attractive as ever

The fact that Princess Beatrice was the daughter of the legendary Queen Victoria was a source of unending amazement to some of the simpler, *platteland* farmers whom they met on this tour. At one wayside station, while poor Princess Beatrice was sitting at her carriage window trying to finish a watercolour sketch, the local inhabitants stood staring at her in open-mouthed wonder. One or two of the braver souls even ventured to shake her hand. When her disconcerted lady-in-waiting begged the policeman on duty to ask them to leave the Princess in peace, he answered that he could not possibly do that. 'You know,' he explained painstakingly, 'they have never seen one before.' And Princess Alice admitted herself 'very moved' when a farmer's wife, with tears streaming down her cheeks, exclaimed, 'To think that I have seen Queen Victoria's daughter.'[33]

Princess Alice's cousin Thora, Princess Helena Victoria, the daughter of Princess Christian, spent a holiday with them and so did Princess Alice's niece, her brother's eldest daughter, Princess Sibylla of Coburg. In 1932, the blonde and lively Princess Sibylla was to marry Prince Gustaf Adolf, the heir to the Swedish throne. 'I like to think,' says Princess Alice, 'the six months' liberal education of sharing our lives [in South Africa] fitted her for her future position in Sweden.'[34]

A relation-to-be who spent some time at Government House was Lady Alice Montagu Douglas Scott who came out in February 1926 for the marriage of her sister, Lady Margaret, to the Athlones' dashing aide-de-camp, Captain Geoffrey Hawkins. Some ten years later, in 1935, the pretty Lady Alice was to marry Lord Athlone's nephew, Prince Henry, Duke of Gloucester, the third son of King George V. Like so many other guests – and members of staff – at Government House, Lady Alice Montagu Douglas Scott was forced to 'disappear'[35] whenever Princess Alice was on the look-out for a companion for yet another ascent of Table Mountain.

Another member of the royal family to experience Princess Alice's excessive love of climbing mountains was the future Queen Elizabeth, afterwards Queen Elizabeth the Queen Mother. She remembers how, on her first stay at Balmoral as the newly-married Duchess of York, 'Aunt Alice' once greeted her with a rousing 'Good morning. Lovely day. Come along . . .' and dragged her up Lochnagar. On the summit, however, the day was no longer lovely. They were caught in a snowstorm and forced to take shelter.[36]

But far and away the most important visitor was Lord Athlone's nephew Edward, Prince of Wales who arrived on an official tour of South Africa at the end of April 1925.

For the past six years, from the age of twenty-five, this debonair young prince had been travelling the world. Slim, slight, good-looking, with an enduring boyishness that belied his years, the Prince of Wales was the prototype Prince Charming. No heir to the British throne had ever been more popular, no international personality was better known, no country boasted a better roving ambassador, no bachelor in the world was more eligible. The world was his oyster, and wherever he went, this blond, blue-eyed, wistful-looking Prince moved in an aura of admiration.

It had been General Smuts who had first suggested that the Prince of Wales visit South Africa. The tour had been arranged for 1924. But with the fall of the Smuts Government in April that year, it was thought that the tour might be cancelled. General Hertzog, however, was quite ready to welcome the Prince and on 2 July 1924 the Earl of Athlone was able to send a telegram to the Secretary of State for the Colonies, inviting the Prince of Wales to visit South Africa.

The Secretary of State replied to the effect that although the Prince could not accept the invitation for that year, he would gladly do so for the next, and would be able to spend three months in South Africa.

Arriving on 30 April 1925, the Prince of Wales stayed for four days with the Athlones at Government House. Among the varied activities of those crowded days, including a ball at Government House at which he shook hands with every one of the two thousand guests, the Prince found time to climb Table Mountain with Princess Alice. 'I am proud to say,' claims the Princess, 'that I quite wore him out.'[37]

Only after the Prince had left on his special train to tour the country did Princess Alice find time to send the always apprehensive Queen Mary a favourable report.

'He got a very good reception from Cape Town,' she wrote. 'Usually the Coloured are quite apathetic but they cheered him as wildly as the white people and so did the Malays and Indians. I never knew there were so many people in South Africa as there were filling every street, and the enthusiasm was kept up all day and all night. David was awfully good, talking to all the right people – indeed there was nothing to criticise. . . .'[38]

The Prince's greatest triumph, though, was his speech to the assembled Members of Parliament. Whatever his political limitations might have been, the Prince of Wales was fully alive to the delicate political situation in South Africa. He was in the country as the representative of the British Crown, while among his hosts – the Government in power – were many who were living for the day when even that purely symbolic link with the Empire would be broken. So, at a banquet given in the Houses of Parliament, the Prince delivered an important policy statement on the imperial connection.

The speech, which had no doubt been drafted for him in London, has been described as 'the happiest and most valuable'[39] of his tour. It had the added advantage of helping to clarify Lord Athlone's position. For by his defining of the relationship between the Crown and the Commonwealth, the Prince of Wales was defining the role of South Africa's Governor-General.

The Prince spoke that evening with great authority. His visits to the other dominions, he said, had opened his eyes to the great developments taking place in the constitutional status of the various self-governing parts of the British Commonwealth. This development had been strikingly illustrated by the fact that each dominion had sent its own representative, to sign on its own behalf, to the Peace Conference at Versailles. In addition, each dominion, in its own right, was a member of the League of Nations. And this development towards greater autonomy was going on all the time. The full conception of what was meant by a 'Brotherhood of Free Nations within the Empire' had still to be worked out.

'I realise that the welcome which you extend to me is in recognition of the fact that I come to you as the King's eldest son, as Heir to a Throne under which the members of that Commonwealth are free to develop each on its own lines, but all to work together as one. No Government can represent all parties and all nations within the Empire, but my travels have taught me this, that the Throne is regarded as standing for a heritage of common aims and ideals shared equally by all sections, parties and nations within this Empire.'[40]

If, concluded the Prince, his visit served in any degree to add to a mutual knowledge and co-operation, he would be content.

His listeners, bursting into applause, realised that he had not quite finished. Haltingly, and to the delight of the Nationalists, he spoke a sentence in Afrikaans. 'Gentlemen, I am glad to meet you, and

I thank you again for your warm welcome.'[41] The cheers were deafening.

'Alge,' reported an ecstatic Princess Alice to Queen Mary, 'will have told you what a great impression David made with his speech when he dined with the Senate and Members of Parliament, and I hear now that this impression is still lasting with the most rabid Nationalists. They were quite delighted with him.'[42]

But the situation, alas, was far too complicated for such simple remedies.

CHAPTER ELEVEN

1

Princess Alice's opinion of General Hertzog, the Nationalist Prime Minister of South Africa, was that he was 'very friendly and personally was a most courteous man and correct in his relations with Government House'.[1] For his part, Hertzog had no personal quarrel with the Athlones. 'He has great admiration and sincere regard for the present Governor-General and his tactful, charming wife, Princess Alice,'[2] wrote one Member of Parliament. Indeed, a rumour has persisted to this day that General Hertzog was, in a particularly South African turn of phrase, 'a little bit sweet on'[3] Princess Alice: this meant, in this instance, that he was very fond of her. 'But in his heart of hearts,' continues the Member of Parliament, 'he considers their presence, in their official capacity, unnecessary, because they represent England and in a measure constitute a bond between South Africa and the Empire.'[4]

James Barry Munnick Hertzog,[*] fifty-eight at the time of his coming to power in 1924, was a polite, honest and painstaking politician who always knew his own mind. This logical, if narrow, mind was set on two political objectives at this time: to secure the constitutional independence of the Union and to ensure the continued predominance of the white man. Fortunately for him, his first years in office coincided with, and indeed contributed to, a period of tremendous economic and industrial development. With this material prosperity running in his favour, Hertzog was able to concentrate on his cherished ideals.

Almost immediately, by a series of symbolic gestures, Hertzog began to loosen the ties which bound South Africa to Britain. A policy of compulsory bilingualism (English and Dutch or Afrikaans) was introduced into the Civil Service. South Africans were forbidden to accept any titles from the Crown. In 1925 Afrikaans was recognised as an official language and, in the following year, it was proposed that the Union Jack be replaced by a new South African flag. The proposal caused such an uproar among the

---

[*] Hertzog's Christian names were those of Dr James Barry, the controversial Army surgeon and Inspector-General of hospitals, at one time private physician to the British Governor of the Cape, whose effeminacy led many to believe that he was actually a woman masquerading as a man. On his death, Barry was, in fact, declared to be a woman. Princess Alice was always fascinated by the Dr James Barry story.

English-speaking community, with the province of Natal threatening secession and even civil war, that it was temporarily shelved.

But Hertzog's greatest triumph came at the Imperial Conference of 1926. With the help of the Canadian Prime Minister, W.L. Mackenzie King, Hertzog ensured that the independent and equal status of the dominions was formally and legally recognised. From now on the British Government would have no more say over South African affairs. This, claimed General Hertzog, fulfilled all his aspirations. 'The liberty of our country as a dominion within the British Commonwealth was all that the most ardent patriot could want.'[5]

It was not. If Hertzog was prepared to stop short of a republic free of all imperial associations, there were a great many of his fellow Nationalists who would never do so.

The Prime Minister tackled the 'colour question' with equal dedication. In 1926 the infamous Colour Bar Act was passed, whereby skilled and semi-skilled jobs would be reserved for whites and Col-oureds, with the blacks being allowed to do only lesser-paid work, no matter what their abilities. The Native Administration Act and the Riotous Assemblies Act further strengthened the Government's hand. But Hertzog's various other bills, aimed at a complete separation of the races, failed to gain the two-thirds majority necessary for their passing. That was to come later.

2

What was the attitude of Government House, or more particularly of Princess Alice, during this turbulent political period? Her attitude was very much that of her time and her circle. She failed to grasp – as the majority of British people or English-speaking people in South Africa failed to grasp – the strength of the two main political forces in the country: Afrikaner Nationalism and Black Nationalism. She could see no good reason why the English-speaking and Afrikaans-speaking white South Africans could not simply sink their differences and live happily together under the imperial umbrella. 'Surely,' she argued, 'it should not have been beyond the genius of two great nations like the Dutch and the English to maintain the harmony which prevailed between them for so many years after the formation of Union?'[6]

She tended to look upon the Afrikaners (who, understandably, she always referred to as the Dutch or the Boers) as a simple, friendly, hospitable people, well-disposed towards the British, who were being led along the wrong path by their leaders. She considered the republican sentiments of some of these leaders to be 'outrageous'.[7] What more, after the winning of South Africa's autonomy at the Imperial Conference of 1926, could they possibly want? Hertzog's claim that they had 'gained their freedom' rang hollow to her. 'As they had had it since 1910,' she argued, 'this did not seem to us to be worth boasting about. . . .'[8] And, try as she might, the Princess could not help being caught up in the tumult surrounding such things as the removal of the King's head from the stamps or the proposed rejection of the Union Jack in favour of a South African flag. More than most, she would have felt this insult to the British Empire and the British sovereign.

In later years she was to admit that the political issues which had seemed so burning at the time now seemed insignificant. 'It is like watching the actors on a stage through the wrong end of one's opera glasses – whereas thirty or forty years ago we examined them through a microscope.'[9]

It was with sorrow and incomprehension that she watched, first the gradual erosion of the apparent Boer-British harmony of her early years, and then the split in the white population along largely racial lines. But not until long after she had left South Africa would Afrikaans Nationalism achieve its triumphant climax in the declaration of a republic in 1961.

Princess Alice's views on that other, and ultimately more important political question – the position of the black South African – again mirrored those of her *milieu.* She would have seen the Africans as most white South Africans preferred to see them: as a simple, unspoilt, staunchly tribal people, content to brew their beer, herd their cattle, hoe their fields and shake their heads in wonder at the superiority of the white man's ways. The great *indabas,* or tribal gatherings, which the vice-regal couple attended, would have confirmed this view. Standing beside her splendidly uniformed and helmeted husband, Princess Alice would gaze out across the great sea of tribesmen, hardly less resplendent in ostrich plumes, beads, animal skins, assegais, knobkerries and hide shields. She would listen, with admirable patience and undoubted satisfaction, to the long, laboriously translated speeches in which this or that chief intoned his people's gratitude for the blessings of peace and prosperity bestowed on them by the Government.

With the Africans in the cities – the partly educated, industrial proletariat living in slum conditions on the fringes of the white communities – she would have had very little contact. This is not to say the Princess was blind to the needs and sufferings of the urbanised black and coloured peoples. On the contrary, she did valuable work among the Cape Coloured community and gave active encouragement to such people as the selfless Dorothy Maud, who lived and worked in the tempestuous African township of Sophiatown, near Johannesburg. On one occasion the Princess gave Dorothy Maud's endeavours the official stamp of approval by visiting her little Sophiatown house and clubroom, where she planted a tree. And she allowed the new hospital in the township to be named after her. Concerned and kind-hearted, Princess Alice was not alone in believing that serious social ills could be cured by acts of charity.

But it is doubtful whether such things as the Colour Bar Act of 1926, by which the urban black workers were legally denied any chance of economic advancement, would have incensed her to the extent that, say, the proposal to replace the Union Jack – the Flag Act–incensed her. The writer Margery Perham, visiting South Africa at this time, professed herself astonished by the reactionary tone of the talk at Government House. 'I had a long talk with Princess Alice, who delivered herself of her views on the native question . . .' writes Margery Perham. 'I realised that the views of both the Governor-General and the Princess were very conventional but I soon saw that it would be silly to attempt an argument. . . . Perhaps it was silly of me to have expected so much more and to be depressed about the views held at this high level.'[10]

And Princess Alice herself admits that her husband's opinion of that far-seeing South African politician, John X. Merriman, who was able to appreciate both the injustice of Britain's earlier attitude towards the Boers and the present injustice of the whites towards the blacks, was that he was 'rather shifty'.[11]

But whatever Their Excellencies' private opinions might have been, their public attitudes were always impeccable. With General Hert-zog's achievement of autonomy in 1926 reducing the Governor-General's status to merely that of the personal representative of the King (with future Governors-General being appointed on the advice of the Union Cabinet) Lord Athlohe's task became largely ceremonial. Yet within strictly constitutional bounds, the couple did whatever they could to promote harmony.

The tact with which they handled the Afrikaans-speaking members of the community was masterly. Once, for instance, they found themselves at the remote settlement of Oudefontein, on the banks of the Orange River, for the celebration of the most hallowed day in the annals of Afrikanderdom – Dingaan's Day, the anniversary of the occasion on which, in 1838, the Voortrekkers won a great victory over the Zulu. Lord Athlone made a short speech in Afrikaans in which he thanked the assembled crowd for their welcome.

This little speech was received with great approval, and at the conclusion the large gathering joined in singing the third verse of Psalm 134, Princess Alice joining in. It is a scene which time cannot efface from the memory – the uplifted heads, the bearded faces, the shades of evening falling, as the solemn notes echoed among the mimosa trees and along the banks of the river.

In the evening Their Excellencies and staff attended a concert given by a band of amateur actors from Bethulie, who produced the play "Magrieta Prinsloo", an Afrikaans drama. . . . The marquee with its platform served as a hall and every member of the audience had to bring his or her own chair. Storm lamps served for lighting up the stage and tent.

The royal party, as well as General Hertzog, had seats in the front row. In front of them on the ground were several little girls, who evidently were beginning to feel sleepy at the length of the programme. Princess Alice lifted up one little girl with black, bobbed hair and held her on her lap, allowing her to rest her head on her shoulder. Lady May Cambridge also had a little girl comfortably ensconsed in her arms. The royal party closely followed and was most keenly interested in the play, their appreciation being manifested in the applause led by Princess Alice. . . . [12]

When the flag controversy was at its height, it was Lord Athlone who set in train the discussions that eventually led to a compromise solution. 'The Governor-General', runs one account of Lord Athlone's intervention, 'asked General Smuts to come and see him. He then told General Smuts that he was convinced that the Prime Minister, General Hertzog, desired a compromise on the flag question, and suggested to General Smuts that he should approach General Hertzog accordingly. The secret of this intervention was admirably kept so long as secrecy was indispensable. . . .' [13]

Between them, Hertzog and Smuts worked out a compromise: a new South African flag would fly side by side with the Union Jack.

An appreciation of Lord Athlone's achievements appeared in *The Times* of 15 November 1927. 'The Earl of Athlone, since he has been Governor-General of the Union, has been a very conspicuous success. Modest and unassuming, entirely approachable, easy in his talks with every kind of man or woman whom he meets in his constant journeys through the Union, the Governor-General has shown himself, too, irreproachable in all his dealings with the rival political leaders and parties. No suspicion of partisanship has ever attached to him – no small achievement in a country like South Africa in times like these.'[14]

For the most part all that the Athlones could do was to treat everyone – English, Afrikaans, Coloured, Malay, Indian and African – with equal warmth, courtesy and respect. Their behaviour was always strictly impartial. No matter how grossly fat the English-speaking mayor with whom she had to dance, nor how long-winded the Afrikaans farmer to whom he was obliged to listen, nor how tongue-tied the African child whom she was questioning, the Athlones were never anything less than charming.

And even Margery Perham had to admit that they carried out their public duties with great style. 'The Governor-General and his wife looked magnificent,' she noted at the official Opening of Parliament in Cape Town. 'They came up the steps through a guard of bluejackets. . . . Princess Alice, all in hydrangea blue, smiled, but rather wanly. I could hardly recognise my friends, the members of the staff, sweltering and alert in epaulettes, scarlet, pipeclay and the rest.'[15]

Some indication of the esteem in which the couple were held came towards the end of their five-year term in 1928. The Government asked them to stay on for another two years. They agreed. When the announcement to this effect was made, the public reaction was overwhelming. 'No news could be more welcome than the announcement that the King has approved of the extension for two years of the term of office of the Earl of Athlone as Governor-General,' claimed the *Argus* of Cape Town. 'From the moment when Lord Athlone and H.R.H. Princess Alice landed in the country they have been engaged in accumulating a store of goodwill and admiration such as the greatest in the world might envy and it has seemed almost impossible to think of a successor who could fill the post with equal ability, tact and good humour.'[16]

Letters and telegrams, from individuals and public bodies, poured into Government House by the thousand. 'It was,' says Princess Alice with characteristic modesty, 'most gratifying and encouraging.'[17]

3

More than anything, perhaps, the Athlones enjoyed their journeys through South Africa. No previous vice-regal couple had travelled so widely through the country. Sometimes these journeys were simply weekend trips, sometimes they were official train journeys, sometimes they were long tours by car, sometimes they were hunting safaris. By the end of their seven-year term of office, there were very few areas of the country that they had not seen.

Often they would stay as guests on farms belonging to friends: it might be in a gracious Cape Dutch homestead in the Western Cape or in some farmhouse in the arid, scrubby interior of the Cape Province-what the Princess called 'our beloved Karoo'.[18] One of their friends was the redoubtable Lady Phillips who lived in the beautiful house, Vergelegen, not far from Cape Town. The dynamic Florence Phillips, with her burning interest in the cultural life of South Africa, was highly appreciative of the way in which the Athlones had identified themselves with so many aspects of the country's development. The couple always enjoyed their visits to Vergelegen.

One of their holidays had its less happy moments. The Earl of Athlone had been ill and, with Lady Phillips away, the Athlones had accepted her invitation to spend two weeks at Vergelegen. One April morning Princess Alice, Lady May Cambridge and Norman McLeod, a local guide, set out to climb the Helderberg mountain rising behind the homestead. Later that afternoon Lord Athlone drove to the foot of the mountain to meet them. He waited, in mounting anxiety, until it was dark. Hurrying back to the house, he organised search parties. All night they scoured the mountainside but there was no sign of the little party. Not until dawn did an immensely relieved and utterly exhausted Lord Athlone see the trio picking their way down the slopes.

Princess Alice, who seldom panicked, denied that they had ever been lost. Lady May's dog had delayed them on the way down and, when night fell, the guide had sensibly suggested that they stop. 'We weren't lost,' Lady May said afterwards, 'it was the search parties that had gone off in the wrong direction.'[19]

'However,' said Norman McLeod's daughter half a century later, 'all ended well, and we often looked at the signed photographs of the two ladies given to my Dad in remembrance of their adventure.'[20]

It was again mountains that would bring the Government House party to the Bain's Kloof Hotel, a modest, corrugated-iron roofed hotel high in the mountains of the Western Cape. The party usually consisted of Lord Athlone, Princess Alice, Lady May, a lady-in-waiting and an A.D.C. Taking a packet of hotel sandwiches they would set out for the day, to walk along the mountain trails or to fish for trout in the clear waters of the Witte river. On their return they would have tea with the owners of the hotel.

Sometimes, says the owner's wife, the Princess would remain behind while the others went fishing. Settling herself on an upturned beer crate behind the hotel, she would sit watching the baboons washing their young in the river below. If she were offered a more comfortable chair, she would refuse. 'This seat is fine, thank you,'[21] the Princess would say smilingly.

On official journeys, the Governor-General usually travelled in his famous White Train. For many country people it was the thrill of a lifetime to see the gleaming, white-painted carriages come gliding into the sun-baked railway siding. The routine was always the same. The train would stop (a Middleburg housewife once flung her passage carpet on the platform only to find that the vice-regal party alighted further along); the serge-suited station-master would move apprehensively forward; a knot of local dignitaries would shift expectantly; a couple of A.D.C.s, all neatly-combed hair and grand accents, would alight, followed by a cloche-hatted lady-in-waiting; then came His Excellency, tall and distinguished, wearing a tussore-silk suit; and finally, framed in the carriage doorway, Her Excellency, looking exactly like everyone's idea of a princess: small, pretty, romantically elegant. A little girl, with fringed hair and a sleeveless dress, would move shyly forward to present a bouquet to this apparently delighted lady; and, with the clicking of half-a-dozen box Brownies, a slightly blurred version of the moment would be caught forever.

In May 1926 the Athlones toured the semi-desert districts of the North-Western Cape. Leaving their train at Calvinia, they drove through clouds of dust over the most appalling roads to Upington on the Orange River. At night they slept on the ground beside their car. Only at weekends, to enable them to attend a Dutch Reformed Church service on Sundays, did they stay anywhere for more than one day. For most of the time the landscape stretched parched and barren all around them; occasionally they would come to a sun-baked *dorp* – usually no more than a scattering of houses and a low, verandah'd building combining the functions of hotel, bar and general store.

The owner of one such establishment, in the village of Bowesdorp, was Mr Abe Schapera. He has left a simply written but strangely moving account of the day that the Athlones passed through this remote settlement.

Now unfortunately for us the V.I.P.s were not going to stay over in our village, therefore no form of welcome was organised. On the afternoon of the day they were to arrive, my sister-in-law Minnie Schapera managed to arrange a pretty bouquet from the homegrown flowers, grown in the paraffin tins on the stoep in front of the hotel.

Minnie, her little daughter Marian aged three, and I, went to stand at the side of the main road on the outskirts of the village, and we waited patiently. We were the only people there. Presently two large cars came slowly down the hill. We stepped forward into the road, Marian clutching the bouquet. The leading car stopped. A lady and gentleman, both rather distinguished looking, and wearing khaki safari clothes, were sitting in the back of the car.

They smiled so warmly at us, and Marian presented the simple little bunch of flowers to the lady, who kissed her tenderly. We all shook hands, and on that deserted country road there followed a delightfully informal and pleasant conversation for about ten minutes. The genial couple asked us about our mode of life in the village and from where we had come originally, and they seemed sincerely interested. We then bade farewell and a happy holiday to two charming and gracious people. . . ."

Princess Alice's interest in the Schaperas' origins is typical. She was always fascinated by the extraordinary variety of people who had settled, or whose forbears had settled, in South Africa. Many of the farmers whom they met on this journey 'had Irish and Scottish names like Kennedy and Cameron, but could not speak a word of English'.[23]

She was equally fascinated by the fact that anyone could survive in this desolate-looking veld. 'Her Royal Highness could not understand how people could make a living in such a barren area devoid of any cultivation and where one seldom saw any animals,' remembers one inhabitant of such a district. 'My father explained to her that it was a sheep farming area, where large tracts of land were required for grazing sheep. The town depended entirely on the surrounding district and the spending power of the farming community. According to my Dad, she listened politely, but was probably not really convinced that people could achieve or survive in such a stark countryside.'[24]

Even in the most far-flung *dorps,* however, Their Excellencies had to play their expected role. When they visited Kenhardt for a two-day stay, they were duly welcomed by the mayoral couple, a Mr and Mrs J.G. Wolhuter, a handful of local dignitaries and the entire population for miles around. Ten school cadets, none with uniforms and most without shoes, were lined up for inspection. Lord Athlone inspected this 'oddest honour guard he and Princess Alice had ever seen . . . unhurriedly, gravely and with dignity'. In his reply to the mayor's welcome, Lord Athlone speaking, to general astonishment, in Afrikaans, said, 'My wife and I are very happy to be here.'

So impressed by His Excellency's prowess was the local blacksmith, who had never before been known to utter one word of English, that he was moved to shout, 'He done it well! He done it well!'

The royal couple spent the night in one of the two local houses that boasted gas lighting and the following day attended a garden party in the park and a ball in the Kenhardt Hotel. To the strains of the Railway Dance Band, which had travelled over seventy miles from Upington for the occasion, Princess Alice and Mayor Wolhuter opened the dance. His worship, conscious of the fact that Queen Victoria had had to propose marriage to Prince Albert, had imagined that Queen Victoria's granddaughter would ask him to dance. No, explained, an aide-de-camp, 'You ask Her Royal Highness for the first dance and the Earl of Athlone will then ask Mrs Wolhuter.'

'And that,' reports Mr Wolhuter's son, 'is how it happened. All went off without a hitch, and the Princess looked beautiful just like everyone thought she would.'[25]

Some weeks after this momentous visit the mayoral couple received two autographed and framed photographs from Their Excellencies. They treasured them for years until, alas, the Hartebeest River burst its banks and the photographs were swept away on the flood waters.

One summer, in searing heat, the Athlones travelled over six hundred miles through the drought-stricken Western Transvaal visiting *dorps* and diamond diggings. Two things about this journey stuck in the Princess's mind. At Lichtenburg a party of Africans presented her with salt and asked her 'to make rain.'[26] And while staying on the late General de la Rey's farm, she was obliged to walk through a living-room full of fellow guests whenever she wanted to go to the outside lavatory.

With her ear ever open for a funny story, Princess Alice delighted in some of the jokes that she heard on her travels through the *platteland*. One, which she loved to tell, concerned the rail junction of Fourteen Streams, in the grey-green vastness of the Karoo.

'I have never passed through this important rail junction without thinking of the story of the Boer farmer who was appraising a young man who wanted to marry his eldest daughter. Asked where he came from, the youth replied "Tweefontein".

They were married and produced twins. Later, when another young man was courting the second daughter, the father again asked, "Where do you come from?" Her suitor answered, "Driefontein." Within a year they had triplets. Finally a third swain asked for the hand of the youngest daughter and when her father demanded where he came from the lad replied, "Fourteen Streams." "That," said the farmer, "is too much! You cannot marry my daughter!"[27]

Perhaps the most adventurous journey was their hunting expedition to Northern Rhodesia* in 1926. Throughout their years in South Africa the Athlones were enthusiastic big game hunters. The Princess was an excellent shot (it was yet another of her accomplishments that endeared her to the backveld Boers) and was often to be found, rifle in hand, striding across the veld in boots and jodhpurs. There were the inevitable narrow escapes: from a charging rhinoceros, from a wounded wildebeest. At Malamala, in the Transvaal Lowveld, she shot a lion and, in her honour, the area of thick vegetation in which it was shot became known as 'Princess Alice Bush'. *

On this Northern Rhodesian expedition the Government House party first travelled up by train through Southern Rhodesia† to Bulawayo where

---

* Now Zambia.

* 'I remember it all as though it were yesterday', said the Princess to Mrs Madeleine Varty almost half a century later.

† Now Zimbabwe.

they visited the dramatically sited grave of Cecil John Rhodes in the Matopos and then went on to the little capital city of Salisbury. From there they went to the Victoria Falls. A launch took them from this wild and thunderous cascade up the wide, placid waters of the Zambesi River to their camp site on the west bank. The camp was a collection of grass huts enclosed by a *boma* or grass palisade. Their bunks were sheets of canvas stretched across rough wooden frames (His Excellency, much to his son's delight, fell through his); the floors were covered with reed mats. They cooked their food over a camp fire.

These primitive conditions bothered Princess Alice not at all. In fact, she revelled in them. 'I have never enjoyed myself so much', she said. [28] Surrounded by those with whom she felt most at ease – her devoted husband, their two children and their Government House staff – Princess Alice felt supremely happy. For her, with her love of colour and adventure, this was the almost idyllic life. By day they would venture out, by horse or on foot, across the grassy plains in search of sport. The party bagged a great quantity of game: buffalo, eland, impala, sable antelope and even lion. At night they would sit in exhausted contentment around the flaring fire, the air pungent with the smell of grilling meat, the dark veld full of strange and menacing sounds and, above them, the great black African sky, filled with glittering stars.

4

A source of great joy to Princess Alice during these years in South Africa was the presence of her two children. Lady May Cambridge and Lord Trematon.

Like her mother, Lady May was small, slim and fine-boned. Her face had an appealing, piquant quality; 'she was pretty,' writes one member of the young Government House set, 'in a pink and white and goldish way.'[29] Although, in time, Lady May was to become as assured, charming and articulate as Princess Alice, at this stage of her life she was still rather shy, which was only to be expected. It could not have been easy for a girl of barely eighteen, with no close friends of her own age, to be pitchforked into so prominent a position. Nor did it help to have quite so socially accomplished a mother. 'Many a time,' writes one witness, 'I have seen H.R.H. give her a hard push, or pull her back, trying to make her mix more freely with the guests.'[30]

But in private, and away from the merciless public gaze, it was quite another matter. Then Lady May was utterly natural and uninhibited. She could be as high-spirited as the rest of them. She was an enthusiastic tennis player and a tireless dancer and there is a story of her washing one of the A. D. C. 's faces with a slice of water-melon and another of her kicking a hotel bathroom sponge under a wardrobe during a riotous game of bedroom football with members of the Government House staff.

She had 'a gorgeous sense of humour',[31] says one hostess.

There was never any talk, though, of a romance. The rumour of a possible match between Lady May and her second cousin, Prince Olav, afterwards King Olav V of Norway, came to nothing. No matter how dashing the aide-de-camp who partnered her at tennis, or how attractive the naval officer who squired her at Government House dances, Lady May Cambridge remained romantically unattached. Or rather, she remained so for the first five years of her parents' term of office.

Unfortunately, the Athlones saw much less of their son. In September 1925 Princess Alice had paid a hurried visit to England in order to settle the 18-year-old Lord Trematon into Trinity College, Cambridge. In the years that followed, Lord Trematon was able to spend several months each year with his parents in South Africa. In spite of his physical handicap, he developed into a tall, well-built, good-looking, adventurous young man, full of *joie de vivre*. Like his sister Lady May, Lord Trematon had a certain delicacy of feature. Unlike her, he was very dark.

'Generous and kind-hearted in the extreme,' says one of his friends, 'he would far rather be taken in than refuse to help anyone in need . . . he was a general favourite, not only on account of these qualities, but also from a singular charm of-personality inherited from both his parents.'[32]

A great deal of his time in South Africa was spent hunting; sometimes with his parents on their safaris, sometimes with companions in Zululand or the Karoo. Like both his parents, he had an enquiring mind. Wireless and engineering were his especial interests; he hoped, he once told a dinner guest at Government House, to become an engineer. But Lord Trematon's chief passion was for the relatively new sport of flying. On the formation of the University Air Squadrons at Oxford and Cambridge, Lord Trematon became an enthusiastic member.

'Although he was never strong,' writes Sir Geoffrey Butler, the Member of Parliament for Cambridge University, 'he flung himself into the movement with an ardour that nothing could quench. Perhaps a little fearful that he might not obtain the medical and parental permission to fly, which the Air Ministry and the University had made obligatory, I remember that he gave the authorities of the Cambridge Air Squadron – by his boyish endeavours harmlessly to circumvent their precautions in this respect – some anxiety. . . .'[33]

'No one,' testified a friend, 'could describe a flight through the air in a more graphic and intelligent way.'[34]

Lord Trematon was also, apparently, developing a taste for politics. In South Africa, where political discussion is the bread of life, he found himself becoming increasingly interested in that country's complex problems; while in England he was 'on many occasions a most attentive listener in the House of Commons'.[35]

In short, Lord Trematon was very much the son of his parents: sincere, enquiring, enthusiastic. He had grown, says his proud mother, 'into such a marvellous companion and was so loving and full of vitality'.[36]

On 1 April 1928, when they were in residence at Government House, Cape Town, the Athlones heard that Lord Trematon had been involved in a motor-car accident in France. He had been driving with two Trinity College friends, Kenrick Madocks and John Stewart-Clark, on the main road between Paris and Lyons. Near Belville-sur-Saone, while overtaking another car, their car had skidded and crashed into a tree. Kenrick Madocks had been fatally injured and died, soon afterwards, in Belville hospital. John Stewart-Clark had merely suffered slight burns and scratches. Lord Trematon, too, did not seem to be very seriously injured.

Princess Alice was thrown into an agony of apprehension and indecision by the news. She knew that for her haemophilic son even an apparently minor accident could prove fatal. Should she go to France? The weekly liner took fourteen days to reach Southampton; and it was due to sail in a few hours' time.

She decided to stay. The report, after all, had been very reassuring and her son had recovered from such slight injuries before. On the last voyage home on the *Windsor Castle* he had injured his knees in the swimming-pool, and a few days in bed were all that had been necessary for his recovery.

For the following few days the medical bulletins gave no cause for alarm. The parents were further reassured by the fact that their son's physician, Dr Howitt, had immediately left England for France and that their son's old nurse was likewise in attendance. But then the news worsened. After being in hospital for some days, Lord Trematon began to suffer from severe aural haemorrhaging. Princess Alice's cousin and close friend, Queen Ena of Spain, who understood the nature of Lord Trematon's illness only too well, sent her son's specialist to attend him. The bleeding was arrested and the patient seemed once more to be improving.

But it did not last. 'One night', says Princess Alice, 'he had a nightmare in which he dreamt he was involved in an Atlantic air-flight accident and woke up screaming. Dr Howitt, who was in an adjoining room, rushed to his assistance, only to find that in his agitation he had dislodged his bandages and the bleeding began all over again.' [37]

Lord Trematon died at three o'clock on the morning of 15 April. Even if his mother had set sail immediately on hearing the news of his accident, she would not have reached him before his death. Lord Athlone, she says, 'was absolutely broken-hearted and I thanked God that I had not started for England and we were together.' [38]

Their son's death, says Princess Alice simply, was 'the greatest tragedy of our lives'.[39] Two things only helped console her. One was the fact that he had had 'such a happy life while it lasted'.[40] The other was

299

her Christian faith. All her life, Princess Alice was a devout and unwavering Christian; during this period her faith was a great consolation. She would often be seen walking up through the Bishopscourt woods to talk to the Archbishop of Cape Town and, many years later, on sympathising with a friend on the death of a loved one, she wrote, 'I know how it feels, and that strength and comfort can only come through one's faith and personal courage.'[41]*

King George V arranged for the destroyer *Tempest* to carry Lord Trematon's body from Calais to Dover. The funeral took place, on 20 April, in St George's Chapel at Windsor. It was a movingly simple ceremony, attended by the King and Queen, the Prince of Wales and other members of the royal family. A guard of honour was supplied by the boys of Princess Alice's Own Troop of Boy Scouts from Islington. On the coffin was a cross of white flowers from Princess Alice and the Earl of Athlone, and wreaths from the King and Queen and Lady May Cambridge. Lord Trematon was buried in the private cemetery at Frogmore.

In Cape Town on the day of the funeral the heartbroken parents attended a quiet service in the

---

* I remember her saying how grateful she was for the strictness and discipline with which she was brought up, how it helped her when terrible sadness and bereavement had to be endured,' writes one family friend. 'She thought young people of the modern age had nothing to sustain them at such times and blamed nervous breakdowns etc. for this. "In my day", said H.R.H., "we did not have such things. We were told to pull ourselves together."' (Mrs A. Maddin to the author).

Archbishop's private chapel. At noon that day there was a memorial service in Cape Town Cathedral. Shops were closed, flags flew at half-mast, crowds of sympathisers lined the streets. The Cathedral was packed to overflowing – with cabinet ministers, Members of Parliament, government officials, representatives of the Army and Navy and with 'people of every race and walk in life'.[42] The service was conducted by the Archbishop, assisted by ministers of the Dutch Reformed and Presbyterian Churches.

'Such a tribute of sympathy as that paid to the sorrow of the Earl of Athlone and Princess Alice, shared by all classes of the community,' reported the *Cape Times,* 'is unprecedented here.'[43]

Unprecedented, too, was the number of messages of sympathy which poured into Government House from all over the world. Of all these it was characteristically one which struck a somewhat more optimistic note that Princess Alice found most moving. It came from the Paramount Chief of the Transkei. 'Be consoled!' ran his letter to Lord Athlone. 'May you and your Princess find it possible soon to emerge from your retreat in the sombre shades of the forest and come again into the sunlight.'[44]

During the rest of her long life Princess Alice is said to have mentioned her dead son very rarely.*

---

* A previous Governor-General, Lord Buxton, who served in South Africa from 1914 to 1920, had lost his son in action in 1917, and in 1935 the eldest son of the then Governor-General, Lord Clarendon, was killed in a motor accident. "This is the third time in succession that our Governor-General loses his only or

5

On 31 May 1928 – the anniversary of both the signing of the Anglo-Boer War Peace Treaty in 1902 and the formation of the Union in 1910 – Lord Athlone unfurled the new South African flag over the Houses of Parliament in Cape Town while Princess Alice was in Pretoria performing a similar ceremony at the Union Buildings. Although the Union Jack would still fly beside the orange, white and blue of the South African flag, Princess Alice could not easily reconcile herself to the change. Her task of unfurling the new flag, she said tersely, 'was not a pleasure'.[45]

A relief from the thundery political atmosphere which had characterised so much of their time in South Africa came two weeks later, on 15 June, when the Athlones sailed to England on six months' leave of absence. In England they were to divide their time between Bran-tridge Park and Kensington Palace.

On the day after their arrival, King George V invested the Earl of Athlone with the insignia of a Knight Companion of the Most Noble Order of the Garter. In September, the Athlones spent a couple of weeks as the King's guests at Balmoral and in October they were guests at Sandringham. But in November King George V was suddenly taken ill with acute septicaemia accompanied, according to the bulletin, 'by a decline in the strength of the heart'.[46] By the time the Athlones were

---

eldest son,' wrote a shocked General Smuts. 'Buxton, Athlone, Clarendon.' *(Smuts Papers:* Letter to M.C. Gillet, 27 April 1935.)

due to sail back to South Africa, on 24 November, the King was seriously ill. The Prince of Wales, then on holiday in East Africa, was summoned home and it was in a 'terribly distressed'[47] state that the Athlones took their leave. It was doubted whether the King would live.

But he recovered. It was not until the following summer, though, that he was again well enough to take up his duties. By then the Athlones had prevailed on General Hertzog to invite him to complete his convalescence in South Africa, but King George V could not possibly get away, and a plan for Queen Mary to come out on her own never materialised. 'This was a great pity, as I thought they would have liked such a jewel of a country with its fascinating history and vast spaces,' says Princess Alice.

The visit, she adds, 'would have done so much to eliminate the absurd [white] racial differences which were entirely due to political rivalries and party expediency.'[48]

The Princess was being too optimistic by half. It would have needed more than a royal visit to still the ever more violently churning waters of South African politics. The year 1929 was election year and the campaign was being fought on the emotive issue of the preservation of a 'white' South Africa. The campaign was particularly vicious. Determined to push through his bills for the complete political separation of the races, Hertzog employed the always effective *Swart Gevaar* – Black Peril – tactics. They worked, and his National Party was returned with an even greater, majority. Once again, Lord Athlone found himself obliged to work hand-in-glove with the country's largely anti-British element. And once again he distinguished himself by the tact and diplomacy with which he carried out his delicate task.

An appreciation of the Athlones' contribution to national life came on 9 February 1929, on the occasion of their Silver Wedding. In presenting the couple with a magnificent silver tea and coffee service and a cheque for £5000* – made up of shilling subscriptions from all sections of the community – General Hertzog paid heartfelt tribute to the Governor-General's abilities. Lord Athlone had 'held the scales equally and impartially,' declared the Prime Minister. 'The Earl and Countess of Athlone,' he continued, 'have not made their stay in South Africa as strangers, but have identified themselves with the interests and aspirations of the people of South Africa and have captured the hearts of the people.'[49]

In his reply, Lord Athlone claimed that they had spent some of the best years of their lives in the country; 'but, as you know,' he added, 'it is in South Africa that we have suffered our heaviest sorrow. You have shared with us in uncommon degree both the sunshine and the dark days. . . .'[50]

6

---

* The bulk of which the Athlones donated to the cause of health education in rural districts.

At the time that her parents were celebrating their Silver Wedding, Lady May Cambridge was beginning to think about her own future. Aboard the ship on which the vice-regal party had sailed back from England to South Africa in November 1928 had been Lord Athlone's new aide-de-camp, Captain Henry Abel Smith of the Royal Horse Guards. The son of a banker, the 28-year-old Captain Abel Smith was a tall, handsome and lively young officer. 'I think,' said one observer, 'May fell in love right away.'[51] Certainly, within a very short time, the young couple were becoming very attached to one another.

Lady May's parents were not altogether happy about the romance. It was not that they had any objections to Henry Abel Smith as a person; indeed, as well as being attractive he was both intelligent and capable. It was simply that they felt their daughter had fallen in love with the first really eligible man to come her way. Realising that the confines of colonial Government House society seriously limited her choice, they were anxious for her to meet other men.

The rumours about Princess Alice's objections to the match on the grounds of Captain Abel Smith's somewhat less elevated social position (Lady May, after all, had been born a princess) were untrue. What the Athlones wanted was their daughter's happiness. And they were anxious for her at least to have an opportunity of finding it with someone from a wider circle.

So the young couple agreed to wait for a year or two before marrying.

7

Early in 1930, the Athlones once again expressed that 'identification with the interests and aspirations of the people' in a most practical way. They launched the Citizens' Housing League Utility Company with an investment of £1000. Some weeks later, having personally investigated the slum conditions in Cape Town, Princess Alice had given vital stimulus to the cause of housing reform among the Coloured community. 'Princess Alice's surprise visit to the slums of District Six pricked the civic conscience of Cape Town for its housing neglect more than all the speeches of a generation,'[52] reported the *Argus*.

Their Excellencies' investment of £1000 pricked it even further. 'By the transparent sincerity of their interest in the poor and the unfortunate,' remembered that great worker for Coloured advancement, Dean (later Bishop) S. W. Lavis, 'they have made thousands of others glad and proud to follow their example.'[53]

And, in the year or so that remained to them in South Africa, the Athlones involved themselves as closely as ever with the community. Their round – of ceremonial duties, of official engagements, of charitable obligations, of private visits – continued. Their energy, wrote one observer, 'is marvellous and quite natural to both of them. They move perpetually . . . they have never flagged in their activity. They have never shirked their duty. The mere physical feat of their life in South Africa has been record-breaking.'[54] For this unstinting giving of themselves, the couple had become, not only greatly admired, but greatly loved.

When they finally took their leave – from Cape Town on 6 November 1930 and from Pretoria on 9 December 1930 – the Athlones were almost overwhelmed by the spontaneous demonstration of affection by all sections of the population. Princess Alice was particularly moved. As she left the Cape Town City Hall after the city's official farewell ceremony she was obliged to hold her newly-presented ostrich feather fan in front of her face: the Princess's cheeks, noticed the watching Norah Henshilwood, were wet with tears.

Their last drive, from Westbrooke to Cape Town station, was a triumph. In an open car they travelled for mile after mile through cheering crowds. In the suburb of Mowbray, as they passed the Princess Christian Home, for which Princess Alice had done so much, the Princess stood up in the car to wave to the old ladies gathered at the roadside in their chairs. 'Without wishing to derogate in the slightest from what is due to His Excellency,' wrote one Member of Parliament, 'it is no presumption to say that he could not have succeeded to the same extent in winning the hearts of the people without the gracious presence and influence of Princess Alice.'[55]

In Pretoria there were the same heart-wrenching farewells, both official and unofficial. At a banquet the Prime Minister paid a moving tribute to the Governor-General's great qualities. 'It is in the hearts and memory of the people of South Africa that you and Princess Alice will continue to live in happy remembrance for many a long day,' said General Hertzog. 'Overmastered by the all-embracing spirit of the veld, you and Princess Alice have in such a manner and such a degree, both in thought and action, identified yourselves with the interests of the country over the welfare of which you were called to preside that South Africa will continue to claim you among her own. . . .'[56]

When, on 9 December 1930, the Earl of Athlone, Princess Alice and Lady May Cambridge drove from Government House to Pretoria station (they planned to travel back to England overland, the length of Africa) dense crowds lined their route. Flags and bunting rippled in the bright sunshine and across the entrance to Church Square stretched a banner bearing the message, 'Pretoria's wish – Totsiens'. Princess Alice, who had always done so much for children, was showered with rose petals as she passed a line of schoolgirls. On the station platform to see them off were General Hertzog, his ministers, Members of Parliament, representatives of the Diplomatic Corps, of the Transvaal Administration and various other dignitaries. As the train moved slowly out, the royal salute was given by the guard of honour, drawn from the Pretoria Regiment, of which Princess Alice was the Colonel-in-Chief.

In his farewell message, Lord Athlone said that he and Princess Alice would never forget the interests and problems of South Africa. They would remember 'with deep affection' and gratitude the warmth, kindness and hospitality which they had received.

'We shall continue to hope and pray,' concluded Lord Athlone, 'that throughout the length and breadth of this land, in all places, at all times, and among all people, there will continue to increase that spirit which inspires "unity in all things essential, toleration in all things uncertain, and in everything charity".'[57]

PART FOUR
BRANTRIDGE PARK

CHAPTER TWELVE

1

For the following five months, from the time they left Pretoria until they arrived in England on 5 May 1931, the Athlones were on the move. Their mammoth journey – by rail, road, river and sea – took them up Africa, through the Middle East and across Europe. There were only five members of the party: Lord Athlone, Princess Alice, Lady May, a lady's maid and a valet. They took very little luggage. As their accommodation was to range from the most primitive overnight stops to longer spells in the grandest of government houses, the choice of suitable clothing presented something of a problem. In the end the Princess took a safari coat-and-skirt, a few cotton dresses, one 'most useful chiffon dress'[1] and a lace evening dress that needed no ironing.

Travelling by train through Southern and Northern Rhodesia, they were still on familiar British-administered territory, but on entering the Belgian Congo, near Elisabethville, they came into contact with a different colonial system. With King Leopold H's ruthless exploitation of the Congo now at an end the Belgian authorities were endeavouring to run the country on more enlightened lines. Just two years before, King Albert and Queen Elisabeth, with whom the Athlones had shared so many wartime experiences, had toured the Congo. In a speech made in Elisabethville, King Albert had emphasised to his listeners that nothing great or lasting could be achieved without fruitful collaboration between the races.

The visitors could now see these sentiments being put into practice. The differences between the Belgian and the South African systems were immediately apparent. In industrial South Africa, not only were African men denied the opportunity of doing any skilled work but they were forced to live in hostels, apart from their families. In the Congo the Athlones were interested to see that even the operation of complicated machinery was done by Africans. They lived with their families and their children were able to attend good local schools.

Lord Athlone took the opportunity to write to General Smuts to tell him how impressed he had been by the ability of the Africans, once they had been given the opportunity to do skilled work.

Their visit to the Congo also brought them into a different sort of terrain. They had left the open savannah of South Africa behind and were now in tropical Africa. Here was a world of steamy heat, palm plantations, paddle boats, trained elephants, chattering monkeys and trees so tall and dense that they seemed to go on and up forever. The towns of Elisabethville and Stanleyville were beautifully laid out: the white buildings so elegantly shuttered and verandah'd, the wide avenues lined with flowering trees.

There were the usual hilarious incidents: the dressing-table that collapsed because white ants had eaten away the inside of the legs; the geyser that exploded, filling the room with smoke and water; the cockerel that flew squawking over Lord Athlone's head as he was settling down on the seat of the outside lavatory and sent him scurrying out in fright 'holding up his trousers as best he could'.2

From the Congo the party crossed into Uganda. Here they were the guests of the Governor, Sir William Gowers, in Government House, Entebbe, on the shores of Lake Victoria. Uganda was a paradise for game and the Athlones spent a great deal of time photographing it – and shooting it. They found few things more exhilarating than the sight of herds of animals in the almost park-like landscape: elephant, lion, giraffe, buffalo, zebra, and varieties of buck. And there were more exotic things to be seen as well: crocodiles, iguanas, situtunga buck and Colobi monkeys.

It was in Uganda that Lady May shot a lioness in an extraordinary fashion. The beast had come bounding towards the party, her mouth open in a great roar. Lady May stood her ground, fired, and the lioness fell dead. Yet there was no trace of blood. The bullet had gone straight through her mouth into her skull.

For the rest, there were launch trips on the vast waters of Lake Victoria, a visit to the Kabaka of Uganda, a tour of the hospital, the cathedral and the burial place of the chiefs, a glimpse of Mount Ruwenzori without its usual blanket of cloud, and more than a glimpse of an unashamedly naked chief who, in their honour, was sporting a necklet of goat's skin and the medal presented to him by King George V in commemoration of his Coronation.

Leaving Uganda they travelled north into the Sudan and down the White Nile by paddle steamer. Through the dense, swampy 'Sud' they chugged, stopping every now and then to shoot game or photograph the trumpeting herds of elephant or the lanky Dinka tribesmen, covered in ash to repel the clouds of mosquitoes and standing, on one leg, resting on their spears. 'I tried it,' says Princess Alice briskly, 'and found the attitude comfortable and restful.'[3]

In Khartoum things took on a more formal aspect. As they were again the guests of the Governor, the 'lace evening dress that needed no ironing'[4] was brought out once more. Lord Athlone inspected the British regiment stationed there and there was a tour of the battlefield of Omdurman. For Princess Alice, who had known, or known about, so many famous historical figures during her girlhood at

Queen Victoria's court, such sites were always doubly interesting.

From Khartoum they went by train to Wadi Haifa, then again by steamer, visiting the famous temple of Abu Simbel, the temples of Karnak and Luxor and staying at the Winter Palace Hotel in Luxor; 'which cost us more than we had spent in accommodation all the way through Africa.'[5]

Cairo, where they were the guests of the British Ambassador and Lady Lloyd, again left the Princess with a multitude of memories: of fascinating archaeological tours, a ball at the Embassy, a visit to King Fuad, the collection of cacti belonging to Prince Mohammed Ali, whom she had last seen at luncheon with Queen Victoria.

The 'crowning point'[6] of the journey, though, was their visit to Jerusalem. With her strong religious faith, Princess Alice found her stay in the Holy Land a most moving and interesting experience. 'When you are there,' she says, 'the atmosphere is so biblical that you live, as it were, in the time of Christ.'[7] The party were in Jerusalem for Easter Week and were able to steep themselves in all the mystical and colourful ceremonies that mark that sacred time: the 'Washing of the Feet', the 'Looking for Christ', the 'Ceremony of the Holy Fire'. Though fully conscious of the garishness of some of the religious observances and the vulgarity of some of the ecclesiastical architecture, Princess Alice could not help being caught up in the excitement and emotion of it all.

From Jerusalem they toured the various Holy Places: Bethlehem, Jericho, Nazareth, the Dead Sea, the Sea of Galilee. For Princess Alice, the Sea of Galilee was made even more memorable by the fact that while crossing it in a small steam launch with a party of clergymen, a strange man suddenly stood up and, in a loud voice, announced to his astonished fellow passengers that, 'This is the very place where the late J.C. stepped overboard and walked home.'[8] The Princess loved to repeat the story.

On another journey they travelled, by train, car and horse, to the marvellous hidden city of Petra, in Jordan. Emerging from a narrow gorge, 'we were faced by the setting sun lighting up a Roman temple literally carved out of the red rock. On either side are high cliffs with the remains of other buildings of the same lovely cream and pink and red sandstone,'[9] enthused the Princess. But the tents in which they slept, she adds no less typically, were alive with fleas.

More wonders awaited them in the Lebanon: the massive ruins at Baalbek ('the most romantic and beautiful of all the gigantic buildings of the past'), the French elegance of Beirut, the Crusader Castle of Cracque des Chevaliers, looking like 'a miniature Windsor Castle'.

In Ankara, they put up at the Ritz Hotel. Here, for the first time, some of the magic faded. Ankara was far too ordinary for Princess Alice's taste. She found the surrounding countryside uninteresting, and the town dreary. Any such dullness, however, was more than compensated for by the personality of Mustapha Kemal, the famous Atatürk, who was then energetically transforming Turkey into a modern Western state.

The Athlones saw a great deal of the dynamic Atatürk. 'He was a short, well-built, stocky man with piercing blue eyes and the general appearance of a hard-bitten police officer', notes the Princess. Unhampered, as she puts it, by a wife, Atatürk satisfied his sexual needs with a series of' adopted daughters' whom he would marry off to one of his officials as soon as he tired of them. He seems, during the Athlones' stay, to have taken rather a fancy to the fair-skinned and vivacious Princess Alice. He danced attendance on her and when, during a ball on her last evening, she explained that they had to go as they were due to leave early the next morning, he would not hear of it. '*Il ne faut pas partir*,' he snapped, cutting short her explanations. When she insisted, he grabbed her by both wrists and, dragging her through several rooms full of people, plumped her down on a sofa.

There they sat, the Princess with her wrists in Atatürk's iron grip. When the Princess begged the worried British Ambassador, Sir George Clark, not to desert her as Lord Athlone had – very diplomatically – deserted her, all the Ambassador could mutter was that 'this is most unusual.' Only on the insistence of his latest adopted daughter would Atatürk let the Princess go.

'He gave me a great fat book about himself,' is Princess Alice's last word on Atatürk, 'which I have never read.'

A stay in Istanbul marked their return to Europe and on 5 May 1931 the family finally disembarked at Dover. Like so many returning travellers, the Athlones were met by a disconcertingly cool reaction on the part of their friends.

'Oh, I haven't seen you for a long time,' they would say. 'Where have you been?'[10]

And when one tried to tell them, they would show a firm and deflating lack of interest.

2

For the first time since moving to Brantridge Park, almost ten years before, the Earl of Athlone and Princess Alice were able to regard it as home. The couple were beginning to feel the need of a permanent base, and the Brantridge Park house certainly had the required air of permanence. Commanding long views over wide, gently sloping lawns, it was an imposing-looking house; a cheerful conglomeration of Georgian, Victorian and Edwardian styles, grey-walled, creeper-covered, many-windowed. The main central block was three-storied; to this had been added a haphazard arrangement of wings, verandahs and outbuildings. The house boasted twelve bedrooms and five bathrooms, and there were extensive kitchens and servants' quarters. It was, admitted

Princess Alice, far too large for their needs, but then they were seldom without guests.

With characteristic vigour, Princess Alice set about making it more habitable. The rooms were re-decorated and rearranged. Much of the furniture had come from Princess Alice's childhood home, Claremont House, and they were able to add the things which they had collected on their travels: paintings from South Africa, carpets from Syria, vases from Egypt. The general effect was one of elegance, comfort and individuality.

As the couple spent much of the season in London, in their Kensington Palace apartment, Brantridge Park would be their home during late autumn, winter and spring. The Princess was an excellent hostess. Unlike so many women in her position, who were content to leave matters in the hands of the housekeeper and the staff, she took an active interest in the running of the home. She kept an eye on everything; the staff were always amazed by her practical knowledge of housekeeping. Whenever guests were expected she would arrange flowers in their rooms and personally check such things as drawer space, soap and towels.

The park had been neglected during their long absence in South Africa and with the help of an accomplished young gardener called William Brodby, Princess Alice set about landscaping the grounds. She was particularly fond of rock gardens; with the help of the equally enthusiastic Brodby, the

Princess converted a hollow near the house into a spectacular rock garden – a charming arrangement of winding paths, shallow steps and cascading water. Throughout the spring and early summer, when the flowering shrubs were in full bloom against a background of trees, the garden was a magnificent sight. It was no less magnificent in the gold and bronze and red of autumn. The nearby oak wood, carpeted in bluebells, never failed to delight the Princess's South African visitors.

The first great occasion at Brantridge Park was the wedding of Lady May Cambridge to Captain Henry Abel Smith. The engagement had been announced on 7 August 1931, three months after the family's return. Any hopes that Princess Alice might have harboured of her daughter falling in love with someone else had proved in vain. With a good grace, the parents had accepted the inevitable. 'As it turned out,' Princess Alice afterwards admitted,'[they] knew best. . . .'[11] They did indeed. The marriage turned out to be a happy and successful one.

The wedding was held in the village church of St Mary, in nearby Balcombe, on 24 October 1931. Among the twelve bridesmaids were Princess Elizabeth of York, the future Queen Elizabeth II; Princess Ingrid of Sweden, the future Queen Ingrid of Denmark; Princess Sibylla of Coburg, the future Crown Princess of Sweden; and Lady Alice Montagu Douglas Scott, the future Duchess of Gloucester.

In fine autumn sunshine, thousands of sightseers lined the steep banks on either side of the road which winds from Brantridge Park to St Mary's Church. Their curiosity was amply rewarded by glimpses, not only of the bride wearing the Brussels lace veil once worn by Queen Mary and Princess Alice at their weddings, but of Queen Mary herself, unmistakable in an ankle-length coat and uncompromisingly set hat. Also present was that darling of the crowds, the Prince of Wales.

The revised marriage service, omitting the word 'obey', was used for the first time by a royal bride at Lady May's wedding. The royal, velvet-bound register, brought specially from the Lord Chamberlain's Office for the occasion, was signed by Queen Mary, the bride's parents, Mrs Francis Abel Smith and the best man – one of Lord Athlone's South African A.D.C.s – the Hon. Cecil Weld-Forester.

In a large blue and white marquee set up on the lawns outside the house, the Prince of Wales proposed the toast to the newly-married couple. Queen Mary was the first to taste the wedding cake, which was decorated with 'hunting figures' and the regimental shield of the Royal Horse Guards. Together with Princess Alice, Queen Mary stood in the doorway waving to the couple as they drove off to Didlington Hall, Norfolk, for their honeymoon.

The parents did not really have much time to feel the loss of their only surviving child. For, all the while, the duties and the distinctions continued. On

3 June 1931 Lord Athlone had been made a Privy Councillor; in July he had received the Freedom of the City of Edinburgh; in August he had been appointed Governor and Constable of Windsor Castle. On 1 February 1932 he was installed as Chancellor of the University of London, an important post which he was to fill with great distinction in the years ahead. 'If I have at any time been of any little help to my country and my fellow men,' he said gallantly in his installation speech, 'seventy-five per cent of the credit, at the very lowest estimate, is due to Princess Alice.'[12] Later that year he was awarded honorary doctorates at Oxford and Cambridge. He was involved in endless charitable works; he was a director of various companies.

Princess Alice was no less busy. She was, or was to be, concerned, among other charities and organisations, with the National Children's Adoption Society (interestingly, the Princess was the first member of the royal family to come out in open support of birth control), the Royal School of Needlework, the King Edward VII District Nursing Association, the Royal Holloway College and the late Duchess of Albany's Deptford Fund. She was appointed President (later Commandant-in-Chief) of the Women's Transport Service, also known as the FANY – First Aid Nursing Yeomanry.

Another of her interests was the Girl Guide Association. The Princess, says the Chief Guide Lady Baden-Powell, was 'a hardworking President of the Imperial Committee'. They had met in South Africa in 1926, when the Baden-Powells had been touring the country. Sir Robert, on that occasion, had been recovering from an illness and on their arrival at Government House in Pretoria, the Princess not only helped them unpack but arranged for the making of a nourishing rice pudding.

On her return to England, the Princess saw a great deal of Lady Baden-Powell in the course of her Guiding activities. 'She nas always been sweet and demonstrative,' wrote Lady Baden-Powell, 'and at times it is difficult to know what to do first on meeting her – salute, curtsey or be kissed.'[13]

But not even this manifold activity could exhaust the Princess's remarkable energy. She yearned for a more active existence. She was simply not prepared to settle down to the sedate, predictable, well-ordered life of the usual royal figure. Her sense of adventure was too keen. 'After moving about so much in South Africa,' she admits, 'we had caught the wanderlust, as well as a craving for sunshine which we missed during our dear English winters!'[14] It was a return visit to South Africa, early in 1933, to open the Princess Alice Orthopaedic Hospital, that reawakened all her appetite for travel. From then on, for almost the following half-century, and with the exception of the Second World War years, Princess Alice was to be constantly on the move in search of sunshine and colour and excitement.

3

The first of her journeys took Princess Alice to another of those places with which she was to fall in love: the West Indies. Sir Bede Clifford, who had been Imperial Secretary to Lord Athlone in South Africa, was now Governor of the Bahamas, and early in 1934 the Athlones accepted his invitation to spend a holiday at Government House, Nassau.

The couple sailed to New York in the *Mauritania*. 'It was one of her worst crossings,' says the Princess, 'a full gale all the way.' In New York there was the customary ebullient reception from the Press. The 60-year-old Earl of Athlone was headlined as 'Queen Mary's Kid Brother', and the always impeccably behaved Princess Alice was likened to her cousin, the flamboyant Queen Marie of Romania, who had recently completed a controversial fund-raising tour of the United States.

Their three-day stay in New York was no less hectic. They were there as the guests of the immensely wealthy Mr and Mrs Harold Pratt and their time in this vibrant city was a blur of overheated rooms, overwhelming hospitality, relentless sightseeing and endless introductions. They had hoped to avoid that *grande dame* of American society, the redoubtable Mrs Cornelius Vanderbilt (known, for her dedicated pursuit of visiting royals, as 'the King-fisher'), but Mrs Pratt begged them to accept Grace Vanderbilt's invitation to tea: her life would not be worth living, protested their hostess, if she kept her royal guests to herself. So the Athlones went to Mrs Vanderbilt's Fifth Avenue mansion where they were duly impressed by the lavish decor and duly introduced to the horde of fellow guests.

Another rough passage took the Athlones to Nassau. Here, at Government House,* with Sir Bede and Lady Clifford and their young family (the Princess was godmother to their Bahamian-born daughter, Alice Atalanta), the couple felt thoroughly at home. The Princess was highly amused at Lady Clifford's servants: the house cleaning and the gardening were done entirely by convicts. When Princess Alice admitted to being somewhat apprehensive about the safety of her belongings, Sir Bede reassured her. Nothing would be stolen, he said; the convicts were all honest men, serving life sentences for murder.

Princess Alice enjoyed her West Indian sojourn immensely. The bright sunshine, the towering palms, the flowering trees, the white beaches, the coral reefs, the 'multi-coloured, transparent seas',[15] the exotically coloured fish, the open-hearted people, indeed, the whole atmosphere of warmth and brilliance and gaiety appealed to her enormously.

Never one for simply idling in the sunshine (and she belonged to a generation that kept the sun off their skins) the Princess filled every hour of every day.

---

* It was this same Government House which, half a dozen or so years later, the Duchess of Windsor, as the newly appointed Governor's wife, would declare quite uninhabitable.

327

She visited several other islands, always swimming in the marvellously warm, translucent water. With her head encased in a heavy diver's helmet, she walked along the bottom of the sea to watch fish swim in and out of a wall of coral. The party flew to nearby Florida to attend a race-meeting at Hilean Park at which the Princess was asked to present the Bahamas Cup. At the race-track she was fascinated to see the way in which the flocks of pink flamingos simply ignored the wildly galloping horses. She was equally fascinated when her husband and Sir Bede Clifford went driving off with the famous Dolly Sisters to attend a charity show. The occasion was made memorable for Lord Athlone by the fact that one of the Sisters, quite unselfconsciously, put her hand on his knee to steady herself as she leaned across him to talk to someone.

Having spent a month in the Bahamas, the Athlones sailed home on the cruise ship, the *Duchess of Bedford*, calling in at several other Caribbean islands on the way. In later years, both with Lord Athlone and alone, Princess Alice was to sail through these shimmering waters many, many times.

4

There was some talk, at this time, of the Athlones being appointed to the most prestigious imperial post of all: that of Viceroy and Vicereine of India. Nothing had been said officially but it was widely believed that they were in line to succeed Lord and

Lady Willingdon. With their undeniable diplomatic and social gifts, the Athlones would have made a most impressive vice-regal couple. The rumour was given weight when they were invited, early in 1935, to stay with the Willingdons in Delhi. Only later would the reason why they had not been appointed become apparent.

They landed in Bombay on 1 February 1935 and for the following two months toured the great sub-continent. This was Lord Athlone's first visit to India since, as a young subaltern, forty years before, he had served there with the 7th Hussars.* Princess Alice had never visited India. Like so many travellers to that great country, she was struck by its vastness and its variety and its splendours. The couple moved, of course, in great style. They travelled in vice-regal railway coaches, they stayed in Lutyens's majestic Government House, they were entertained by maharajahs, they sailed in luxuriously-appointed launches, they rode on the backs of elephants in tilting howdahs, they slept in flamboyant palaces and strolled in formal gardens, sweet with the scent of flowers and hushed with the sound of splashing fountains. 'The kindness of everyone,' says the Princess, 'had to be experienced to be believed.'

---

* While in South Africa Lord Athlone had been appointed Colonel of the 7th Hussars by King George V. 'This gave him very real pleasure,' says Princess Alice, 'as he considered that the greatest reward that a soldier can earn is to become Colonel of his old regiment.' (Princess Alice: *For my Grandchildren*, p. 174.)

While staying with the Begum of Bhopal, the Princess shot her first tiger. Perched high in a tree, she sat waiting for it to appear. 'It is most exciting and thrilling to wait for one's tiger,' she wrote, 'hearing all sorts of strange noises from birds and other small game. Then, without a sound, this great creature is at your feet – perhaps growling on spotting you. It is indescribable how one feels – at least I felt sick with excitement. . . .'

But even amongst all the magnificence of their Indian tour, Princess Alice had an eye for a human or a humorous story. In Bombay Lord Athlone's old servant of over forty years before travelled a vast distance to come and see him; fully confident, says the Princess, that her husband would pay his train fare. The somewhat masculine Begum of Bhopal was much given to vigorous games of 'bicycle polo'. When staying with the Maharajah of Bikaner, the Princess was obliged to dress in her tiny bathroom as all women of the establishment sat watching her from behind the marble lattice-work that decorated the top of her bedroom walls. And in Lady Willingdon, apparently, the tireless Princess Alice met her match. 'Lady Willingdon was too energetic,' she complains, 'up at cock-crow to bathe and play tennis while we were still abed.'

The Indian journey was not all play, however, As Overseas Girl Guide Commissioner, Princess Alice frequently had to put on her Guider's uniform in order to hold inspections of India's polyglot Girl Guides.

Here, she says, 'was Guiding at its best, uniting all parties, and I a Christian among Hindus, Muslims and Untouchables – all joined in one band.'[16]

The couple returned to England to face an increasingly serious situation that was developing within the royal family. And to come to an understanding of why Lord Athlone could not possibly be considered as Viceroy of India; or, for that matter, as Governor-General of Canada. King George V's health was not good. In February that year, while the Athlones had been in India, there had been a renewal of the King's bronchial trouble and he had spent most of March convalescing. In the event of his death, the King wanted Queen Mary's brother, Lord Athlone, close at hand, i want nothing to take her brother from her side,'[17] he said emphatically.

For by now King George V suspected that his Queen, and the British monarchy, was soon going to need as much support as possible.

5

A frequent visitor to Brantridge Park during these years was Queen Mary. With her abiding interest in houses, gardens and sightseeing generally, the Queen greatly enjoyed her annual October visits to her brother's home. Several of the trees in the park were planted by her. The Queen loved being driven around the beautiful Sussex countryside, and nearby Brighton, with its scores of antique shops, drew her like a magnet. The two royal sisters-in-law – the stiff, unbending Queen Mary in her dated clothes, and the lithe, alert and always fashionably dressed Princess Alice – made an incongruous pair as they poked about the *objets d'art*.

The Queen spent many happy hours among the fantasies of the Brighton Pavilion. Once, says Princess Alice, Queen Mary's sharp eye noticed that some pilasters were missing from the panelling in the small oval drawing-room. Deciding that they must have been taken to decorate the Belgian Suite at Buckingham Palace, she promptly arranged for their return to the Pavilion.

Although none of the three of them – Queen Mary, Princess Alice and Lord Athlone – were given to parading, or even discussing, their personal griefs and problems, it is highly probable that the Queen sometimes spoke to her brother and sister-in-law about her eldest son David, the Prince of Wales. As the three of them sat in the light-filled drawing-room at Brantridge Park, the women with their heads bent over their tapestry frames, the Queen would almost certainly have opened her heart to these two trusted relations. Princess Alice was known to be the Prince of Wales's favourite Aunt and the Queen might have hoped that her sister-in-law would be able to exert some influence on her wayward son. She herself had never been able to establish a close relationship with him. Princess Alice certainly knew that the Queen was worried about the Prince of Wales's seeming inability to choose a wife, and even more worried by the sort of wife whom he was likely to choose.

On the engagement of the "Queen's third son Henry, Duke of Gloucester, to Lady Alice Montagu Douglas Scott, Princess Alice wrote to say that, 'This is indeed good news and I congratulate you on settling another son and upon getting what I know to be a really splendid daughter-in-law.' If only David could follow his example, she wrote, but she was afraid that he had missed his best chances. 'But never mind,' she continued, 'one must look on the blessings and has to be thankful for them.'[18]

For by now, at the end of August 1935, Princess Alice must have been well aware of the Prince of Wales's friendship with Mrs Wallis Warfield Simpson.

King George had recovered sufficiently from his illness earlier that year to take part in his Silver Jubilee celebrations in May 1935. On 6 May the King and Queen drove through the clamorous streets of their capital to attend a Thanksgiving Service in St Paul's Cathedral. In their procession drove the Earl of Athlone and Princess Alice. For the Princess, with her staunch belief in the institution of monarchy, the spontaneous enthusiasm of the public throughout the week-long Jubilee celebrations was extremely gratifying. And not only gratifying but surprising. Like the King himself, Princess Alice had not expected the public reaction to be quite so rapturous. She had seen the fall of so many thrones during the past seventeen years; only four years previously King Alfonso

XIII had been forced to flee his Spanish kingdom and Princess Alice's close friend and cousin, Queen Ena, was now living in exile.

But the British throne seemed more secure than ever; thanks, not only to the personality and dedication of the monarch himself, but to the highly developed sense of duty of the other members of the royal family – not least among them, the Athlones.

In just over six months, however, this apparently unassailable throne was beginning to show signs of weakening. King George V died, at the age of seventy, on 20 January 1936. 'His death . . .' writes Princess Alice, 'was a grievous blow, especially for poor [Queen Mary] but it was not unexpected.'[19] Yet it was Queen Mary, she claims, who set the rest of them an example in fortitude and self-control. At the King's funeral, in St George's Chapel at Windsor, Princess Alice was particularly struck by the tribute paid to Queen Mary by the Archbishop of Canterbury, Dr Lang.

'The one who might have been expected to be most overwhelmed,' he declared, 'was the one who radiated calmness and strength to all others.'[20]

Lord Athlone's nephew, the slight, fair-haired, 41-year-old David was now King Edward VIII. Having already lived during three reigns – those of Queen Victoria, King Edward VII and King George V – Princess Alice was about to experience her fourth: the short, turbulent and, for the family, distressing reign of King Edward VIII.

CHAPTER THIRTEEN

1

'The events which led up to the Second World War bore a marked resemblance to those which preceded the First,[1] wrote Princess Alice in her old age. In this instance she was referring to the general political situation, but there was another, more personal way, in which the pattern was being repeated. Once again her brother Charlie, the Duke of Coburg, was being caught up in the maelstrom of events.

The rise to power of Adolf Hitler had thrown a great many German royals into a quandary. On the one hand they could hardly approve of this vulgar upstart with his rabble-rousing tactics and his pagan, nihilist philosophy, while, on the other, they would not be sorry to see the end of the decadent and bankrupt Weimar Republic and the return to the order, nationalism and patriotism of their own heyday. Among the Prussian royal family – the Hohenzollerns – there was a widespread belief that Hitler might one day restore the monarchy. Princess Alice's cousin, Kaiser Wilhelm II, was still alive and living in exile at Doom in Holland: he had certainly been led to believe that Nazi triumph in Germany would mean a royal restoration. What all these hopeful people failed to appreciate was that the Nazis were not old-fashioned conservatives; they were radical revolutionaries of the Right.

Kaiser Wilhelm H's daughter, Princess Viktoria Luise, Duchess of Brunswick and Luneburg, gives an indication of the attitude of certain members of her family towards Adolf Hitler. 'We regarded the rise of National Socialism – which was soon to become the largest political party – more or less in the same light as millions of others in all strata of our society. . . . Our people's misery and the failure of government were the reasons why my family could not stand aloof from politics but had to take part in them.'

The Kaiser's sons had all joined the *Stahlhelm,* an organisation of ex-soldiers, dedicated to the upholding of 'order and discipline', which was later absorbed into the Nazi movement. 'Those days in the *Stahlhelm* were wonderful, so exalting,' claimed Prince August Wilhelm, the only one of the Kaiser's sons who actually went on to join the Nazis. 'Had superb billets, fifteen men. Coffee morning and evening. We're on the march for two hours. . . . Alexander [his son] stood for four hours in the stadium during a splendid tattoo, 2200 flags, about 100,000 spectators, and for seven hours on Sunday without food! The population, too, were greatly enthusiastic. Charlie, too, stayed for seven hours.' In fact Charlie, the Duke of Coburg, was every bit as elated by this resurgence of 'national fellowship' and by these 'clean young men marching in fine harmony'.[2]

Ever since being forced to abdicate his dukedom in 1918, the Duke of Coburg had been associated with 'almost every reactionary and militarist organisation which sprang up'.[3] In 1931 he took part in the massive demonstration known as the Harzburg Front, when various conservative elements decided to join forces with the Nazis in order to overthrow the Republic. Yet the Duke of Coburg had not, at that stage, felt ready to emulate the younger members of his family by joining the Nazi movement. On 20 October 1932 his eldest daughter, Princess Sibylla, married Prince Gustaf Adolf of Sweden at a brilliant wedding ceremony in Coburg, and when a message from Hitler was read out, in which he thanked the House of Saxe-Coburg-Gotha for its support, the Duke was somewhat discomfited. He was said to have been equally disapproving of the saluting Brownshirts who lined the processional route and of the four thousand Nazis who marched in torchlight procession through the streets of Coburg that evening.

Not until 1935, in the belief that only Nazism could save Germany from Communism, did the Duke of Coburg join the Nazi party. Although it is unlikely that he was ever a force, or even an influence, in the Nazi hierarchy, the Duke's small, neat, uniformed figure, sporting a swastika armband, was usually to be seen on ceremonial occasions.

His chief obsession seems, understandably enough, to have been the fostering of an Anglo-German alliance. As an Englishman-turned-German, as a member of the British royal family and as President of the Anglo-German Fellowship, the Duke felt himself to be in a unique position for the furthering of his objectives. Nor was he alone in wanting a closer understanding between Great Britain and Nazi Germany: there were a great many prominent people in both countries during the 1930s who were just as anxious for some sort of Anglo-German *entente.*

At the time of King George V's death, the Duke and Duchess of Coburg were staying with the Athlones at Kensington Palace. Princess Alice says that her brother had come over to watch 'the first football match between Germany and England since the war,'[4] but, possibly unbeknown to her, he seems to have come to England to explore the possibilities of an Anglo-German agreement. He certainly sent Hitler a report of his findings.

Various prominent personalities – Anthony Eden, Duff Cooper, Neville Chamberlain and J.J. Astor, the proprietor of *The Times* – were invited to Kensington Palace to meet the Duke of Coburg. As the Duke was known to be a member of the Nazi party, his visitors would have been very wary of what they said, but in his self-congratulatory report to the Fuhrer, the Duke laid great stress on the fact that, as an old Etonian himself, he was in a very valuable position to sound out the views of other old Etonians.

It was, though, on the new King, Edward VIII, that the Duke of Coburg placed his highest hopes. These hopes were shared, apparently, by Hitler. The Fuhrer had considerable faith in the value of the ties between the British and German royal families. He had once instructed the Kaiser's daughter, Princess Viktoria Luise, to 'explore the possibilities' of bringing about a *rapprochement* with Britain and, through von Ribbentrop, had asked her to 'arrange a match' between the future King Edward VIII and her daughter, Princess Frederika.* Understandably, the Princess professed herself 'astounded'[5] by Hitler's proposal.

Now, in London, the Duke of Coburg had several discussions with King Edward VIII and from him he gathered that the new British monarch was very kindly disposed towards the idea of an Anglo-German alliance. It was *'for him* an urgent necessity and a guiding principle for British foreign policy,'[6] reported the gratified Duke. It is now known that King Edward VIII was indeed very warmly disposed towards Germany and that, in the future, there was to be considerable hobnobbing with the Nazi hierarchy. The Duke ends his report by writing that, 'The King asked me to visit him frequently in order that confidential matters might be more speedily clarified

---

* Princess Frederika (1917–81) afterwards married the future King Paul I of the Hellenes (1901–1964).

in this way. I promised – subject to the Fuhrer's approval – to fly to London at any time he wished.'[7]

It is highly unlikely that Princess Alice knew anything about her brother's commission for the Fuhrer – 'the infamous Hitler'[8] as she called him. She would have known that, as President of the Anglo-German Fellowship, her brother was anxious to promote understanding between the two countries but as his commission for the Fuhrer was a highly confidential one, the Duke would hardly have told his sister about it. Her only published comment on the political aspects of her brother's stay is a mention of a luncheon at the German Embassy as the guest of Joachim von Ribbentrop, the German Ambassador. She described his bombastic references to the 'new Germany' as 'most objectionable.'

She has another, characteristically amusing, aside as well. Recognising one of the paintings in the Embassy and knowing something of the Nazis' propensity for helping themselves to other people's works of art, she greatly disconcerted Ribbentrop by pointedly asking 'how he came by a picture belonging to my Uncle Willy Wurttemberg'.[9]

2

To the distress and embarrassment caused by her brother's association with the Nazis there was now added the distress and embarrassment caused by King Edward VIII's association with Mrs Simpson. But whereas the Duke of Coburg's behaviour affected the British monarchy only marginally, King Edward VII's behaviour affected it very drastically indeed.

The story of King Edward VII's abdication is too well known to bear repeating here. The Athlones' part in it is concerned mainly with Queen Mary; throughout that fateful year, they gave her all the comfort and support they could. 'I thought how wise King George had been in not wishing this much-loved brother to be separated from her,'[10] said Queen Mary's lady-in-waiting and friend, the Countess of Airlie.

Never easy in the company of her own children, the Queen came to lean more and more on her brother and his wife. That summer she came to stay with them at Brantridge Park and one may be sure that the Queen discussed her son and Mrs Simpson. Following his much-publicised cruise on the *Nahlin*, when he and Mrs Simpson were seen openly together, Queen Mary began to receive countless letters from British residents abroad, all shocked by what they had read in their papers about the King (the loyal British Press was keeping a discreet silence on that matter) and urging her to do something about it before it was too late.

There was nothing she could do. On 3 December 1936, the British Press finally broke its silence and the news of the King's wish to marry Mrs Simpson appeared in all the London papers. The hitherto unsuspecting British public was surprised and horrified.

The Athlones had moved to Marlborough House to be with Queen Mary during this agonising time (they were to remain with her throughout the abdication crisis) and the three of them were equally stunned by the virulent tone of the Press. The very institution of monarchy seemed to be under attack. Typically, Queen Mary decided that some sort of public gesture of reassurance was called for. Accompanied by her brother and sister-in-law and by her daughter the Princess Royal, the Queen drove out on the afternoon that the news broke to see the smoking ruins of the Crystal Palace. The sight of these four members of the royal family viewing the burnt-out shell of the Crystal Palace as though nothing in the world were wrong had the intended effect on public opinion.

And Lord Athlone and Princess Alice were still by the Queen's side when the final scene in the Abdication drama was played: the ex-King's farewell broadcast to his former subjects. King Edward VIII had signed his Instrument of Abdication on 10 December 1936 and on the following evening he invited the members of his family – the new monarch, King George VI (the new Queen was ill with influenza), Queen Mary, the Princess Royal, his two other brothers, the Dukes of Gloucester and Kent, and Lord Athlone and Princess Alice – to dinner at White Lodge. After dinner he drove up to Windsor Castle to make his broadcast and then came back to say his farewells. He left the country at midnight.

'The shock of the abdication . . .' says Princess Alice, 'was a terrible disappointment to poor sorrowing [Queen Mary].[11] It was hardly less of a shock to the Princess herself. With her own emotions under such rigid control, she found King Edward VIII's decision all but inexplicable. She might have sympathised with his dilemma but she would never have condoned his action. Princess Alice always maintained – mistakenly – that one had to have been born royal in order to cope with the strains of what she called an arduous profession. So for the King to forswear his royal birth and his royal training was inexcusable. Lord Athlone was equally disapproving. He would speak bitterly of his nephew's 'absolute folly in mucking up his life and position'.[12] In later years, Princess Alice's comment on what she regarded as the King's shameful dereliction of duty was to be typical. 'He was *very* naughty,'[13] she would declare. And, to the end, she would always refer to the Duchess of Windsor as *'that woman'*.[14]

3

Two more joyous royal occasions took place during the next few months. The first was the wedding, in January 1937, of Princess Alice's cousin once removed, Princess Juliana of the Netherlands.

On a day of bright winter sunshine – 7 January 1937 – the 27-year-old Princess Juliana was married to the 25-year-old Prince Bernhard of

Lippe-Biesterfeld. There were two ceremonies in The Hague that day: a civil ceremony in the Town Hall and a religious ceremony in the Jacobkerk. The Calvinistic severity of the church – no altar, no choir, no decorations, very little stained glass – served as an excellent background for the brilliance of the uniforms and dresses. And looking even more decorative and distinguished than most were Lord Athlone and Princess Alice: he in a scarlet tunic, she in a gown of pastel blue, sporting the orange ribbon of the Order of Orange-Nassau.

Prince Bernhard, in agreeing to take Princess Juliana as his wife, gave his resounding *Ja* 'in a tone which rang through the church and was heard from loud-speakers all over The Hague and beyond, to the delight of the crowds'.[15]

A few months later, on 12 May 1937, the Athlones played their parts in the Coronation of yet another of Lord Athlone's nephews – King George VI.* While Princess Alice drove in the carriage procession with Prince and Princess Arthur of Connaught, Lord Athlone rode with the rest of the sovereign's personal aides-de-camp: the Duke of Gloucester, the Duke of Kent, Lord Louis Mountbatten and the Earl of Harewood. Of the four Coronations that the Princess was to attend during her lifetime, she considered King George VI's Coronation to be the most moving. More than most, perhaps, she appreciated

---

* In this Coronation year. Princess Alice was awarded the GBE (Dame Grand Cross of the Order of the British Empire).

the anguish of the events that had led up to this scene of 'unforgettable splendour'.[16] She realised, too, what it was costing her husband's tense, insecure and diffident young nephew to be crowned King. 'I thought Bertie looked too wonderful,' she says, 'as he stood at the altar divested of his robes and wearing only knee-breeches and shirt, which suited his fine figure.'[17] Wonderful, but also very vulnerable.

Yet, again more than most, Princess Alice realised that the new King had certain things in his favour: a brand of quiet courage, an unshakable sense of duty and a family on whose support he could always rely. This family was composed of two parts: the greater royal family of which the Athlones were such stalwart members, and the King's more immediate family – his mother, the magnificent Queen Mary, his two charming little daughters, Princess Elizabeth and Princess Margaret Rose, and his wife, Queen Elizabeth, who had, like Princess Alice, the charm, optimism and serenity of spirit that helps make the royal burden a little less heavy to bear.

4

While Europe moved ever more surely towards war, the Athlones were able to enjoy, for a few weeks at least, a spell of pure escapism: early in 1938 they visited Saudi Arabia. For Princess Alice, this was to be a 'wonderful Odyssey, as romantic as the Arabian Nights'.[18]

The visit had come about through an accidental meeting with Crown Prince Saud, at Ascot, some eighteen months before. To make conversation, the Princess had said how sorry she was never to have been to Saudi Arabia. Immediately the Crown Prince suggested that she visit the country. But surely, she demurred, no European woman ever visited Saudi Arabia. That, he said, would make no difference. The only problem would be that she would have to sleep in tents. As sleeping in tents – or even in the open without tents – had never bothered the intrepid Princess Alice, the Crown Prince's invitation was accepted.

In the months that followed, this casually extended and cheerfully accepted invitation took on a more formal aspect. The Foreign Office decided that the Earl of Athlone and Princess Alice would pay an official visit to King Abdul Aziz, better known as Ibn Saud, as the representatives of the British sovereign. The visit, it was said, would be without political significance. But no royal visit, other than a strictly private one, is ever without political significance and the Athlones' Saudi Arabian journey was no exception. By this exchange of royal courtesies the Foreign Office hoped to strengthen the Anglo-Arab *entente.* Certainly this was how Mussolini viewed the projected tour. The Italian Press saw it in terms of a nefarious British plot to counteract Italy's recent conquest of Abyssinia.

And so, for the first stages of their Middle-Eastern journey, the Athlones were given what Princess

Alice called 'the usual V.I.P. treatment'. With Lord Frederick Cambridge[*] as aide-de-camp, they sailed from England in the P. and O. liner *Narkunda*. In Gibraltar there was a luncheon at Government House; at Port Said they were met by Prince Mohammed Ali, a host of British and Egyptian notables and what the Princess describes as 'thousands of photographers'; and in Cairo they were entertained by King Farouk.

Princess Alice and Lady Lampson, wife of the British Ambassador Sir Miles Lampson, visited King Farouk's 16-year-old Queen. She was 'very sweet and gay . . . dressed in semi-evening with lots of diamonds, of which she was very proud', writes Princess Alice.

The Athlones' reception at Jeddah, where they arrived from Port Sudan in the *Enterprise* on 25 February 1938, was even more formal. To the thudding of a 21 – gun salute, a royal launch carried them from the *Enterprise* to the shore, where they were officially welcomed by King Ibn Saud's second son, Emir Faisal. Dressed in billowing robes of black and gold and surrounded by 'wild-looking creatures in long garments and with long hair, carrying rifles and swords'. Emir Faisal led them through a jostling crowd to a semi-circle of gilt, Louis XVI chairs where they were served with the customary coffee and

---

[*] Lord Frederick Cambridge born in 1907, was the second son of Lord Athlone's late brother Dolly, Marquess of Cambridge. He was to die, unmarried, in 1940. His elder brother George, 2nd Marquess of Cambridge (1895–1981), was always 'a tower of strength' to the Athlones.

sherbet. After the presentation of various dignitaries they were driven to the Kandara Palace.

To Princess Alice, as she took in the details of this fascinating scene – the narrow streets, the picturesquely-robed Arabs, the hordes of pilgrims, the houses with their high wooden balconies – it all seemed 'like *Chu Chin Chow* without the naked ladies'.

On the following day they met the King. The 58-year-old King Ibn Saud was one of the great characters of the Middle East. His climb to power had started almost forty years before when, as a very young man leading a handful of followers, he had captured the fort of Riyadh from a rival dynasty. Since then, and with British encouragement, this astute and ruthless warrior had created a united and powerful kingdom, covering the greater part of Arabia, out of a collection of sheikdoms and emirates. By now he was the absolute ruler of the independent and internationally recognised country of Saudi Arabia. His relations with Britain, with whom he had concluded a series of agreements during his rise to eminence, were extremely cordial.

The Athlones were captivated by King Ibn Saud. He was every Englishman's idea of a desert chieftain: huge, hawk-nosed, courteous, courageous, masterful. The couple became, says Princess Alice, the King's 'hero-worshippers'. Everything about him seemed tinged with romance: the way he sat cross-legged on the floor, the way his tough bodyguard with their 'fierce bird faces' never left his side, the graphic way he told them about his seizure of Riyadh so many years before.

'It really was thrilling to watch his expressive face, more often than not amused at himself and gesticulating with his fine hands, with very turned-back thumbs.'

At the various official functions Princess Alice soon grew accustomed to being the only woman present. For the King's dinner party she wore a demure black dress. 'I felt the King would be less disgusted with me in that attire, as he had never in his life sat next to any woman at meals. I wondered afterwards if he might not have heard some lurid tales from his son about semi-nude English ladies at banquets and was disappointed with me!'

There were other things to which the Princess had to accustom herself: the gigantic meals at which sixteen whole sheep, complete with eyes, would be roasted; the huge picnic tents with their carpets and sofas and cushions; the attendants who hung onto their rifles or daggers even when serving coffee; the lavatory tents with their two holes dug side by side in the sand.

After five days the official part of the Athlones' visit came to an end. They took their leave of the 'entrancing' King Ibn Saud and, on his suggestion, the Princess went to say goodbye to two of his wives. Both were exquisitely dressed in gold-embroidered gowns, spangled veils and glittering jewellery. Three of the King's fifty-nine children were also brought in to greet the visitor.

'Scent was poured on our hands and we ate sweets, and incense was burned . . .'[19] says Princess Alice.

For the following three weeks the party travelled in a convoy of cars and lorries across the Saudi Arabian desert to the Persian Gulf. Both Lord Athlone and Princess Alice wore Arab dress. Enveloped in an abba and heavily veiled, the Princess was indistinguishable from any other Arab woman except when a sudden gust of wind lifted her garments to reveal, as she puts it, 'my very English coat and skirt'.[20] Lord Athlone looked magnificent in his robes.

The couple were equally well prepared for what they were to see. Both were conscientious travellers and before leaving London had read extensively on the subject of Saudi Arabia. In Jeddah they had listened to a talk by the famous Arabist and explorer, H. St J.B. Philby.* Philby, reported Princess Alice, – 'was not liked by the English colony, as he had become a Muslim and took meals twice a day with the King.'[21]

Their journey was an amalgam of discomfort, adventure and high romance. Crossing desolate plains they were bogged down in deep sand, and suffered the attacks of swarms of flies; they drank coffee that tasted like earth and ate food that gave them, as the Princess so graphically put it, 'a bad go of "teasy weazy in the trash box" at dawn'.[22] But there were marvellous compensations: lavishly furnished tents, crystal-clear air, romantic palm groves, lush oases,

---

* The father of the notorious spy, Kim Philby.

350

rocky banks of lavender, medieval-looking towns, picturesque mosques, white-washed forts (including the legendary one captured by King Ibn Suad at Riyadh [†]), overwhelming hospitality. They rode on camels, they shot sand-grouse, they slept in palaces, they shopped in souks, they took endless photographs.

To Princess Alice, it was all enchantment. When, finally, they arrived at the Caltex Oil Company's camp on the Persian Gulf, with its barbed-wire barricade, spotless grounds, neat bungalows, and bland American meals they seemed to have come to another world. The contrast was even more pronounced when the couple flew back over part of the same primitive, timeless, romantic desert kingdom in a Royal Air Force plane to Cairo. [*]

In just over a year, the indefatigable Athlones were back in the Middle East. They went to Teheran to represent King George VI at the civil marriage ceremonies of the Crown Prince of Iran, Shahpur Mohammed Riza [†] and Princess Fawzia of Egypt. The religious ceremonies had already taken place in Cairo. For four days the Athlones played their part in the extravagant ceremonial and, when it was over, very characteristically set off on a nine-day tour of Iran. They arrived back in London, by air, on 14 May 1939.

[†] Princess Alice was only the third European woman to enter the 'forbidden city' of Riyadh.
[*] A full account of the journey is given by Princess Alice in her book *For my Grandchildren* (Evans Brothers, London, 1966)
[†] Afterwards the Shah of Iran (1919–1980)

5

Unlike most members of the royal family, Princess Alice always had a wide circle of friends. For those on, or near to, a throne, it is not always easy to cultivate friendships beyond the confines of the family. In fact it is not even advisable. The mystique of monarchy is best served by keeping a certain distance between Crown and people: too much familiarity may well breed, if not exactly contempt, a lack of proper awe or even proper respect. For this reason most reigning families remain somewhat guarded, somewhat aloof, somewhat loath to establish everyday relationships with outsiders. This was, and is, particularly true of most members of the family of King George V and Queen Mary.

But Princess Alice's position had always been slightly different. Born a fringe member of the royal family, and raised in a relatively enlightened way, she was able to lead a fairly normal private life and to travel in a fairly informal fashion. Not always having to watch every word she said and being, by nature, gregarious, friendly and enquiring, Princess Alice had been able to form several close and lasting relationships.

She brought to these friendships a great warmth of heart. For underneath the superficial characteristics – the cheerfulness, the heartiness, the impishness – was a strain of seriousness, a great depth of feeling. More and more, during the Princess's middle years, did people remark on her kindness, her tenderness and her fund of sympathy for those in trouble. She was never too busy to write a line to someone in distress. And this did not apply only to her close friends. People with whom she had a mere passing acquaintance were often astonished to receive a letter from Princess Alice sympathising with them in some grief about which she could only have heard in a roundabout fashion. Nor was this simply *noblesse oblige;* such sentiments clearly came from the heart.

To those whom she knew well, this unfeigned sympathy was always a source of great solace. Her letter to Gwelo Goodman's widow, on hearing of the death of the South African artist, was typical.

My dearest Margaret,
You have been constantly in my thoughts these past weeks, and when I think of what it must mean to you losing your beloved husband my heart breaks for you. Someone so vital, so interesting and gifted and withal so difficult to manage must leave a blank in your life perhaps no one but you can measure, although all those who love you both can apprehend a little of what it must mean.

Your delicious home was always a centre for what counted in South Africa and without, for all that was delightful and interesting and gay and lovely. The passing of Gwelo will leave a great emptiness which all his friends will greatly feel. You know how fond both my husband and I were of him and I rejoice to think he considered us true friends of his.

In all your grief and loneliness it must be a consolation to realize how much you were to him and in what a marvellous way you sheltered him and smoothed life for him and sustained him in all difficulties. You indeed complemented Gwelo; you were a fascinating pair.

And now Cape Town will never be the same, to me, at least. I do pray and hope that you will feel the sheltering love of your friends in your sorrow, and that you will in time be able to pick up the threads of life again, for there are so many who need you and your ever-ready sympathy. . . .

With much love from both my husband and myself and our deepest, truest sympathy.

Yours affectionately,
Alice[23]

This was just one of many such letters – vivid, sensitive, heart-felt – that Princess Alice would write throughout her long life.

The same warmheartedness was evident in the Princess's dealings with the evacuees just before and during the Second World War. Before the outbreak of war, the Government decided that women and children living in dockside areas should be moved out of London to escape the anticipated bombing. As Brantridge Park lay forty-one miles from London, the Athlones immediately offered to take a contingent. The staff was moved into the main house and their quarters made ready, with extra furniture, bedding and household equipment, to receive the evacuees. The Princess was told to expect a batch of schoolchildren in the care of a headmistress; what arrived on 1 September 1939 was a party of mothers with little children hanging on to their skirts and with babies in their arms.

This influx from London's East End brought the Princess into contact with a new, very different, world. The sight of this doleful collection of evacuees 'wrung one's heart'.[24] They were pale, they were dirty, they were pathetically ill-clothed. The mothers had very little idea of how to run a home; of how to cook or sew or shop. Crushed and lethargic, they had obviously known little happiness. The Princess's heart went out to one particular woman: never having known any tenderness, she simply could not understand why the Princess and her staff were being so kind to her.

All this opened, perhaps not before time, Princess Alice's eyes to the conditions under which so many of the poor lived in the great cities. She found it 'a sad reflection on social conditions in London in 1939'.[25]

Princess Alice did all she could for the evacuees at Brantridge. She had always been good with children: she was able to enter into the spirit of their games and to communicate to them her interests and enthusiasms. She would take these slum-bred children for long walks through the woods and lanes, explaining to them something of the mysteries and joys of country life. She would teach them the names of trees and flowers, she would stop them from eating green apples and explain away their terror of owls. She made their first wartime Christmas magical with a huge Christmas tree, lights, decorations, presents and carols. She was delighted to notice that by going early to bed instead of being allowed to play in the London streets until all hours, the children soon lost their wan, exhausted look. In the end, she says, she became devoted to them.

In those tense, strangely unreal months just before and just after the outbreak of the Second World War, the Athlones continued to carry out, as one observer has put it, 'the round of duties which make but little show and yet count for so much in the life of a country.'[26] At sixty-five Lord Athlone was too old for active military service. He had to be content with issuing appeals, making speeches, accepting the post of Commandant of a Balloon Section. Both he and Princess Alice felt the lack of meaningful employment very keenly and longed to be serving their country in a more useful fashion. There surely had to be some way in which their considerable experience and still unimpaired energies could be put to use.

There was a way. In February 1940 Lord Tweedsmuir,* the Governor-General of Canada, died after an operation. There was very little doubt, in official circles, as to who should succeed him. Both the Canadian Prime Minister, William Lyon Mackenzie King, and the High Commissioner for Canada in London, that ardent royalist, Vincent Massey, favoured the Earl of Athlone. In fact, during King George VI's tour of Canada the year before, Mackenzie King had suggested to him that Lord Athlone succeed Lord Tweedsmuir. Now, on Lord Tweedsmuir's death, the Canadian Prime Minister cabled the King to ask if he could submit Lord Athlone's name as Governor-General.

In his discussions with King George VI, Lord Athlone was characteristically modest about accepting the post: he wondered if his nephew should not try for a younger man. But in the end he agreed to accept it for two years only. He was to stay for six. 'We both appreciate the compliment,' reported Lord Athlone to his sister Queen Mary, 'and I hope in spite of age I shall be able to carry out the work.'[27] On 3 April 1940 an official announcement from Buckingham Palace let it be known that the Earl of Athlone had accepted the office of Governor-General of Canada. Over a quarter of a century since last being selected for the same position – in the

---

* John Buchan, the novelist.

summer of 1914 – the Athlones were once more preparing to take it up.

'We feel that we shall love Canada,' announced Lord Athlone, 'and hope to be worthy of the great privileges and the opportunity which lie before us.'[28]

The Athlones' natural distress at leaving their home, their family, their friends and their country was heightened by the dramatic events which happened to coincide with their time of departure. Their last few weeks in England were coloured by horrifying news of the German victories in Western Europe. They had only just set sail, in strict wartime secrecy, when they heard of the fall of France.

It was in what Princess Alice has called 'this desperate time'[29] that they steamed into Halifax, Nova Scotia, after a zigzag voyage across the Atlantic. To keep the time of their arrival secret it had been decided to break the tradition whereby a new Governor-General is sworn in on first landing on Canadian soil. The ceremony was to be performed, the following day, in Ottawa. So it was in far from jubilant circumstances that the Athlones arrived in Canada. 'The whole proceeding, accompanied by torrents of rain, was quite mournful,' says the Princess, 'as we were all oppressed by the fall of France and our own serious predicament.'[30]

It was an inauspicious start to what would prove to be yet another splendid chapter in the life of Princess Alice.

PART FIVE
RIDEAU HALL

CHAPTER FOURTEEN

1

The Earl of Athlone was officially installed as Governor-General of Canada on 21 June 1940. At half past eleven that morning the viceregal couple arrived at Union Station, Ottawa and the brilliance of the official welcome to the nation's capital more than compensated for the bleakness of their arrival at Halifax the day before.

To the applauding Canadians thronging the station entrance, the Plaza and Parliament Hill, the first sight of the Earl of Athlone and Princess Alice came as something of a surprise. At a time when the reproduction of colour photography was still comparatively rare, people had been accustomed to seeing the couple pictured in black and white; both tended to look rather stiff, formal and unsympathetic in official portraits. Surprisingly, for someone of her assured and extrovert nature, Princess Alice photographed particularly badly: except in casual pictures, she wore a severe and guarded look.

361

Now, seen in the flesh on this sparkling summer's day, the Athlones created an entirely different impression. In morning suit and carrying a top hat, Lord Athlone looked not only dignified and impressive but handsome and genial. Princess Alice looked enchanting. 'I thought I was very smart',[1] she says in her engagingly frank fashion. And so she was. Bright-eyed, silver-haired and gaily smiling, she exuded warmth. The frequently expressed fears that 'the simple democratic atmosphere of the capital city will be damaged by the introduction of Old World pomps and celebrations'[2] were instantly dispelled by the sight of these two good-looking, unpretentious and friendly people.

From the station the Athlones drove to the superbly situated Parliament Buildings. Here, in the Senate Chamber, the Earl of Athlone was formally installed as the sixteenth Governor-General of Canada. In his low, clear voice Lord Athlone replied to the Prime Minister's address of welcome, ending his speech with 'a strong belief in ultimate victory for the Allies and the restoration of peace in the world'.[3] From the Parliament Buildings the couple drove to their new home, Rideau Hall.

Situated high above the junction of the Ottawa and Rideau Rivers, Rideau Hall had served as Canada's Government House for some sixty-five years. Built as a home for Thomas Mackay, the founder of the settlement that became Ottawa, the house had been greatly altered and extended through the years. It was now a vast, rambling, irregular building, described, by one Governor-General, as 'a very big, comfortable English country house'[4] and by another as having 'a certain lovable eccentricity'.' A quarter of a century or so before, the house had been given cohesion by the erection of a new façade – a flat, formal, pcdimentcd grey stone front sporting a huge coat of arms. Its style was described, somewhat guardedly, as 'adapted Florentine'.[6] The result was not unimpressive, but the interior remained the cheerful hotchpotch of rooms – some splendid, some awkward – that it had always been. The house was set amid sweeping lawns and spacious, well-wooded grounds.

Princess Alice's first impression of Rideau Hall was slightly disconcerting. Although it was a beautiful summer's day, all the blinds had been drawn and the lights were on. Canadians, she decided, turned in early. Nor was the arrangement of the furniture much to her taste. With typical energy, the Princess almost immediately set to work reorganising things. 'I turned all the furniture upside down,'[7] she says. In the Long Gallery, where all the chairs and sofas were solemnly ranged against the walls, she made what she called three encampments: 'so that you could sit and talk in groups and feel more comfortable.'[8] Over the fireplace in the main drawing-room she hung a Laszlo portrait of herself.

Because of wartime restrictions, the Princess could make few radical changes but she was able to get rid of at least some of the last vestiges of the

363

Willingdon regime. Lady Willingdon, whose husband had been Governor-General from 1926 to 1931 (and who went on to become Viceroy of India), had had a passion for mauve. Everything, it is said, 'from her writing paper to the exteriors of their railway carriages'[9] was mauve. With Lady Willingdon, sighed Sir Edwin Lutyens, it was a case of 'mauve qui peut'.[10] Princess Alice had the satisfaction of banishing the last of Lady Willingdon's favourite colour by dying a quantity of mauve satin curtains.

As in South Africa, Princess Alice quickly established herself as an interested and practical mistress of the house. She organised things more efficiently, she eliminated waste, she paid daily visits to the kitchen, she discussed things with the Comptroller and the housekeeper, she saw to the flowers, she kept an eye on all arrangements. 'She knew if a duster was misplaced',[11] claims one member of the staff. A small pad and a silver pencil lay always beside her place at table for the jotting down of notes about the running of the household. In next to no time she was busy laying out one of her beloved rock gardens; she never travelled without a garden trowel for digging up plants to take back to Rideau Hall. And if gardening in the short Canadian summer proved less rewarding than in Britain or South Africa, the five hothouses at Rideau Hall made up for any lack of outdoor flowers.

The Athlones were fortunate in their staff. Despite the wartime lack of candidates, they had managed to retain or employ the services of a highly qualified team. Lord Athlone's Secretary was Sir Shuldham Redfern, who had been with the previous Governor-General, Lord Tweedsmuir. The Deputy Secretary was Mr F.L.C. Pereira. Major Geoffrey Eastwood was Comptroller of the Household; Colonel Willis O'Connor was Senior aide-de-camp and the other aides were Capt. Edson Sherwood RCNVR, Lieut, the Hon. Ernle Chatfield RNVR, Capt. Tom Goff and Lieut. Dunn Lantier RCN.* The Princess's lady-in-waiting was the Hon. Ariel Baird who was to be succeeded by first Miss Vera Grenfell and then Miss Sylvia Evans WRCAF.

With the Statute of Westminster – the formal recognition of the Dominion Status won by Hertzog and Mackenzie King at the Imperial Conference of 1926 – having reduced the Governor-General's status to purely that of the representative of the Crown, and with the diplomatic representative of the British Government now being the British High Commissioner in Canada, it was decided that it was no longer necessary for the Governor-General to retain an office on Parliament Hill. He could do all his work at Rideau Hall. So the former state cloakrooms at the back of the house were converted into offices and it was from here that Lord Athlone conducted affairs.

---

* Among later aides-de-camp were Captain L. Leveson-Gower, Captain Mark Clayton, Flying Officer W. O'Brien RCAF, Squadron Leader P. Leath RCAF, Captain Neville Usshcr and Captain the Earl of Harcwood.

Thus efficiently and comfortably installed at Rideau Hall, the Athlones embarked on their six-year-long term of duty in what was, after the Soviet Union, the largest country in the world.

2

In Canada, the Athlones faced almost as complex a situation as they had in South Africa. There might not be a similar colour problem (the Indian tribes formed a minority group) but there was certainly a similar racial one. Of Canada's population of almost twelve million, fifty per cent were of Anglo-Saxon stock, thirty per cent of French stock and twenty per cent of more recent European origin – Ukrainians, Poles, Germans and Scandinavians. The most serious division was between the English-speaking and French-speaking Canadians. 'I expected to find a contest between a government and a people', ran the famous passage in Lord Durham's report of a century or so before. 'I found two nations warring in the bosom of a single state. I found a struggle, not of principles, but of races.'[12]

His Lordship's findings were hardly less true now. The French-Canadians – or Canadians of French origin as they preferred to be known – living chiefly in the province of Quebec, remained determined to resist the cultural, economic and religious encroachments of the English-speaking section. *La survivance* was their rallying cry. There was even a section amongst them who resented becoming embroiled in what they regarded as a British war.

As with the Afrikaners in South Africa, the Athlones showed great tact in their dealings with these French-Canadians. Their annual visit to Quebec City ensured that the community had no cause to feel slighted and, speaking fluent French, the couple were able to establish friendly contact with all sorts of French-speaking Canadians. In any case, the issue of separation, for all its importance, was not in those days quite the burning issue it was to become during the 1960s.

Nor were all English-speaking Canadians unequivocally pro-British. On the contrary, for well over half a century Canada had been trying to free itself from British domination; and since the end of the First World War a strong tide of nationalism had been sweeping through the country. At the Imperial Conference of 1926 Canada's Mackenzie King had been every bit as determined as South Africa's Hertzog to establish his country's autonomy. Through their unremitting efforts the old Empire had been re-defined as 'a group of autonomous communities within the British Empire, equal in status, in no way subordinate one to another in any aspect of their domestic or external affairs, though united by a common allegiance to the Crown, and freely associated as members of the British Commonwealth of Nations'.[13]

Throughout the 1930s Canada had become increasinlgy isolationist, increasingly anxious not to become involved in a European war, increasingly North American, rather than British, in character. Although there was never any serious doubt that, in the event of a war, Canada would support Britain, she had made no more effort than anyone else to prepare for such a war. Comforted by the presence of the powerful United States, separated from Europe by the Atlantic Ocean, placing her trust in the League of Nations, the country undertook no long-term military preparations.

Yet, once war broke out, the Canadian response was immediate and impressive. There was what one member of Lord Athlone's staff described as a surge of power to the centre, with all local, racial and political issues being subordinated to the national war effort. Canadians, including many French-speaking Canadians, volunteered in vast numbers to fight abroad and, by her massive wartime contribution, Canada earned for herself the title of 'the arsenal of democracy'. Throughout Lord Athlone's term of office, Canada was, above all else, a nation at war.

3

Guiding the Canadian ship of state through these various crosscurrents was the Prime Minister, William Lyon Mackenzie King. He was a strange man. Exactly the same age as Lord Athlone, King had first become Liberal Prime Minister almost twenty years before and was to be the dominant figure in Canadian politics for well over a quarter of a century.

A short, podgy, unimpressive-looking bachelor ('Our dear little roly poly friend'[14] was one previous First Lady's sardonic description of him) Mackenzie King had gained a formidable political reputation. The over-riding aim of his political life was national unity. To achieve this far from simple aim King employed a bewildering variety of tactics, ranging from those of the utmost caution to those of complete ruthlessness. His ploy was to avoid all divisive issues. Everyone, and particularly the French-Canadians, from whom the Liberal party drew some of its strength, must be kept sweet in the cause of a united Canada. But even those who appreciated and applauded King's achievements found themselves disconcerted by his methods: by his unpalatable blend of timidity, astuteness and hardness.

Lester Pearson, the young diplomat who was himself to become Canadian Prime Minister one day, speaks of Mackenzie King's 'enigmatic and contradictory personality, with that combination of charming friendliness and self-centred calculation, of kindness and ruthlessness, of political vision and personal pettiness'.[15]

Mackenzie King's attitude towards the Athlones, as towards everything, was ambivalent. A dedicated worker for a Canada free from British influence, he was a no less dedicated upholder of the Crown. He was highly gratified by the thought that he, the grandson of William Lyon Mackenzie, that fiery rebel against British rule, should be the one to advise the King to appoint the husband of Queen Victoria's granddaughter as Governor-General of an autonomous Canada. Yet he resented having to give precedence to Lord Athlone. It was, he confided to his diary, 'an absurdity for a Prime Minister of a country to have second place in the public eye to anyone in official position not belonging to one's own country and in fact appointed by the Government of the country itself.'[16]

On a personal level, relations between the Athlones and Mackenzie King were cordial enough. Princess Alice found him 'very easy to talk to and very sympathetic',[17] while the Prime Minister, in turn, found the Governor-General 'companionable, with no affectation or side. He knows a good deal about military affairs, is first and foremost a soldier.' Princess Alice, continued Mackenzie King in his diary, 'is exceptionally clever, very charming; exceedingly intelligent and active.'[18]

Yet the Prime Minister was quick to take offence at whatever he – quite mistakenly – considered to be a royal snub. Once, after an electoral victory, he bitterly resented the fact that Lord Athlone had not written to congratulate him. And worse still, confided King to his diary, the Governor-General 'said very little in the way of congratulations in my talk with him'. The Princess, he adds, 'who was in the garden, did not come in to extend her congratulations, as I would have thought they both would have, our relations being as close as they are. The trouble with these people is that their concern lies with what is going best to meet their own convenience. There are few if any wiser sayings than: "Put not your faith in Princes." I am beginning more and more to see that the upholding of monarchy is a form of idolatry.'[19]

The Prime Minister's attitude was indefensible. What he was forgetting was that in party politics princes must always remain impartial. Lord Athlone, and Princess Alice for that matter, were always meticulous about keeping within their constitutional limits; it was certainly not for them to write and congratulate him on a party political victory. Impartiality had been one of Lord Athlone's strengths in South Africa; and it was no less one of his strengths in Canada.

Although, for most of the time, the political relationship between Governor-General and Prime Minister was amicable, there were occasional moments of friction. Politically, says Princess Alice, 'Prime Minister Mackenzie King was not always easy to get along with.'[20] Both Lord Athlone and Mackenzie King had quick tempers; Princess Alice speaks of her relief when raised voices behind the study door did not mean a quarrel. The Earl of Athlone, an upright, unsubtle, transparently honest man intent on upholding the British connection and of doing everything in his power to support embattled Britain, could well have found the Prime Minister's methods too tortuous. King was, as Princess Alice puts it, 'somewhat unpredictable where politics were concerned'.[21]

Nor, in Lord Athlone's opinion, did the Prime Minister keep him well enough informed on what was going on. 'Prime Minister,' the Governor-General would say, shaking his finger at Mackenzie King, 'you've been very naughty lately.'[22] And it is significant that when, at one stage during the war, Mackenzie King was visiting England, King George VI asked him how often he reported to the Governor-General. Churchill, claimed the British monarch, came to see him every week. Had Lord Athlone complained about Mackenzie King's neglect?

Mackenzie King, on the other hand, felt that his efforts on behalf of Britain were not enough appreciated. 'Churchill is pretty much alone in having given any recognition in a personal way of what I have done for the British Crown, its people and the Empire, throughout the years of my life,' he grumbled. 'Is it any wonder that so many of our people feel much more in touch with the United States than with the United Kingdom, and that it is so difficult to keep the two together?'[23]

Yet at no stage, apparently, did Lord Athlone ever suspect that Mackenzie King was harbouring such resentment. 'Totally self-confident, it would never have occurred to him,' says one of the Governor-General's aides, 'that anyone might not have been happy with him.'[24] Nor were Lord Athlone's political attitudes simply blimpish or jingoistic. After a lifetime of service to the Crown he understood the Canadian, as well as the imperial, situation very well indeed.

'There was, I believe, at one time a slight prejudice against the use of the word "Empire" in relation to Canada,' he once said in a speech at a Joint Meeting of the Canadian and Empire Clubs in Toronto. 'It was, I think, a natural prejudice, for such expressions as "Empire" and "Imperial" carry with them a flavour of dominion on the one part and subservience on the other. My own feeling is that Canada has by now reached such a degree of complete independence and self-assurance as to render unobjectionable the use of a word which connotes a brotherhood of peoples of which we are justly and mightily proud. . . . We must never forget that the Throne, as we know it and have made it, is far greater than anyone who can ever occupy it. It is the keystone of the way of life and system of government, with all its imperfections, we believe to be the best that has yet been devised.'[25]

And, as a representative of the Crown, Lord Athlone carried out his duties impartially, impressively and tirelessly. The powers and the prerogatives of his office might have been curtailed but he could still wield considerable influence. 'He had many qualities fitting him for the post,' claimed Vincent Massey, who was Governor-General from 1952 to 1959. 'He shared his family's ability to come down by a sort of instinct on the right side of a public issue. Like his sister Queen Mary, he had an unbending sense of duty.

He possessed an endearing nature and the engaging attributes of warmth and personal modesty. [26]

Added to this, his dignified bearing and military background made him, in the words of one of his staff", 'the perfect wartime Governor-General.'[27]

4

'Lord Athlone,' wrote Vincent Massey, 'was brilliantly supported by Princess Alice. Government House has rarely had a chatelaine with her perception, imagination, and capacity for friendship – and a trait no less endearing: frankness and candour.'[28]

Princess Alice's life in Canada bore little resemblance to the life she had lived in South Africa. So many things – the climate, the terrain, the people, the wartime conditions, the fact that she was older – were different. The times were more desperate; the tone of the regime was more solemn. There were fewer private visits, fewer informal occasions, fewer parties. The Princess was often in uniform: 'our chief preoccupation,' as she puts it, was inspecting 'endless, endless war factories'.[29]

The Athlones' concern about the war seldom left them. They worried about its general progress and they worried about its more personal aspects: the plight of their various continental relations, the fortunes of Lord Athlone's sister Queen Mary, the bombing of Buckingham Palace and of Kensington Palace. The first news of the Kensington Palace bombing was that the building had been 'gutted';[30] only later did they hear that their apartments had not suffered too severely and that at least their pictures and furniture were safe.

Lord Athlone's reaction on first hearing the news of the Kensington Palace bombing – by telephone from his Secretary – was typical. Not only did he show no emotion; he did not even comment on it. His Secretary, expecting some expression of shock or distress, was astonished to hear Lord Athlone (who was about to visit the United States) casually remark that 'Roosevelt says that we needn't bring tail coats'.[31]

But things were not all gloom. If Canada was different from South Africa in many ways, it was not unlike it in some. There were the same vast, in fact vaster, distances to be travelled; there was equally spectacular scenery; there was the same warm welcome wherever they went. If the English-speaking Canadians were less demonstrative than the English-speaking South Africans, they were just as hospitable and just as friendly. And wherever she appeared, Princess Alice radiated the same charm and good humour and approachability. Throughout Canada she has left countless memories of her easy-going informality, her unfeigned interest and her spontaneous acts of kindness.

'Human-beings,' she once said, 'are the most fascinating study in the world; besides, I like them.'[32] It was this fascination with, and like of, human-beings, that made Princess Alice so fascinating and likeable to the Canadians.

Most of the Athlones' time was spent at Rideau Hall. Ottawa, which had been especially chosen by Queen Victoria as a compromise capital which would favour neither the English- nor the French-speaking Canadians, was a small city. In spite of its impressive, mock-Gothic Parliament Buildings with their jade-coloured turrets and soaring Peace Tower, Ottawa had an almost rural air. It has also the dubious distinction of being one of the coldest capital cities in the world.

Yet the summers in Ottawa could be hot. This was when the vice-regal couple would spend a few weeks each year in their Quebec home, the Citadel. The Citadel was a massive, star-shaped stone fort perched high above the St Lawrence River. Built by the British on top of the old French fortifications, the Citadel was entirely military in character: a conglomeration of cannon, ramparts, parade grounds, sentry-boxes and barracks. In fact, the Governor-General's residence was merely the eastern end of a long, utilitarian military building dating back to the early nineteenth century. It had been entirely modernised and redecorated some ten years before by the ineffable Lady Willingdon. 'Those who are familiar with Lady Willingdon's colour preferences,' wrote the *Canadian Homes and Gardens* gamely, 'would expect the lilacs, amethysts and soft greens. . . . [83]

During their many tours of this immense country, the Athlones would sometimes stay in the Government Houses of the various Lieutenant-Governors of each province but, more often, they remained on their train. This was the luxurious train which had been built for the Canadian tour, in 1939, of King George VI and Queen Elizabeth. The Governor-General's accommodation consisted of two coaches: a drawing-room and two bedrooms with bathrooms in one, and a dining-room and an office in the other. As in South Africa, there would be occasional breaks in this routine, when the vice-regal couple would be able to spend the sort of casual holidays they both loved.

But there was certainly no lack of informal occasions at Rideau Hall. By their first winter Lord Athlone was not only learning to skate to recorded Strauss waltzes ('we simply turned the hose on the tennis court to make a skating rink,'[34] remembers Lord Harewood, who was one of his aides) but the couple were enthusiastically tobogganing at Rockcliffe Park or walking in the nearby Gatineau Hills. When the weather was too bad they played tennis or badminton on the indoor courts.

The Athlones enjoyed an excellent relationship with their staff 'They gave us every kind of consideration,' says Neville Ussher, one of Lord Athlone's later aides. 'I was only twenty-five and had never seen the world at that level, but they were always on hand with guidance and advice. They were wonderful that way.'

Little pencilled notes, addressed to the aide-in-waiting, in Lord Athlone's beautiful handwriting, would draw their attention to this or that duty; and after some great occasion, like the Opening of Parliament, His Excellency would thank them in his characteristically bluff, if oblique, fashion. 'It went quite well, don't you think? It went quite well.'" Whenever he attended a public function or addressed an audience, Lord Athlone took endless trouble to introduce his aides as though they were personal friends or equals.

The whole atmosphere at Rideau Hall, which could have been so different, was one of 'warmth and liveliness and conviviality'.[36]

5

Within a week of the Athlones' arrival in Canada, their daughter, Lady May Abel Smith, with her three children, Anne, Richard and Elizabeth,* had arrived from England and moved into Rideau Hall. With Major Abel Smith in the Middle East on active service, it had been decided that his family would be better off in Canada. They were joined by Princess Alice's Dutch relations, Princess Juliana and her two daughters, Princess Beatrix and the 10-months-old Princess Irene. Princess Juliana's lady-in-waiting, Mrs Roell, had a little daughter with her as well. So there was certainly no lack of young company in the house. During those first weeks and months in Canada, when the news from Europe was so bad, the children 'made merriment in

---

* The Abel Smith children were Anne Mary Sibylla, born 5 September 1932; Richard Francis, born 11 October 1933; Elizabeth Alice, born 5 September 1936.

the house'; 'they helped take our minds off the seriousness of those tragic times,'[37] says the Princess.

Princess Juliana and her two daughters had been escorted to England by her husband, Prince Bernhard, just before the fall of the Netherlands on 15 May 1940. She had been followed, with the greatest reluctance, by her mother, the redoubtable Queen Wilhelmina. Little Princess Irene, who was to have been christened in state in Amsterdam that May, was christened instead in the chapel at Buckingham Palace; her godparents were Queen Elizabeth and 'the Dutch armed forces'.[38]

With the Dutch royal line of succession being so tenuous (Princess Juliana was an only child) and with the German invasion of, or at least the heavy German bombardment of, Britain being a distinct possibility during those dark days of 1940, it was decided that Princess Juliana, as heir to the Dutch throne, should move to a safer place. Canada was the obvious choice. For one thing it was important that, in the event of Queen Wilhelmina's death. Princess Juliana should be living in an Allied country where she would be allowed to exercise her royal powers: 'in a neutral country,' reckoned Queen Wilhelmina, 'this would not have been quite so certain.'[39] For another thing, Princess Juliana was related, through two of her mother's aunts, to both Lord Athlone and Princess Alice. So, on 2 June 1940, Princess Juliana and her two daughters set sail in the *Sumatra* for Halifax. Her mother and her husband remained in England. Prince Bernhard would come over to Canada whenever his military commitments allowed him to.

Princess Juliana was very much a person after Princess Alice's own heart. Unaffected, energetic and with a keen sense of humour, she wasted no time on vain regrets. 'Juliana,' says Princess Alice, 'was really magnificent. She never once complained or expressed unhappi-ness, but threw herself into everything that was being done for the war.'[40]

Always careful not to steal any of Princess Alice's thunder, Princess Juliana carried out only such official duties as concerned her Dutch fellow-countrymen. She helped with the Red Cross, she was a regular blood donor, she organised sales of work, she kept in touch with and was a source of inspiration to those of her countrymen who either lived in Canada or who were still in the fight. Both in Canada and the United States, Princess Juliana came to symbolise Dutch resistance to the Nazis.

'In Juliana,' wrote Queen Wilhelmina afterwards, 'we had a source of strength for the Dutch cause across the ocean, and a forceful representative of the nation with two of our most important allies.'[41]

In time, Princess Juliana and her family moved from Rideau Hall to a home of their own in Rockcliffe Park.

6

'The whole country,' says Princess Alice of Canada during those years of war, 'threw itself into war work and it was very inspiring to be there at that time.'[42]

But few threw themselves more wholeheartedly or were a greater inspiration to others than the Athlones themselves. During these years, when Canada was earning its title of 'the arsenal of democracy', Lord Athlone and Princess Alice were to be seen wherever efforts, great or small, were being made towards the ultimate achievement of victory.

'With simple dignity, befitting wartime conditions,' wrote one observer, 'they kept in touch with the vast variety of war effort in this wide land. They repeatedly visited hospitals, factories, the establishments of the services, Red Cross centres – all institutions and societies dedicated to winning the struggle. Nor were these duties mere formalities. The visitors brought with them the stimulation of a genuine and appreciative interest, and a desire to meet and to learn from those by whom all these efforts were being carried on.'[43]

But no matter how exhausting their daily schedule, the Athlones would never admit, not even to their staff, how tired they were. Nor did they ever complain about anything else. On the contrary, they set their much younger staff an example in vigour and cheerfulness. 'What are we doing tomorrow?' they would ask eagerly after a long day's activity. 'When do we start?'[44]

In speech after speech, Lord Athlone would urge greater efforts towards the winning of the war. 'We are not fighting only our own battles for our own freedom,' ran one of his wartime speeches. 'Never have we shouldered such an immense responsibility, never has so much depended on how we acquit ourselves. Let us have "no craven fear of being great" but let us . . . prove to mankind, as we are proving every day, that we have never been so great as in this hour of trial, and let us pay the debt we owe to our fathers that begat us by ensuring that each of our children and their children and all those who now suffer humiliation and defeat will be beholden to us for their salvation, their freedom and civilisation.'[45]

But there were occasions when he felt things so intensely that he discarded such formal phraseology and spoke from the heart. To an audience in Victoria he once declared that the importance of winning the war transcended any colonial squabbling, and that it was everyone's duty to rally round Britain. His impassioned outburst won him a standing ovation but the authorities insisted that reporters confine themselves to the undelivered, less controversial, text.

Princess Alice was equally committed to her wartime tasks, and was tireless in carrying out her often boring and exhausting duties. She spent hours in munitions plants, she tramped through shipyards, she clambered into aeroplanes, she rode in tanks, she comforted the wounded, she organised women's groups, she made speeches, she launched appeals, she chatted to thousands upon thousands of nurses or servicemen or voluntary workers. Yet she never allowed herself to look anything less than cheerful and confident. Time and again those who spoke to her, or even caught glimpses of her, mention her charm, her interest, her likeableness, and her enthusiasm.

They also mention her common sense. When, for instance, she went to Halifax to see the new naval barracks that were being built for the ratings she proved equally practical. Turning to the accompanying Admiral, she remarked briskly. 'There aren't enough hatches between the kitchen and the dining-room.'[46]

Even the Rideau Hall staff were amazed by her efficiency. She could change her outfit, they said, in ten minutes. Nor did her always fashionable appearance depend on expensive clothes. Once, when Lord Athlone was being complimented on the dress which the Princess was wearing, he admitted that it was an old one which had been 'made over'.[47] Unlike her husband, she wrote most of her own speeches, and her delivery was equally confident. All she asked was that she never be expected to speak without warning: whatever she did must be done as perfectly as possible, she maintained.

The servicemen who were invited to her regular tea dances at Rideau Hall were always delighted by the way she cheerfully joined in the dancing. 'Who', one unwitting young Air Force cadet was once heard to ask, 'is the precious white-haired lamb I've been rushing all afternoon?'[48]

And Princess Alice was no less impressed by the Canadians. Addressing the National Chapter Imperial Order Daughters of the Empire, she once spoke of the 'wonderful privilege' of being associated with a people 'who had devoted their every energy of body and mind to so stupendous a task in connection with a war carried on thousands of miles away from their shores, but who had done so in support of principles for which the British people had always been ready to sacrifice their all'.[49]

In addition to all this daunting wartime activity there were the customary vice-regal duties to be carried out: the levees, the dinners, the Openings of Parliament, the tours, the receiving and entertaining of important political figures – President Roosevelt, Winston Churchill, Charles de Gaulle, General Smuts,[*] Anthony Eden and the inimitable Madame Chiang Kai-shek, who was fondly remembered by the staff at Rideau Hall for the size of the tips when she left.

One of Churchill's visits took place in the depths of winter. Visitors coming in from the freezing cold outside often found that the friction of their shoes on the entrance hall carpets would cause an electric spark as they shook hands. And, true enough, as Lord Athlone's and Winston Churchill's fingers touched, a spark flew between them.

Churchill remained imperturbable. 'This wouldn't be a good house for courting couples,'[50] he remarked wryly.

---

[*] Smuts, always so interested in flowers, asked one of the aides to meet him an hour before breakfast so that he could be conducted round the Rideau Hall garden. The Athlones, who had hesitated to suggest something like that themselves, were delighted.

It did not take Canadians long to discover yet another facet of Princess Alice's personality: her knowledge of, and interest in, the arts. She attended, says the historian of Rideau Hall, 'literally every concert and exhibition in Ottawa'.[51] Among the recitals she attended were those of Portia White, the black contralto, Witold Malcuzynski, the exiled Polish pianist, and Yehudi Menuhin. When the cellist Gregor Piatigorsky spent the night at Rideau Hall he was discovered, the following morning, in bed with his cello: he was protecting it, he explained earnestly, from the dry air of Ottawa.

Princess Alice played hostess to the numberless actors and actresses who came to perform at charity concerts; not only to such long-established stars as Sir Aubrey Smith and Sir Cedric Hardwicke but to distinctly more dashing personalities like Maureen O'Sullivan, Anna Neagle, Greer Garson, Kate Smith, Jack Benny, Ronald Colman and James Cagney.

When Sir Cedric Hardwicke was presented to Lord Athlone, the Governor-General said casually, 'I was talking on the telephone to my sister in England last night. She sends you her regards.' Sir Cedric was 'pulled up short,' he says, 'by the realisation that the sister he mentioned was Queen Mary.'[52]

Yet, incredibly, Princess Alice still found time to make those totally unexpected gestures that brought so much pleasure. A Mrs Eflfie Almon, who owned a hotel in the small South African seaside village of Port St John's, was astonished to receive a letter from

Princess Alice, to whom she had once been presented, to say how interested and impressed she had been to learn, indirecdy, that Mrs Almon had two sons and a grandson in the Forces. 'I have always felt that she was a very special person,' writes Mrs Almon's granddaughter, 'since I first saw her letter and realised that she was a very important person, leading a full and busy life, and yet could find time to keep track of, and write, to someone like my granny, who was a passing acquaintance. . . .'[53]

7

Princess Juliana was merely one of the many royals who came crowding into Canada during the Second World War. Through Rideau Hall passed a constant stream of exiled or visiting members of Europe's royal houses. There were Prince Olav and Princess Martha of Norway (King Haakon VII, like his fellow exiled sovereign, Queen Wilhel-mina, now had his headquarters in London); there were the Grand Duchess Charlotte and Prince Felix of Luxembourg; there was the gallant King George II of the Hellenes and the young King Peter II of Yugoslavia; there was Lord Athlone's nephew, the debonair Prince George, Duke of Kent; and there was even a royal prisoner-of-war, Princess Alice's godson, Prince Friedrich of Prussia, Kaiser Wilhelm II's grandson, who would be allowed out from Camp L on the Plains of Abraham to have tea with his godmother in the Citadel, Quebec City.

A strange young member of Princess Alice's family at Rideau Hall was 28-year-old Alastair, 2nd Duke of Connaught, grandson of Queen Victoria's long-lived son Arthur, 1st Duke of Connaught. A pleasant but utterly vague and feckless young man, he had been sent to the Athlones in the hope that a spell at Rideau Hall would help give some shape to his amorphous personality. It did not. The Duke of Connaught's irresponsibility was such, in fact, that it killed him. He was found dead on the floor of his room at Rideau Hall on the morning of 26 April 1943. He had died, apparently, from hypothermia.

Perhaps the most bizarre royal visitor was the Empress Zita of Austria who, with two of her daughters, Princess Charlotte and Princess Elizabeth, spent some time at Rideau Hall.

In many ways the Empress Zita, although only just fifty years old, was like a relic from another age. Born a member of the stiff-backed Bourbon-Parma family (she had been one of the twenty-four children, by his two wives, of Roberto I, Duke of Parma), the Empress Zita had been the wife of the last Emperor of Austria and King of Hungary, Karl I, who had succeeded his great-uncle, the courtly old Emperor Franz Joseph, during the last tumultuous years of the First World War. He had reigned for less than two years. With the old Austro-Hungarian Empire crashing in ruins about him, the Emperor Karl I had been deposed in 1919. A desperate bid to win back at least his Hungarian throne in 1921 ended in failure and the Emperor died in Madeira a year later.

In Europe between the wars the widowed Empress Zita had seemed anachronistic enough; in wartime Canada she seemed extraordinary. Princess Alice, so modern in outlook and ten years older than the Empress, was intrigued by her appearance and attitudes. All the Empress Zita's dresses were black, floor-length, long-sleeved and high-necked. This same old-fashioned austerity marked her behaviour. Although cultivated and articulate, the Empress was spartan, narrow-minded, ultramondaine. She lived, as Princess Alice puts it, 'in the bosom of the R. C. Church.'[54] Her lady-in-waiting, Countess Kerstenbruck, would have to slip out of the Empress's rooms in order to enjoy a cigarette and a glass of sherry with the aides-de-camp. 'Such indulgences were not permitted in the ascetic apartments of the Empress,' writes the amused Princess Alice.

In time, the Empress and four of her eight children* settled down in a modest home of their own in Quebec. The Empress Zita was extremely strict with her children; her two daughters, who were studying at the university in Quebec, were always chaperoned to and from their lectures by a lady-in-waiting. Princess Alice did what she could to brighten the socially restricted lives of these two young princesses

---

* If the Empress had been married for longer than ten years, the Athlones used to say, she would have exceeded her father's record of twenty-four children.

but nothing would induce the Empress to relax her own austere way of life. To take tea with the Empress was always a sober experience for the visiting Princess Alice. While the Princess and her lady-in-waiting were allowed tea, the Empress Zita insisted that her family and household drink only glasses of water. It was all a far cry from the gaieties of Imperial Vienna and the splendours of the Hof-burg or Schönbrunn.

But the most important royal visitor was Princess Alice's cousin, Queen Wilhelmina of the Netherlands. Twice she flew to Ottawa to see her daughter, Princess Juliana. The first occasion was in June 1942 when the Athlones were away on tour. Although fully alive to Queen Wilhelmina's great qualities and particularly to her magnificent wartime role, Princess Alice could not resist remarking on some of the more amusing aspects of her stay at Rideau Hall. The 62-year-old Queen Wilhelmina had, says Princess Alice, 'a mania for what she called "not giving trouble".'[55] This could have exactly the opposite effect. At Ottawa airport, where the Prime Minister, a group of dignitaries, a guard of honour and a military band were waiting to give her an official welcome, the indomitable Queen emerged from the plane wearing an old raincoat and carrying her own suitcases. This determination to save others the chore of carrying her luggage left her with no free hand with which to shake those of the assembled officials.

Settled into Rideau Hall, and wanting to do some shopping, the Queen telephoned for a taxi. She was assured that there was no need to call for a taxi: a car was available for her use. Having been convinced that by using it she would be giving no trouble, the Queen had to be similarly convinced that by agreeing to the obligatory detective she would likewise be giving no trouble. Yet once she was in the city, she simply could not understand why she – the Queen of the Netherlands – should be kept waiting at traffic lights. 'She peremptorily ordered the detective to get out and stop the cross traffic which had been so ill-mannered as to keep Her Majesty waiting,'[56] says Princess Alice.

Queen Wilhelmina's determination to visit the United States with the least possible fuss caused equal consternation, claims the Princess. She refused to take advantage of the offers of both the President of the United States and the Canadian Government to provide her with a private railway coach for the journey. She would buy her own ticket and travel in an ordinary train, she said. However, an astute member of the staff handed her the highly complicated Canadian Government Railway Timetable and asked her by which train she would like to travel. The baffled Queen capitulated and agreed to go by special coach.

Yet when the Canadian and the United States authorities were trying to come to a decision about the day of her journey, the Queen again revealed her devastatingly regal streak. 'It is not for the Governor-General or the President of the United States to decide,' she declared, 'it is for *me* to decide, and I am *un*decided.'[57]

These anecdotes, which so greatly amused Princess Alice, did not mean that Queen Wilhelmina had been an unreasonable or difficult guest (in the main, the Rideau Hall staff found the Queen both impressive and accommodating); they were simply examples of the Princess's appreciation of a funny situation.

The redoubtable Dutch Queen came again, the following summer, for the christening of Princess Juliana's third daughter, who had been born on 19 January 1943. The ceremony took place in St Andrew's Presbyterian church in Ottawa. The Earl of Athlone and Princess Alice were both present on this occasion, Lord Athlone being one of the child's godparents. The others were President Roosevelt, Queen Mary, Princess Juliana's lady-in-waiting, Mrs Roell, and the Dutch Merchant Navy. The infant Princess was given the name of Margriet, as the marguerite had become the symbol of the Dutch resistance to the Nazi conquerors.

'In choosing this name,' Queen Wilhelmina had said in a broadcast to her countrymen earlier that year, 'it is the parents' intention to establish a lifelong tie between our severely tried people in the occupied parts of the Empire and the new-born child . . .

'May it soon be granted to Margriet to live in her fatherland, among her people, and, like her flowering namesake of the fields, may she represent our living and constantly renewed homage to all those who made the great sacrifice, which will prove to be the seed from which will spring a truly free and great fatherland and empire.'[58]

8

Of considerable comfort and interest to the Athlones during these years were the letters from home. The most regular correspondent was Lord Athlone's sister Queen Mary.

There had been a suggestion, at one stage, that Queen Mary might come to Rideau Hall for the duration of the war, but the old Queen would not hear of leaving Britain. She had gone instead to Badminton in Gloucestershire, the home of her niece (the eldest daughter of her late brother Dolly, the Marquess of Cambridge), the Duchess of Beaufort. Queen Mary was to remain there throughout the war.

From Badminton, in Queen Mary's distinctive handwriting, came all the family news. There was a great deal about 'Bertie and Elizabeth' – the King and Queen, and about their daughters: 'Lillibet much grown, very pretty eyes and complexion, pretty figure. Margaret very short, intelligent face but not really pretty.'[59]

She was also able to tell the Athlones, that the King had received 'such good accounts' of both of them and that he was very pleased that they had accepted the Canadian post.[60]

For Princess Alice, both King George VI and Queen Elizabeth were full of praise. The King told the Canadian Prime Minister that the Princess was always so 'lively and helpful'[61] and, years later, the Queen Mother claimed that Princess Alice had done wonderful work in Canada. 'She had such get-up-and-go,' remembered the Queen Mother. 'She was always very straight, very strong-willed, with a great natural dignity.'[62]

Queen Mary had news of the Athlones' country house, Brantridge Park, as well. It had been lent to Princess Beatrice – 'Auntie B' – and she was delighted to be there; 'it was such a sunny house.'[63] In fact, Princess Beatrice, Queen Victoria's last surviving child, was to die at Brantridge in October 1944 at the age of eighty-six.

Although Queen Mary was in her mid-seventies during the Second World War, she remained as alert and energetic as she had ever been. When Lord Athlone wrote to describe the Empress Zita's mother, the 78-year-old Duchess of Parma, as 'the old lady', he was roundly rebuked by Queen Mary: 'she herself was only three years younger and did not feel at all old!'[64] As though to prove it, Queen Mary told the Athlones about an experience during her recent visit to Bath.

'Some Australian sailors and airmen happened to be there,' she wrote, 'and asked me to be photographed "with the boys". I said yes and they crowded round me and I suddenly felt an arm pushed through mine and an arm placed round my waist in order to make more room, I suppose. It really was very comical and *unexpected* at my age!'[65]

CHAPTER FIFTEEN

1

Each year the Athlones journeyed through Canada. Sometimes by plane, sometimes by car, more often by train, they travelled immense distances, from Newfoundland on the Atlantic Ocean to Vancouver Island on the Pacific, from the Great Lakes in the South-East to the Yukon Territory in the North-West. Across provinces as big as European countries, in climates and terrains of extraordinary variety, through seven time zones, they journeyed with all their customary absorption and enthusiasm.

There was the annual visit to the picturesque, French-speaking city of Quebec. There were official duties to be carried out in Toronto and Montreal. They chugged across the apparently limitless prairies, through great forests and across snow-covered mountains. From the hilltop Government House in Victoria, Vancouver, they had 'glorious views'[1] across that most beautiful of coastlines. They stayed at the celebrated Banff Springs Hotel and marvelled at its incomparable setting. Lord Athlone was made 'Chief Rainbow' of the Ojibway tribe and, followed by whooping braves and squaws, danced hand-in-hand with a genuine Indian chief. Princess Alice gamely put on a squaw's head-dress: 'though I hate,' she says frankly, 'having to remove my hat without a mirror.'[2] New Brunswick, with its 'atmosphere of permanence',[3] she loved; the Mennonite communities, with their 'weird religion',[4] she found intriguing. In Halifax she saw a portrait of her great-grandfather, the Duke of Kent, who had once commanded the British forces in Canada, looking much less 'butlerish'[5] than usual. At Cap Tourmente she was enraptured by the sight of a marsh, covered with a vast flock of twenty-four thousand snow geese, which made it look quite white; on another occasion a moose passed calmly in front of her.

They saw all the famous sights: the Niagara Falls, the emerald waters of Lake Louise ('its fantastic beauty was spoilt by the hideous hotel'[6]), the overwhelming grandeur of the Rockies.

Once, on President Roosevelt's invitation, they visited Alaska. The President was anxious for Lord Athlone to see the American planes and tanks being ferried across the Bering Straits to the Russian allies. It was, says Princess Alice, 'a very interesting experience'.[7] Through an interpreter, they were able to chat to the various Russian pilots who had come over to fetch the planes. To the astonishment of their American hosts the Earl of Athlone, in his straightforward way, established immediate rapport with the

Russians, something which the Americans had had great difficulty in doing.

The Princess's most vivid memory of the Alaskan visit was their first breakfast, brought to them from a nearby 'eatery': ham and eggs on paper plates and coffee in a pickle jar covered with a rag.

(Allies or not, Princess Alice had the greatest difficulty in reconciling herself to the Russian régime. She had, after all, been thirty-four at the time of the Russian Revolution and the murder of so many members of the imperial family, including her first cousins the Empress Alexandra and the Grand Duchess Ella.* Nevertheless, the Russian Embassy in Ottawa was famous for its parties, and the Athlones were frequently obliged to attend them. 'These people killed my relations,'[8] she would mutter as the vice-regal car drew up beneath the spotlit hammer and sickle on the Russian Embassy. But once inside, says Sir Shuldham Redfern, she was her usual charming self.)

These nation-wide tours were accompanied by the occasional, but inevitable, mishaps. On one occasion Lord Athlone gave his apprehensive aides a reassuring wink when, lacking the customary velvet cushion at an investiture, they had had to make do with a hastily procured and distinctly inferior substitute.

On another occasion, in Regina, Saskatchewan, the driver of the vice-regal car so lost his head that

---

* Princess Alix (1872–1918) and Princess Elizabeth (1864–1918) were both daughters of Ludwig IV, Grand Duke of Hesse and Queen Victoria's daughter, Princess Alice.

he drove right past the Town Hall on whose steps the welcoming dignitaries stood waiting.

'What's happening?' demanded the short-tempered Lord Athlone as they went gliding past the frieze of puzzled faces. The aide on duty, young Neville Ussher, did some quick thinking. As there were so many people in the streets hoping to catch a glimpse of Their Excellencies, he explained, it had been decided to drive once round the block before stopping at the Town Hall. This they duly did. By giving the driver a sharp kick, Ussher was able to prevent him from sailing past the Town Hall – and the astonished welcoming committee – a second time. Their Excellencies were highly amused on being told the truth later in the day.

What the Athlones enjoyed most of all were their private holidays. There was nothing that this devoted, well-matched couple liked more than getting away by themselves for a few days walking or fishing or reading. They would often spend two or three days in a fishing lodge at Kamloops in British Columbia. Here, with a couple of aides and a lady-in-waiting, they would live *en famille*. 'They were absolutely splendid with us,' says one of the aides, 'like a private family.' For years afterwards the aides would treasure the coarse woollen sweaters bought for them in a local store by Lord Athlone. Princess Alice, says Neville Ussher, 'never ceased to be interested in everything that went on.'[9]

Early each summer, the Athlones would spend a holiday in the Jasper National Park in the Rockies. Their private railway coach would be shunted onto a nearby siding and here, guarded by a handful of Mounties, they would live for five or six days.

The Superintendent of the Park at that time was Major J. A. Wood, and together with his wife he would take the Athlones for long drives through the immense, thickly wooded area. 'Princess Alice was always very interested in all wildlife, but seemed to have an excellent knowledge of birds and waterfowl in particular,' remembers Mrs Emily Wood. 'She was very interested in the fish hatchery in Jasper and would go and watch the men collect the fish eggs and strip the milt to fertilize the eggs. Then the following year she was keen to see what growth and development in the fish had occurred.'

Lunch would be carried with them in a large box on which the Princess would often sit. Queen Mary, she would tell the Woods, usually sat on the lunch box at picnics in England. On their way back to the siding, the vice-regal couple would ask to be let out of the car so that they could walk the last two miles. 'Princess Alice was always knitting army or navy garments for the war effort,'[10] says Mrs Wood. And about her own, beautifully tailored tweed suits, the Princess was very knowledgeable: she knew exactly from which type of sheep and from which part of the British Isles the wool originated.

On one occasion, the Athlones spent a holiday in Mackenzie King's little retreat at Kingsmere, in the Gatineau Hills. The Prime Minister gives a touching account of the way in which the Governor-General broached the subject of the holiday, when he was visiting Mackenzie King at Kingsmere.

The two men – the tall, distinguished-looking Governor-General and the squat, ungainly Prime Minister – had tea together: Toast and some fresh strawberry jam and cake and tea. The Governor thoroughly enjoyed the jam, took no less than three helpings. Before starting off, in an embarrassed sort of way, he asked me if I had any little cottage I could let him and Princess Alice have for a few days. That they would like to get away by themselves quietly before going out to the West. . . . He said they would be glad to come out by themselves and just look after themselves. After canvassing different situations, the Governor asked me about the little farmhouse here. I at once said: 'Of course, they would be most welcome here, and it would be an honour to the little house to have them stay.' He said, in a quite simple way, 'It is strange, we have wanted to be in that little house and would be so glad to be here for a day or two. . . .'

Finally it was arranged that if I go down to Quebec on Monday week, they will come out and stay here before going to Quebec themselves. . . . I was really touched by the almost child-like delight. The Governor repeatedly said how much this little place appealed to them; the air and the beauty. The peace of it all. I can understand exactly what they want. It is to be away from everybody and everything for a little time.[11]

2

During these years in Canada, the presence of their three grandchildren remained a source of great joy to the Athlones. Their daughter, Lady May Abel Smith, had gone back to England in 1941. With Major Abel Smith having returned from service in the Middle East and now commanding his regiment in England Lady May had, quite naturally, been very anxious to rejoin him. This had turned out to be easier said than done. It was almost impossible to get a passage back to England. Not even the most highly placed personages – Lord Mountbatten, Queen Mary, even King George VI himself – were able to secure a cabin for Lady May on the crowded troopships. Finally, in desperation, Princess Alice asked Lord Athlone's Secretary, Sir Shuldham Redfern, to make one last effort. Not feeling very hopeful, Sir Shuldham went to see the military authorities who were in charge of sailing arrangements. He was directed to a lowly corporal sitting in a tiny, box-like office.

The corporal made a telephone call. Certainly, he then said cheerfully, there was a cabin, with bath, available on Friday week. Would this suit Her Ladyship? It would; and Lady May sailed back to England to join her husband. 'That corporal was far too valuable ever to be promoted,'[12] claimed Sir Shuldham years afterwards.

Very wisely, Lady May Abel Smith had left her children in the care of their grandparents. They could hardly have been in better hands. Both Princess Alice and Lord Athlone were devoted to the children. The Princess had always been good with youngsters, being able, wrote someone who, as a child, had known the Princess, 'to close the generation gap between herself and us children. She would engage in pranks with us, play with us on the swings and with the electric trains and other toys. To me this was perhaps her greatest attribute, the ability to join the children and establish a tremendous rapport with them.'[13]

And Princess Alice, Duchess of Gloucester, tells the story of the day that Princess Alice went out walking at the Gloucesters' Scottish home with young Prince William of Gloucester and their chauffeur's son. Realising that they would be late back, the little party decided to take a short cut. It brought them up against an apparently impenetrable deer fence. Princess Alice refused to admit defeat. She encouraged Prince William to slip through underneath but when she, by then almost seventy years old, tried to squeeze through, she stuck. Only after frantic tuggings and pushings by the two boys was she freed. 'She thought it all great fun,'[14] says the Duchess of Gloucester.

So adventurous and independent-minded herself, Princess Alice was delighted to see that the young

Abel Smiths were acquiring that 'self-reliance natural to Canadian children'.[15]

Lord Athlone was equally good with them. He always tried to be present whenever one of his aides, the amiable Tom Goff, was telling them a story. In fact, Lord Athlone would be every bit as interested in the story as they were. If, for instance, Tom Goff were telling them a story about a character called Bloggins, and the Prime Minister happened to arrive for an important meeting with the Governor-General, Lord Athlone would leave the story-telling with the greatest reluctance. 'Tell me, Tom,' he would ask eagerly on seeing Goff later that evening, 'whatever happened to Bloggins?'[16]

While the Athlones' granddaughters, Anne and Elizabeth, attended the Institut Jeanne d'Arc, under Mère Saint-Thomas, in Ottawa, their grandson Richard was sent to Trinity College School at Port Hope, Ontario. Here he shared a dormitory with eleven other British boys who were in Canada without their parents.

Happy enough at school, young Richard regarded the Sundays that he spent with his grandmother as his greatest treats. Princess Alice would reserve a private dining-room at Lakeview House Hotel at nearby Cobourg on Lake Ontario. Here she would give Richard and a handful of his friends a hearty Sunday lunch and, the minute the great oval table was cleared, would organise games. For one of these games, she would produce either a feather or a ping-pong ball, and divide the boys into teams. The object was to stop the feather or ball from being blown off the table by the opposing team.

All this puffing caused, says the wife of the owner of the hotel, 'a great deal of merriment'. The Princess 'must have put her grandson's guests at ease,' she continues, 'because they were certainly a very happy, merry group.' At half past three exactly, the party would leave so as to be in time for chapel at Trinity College.

Only at the end of the war, late in 1945, would the three Abel Smith children rejoin their parents in England.

3

The most internationally significant events to take place in Canada during the Second World War were the Quebec Conferences of 1943 and 1944. During both these conferences, the Athlones acted as hosts to the delegates.

In the summer of 1943 the British Prime Minister, Winston Churchill, let Prime Minister Mackenzie King know that he would like to have a formal meeting with President Roosevelt in order to discuss the conduct of the war. He suggested that a meeting take place in the Citadel, Quebec. It would be, and this Mackenzie King insisted on, an 'Anglo-American-Canadian' conference.

Lord Athlone, on being told of Churchill's plan, was immediately 'struck by the idea'.[17] The holding of the conference in Quebec would do wonders for Canadian prestige. The Athlones would postpone their official visit to Prince Rupert and the North, they would place the Citadel at the Government's disposal and arrange for some of their Rideau Hall staff to go down to Quebec. The Conference would take place between 17 and 24 August. Churchill (with his wife Clementine and daughter Mary), Roosevelt and Mackenzie King, with their immediate staffs, would all be accommodated in the Citadel; the military staffs would take over the whole of the famous Chateau Frontenac Hotel.

On 17 August 1943 the Athlones arrived at the Citadel to welcome President Roosevelt. Security was extremely strict. An American President, explained Roosevelt's chief detective earnestly to Princess Alice, was assassinated every forty-five years. As the next assassination was due that year, he had to take extra precautions. So the detective insisted on stationing one of his own men on each landing. In this he came up against Lord Athlone. With the weather being hot, the American security men appeared in shirt-sleeves. This was too much for the punctilious Governor-General. As the Americans refused to dress more appropriately, Lord Athlone stationed a scarlet-tunicked, superbly turned-out Mountie beside each one of them. He won his battle. The security was left to the Mounties.

This was by no means the end of the Athlones' trouble with the American detectives. Princess Alice, expecting the President to arrive at any moment, had just had the drawing-room tidied to her satisfaction when two of the Presidents' 'toughs' flung themselves onto the sofa, tossed their legs over the arms and lit up their cigars. To crown this, she says indignantly, they forbade her – as a security risk – to go out onto the terrace to welcome the President. Only the arrival of Churchill, who had already been there for a day or two, saved the situation. 'Come along with me,' he growled and led her out onto the terrace.

Although the Athlones played no part in the official business of the Conference, they spent a great deal of time with President Roosevelt, the Churchill family and their staffs. 'It was wonderful,' says the Princess, 'to meet all the leading men directing the war effort.' They were all 'delightful guests when we were just *en famille,* and we enjoyed many thrilling conversations, off the record, as they say'.[18]

The second Roosevelt-Churchill Conference was held just over a year later, from 10 to 15 September 1944. Again it took place at the Citadel. But this time the atmosphere, as far as it affected Prime Minister Mackenzie King, was not nearly so happy. Quite unsuspected by the Athlones, their attitude during this second Conference brought all Mackenzie King's simmering resentment of them – or of their official position, rather – boiling over. To the vice-regal couple, this was simply another job to be done and another chance to enjoy stimulating conversations with the various personalities attending the

Conference. But to the thin-skinned Canadian Prime Minister, their behaviour appeared suspect.

His edginess had begun a week or two before the opening of the Conference. The vice-regal couple had invited him to spend a couple of days at the Citadel. 'I do not know why I should have felt so completely ill at ease throughout the whole of the visit,' he afterwards confided to his diary. 'I do not recall in my life having experienced more in the way of restraint and this wholly due to some curious subjective force within myself. It was in no way the fault of His Excellency and Her Royal Highness. They did their utmost to make me feel happy and comfortable. Had I been in prison, I could not have felt more constrained or more ill at ease. It cannot be helped but there it is.'

He returned to the theme the following day. "The experience of the Citadel continues to haunt me like a nightmare. I feel so sorry to have not been able to measure up in any sort of way to what would have been expected of me.'

And then he gave what he imagined to be the reason for his sense of insecurity. 'Instinctively, I revolt at anyone from the Old Country exercising even outwardly any semblance of control over Canada.'[19]

Throughout the Conference Mackenzie King felt that he, the Prime Minister of Canada, was being overshadowed, and purposely overshadowed, by the Governor-General and his wife. His achievement in having the conferences recognised as

'Anglo-American-Canadian' affairs seemed to have been undermined by the presence of the Athlones. His resentment came to a head on the Sunday after the Conference. On accompanying Mrs Churchill to the Anglican Cathedral, Mackenzie King found himself greatly put out by the homage being paid to Their Excellencies. Everyone at the church door, he grumbled, 'seemed to regard the vice-regal party as the one element to be noticed and did not come forward even to shake hands.' He was furious when Lord Athlone, in his usual friendly way, said how glad he was that the Prime Minister 'had come along'; for all the world, judged King, as though he need not have been there.

I am determined not to allow the position of Prime Minister of Canada to be blotted out in my own country by those who come from another land. I cannot get rid of the feeling of resentment at Englishmen coming here and holding in the eyes of any body of Canadians a place more honourable or worthy than that of those who have been born in Canada itself and are their chosen representatives.

I have felt right through this Conference, though nothing has been said, that so far as the Governor-General and Princess Alice are concerned, there has been, since the last Conference, a sort of carefully-planned arrangement to be in evidence in relation to the Conference in a way much more conspicuous than they were at the time of the last Conference, or in relation to the Prime Minister of the country, emphasizing in this way before the Americans and people of England and others the place which privileged position and the Crown continues to hold in Canada.[20]

Needless to say, there were no grounds whatsoever for the Prime Minister's suspicions. On the contrary, the Athlones had kept deliberately out of the way. They certainly never suspected that Mackenzie King's feelings were anything but friendly and appreciative; or that he had any reservations about the position held by the Governor-General. To Princess Alice, Mackenzie King was always 'a staunch Imperialist'.[21]

The Canadian historian Bruce Hutchison, in discussing what he calls the 'riddle' of Mackenzie King, claims that Lord Athlone once provided a blunt but eminently sensible solution. 'As Governor-General in King's later years,' writes Hutchison, 'the Earl of Athlone observed him with neutral English eyes and a shrewd common sense little known outside Rideau Hall. After King's death and his own return to London, Athlone delivered a judgement in his jerky, soldier's idiom.

'"Your man King," he said to me. "Knew him quite well actually. Bit of a puzzle. . . . Great man and all that. And you know, he just missed being quite a decent feller."

'A great man who just missed being quite a decent fellow', says Hutchison, 'that was King to the life!'[22]

4

During Lord Athlone's term of office, Princess Alice had several contacts with the United States. At the beginning she was besieged by American matrons, all anxious for her to make speeches, present awards, open fêtes or become patron of this or that society. She was advised against it and as, according to Sir Shuldham Redfern, she was always ready to take advice, she graciously declined. But she did pay several visits, both official and unofficial, to the States.

In October 1940, not long after their arrival in Canada, the viceregal couple had paid a private visit to the Roosevelts at their home, Hyde Park, on the Hudson River. Princess Alice had been fascinated by the Roosevelt household. She found the interior of the home to be 'a delightful old-fashioned muddle'. Franklin Roosevelt she thought utterly charming and possessed of 'real greatness of character'; 'we both fell completely under his spell.' At the wheel of his own car, the President drove them through the autumn woods of his Hyde Park estate. As usual, there was strict security. They were accompanied by two police cars and at every bend in the road stood yet another plain-clothes policeman. Security, sighed the President, was the curse of his office.

The Princess was equally taken with the gaunt, toothy, dynamic Eleanor Roosevelt. She arrived from Seattle 'like a whirlwind' and made so much noise at luncheon that Lord Athlone complained of being deafened. But the most notable character of all was the President's mother, Mrs Sarah Roosevelt. Plump, vivacious and domineering, old Mrs Roosevelt had an energy which belied her eighty-four years. 'She was a great dear, but such a matriarch,'[23] says the Princess.

Princess Alice remained in New York after Lord Athlone had returned to Canada. For several days she was able to indulge in the sort of cultural feast that she loved: visiting art galleries, museums and the theatre. She saw *There shall be no Night,* with Alfred Lunt, Lynn Fontanne and the young Montgomery Clift, the profits from that night's show going towards the Spitfire Fund.

The Athlones' second American journey was in March 1945 when they paid a state visit to Washington. They were given, as Lester Pearson, then Canadian Ambassador to the United States, put it, 'the full, red-carpet, head-of-state treatment'.[24] There was an official welcome at the station by the President and Mrs Roosevelt, a roaring cavalcade through the streets of the capital, and a series of formal luncheons, dinners and receptions. The Ambassador experienced one heart-stopping moment when he thought that Lord Athlone, in toasting the President at a White

House dinner, was going to refer to the beauty of Washington's 'Japanese' cherry blossom; but fully alive to the fact that Japan was the enemy, Lord Athlone deftly substituted 'Oriental' for 'Japanese'.

Lester Pearson was very taken with the Athlones. 'Their natural simplicity and kindliness made them easy and welcome guests. My experience of people has been that the more exalted they are in the social or official hierarchy, the less snobbish and difficult they are with others.'[25] This was certainly true of the Athlones. Pearson considered Lord Athlone to be 'a born tourist, and a very nice, amiable man'.[28] The Princess, though, was an exceptional personality: 'she had surely found the secret of perpetual youth and charm.'

Within a very short time after the couple's return to Canada, Lord Athlone was back in Washington for President Roosevelt's funeral. The President had died on 12 April 1945. This time Lord Athlone came without the Princess and stayed at the Canadian Embassy. He endeared himself to his hosts by asking, just before leaving, to be allowed, to meet and thank the members of their domestic staff.

Heightening the Pearsons' appreciation of their guest's courtesy was the fact that their cook, Pearl, was just then threatening to leave them in order to return to her native Jamaica. Could His Excellency, asked the Ambassador, appeal to Pearl's staunchly pro-British and pro-Royalist sentiments by suggesting that her continued presence at the Canadian

Embassy was essential for ultimate British victory and as proof of her loyalty to the monarchy?

Lord Athlone complied; and Pearl stayed.

Lester Pearson had one final anecdote. One evening at dinner, Lord Athlone asked James, the stiff-backed British butler, the name of the white wine he was serving. It was a Licbfraumilch, but James, deciding that it would be improper to use a German word to a member of the British royal family in wartime, did a quick literal translation before answering.

'Milk of the Virgin, Your Excellency,'2[7] came his unblinking reply.

5

Lord Athlone's term of office should have ended in 1945 but, as in South Africa, he was asked to stay on. It was generally agreed that until the war, and the inevitable period of post-war confusion, was well and truly over, it would not do to change Governors-General. In any case, as King George VI said laughingly to the visiting Mackenzie King, with servants being almost impossible to come by in England, the Athlones would do as well to remain at Rideau Hall as long as they could. So Lord Athlone agreed to stay on until the spring of 1946, when he would be replaced by Viscount Alexander of Tunis.

The day marking the official end of the war in Europe, VE Day, 8 May 1945, found the Athlones on their annual visit to Jasper National Park. They arranged to go to the Superintendent's home to listen to the radio broadcast by King George VI and Prime Minister Mackenzie King. 'When "God Save the King" was played,' remembers the Superintendent's wife, 'the Athlones jumped to attention.' Dutifully, their hosts also rose to their feet. At that moment, a neighbouring doctor happened to call in. At the sight of these four people, standing rigid in the middle of the room, the visitor wondered, as well he might, 'what on earth was going on'![28]

In the autumn of 1945, with the war finally over, the Athlones returned to England for a few weeks. They sailed on a liner which, having brought home a contingent of Canadian soldiers, was going back almost empty. 'Conditions on board were most unsalubrious and the ship was still blacked out,' remembered the Princess. 'However, we were so happy at the prospect of being home after five long years that nothing mattered.'[29]

Their happiness was somewhat marred by the first sight of their Kensington Palace apartments. The fire-bomb damage was much worse than they had feared: the place was quite uninhabitable. 'Our apartments there were in complete chaos,' says the Princess. 'The disastrous fire had destroyed part of our roof and attic rooms, though even greater damage had been avoided by the torrents of water that had deluged the whole place, and the house had remained unrepaired since 1940. No window frames were left and all our furniture, books and pictures were heaped higgledy-piggledy in the drawing and dining rooms.'[30]

Still, there was nothing that could be done at that stage. It would have to remain as a task for the future.

The couple sailed back from Southampton in the *Queen Elizabeth* on 15 November 1945. The ship was packed with over ten thousand returning Canadian soldiers. Also on board were some fifty servicewomen, including seven belonging to the St John Ambulance Nursing Division. Soon after sailing, the women were told that they would be sharing the sports deck with the vice-regal party, and were warned not to speak to either Lord Athlone or Princess Alice unless spoken to first.

In no time, though, Princess Alice was over speaking to the little group of St John Ambulance girls. Utterly natural and charming, she struck the girls as being genuinely interested in all they had to tell her about their years of service abroad.

'As Princess Alice was leaving us,' remembers one of the girls, 'she noticed my camera and *offered* to pose for a picture.'[31] The moment was caught, and treasured forever, in the snapshot. There, on the windy, heaving deck of the *Queen Elizabeth,* stands Princess Alice, in fur coat, scarf and small, smartly tilted hat, carrying a life-jacket and managing to look, as only she could manage to look, both highly distinguished and irrepressibly impish.

No matter how freezing the weather, Lord Athlone would insist on going up on deck for a breath of air. Invariably, he went without his overcoat. Very worried about this, Princess Alice once scribbled a note to his aide, Neville Ussher. 'Please follow H.E. about with a coat,' she wrote. 'Never let him go without one.'[32] So poor Ussher, with a coat over his arm, would have to dog His Excellency's footsteps, keeping out of sight behind lifeboats and ventilation shafts, until such time as he felt it politic to emerge and nonchalantly suggest that – as it seemed to have turned rather cold – the reluctant Lord Athlone put on his overcoat.

That Christmas, their last at Rideau Hall, the Athlones received a charming letter from the always unpredictable Mackenzie King. It was a letter, says Princess Alice, that she would always cherish.

I shall ever recall, with feelings of delight mixed with many tinges of regret, the happy hours spent with Your Excellency and Princess Alice on the afternoon of the 24th [Christmas Eve]. It was a great joy to be again celebrating the festivities of the Xmas season at Government House but one missed the little children* whom one has watched grow up in Canada and one could not but feel how greatly one would miss Her Royal Highness and yourself once your years in Canada were at a close.

---

* The three Abel Smith children had by then returned to England.

There are not many occasions when one feels free to say some of the things that lie nearest to one's heart but when I read on your card of Xmas greetings the words 'With our warmest wishes and affectionate remembrances' I realised how large a place H.R.H. and Your Excellency had had in my life during the first five eventful years and how warm had become the attachment I shall always feel for you both. There will be a great blank space in my little world when you are no longer here. . . . You have both been such true friends in everything that had its relationship to my personal and public life, so considerate, so understanding and so helpful that I am going to miss you terribly.

Canada, too, is going to miss Your Excellency and H.R.H. more than you will ever know. Your years here as representative of the King have strengthened the country's attachment to the Crown. I doubt if that attachment were ever stronger than it is today.[33]

With their departure planned for March 1946, the Athlones' last weeks in Canada were exceptionally busy. There was a great ball at Rideau Hall in honour of General Dwight Eisenhower; there was the Opening of Parliament; there were investitures and receptions and farewell dinners. The Princess had to take leave of so many of those organisations with which she had been associated. In her final address as Honorary President of the Imperial Order Daughters of the Empire, she reviewed her years in Canada and, with an eye on Quebec Province, expressed the hope that Canadians would come to regard the whole of Canada, rather than their individual provinces, as their homeland. 'Canada cannot be a nation,' she said, 'unless Canadians have a national outlook. It is futile to sing "O Canada" unless the whole Dominion is signified and not just an individual province.'[34]

The Princess's concern for Canada's future manifested itself in a more tangible fashion as well. It was customary to present the retiring Governor-General's wife with a gift bought with contributions from women all over Canada: from members of national and local women's organisations, from servicewomen and from individuals. The gift could be one of jewellery, furs or paintings. But Princess Alice asked that her Fund be used to meet the needs of young Canadians. So the Princess Alice Foundation was established 'for the provision of bursaries to young men and women as social workers from all classes of schools and universities so that they may enlarge their capacity as leaders of younger Canadians in the impressionable years between fourteen and sixteen'.[35]

That such social service could indeed 'be rendered in full and happy enjoyment of life,' commented the Ottawa *Citizen*, 'Her Royal Highness has herself abundantly demonstrated.'[36]

The Athlones left Canada on 16 March. The official departure was a most moving occasion. Watched by a vast crowd, Lord Athlone, wearing the uniform of a Major-General in the British Army, laid a wreath of maple leaves and poppies at the foot of the National War Memorial in Confederation Square. The Princess was looking especially soignée in a Persian lamb coat and a dashing black hat, with a spray of orchids pinned to her lapel. Mounties, resplendent in their scarlet tunics and wide-brimmed hats, lined the Square. With the Prime Minister having called for three cheers, the party entered the waiting cars and drove out to Rockcliffe airport. 'En route', runs one report, 'Their Excellencies were repeatedly called upon to respond to crowds and individuals waving them a loyal farewell.'[37]

Until now, Princess Alice had managed to keep her emotions under control. But at the airport, as she said goodbye to the various dignitaries and to the members of the Rideau Hall staff, it was hard, she admitted 'to keep the tears from falling'.[38] It was not only hard; it was impossible. When the band broke into that most touching of airs, 'Will Ye No Come Back Again?' the Princess could control herself no longer. Tears streamed down her cheeks. 'She tried to say a parting word to Mackenzie King but couldn't,'[39] noted one observer.

Turning abruptly, Princess Alice disappeared into the dark interior of the giant Liberator transport plane.

419

PART SIX
KENSINGTON PALACE

Chapter Sixteen

1

The Athlones came back from Canada to a very different world. Princess Alice, at sixty-three, and Lord Athlone, at seventy-two, returned to face a grey and exhausted Britain. The exciting, between-the-wars capital was now 'poor, dear, dirty London'[1] and their Kensington Palace home was uninhabitable. Help, of any sort, was difficult to come by and, as Brantridge Park had been given up, the couple were obliged to make their home with Queen Mary at Marlborough House until such time as their own Kensington Palace apartments could be made ready. There was no question, protested Lord Athlone, of their getting preferential treatment in the restoration of their apartments. 'We must wait our turn,'[2] he would say.

There were more permanent differences as well. The establishment of the Welfare State was bringing changes to every sphere of national life. It was making obsolete much of the sort of charitable work that the Princess had done before the war. The Deptford Fund, for instance, founded by the Duchess of Albany half a century before, was the sort of undertaking that was quite out of tune with post-war Britain: it had to be reorganised, as Princess Alice put it, 'from top to bottom.'[3]

Their first winter back in Britain was the worst for decades. To a country still suffering from food rationing was now added fuel rationing. As electric power was switched off at nine in the morning, they lived, says Princess Alice, 'in overcoats and snowboots'.[4] Marlborough House was like a refrigerator. A friend, meeting Lord Athlone in Pall Mall one day, asked whether he and Princess Alice were accepting invitations out to dinner. 'Oh yes,' answered Lord Athlone eagerly, 'we love going out to dinner. It's too damn cold in Marlborough House in the evenings.'[5]

But Princess Alice was nothing if not resilient. With the help of two or three personal servants, she set about putting their Kensington Palace apartments in order. Even Queen Mary, with a toque on her head and an apron round her waist, helped wash the china. 'We laughed a lot over our tasks,'[6] said the irrepressible Princess.

Only after several months of hard work could the Athlones move back into their home. Their apartments – which they had occupied, off and on, for something like a quarter of a century – were in Clock House, Kensington Palace. As one faced the simple, symmetrical, red-brick facade of the William and

Mary palace, their apartments were on the left of the central Clock Tower. To reach their front door, one passed through the archway under the Clock Tower and crossed to the left-hand side of the great paved courtyard. A few steps led up to their large front door.

The Athlones occupied four floors. In the basement was a stone-flagged kitchen and, leading off it, a large, high-ceilinged room known as the King's Kitchen, the walls of which were crowded with stuffed animal heads – the trophies of a lifetime's hunting. The King's Kitchen, said one member of the household, was 'wonderful for parties'.[7] On the next level up were the entrance hall, an inner hallway through which passed the central staircase, Lord Athlone's study and, a few steps down, the dining-room. Above this was a large double drawing-room, whose windows overlooked Palace Green, the Princess's private sitting-room-cum-study, the Secretary's office, the wide Green Corridor in which the couple would often breakfast or take afternoon tea, the Athlones' bedroom and a couple of guest rooms. On the top floor were more bedrooms and servants' rooms. To the side of the Palace lay the Athlones' private garden – a stretch of tree-shaded lawn, surrounded by a wide border and entirely enclosed by a high brick wall. As always, Princess Alice devoted a great deal of her spare time to working in the garden.

In time, the couple were able to assemble a large enough staff to help run this sizeable establishment. One pillar of strength was the butler, the redoubtable

425

Mr Bennett; another was the couple's new secretary, the slim, elegant, efficient and Canadian-born Miss Mary Goldie, who joined them in 1946. Mary Goldie could hardly then have guessed that she was to remain with Princess Alice for well over thirty years.

Gradually, the Athlones' life resumed some sort of pattern. They stayed with the Abel Smiths, now living at Barton Lodge near Windsor and, when Lady May brought the children up to London, there were lunches or teas at Gunters in Curzon Street ('the only place where one could get decent food at that time'[8]). There were countless visits, with that passionate playgoer Queen Mary, to the theatre. There were weekends in the country with friends. There was a Christmas at Sandringham with King George VI, Queen Elizabeth and their two daughters, where Lord Athlone was able to enjoy the shooting. 'There was something unique about the King's home life,' claims Princess Alice. 'It was just a small, absolutely united circle of the King, the Queen and their two daughters; they were in the most perfect harmony of thought, sharing the same jokes and at times sharing the same troubles. I am convinced it was both a source of strength and a refuge from his overwhelming burden in his tasks as King. . . .'[9]

In 1946 the Athlones spent a holiday in Sweden. Here, Princess Alice was once more among relations. Although the erect, vigorous, 88-year-old King Gustaf V was not directly related, his son and heir, Crown Prince Gustaf Adolf, had married two members of

Princess Alice's family. Prince Gustaf Adolf's first wife had been the Princess's cousin, Princess Margaret of Connaught. Having borne her husband five children, Princess Margaret had died in 1920. Three years later Prince Gustaf Adolf married again. His second wife had been Lady Louise Mountbatten,[*] whose mother – Princess Victoria of Hesse – had been yet another of Princess Alice's cousins.

Crown Prince Gustaf Adolf and Crown Princess Louise were a delightful couple. He, tall and bespectacled, had the look of an amiable professor; indeed, Crown Prince Gustaf Adolf was a highly civilised and intelligent man, interested in the arts and archaeology as well as in contemporary affairs. As such, he suited Crown Princess Louise perfectly. Thin, toothy, sharp-featured, she was equally cultivated and well-informed. It was in their enchanting seaside palace at Solfiero that this unpretentious couple entertained the Athlones. Here the Crown Prince and Princess could get away from the cares and responsibilities of their position and lead the sort of relaxed and informal life that they preferred. As gardening was one of their passions, that equally enthusiastic gardener, Princess Alice, delighted in the superbly laid-out grounds at Sofiero. She was able to enjoy, she says, 'my pet hobby of weeding'.[†]

---

[*] Lady Louise Mountbatten was one of the four children of Prince Louis of Battenberg, afterwards the Marquess of Milford Haven. She was a sister of Earl Mount batten of Burma.

[†] Princess Alice, Duchess of Gloucester, assured me that Princess Alice, Countess of Athlone was 'a *great* weeder'.

Princess Alice had another close relation at the Swedish court. This was her brother's daughter, Princess Sibylla of Coburg, who had married the Crown Prince's eldest son, another Gustaf Adolf – known in the family as Edmund. At the time of the Athlones' visit to the exquisite Haga Palace in Stockholm the family were feeling highly gratified. In April that year, 1946, after having given birth to four daughters, Princess Sibylla had finally produced a son. In 1973 this son would ascend the Swedish throne as King Carl XVI Gustaf.

Princess Alice was devoted to Princess Sibylla and her husband: 'dear, nice Edmund' she always called him. But sadly, a few months after this visit, on 20 January 1947, Prince Gustaf Adolf was killed in a flying accident, leaving Princess Sibylla to bring up her five children alone.

From Princess Sibylla, Princess Alice would have heard some firsthand news of her brother Charlie – Princess Sibylla's father, the Duke of Coburg. At the end of the war Coburg had falled into American hands. The Duke of Coburg and his family had been living in Coburg Castle at that time and despite the fact that the Duke had been a member of the Nazi party, General Patton had allowed him to remain there. But, on the arrival of a less sympathetic general, the Duke was imprisoned. Along with several other 'old generals and officials', the Duke of Coburg was put into a primitively equipped old Serbian prisoner-of-war camp. 'As he was crippled with arthritis,' says

Princess Alice, 'he found conditions almost unbearable. . . . Many of his fellow prisoners died there, but he was tough and somehow survived, though more crippled than ever . . .'

'No doubt,' says Princess Alice, 'their jailers had seen some of the ghastly German concentration camps and were determined to treat these old officers with the utmost severity.'[11]

In 1946 the Duke of Coburg was released. Together with his wife, Princess Victoria Adelaide, he went to live in a miserable little cottage attached to the stables of Schloss Callenberg, near Coburg. Although agonised by her brother's predicament, there was not a great deal that Princess Alice could do about it; this was hardly the time to be pleading the cause of a one-time active supporter of the Nazi party. The Princess would have to bide her time.

The first post-war royal occasion to capture something of the brilliance of those great family gatherings of pre-war days was the wedding, on 20 November 1947, of King George VI's elder daughter, Princess Elizabeth, to Lieutenant Philip Mountbatten, born Prince Philip of Greece and newly created Duke of Edinburgh. For Princess Alice, one of the chief joys of the wedding was the chance to meet the various members of foreign royal families, many of whom she had not seen for almost a decade. Among this royal galaxy were two especially close friends and relations — the widowed and exiled Queen Ena of Spain and Princess Juliana of the Netherlands. There were old associates among the visiting dignitaries as well: Field Marshal Smuts of South Africa and Mackenzie King of Canada. The Athlones, looking as distinguished as ever, played their part in all the ceremonial: driving in the carriage processions, signing the register, appearing on the balcony of Buckingham Palace.

On the day after the wedding the Athlones were visited by King Peter II of Yugoslavia and his wife, Queen Alexandra.* The young King had lost his throne soon after the end of the war and the couple, who had married some three years before, were already embarked on the rootless, hopeless, feckless and ultimately impoverished life of so many royal exiles. But on this visit to Kensington Palace the conversation was entirely about the previous day's wedding: 'How pretty Margaret had looked as chief bridesmaid; how vivacious Aunt Elizabeth [the Queen] had been; what a wonderful frock Aunt May [Queen Mary] had worn, all gold and blue. . . .'[12]

Queen Alexandra, whose father had been the short-lived King Alexander I of the Hellenes, was a first cousin once removed to Prince Philip and was able to tell the Athlones a great deal about him. 'We think him a very charming young man,' said Princess Alice, 'but, of course, we don't know him as we know Elizabeth.' It was a 'great thing', she continued, for

---

* King Pctcr II (1923–1970) was the grandson of Princess Alice's cousin. the flamboyant Queen Marie of Romania; Queen Alexandra (born 1921), was the grand-daughter of the Princess's cousin. Queen Sophie of the Hellenes.

King George VI and Queen Elizabeth to know that their daughter was marrying a man with whom she was in love. 'She will need a husband who can give her much happiness . . . A marriage that was unhappy would be doubly so in our family.'[13]

2

At an age when most people are beginning to take life at a more leisurely pace, the Athlones remained constantly on the move. 'We were tremendously busy with engagements day and night,' said Princess Alice at an even greater age. 'It makes me quite giddy remembering those days.'[14]

Because, of course, no sooner had the Princess returned to England than she was once more involved in a hundred and one royal duties. Every other day seemed to bring the unvarying routine: the mathematically planned schedule, the drive in the Daimler, the saluting police, the cheers, the fluttering flags, the flashing press cameras, the bouquet, the introductions, the small talk, the speech, the trophy to be presented or the stone to be laid or the tape to be cut, a word or two with some delighted member of the crowd, the farewells, the final wave, and the drive back to Kensington Palace. The wonder was that she did it all with such verve and freshness.[†]

[†] In 1948, Princess Alice was created Dame Grand Cross of the Royal Victorian Order.

One of Lord Athlone's most important posts remained that of Chancellor of the University of London. Although no academic, he brought that office back, writes one of his colleagues, 'to be a living part of the University and restored its prestige as no one else could have done. And admirable as he was as Chancellor, he was by no means a Chancellor for formal occasions only. By the humanity and friendliness which he added to his dignity, he established himself at once in the affections of all who met him.'[15]

Not long after Princess Elizabeth's wedding, the Athlones were invited by Field Marshal Smuts to spend a holiday in South Africa. They accepted with great pleasure. Having had Christmas on board ship, they arrived in Cape Town early in January 1948. By now Smuts was once again Prime Minister and another old friend, Gideon Brand van Zyl, was Governor-General. From the moment that they stepped ashore, eighteen years after their official departure, the Athlones were made to feel at home. 'After all the years since we had left South Africa, it was wonderful to be welcomed so warmly and lovingly by countless friends in every walk of life,' says the Princess. 'The people in the streets waved and smiled and we were recognised in the shops as if we had never left.'[16]

'The Athlones are enjoying themselves here and will spend next weekend with me,' wrote Smuts to a friend. 'I think this is a happy visit and change and a rest for them. I shall take them out to Du Toit's Kloof

[Pass] which is now in order and one of our new glories. . . .'[17]

'We went everywhere,' says Princess Alice. They toured the whole country, from Cape Town in the south-west to White River in the north-east, staying in Government Houses or with their many friends. 'It was really heart-warming,' writes Princess Alice, 'to be the recipients of so much love and also very humbling.'[18]

And if the Athlones were charmed by South Africa, South Africa was no less charmed by them. Lord Athlone, in his cream-coloured summer suits, bought for five pounds each in Cape Town, looked as handsome as ever. Princess Alice, in her silk summer dresses and flower-trimmed straw hats, was the same graceful, vibrant personality she had always been.

Stories of their charm and their thoughtfulness are legion. On one occasion, for instance, while they were staying at Admiralty House in Simonstown, the Admiral's wife, Lady Packer, suggested that they visit a nearby farm cottage, then occupied by Commander and Mrs Pearce. Mrs Zella Pearce, having been asked to give them tea, instructed her Coloured maid, Nellie, to wear her best black uniform with white cap and apron. Only as tea was being served did Zella Pearce notice that Nellie was sporting her 'beloved' pair of bright red shoes with her uniform.

As they were leaving, Lord Athlone, in his always courteous way, asked Nellie about her children. How many did she have? Six. What were their names? She rattled them off, ending with the name of her baby – Winston. And after whom had she named him?

'Sir Winston of England, Sir,'[19] came Nellie's unhesitating answer.

But just before taking final leave of Nellie, Lord Athlone had one more comment.

'I like your shoes very much,'[20] he said.

Having spent three months in the South African sunshine, the Athlones sailed back in, appropriately enough, the *Athlone Castle* which Princess Alice had launched several years before.

In September that year they travelled to Amsterdam for the inauguration of Princess Alice's cousin once removed, Princess Juliana, as Queen of the Netherlands. Now that Queen Wilhelmina was almost seventy, she had decided to abdicate in favour of her only daughter. The old Queen had told her cousin Princess Alice that 'she was not going to hang on like the old King of Sweden' when her daughter was 'quite capable of carrying on herself.[21]

Queen Juliana's inauguration, on 6 September 1948 in the Nieuwe Kerk in Amsterdam, was a most impressive ceremony. The stark Protestant simplicity of the interior of the great Gothic pile was more than compensated for by the congregation – the jewels, feathers and shimmering fabrics of the women and the dashing uniforms of the men. Although held in a church, it was a strictly secular ceremony. The new Queen was not crowned. With the crown and orb and sceptre lying before her, Queen Juliana made a vow to uphold the constitution.

'Juliana had a wonderful purple dress draped close to her figure, no tiara but a Juliette cap studded with huge stones and diamonds. She wore the ermine and crimson royal mantle about her shoulders,' writes Princess Alice.[22]

After Queen Juliana herself, the most popular figure with the Dutch crowds was the 18-year-old Princess Margaret, who had come to represent her father, King George VI. Almost overnight, it seemed, this young Princess in her floor-length pink dress and pink ostrich feather hat had developed into a stylish and beautiful Princess: 'too sweet, charming and shy, and lovely to look upon', as Princess Alice puts it.*

The crowds, says Princess Alice, 'were enchanted, and cheered and shouted "Margriet" wherever she drove.'[13]

3

Princess Alice's next journey was distinctly more harrowing. From Amsterdam the Athlones went on to Coburg to visit the Princess's brother. In ever-deepening depression and with a heavy sense of foreboding, they travelled across the war-shattered German landscape. Their apprehensions were fully justified. The 64-year-old Duke of Coburg and his Duchess

---

* Princess Alice was always very fond* of Princess Margaret. 'I do wish they would leave poor Princess Margaret alone', she once wrote to mc when the Press was being particularly voluble on the subject of the Princess.

(known, in the odd fashion of royal families, as 'Dick') were living in the most unhappy conditions in their stable cottage at Schloss Callenberg. 'It was all so sad and sordid,'[24] sighed the Princess. With the Duke of Coburg too crippled by arthritis to do much to help himself, the Duchess was obliged to shoulder a rucksack each day and walk or cycle three miles to the nearest shop for food. Schloss Callenberg itself was packed with refugees. Adding to the couple's sense of desolation had been the death of their second son, Prince Hubertus, in Russia in 1943.

Putting up at a local hotel, the Athlones did everything they could to alleviate the Duke's and Duchess's sufferings. They badgered the American and German authorities to provide the couple with better living quarters. Eventually, after endless rebuffs, disappointments and humiliations, they were successful: the Duke was allowed to move into part of one of his own houses, closer to the market where the Duchess could do their shopping. Princess Alice was able to return to England in the knowledge that, if nothing else, her brother would now be more comfortably accommodated.

In the post-war period, the Duke of Coburg had several times faced trial for his alleged Nazi activities. Yet according to the Duke's British relations, his support for the Nazis had not been for any ideological reasons. The change in his attitude – from initial disapproval to acceptance of the Nazi régime – had been due to his conviction that Hitler had saved Germany from Communism. Throughout the war, the Duke of Coburg had confined himself to the humanitarian and uncontroversial activities of the Red Cross, of which he was President.

Nonetheless, in August 1949, the Duke of Coburg was classed by a dc-nazification appeal court as a 'Nazi camp-follower',[25] category four, and fined the equivalent of £100. He was accused of having been a member of the Nazi party since 1935, the President of the German Red Cross under the Nazi regime, a *Gruppenführer* in the S.A. and a Reichstag deputy from 1937 until 1945. As the Duke was in hospital with an eye ailment at the time, he was tried *in absentia*. An immediate appeal against the verdict was lodged by the State Prosecutor, on the grounds that it was too lenient.

A broken and bewildered man, the Duke of Coburg was to die some five years later, on 6 March 1954, at the age of sixty-nine.

Not unnaturally, Princess Alice was always very reticent about her brother's controversial career. She could only say, in relation to him, that 'Fate plays a part in our lives and sometimes forces us into situations to which we have to adapt ourselves – often against our inclinations. Several members of my family, including my own brother, found themselves so encompassed by the fatal hands of fortune. . . .'[26]

For Princess Alice, it was another of the prices to be paid for being royal. Born and raised during a period when the royal families of Europe formed a great international freemasonry, she was obliged

437

to suffer whatever disadvantages such intertwined relationships might bring. Few families are without a skeleton in the cupboard; the unfortunate thing is that royal families are never able to keep theirs in the cupboard.

4

Between leaving Canada in March 1946 and returning to England, the Athlones had spent a few weeks in the West Indies. They had again stayed with Sir Bede and Lady Clifford, who were now in Trinidad, and they were able to visit various other islands. The holiday awakened all Princess Alice's enthusiasm for this captivating part of the world. She then little thought, she admits, that for the following quarter of a century or so, she was to be closely associated with the West Indies.

Princess Alice had not been back in England long before King George VI invited her to accept the position of Chancellor of the still-to-be-established University College of the West Indies. The University, which was to be attached, initially, to London University, was being planned by Sir James Irvine, Vice-Chancellor of St Andrew's University, Sir Raymond Priestley, Vice-Chancellor of Birmingham University, and Dame Lilian Penson, Vice-Chancellor of London University. 'I accepted joyfully,' says the Princess, 'though with much trepidation. To be invited to preside over the launching of such an original enterprise as this scheme for providing higher education for the people of the West Indies was indeed an honour and a task of unique interest.'[27] The University was to be established, in the first place, at Kingston in Jamaica. Princess Alice would be the first woman Chancellor of any university.

For the first two or three years Princess Alice was concerned only with the planning stages of the venture, but early in 1950 she travelled to Jamaica for her formal installation as Chancellor. Lord Athlone, as Chancellor of the University of London, the degree-granting body for the new college, went with her. The inauguration was a happy blend of the unpretentious and the impressive. The members of the founding committee sailed to Jamaica in the little banana boat, *Beano,* and the majority of them were violently seasick. The magnificent site, set against a mountainous backdrop at Mona, six miles from Kingston, was nothing but 'a jungle of bush and grass'[28] with a huddle of wooden huts which were to serve as the temporary homes of the various departments. But among the great crowd attending the installation ceremony on 16 February 1950 were brilliantly uniformed governors of the British West Indies, a number of Anglican and Roman Catholic bishops and several leading British Caribbean political figures. Lord Athlone, sitting beside Princess Alice in the robes of the Chancellor of the University of London, looked magnificent.

But it was Princess Alice who held every eye. 'She is one of the loveliest women I have ever seen and in spite of increasing age she retains that wonderful quality of spirit which makes real beauty,' enthused the watching Lady Huggins, wife of Sir John Huggins, then Governor of Jamaica.[29]

In her inaugural speech the Princess spoke of several things that lay near to her heart. 'No one,' she said, 'will dispute the fact that in the pursuit of truth and in the guardianship of the wisdom of mankind – and I put those first among the responsibilities of a University – integrity, perseverance, patience, courage and unselfishness are qualities that are absolutely essential. But they are not enough by themselves to withstand the dangers and vicissitudes by which they will be constantly assailed. They must be strengthened and vitalised by a spiritual grace. Their work must be fortified by the warmth and energy of religious faith.'[30]

Amid what she calls a jungle, Princess Alice laid the foundation stone of the Senate House, Lord Athlone that of the hospital and Sir James Irvine that of the first hall of residence. 'Faith and enterprise,' she admitted, would be required to convert this straggle of temporary structures into a fullyfledged seat of learning. Fortunately, both the first Principal, Dr Thomas Taylor, and the Vice-Principal, Philip Sherlock, had those particular qualities in abundance. And so, of course, did Princess Alice. For twenty-one years the Princess carried out her duties as

Chancellor of the University of the West Indies with all her customary vigour, professionalism and dedication. Year after year she came to the West Indies to confer degrees, attend meetings, discuss problems, make speeches, dance at graduation balls and lay more foundation stones as the University of the West Indies spread and developed.

'She exercised the most remarkable control of affairs,' testifies one Governor of Jamaica, 'dealing quietly and efficiently with every problem that arose – and there were plenty of them.'[31] On one occasion, for instance, a leading university figure had threatened resignation just before the Princess's annual visit. Immediately on arrival, she asked the Governor to arrange a private meeting between herself and the recalcitrant staff member. 'The day arrived,' writes the Governor, 'and, after the interview was over, I asked her how it had gone.'

'It's quite all right,' she answered briskly, 'he's staying on.'[32]

'The professors at the University of the West Indies . . .' writes one Jamaican resident, 'all, without exception, commented on her fantastic memory, and her command as chairman of meetings. On more than one occasion she is reputed to have commented to one of the speakers that this was not what he had said last year – and she would enquire if he had changed his mind.'[33]

Two years after the official inauguration, the University College Teaching Hospital was opened. To meet this, as well as various other, university expenses, Princess Alice launched an appeal on 25 February 1955. Due very largely to her untiring efforts and to what a published university statement was later to call 'the prestige and the undoubted influence of the royal name',[34] the Princess Alice Appeal was a great success.[†]

'No one laboured more intensively in Britain, Canada, the United States and the West Indies than Her Royal Highness for her beloved foundation,' writes the first President of the Executive Committee of the Guild of Graduates of the University; 'every conceivable and possible source of support was approached on behalf of the institution. . . . And nothing escaped her alert mind and vigilant eye for the proper education, personal comfort and spiritual welfare of the students.'[35]

It was on behalf of this 'spiritual welfare of the students' that Princess Alice made her most formidable efforts. 'Devout,' as one member of the University staff puts it, 'in a natural, easy way,' Princess Alice was determined that there should be a university chapel. When her appeal was launched, she wrote to an old Canadian friend to ask him to donate the money for a chapel. She needed forty thousand dollars.

Jamaican-born Philip (afterwards Sir Philip) Sherlock, as Secretary of the Princess Alice Appeal Fund, was in London soon after the appeal was

---

[†] The Princess was to launch an equally successful Appeal in 1969

launched and one day he had a telephone call from the Princess. Her voice, he remembers, was 'electric with excitement'.

'I have the chapel,' she exclaimed.

'Ma'am,' answered the astonished Sherlock, 'did you say that you have the chapel?'

'Yes. My friend replied to my letter by return air mail. He sent me a cheque for forty thousand dollars. Come up right away and put it in the bank.'

'How wonderful, Ma'am,' enthused Sherlock, 'how wonderful that the first gift to the appeal should be the chapel.'

'That's what my husband said,' answered the Princess. 'So come up right away and put it in the bank.'

Philip Sherlock hurried out and hailed a taxi. 'Kensington Palace please, and quickly,' he instructed.

'The driver looked at me as if I were mad,' he remembers. 'I could hear him thinking, "A coloured man and Kensington Palace; they don't fit." So I assumed an "Oxford accent" and said very firmly, "Kensington Palace please and I am in a hurry. Her Royal Highness Princess Alice is waiting for me." That did it.'

At the Clock House, Sherlock rang the bell. The door was opened, 'in a flash', by the Princess herself. She thrust the cheque into Sherlock's hands.

'Good. Now off to the bank,' she commanded.

'Good,' repeated Sherlock to his bemused taxi driver. 'Now off to the bank.'

'And all the way I clutched the cheque, which was safely tucked away in the inside pocket of my jacket.'[36]

The Princess's concern with the chapel by no means ended with her financing of it. She was determined to see it built and furnished. In this she was being supported, among others, by the Rev. George Fox, rector of St James's Church, Montego Bay. On a Jamaican sugar estate Princess Alice came across the ruins of an old mansion, constructed of massive blocks of cut-stone and featuring gracious archways. The owner immediately agreed to donate the building. The Princess then badgered the Association of Jamaican Builders to make their contribution by transporting the building, stone by stone, to the university campus, and the university architects, through their resident architect Alick Low, to redesign it as a chapel.

The result was a harmonious blend of old and new: 'the building spoke of today as a natural continuation of yesterday',[37] as one contemporary puts it. The building completed, the Princess organised the working parties who furnished and equipped it.

Close to and complementing the newly constructed chapel was an old aqueduct which had once carried water from the Hope River to the sugar fields that had previously covered what was now the university campus. Here and there this graceful line of arches was broken and at one point the builders had knocked down half an archway to make room for a road. The Princess was appalled.

'The vandals!' she exclaimed. 'Don't let them touch it. They mustn't remove another brick!'

The university authorities promised that the aqueduct would be preserved but to make quite sure that they kept their promise, Princess Alice took out her 'little box camera' and solemnly photographed the entire length of the aqueduct. This way, she explained in her mock-serious fashion, she 'would have evidence to use against them if they strayed'.[38]

5

'No holiday,' Princess Alice once said, 'is as agreeable as one which is allied to a purpose.'[39] Now, her purpose being her duties as Chancellor, the Princess was able to spend some of the most agreeable holidays of her life in Jamaica. Each January the Athlones would sail from England in one of Elders & Fyffes banana boats to spend several weeks in 'the heavenly climate' of the Caribbean. We returned to our work, says the Princess, 'like giants refreshed'.[40]

'I think,' says Lady Huggins, 'she really fell in love with Jamaica.'[41] Lady Huggins was right. Not since her years in South Africa had Princess Alice been so enamoured of a place as she was of Jamaica. Each season, having spent ten days or so as the guests of the Governor in King's House, the somewhat haphazardly constructed Government House in Kingston, the Athlones would rent a house on the north coast. This might be The Ridge, belonging to Mrs Alice Màchelin, or Mount Corbett, belonging to Mrs Emma Sewell. The house having first been inspected by the Governor or an aide, the Athlones would arrive with maid, manservant, suitcases and 'crates of books'.[41] (Princess Alice always enjoyed reading biographies and sometimes, on the voyage out, she might be reading a Trollope novel.) Although the owners of the homes would have been only too willing to allow their illustrious guests to live rent-free, the Athlones always insisted on paying.

With its scenic drives, its wooded mountains, and dazzling seashore, its brilliant flowers and fields of pineapples and sugar cane, its coconut palms and banana plantations, Jamaica was, in Princess Alice's words, 'a supremely beautiful island'.[43] During the day they would bathe, go for drives or take long walks. At night they would entertain friends to dinner, play cards or read. On Sundays they always went to church. Princess Alice was especially fond of the sermons of a certain Canon Pronger. 'Where is Canon Pronger preaching today?' she would ask of her hostess. 'I've never followed a rector around like I do this one.'[44] And even in the most violent rainstorm, the Princess would set off for some remote village church to hear her favourite preacher.

On their daily walks, the Athlones would always stop to talk to the islanders. 'Morning, Ma'am,' one of them might call out cheerfully, 'stretching your foot this morning?' On one occasion, a woman drew the Athlones' attention to the state of her roof: it had been all but destroyed in a hurricane. She was waiting, she explained, for the Lord to repair it. The Athlones hurried on, not at all sure if the woman was pinning her hopes on the Lord Almighty or Lord Athlone.

Sometimes, after their stay on the north coast, the couple might spend a few days at the Mona Hotel near Kingston. At this time it was owned by Harold J. Ashwell. On the occasion of their first visit, Harold Ashwell found the protocol both fascinating and unnerving. The hotel owner had given his guests his own, recently remodelled cottage in the grounds and he and his manageress had been fully briefed 'as to where we should stand and how we should receive them when introduced'.

This meticulously planned and well-rehearsed performance was ruined by the fact that the Athlones arrived in a tiny British car out of which the tall and bulky Lord Athlone had the greatest difficulty in extricating himself. Completely forgetting his careful briefing (and possibly emboldened by the glass of whisky with which he had been steadying his nerves) Ashwell dashed forward and, by lifting out first one of Lord Athlone's long legs and then the other, and by hoisting his Lordship into an upright position, got him safely out of the car. When the flustered aide began his introductions, Lord Athlone cut him short.

'I think,' said the wryly smiling Lord Athlone, 'Mr Ashwell has very successfully presented himself.'

Nor was this Harold Ashwell's only contact with Lord Athlone's long legs. Before the arrival of his guests Ashwell had very wisely asked the local Chinese blacksmith to lengthen his Lordship's bed-frame – and the local sempstress to lengthen his Lordship's mattress – by a foot. The owner's foresight was greatly appreciated. 'I was looking for you,' said Lord Athlone to Ashwell on the morning after his arrival, 'to congratulate you on giving me the most comfortable night I have spent since I left my own home. It was the first time that my feet have not hung out of the end of the bed.'[45]

One of the most touching moments during the Athlones' stay was when the couple first entered the hotel dining-room for dinner. Quite spontaneously the other diners, who were mostly American and Canadian, rose to their feet, and remained standing until the Athlones were seated.

At the Mona Hotel, as at every other place where the couple stayed, they would go for a daily walk. Although the Princess remained as vigorous as ever, Lord Athlone, by now in his late seventies, was beginning to slow down, so she sometimes went walking without him. Trailed by one or two puffing and perspiring companions, often less than half her age, the Princess would stride briskly on, keeping the pace up for two or three or even four hours at a time.

On one occasion, when the couple were living in the Màchelin household on the north coast, and the Princess was out walking, Lord Athlone was suddenly taken ill. The Máchelins were greatly alarmed. One messenger was sent dashing off after the Princess and the other to summon the local doctor. The doctor arrived first. Fortunately, Lord Athlone's condition was not serious. It was some time before the Princess could be reached and brought back. Why, she asked Alice Máchelin on arriving home, had they sent for the doctor? And why had she been called back? A flustered Alice Máchelin tried to explain but the Princess, with her refusal to acknowledge illness, was unconvinced.

'In our family,' said Princess Alice firmly, 'we don't panic.'[46]

6

On 6 February 1952, King George VI died in his sleep after a day's shooting at Sandringham. The Athlones heard the news soon after setting out on their annual voyage to Jamaica. The shock, says Princess Alice, was 'intensely personal'. Having 'spent himself so unstintingly for fifteen years,' she wrote, 'his health finally gave way and he had to undergo the sufferings of two major operations, both of which he bore with such stoical courage and cheerfulness that the rest of us could scarcely bring ourselves to realise the magnitude of what he had endured.'[47]

Princess Alice, who had already lived during five reigns, now entered her sixth. Again she was doubly related to the new sovereign, the young Queen Elizabeth II. The Queen was her first cousin, twice removed, on Princess Alice's own side of the family, and her great-niece on Lord Athlone's side: Generally, Princess Alice would be referred to as Queen Elizabeth II's great-aunt. Quite literally, overnight, Princess Alice found herself moved yet another generation away from the throne. During Princess Alice's girlhood, the reigning Queen had been her grandmother; now the reigning Queen belonged to the generation of her own grandchildren.

This sense of things changing and time passing was emphasised, just over a year later, by the death of Princess Alice's sister-in-law, Queen Mary, on 24 March 1953. Although the death of this indomitable old Queen had been expected, it came as a great blow to the Athlones. There had always been what Princess Alice calls 'a special affinity' between Queen Mary and Lord Athlone: 'even when they were thousands of miles apart,' she claims, 'they seemed to influence one another.' Queen Mary's brother and sister-in-law were among the very few people to whom the unnaturally reserved Queen could ever open her heart. And they, in turn, had always appreciated her 'strength of character as much as her infinite capacity for sympathy and understanding.'[48] If others thought that Queen Mary was somehow cold and unfeeling, the Athlones knew her too well to make that misjudgement.

After lying in state in Westminster Hall, Queen Mary's body was brought to St George's Chapel for burial. 'It was a simple ceremony,' remembered Princess Alice, 'as befitted the gentleness of her disposition, and was unaccompanied by the sombre magnificence and military display which are prescribed for the funerals of sovereigns. . . .

'The service ended with her chosen hymn "Abide with Me", sung by that perfect choir without accompaniment, at the conclusion of which her favourite grandchild, Lillibet, now Queen, quietly left her stall and stood alone beside the catafalque which was covered by [Queen Mary's] Garter banner. . . . As the coffin descended into the vault Lillibet bowed over the open space which appeared in the floor and the Lord Chamberlain threw some gravel on to it in accordance with custom.'[49]

It was a great pity that Queen Mary did not live long enough to see her granddaughter crowned, just over two months later, on 2 June 1953, amid scenes of great splendour, in Westminster Abbey. Of all the coronations at which she was present, Princess Alice considered Queen Elizabeth II's Coronation to be 'the culmination of beauty and pageantry'.[50] Lord Athlone, finally too old at seventy-nine to escort his sovereign on horseback, drove to the Abbey beside Princess Alice in the carriage procession of the Princes and Princesses of the Blood Royal. With them, in the first of these coaches, were two more of Queen Victoria's surviving granddaughters: Lady

Patricia Ramsay and Princess Marie Louise.* In the Abbey itself, Princess Alice's train was borne by her old friend, Mrs Muriel Mure, and her coronet was carried by her grandson, Richard Abel Smith. Lord Athlone's page was Gerald Ward.

Even among that glittering assembly of women in Westminster Abbey, Princess Alice looked remarkable. There was certainly no member of the royal family of her generation to equal her for poise, elegance and beauty. With her silver hair dressed high and topped by her coronet, her finely chiselled features, her still slender figure, her gleaming satin dress, her sparkling jewels, including the ropes of pearls and stomacher which she had worn at every Coronation, and her sumptuous, ermine-lined mantle, Princess Alice looked undeniably regal. For the first time, perhaps, a younger generation of the public became aware of the fact that among the new Queen's collection of elderly female relations was one with an outstanding sense of style.

Public recognition of Princess Alice's enduring elegance came some eighteen months later when she was chosen, by the *Evening Standard* Fashion Panel, as one of the ten best-dressed women in Britain. The panel – made up of Loelia, Duchess of Westminster, Lady Diana Cooper, the historian of costume James Laver and the photographer Baron, with the fashion writer Eileen Ascroft as a non-voting chairman

---

* Lady Patricia Ramsay (1886–1974) was the second daughter of Prince Arthur, Duke of Connaught. Princess Marie Louise was the second daughter of Princess Christian of Schlcswig-Holstein.

– unanimously chose Princess Alice as 'the most elegant older woman of the year'.

'At the age of seventy-one,' declared the Panel, 'she still possesses the face and figure of a Dresden shepherdess and her superb carriage puts many younger women to shame.' It went on to list the various features which had caused her to be chosen: her simplicity of style, the perfection of her accessories, her imaginative use of colour (with a pearl grey evening dress she wore pale mauve gloves and had her hair tinted pale mauve), her stylish hats, her lavish furs and, above all, the air of assurance with which she wore her clothes. 'The panel', ran the final summing-up, 'choose Princess Alice for all-round day and evening elegance in dressing which makes her outstanding among women of her age.'[51]

The extraordinary thing was that, a quarter of a century later, the panel's judgement would still have held good.

7

On 10 February 1954 Princess Alice and Lord Athlone celebrated their Golden Wedding. She was seventy, he was seventy-nine. Fifty years ago, under the banner-hung ceiling of St George's Chapel at Windsor, King Edward VII had given away his niece, the elfin Princess Alice of Albany, in marriage to the handsome Prince Alexander of Teck. All in all, the marriage had been a supremely happy one. The couple had so many tastes and interests in common; their personalities were complementary. Although Princess Alice might have had the stronger character ('She was always the boss',[52] claims a close friend) she was never domineering, never aggressive. She knew exactly how to handle her husband. 'They were *very* sweet together,'[53] says one associate. 'I think,' wrote Princess Alice on one occasion, 'there is no closer companionship, no more sympathetic understanding than that which exists between the husband and wife of a long and happy union.'[54]

The Golden Wedding was to have been celebrated with a party for two hundred guests in the State Apartments of St James's Palace. But a week or so before the date, Lord Athlone was confined to bed with influenza. By 5 February it was realised that he would not be well enough to attend and the party had to be cancelled. Instead, a family luncheon was held at Kensington Palace on 10 February. It was attended by Queen Elizabeth the Queen Mother, Princess Margaret, the Duke and Duchess of Gloucester, the Duchess of Kent and, of course, the Abel Smith family. As a gift from Queen Elizabeth II, members of the royal family and a number of friends, the couple were presented with a large painting by Norman Hepple. It was a double portrait, picturing Princess Alice and Lord Athlone sitting in the Green Corridor at Kensington Palace.

'Thank you,' wrote Princess Alice to a friend when the great day was over, 'for your good wishes on our Golden Wedding anniversary. It is a very happy and, even to us, wonderful date to have reached. We were inundated with telegrams and letters and flowers and many very charming presents. . . . It made us very proud to feel we possessed so many faithful friends and well-wishers.'[55]

As Lord Athlone was slow in recovering from his bout of illness the couple travelled to Italy, to the Villa Taranto on Lake Maggiore, that spring. 'We have now come to Italy for him to get thoroughly back to his old form,' the Princess reported to a friend, 'though at eighty one can't expect to be as frisky as a lad.'[56]

In fact, Lord Athlone never really 'got back to his old form'. In spite of Princess Alice's determination not to acknowledge the fact that her husband might be taken from her, Lord Athlone's health gradually began to fail. 'Slowly and peacefully . . . as a candle burns itself out,' she says, 'he failed in health and vigour during the last two years of his life.'[57]

During these years the presence of their family afforded the couple great pleasure. 'Aunt Alice', claims the Queen Mother, 'had a very strong sense of family. She was devoted to them all.'[58] By now their son-in-law, Colonel Henry Abel Smith,* had left the Army. 'He is busy farming pigs, breeding arabs and busy with the administrative life of his district: on the Church, Boy Scouts, Horse Shows and urban Council –

---

* Made Knight Commander of the Royal Victorian Order in 1950 and Knight Commander of the Order of St Michael and St George in 1961.

so he has little time to idle,' reported the Princess in 1954. 'May flourishes and is the same as ever . . . Richard, the only boy, is twenty and now a lieutenant in the Horse Guards; we are very pleased with him as he came 3rd in the "passing out" at Sandhurst . . . 3rd of 300! So I hope he keeps up his standard. I know you would like him, he is so modest and friendly. Ann is out and about and also a sweet person. Elizabeth, seventeen, comes out this summer; she is the pretty one, really pretty. . . .'[59]

These three charming and attractive grandchildren, flitting in and out of Kensington Palace, were the greatest comfort to the dying Lord Athlone. He always looked forward to their visits, when they tried, as they put it, to 'jolly him up'.[60] This meant, says Princess Alice, that 'as he was daily growing weaker, there was no sadness in the house, except deep down in our hearts, as we followed his days to the quiet end. For me it was like watching the weights of a pendulum clock moving slowly to their ultimate extension while realising that neither I, nor anyone else, could wind them up again. . . .'[61]

Lord Athlone died on 16 January 1957, at the age of eighty-two. He was buried, with full military honours, in St George's Chapel, Windsor Castle. From the special train, which had brought it from Paddington to Windsor, his coffin was lifted by soldiers and placed on a waiting gun carriage. To the sound of mournful music and the thudding of a 13-gun salute from the Great Park, the coffin was taken through the King Henry VIII Gateway of the Castle and carried up the steps into the Chapel. The funeral was attended by the Queen, Queen Elizabeth the Queen Mother, Princess Margaret and over a score of other royal mourners. Princess Alice, heavily veiled, sat on the left of the Queen. At the head of the mourners walking behind the coffin was the Duke of Gloucester; among the others were Prince Bernhard of the Netherlands and Admiral of the Fleet Earl Mountbatten. Lord Athlone was buried, alongside other members of the royal family, at Frogmore in Windsor Great Park. [†]

There is no isolation, wrote Princess Alice some years later, 'so desolate as the loneliness of those "first dark days of nothingness" which follow the final separation.'[62] And almost a quarter of a century later, when speaking to someone who had recently lost her husband, the Princess said, 'You will find that the family and friends will remember with you the important dates and the sad events, but now there will be no one to laugh at the happy memories with you. That is the worst of loneliness.'[63]

[†] Lord Athlone left an estate of £34, 112 net. Except for a few small legacies, the bulk of his estate was left in trust for Princess Alice.

CHAPTER SEVENTEEN

1

There is a prayer, written by Sir Francis Drake, which Princess Alice was particularly fond of quoting. 'O Lord God,' it reads, 'when thou giv'est thy servants to endeavour in any great matter, grant us also to know that it is not the beginning, but the continuing of the same unto the end, until it be thoroughly finished, which yieldeth the true glory. . . .'[1]

Few words could more accurately have summed up Princess Alice's attitude to life. It would never have occurred to her to do other than continue 'unto the end, until it be thoroughly finished' anything which she had undertaken. Her husband's death, after fifty-three years of happy marriage, might have left her desolate but she would never, for a moment, have contemplated a permanent withdrawal from public life. Neither her temperament, nor her iron sense of duty, would have allowed her to give up her various obligations. What she could not have guessed was that well over twenty years of life – of active, adventurous

458

and useful life – still lay ahead of her. Princess Alice turned seventy-four in the year of Lord Athlone's death; the 'true glory' had still to be yielded.

As always, travel remained one of the Princess's chief diversions. Fortunately, a few months after Lord Athlone's death, Sir Henry Abel Smith was appointed Governor of Queensland. As the Abel Smiths were to remain in Brisbane for almost eight years, Princess Alice was able to pay them three long visits – in 1959, in 1962 and in 1965. Travelling out to Australia in a cargo boat (on one occasion she flew) she usually spent four or five months in Government House, Brisbane.

The Princess describes these visits as 'unforgettable'. 'I travelled,' she says, 'by rail, by air, by car and on foot throughout that most beautiful country – so different from other parts of the world and yet holding the same enchantment for all who have eyes to see. I learned to know and to make real friends of so many Australians, that frank, hospitable and cultured people.' Indeed, she continues, 'I really fell in love with Australia and its people.'[2]

And Australia fell in love with her. There was something about this doughty, independent, unpretentious yet unmistakably royal old lady that made a tremendous appeal to the Australians. They appreciated her outspokenness. For, as Princess Alice aged, so did she feel less inhibited about expressing her always forthright opinions. To the delight of Australian newspapers, she announced that she could not agree with Queen Elizabeth II's decision to send her heir, Prince Charles, to Gordonstoun. He should go to Eton, declared Princess Alice. 'There he would make many more contacts that would stay with him through life – not just in England but throughout the world.'[3] In Melbourne she said that it was a pity that the Queen would have to undergo the strain of an official tour when she came out to Australia in 1963. 'It would be so much better if she could get out into the country without all the fuss.'[4]

Princess Alice certainly moved about with the least possible fuss. 'I really came to have a bit of a holiday,' she once explained. 'I don't want to be involved in a lot of formalities. There is plenty of that sort of thing at home.'[5] Yet, whenever she was obliged to do 'that sort of thing' she did it with all her customary grace and charm. When, for instance, the Triennial Conference of the International Federation of University Women was held in Brisbane in 1965, Princess Alice consented to act as Patroness. 'Princess Alice,' remembers one delegate, 'who was then eighty-two, officiated at the opening of the Conference the same evening, looking very elegant in a beautiful long evening dress, and giving an excellent speech.'[6]

But, of course, it was on her journeys through the Australian bush that the Princess was happiest. 'We walk for miles every afternoon,' she claimed gleefully. 'There are lovely hills and mountains to climb, and wonderful walks off the main track.' The Princess could hardly have hoped for a better walking companion than Sir Henry Abel Smith. An enthusiastic bird-watcher, he introduced her, she says, 'to some of the strange and beautiful species that can only be found "down under".'[7]

The Princess and Sir Henry would usually be driven in the Governor's Rolls-Royce to some remote area where they would be dropped off by the chauffeur, who would then pick them up at some prearranged point several hours later. On one occasion, when Sir Henry had an important evening engagement, there was no sign of the car at the appointed meeting place. In mounting anxiety and in the fast-fading light, the two of them stood by the roadside waiting for the chauffeur. Finally, from the opposite direction, in a cloud of dust, a vehicle came trundling down the road. As it came closer, they saw that it was a small open truck, loaded with school desks. When Sir Henry hailed it the driver stopped and agreed to give them a lift. Quite unperturbed, Princess Alice clambered up onto the back of the truck and seated herself at one of the desks. And there she sat as they jolted along the dusty, rutted road, until they met the frantic chauffeur in the Governor's Rolls-Royce.

Princess Alice's first visit to Australia, in 1959, was merely one of her calls on a 25,000 mile, round-the-world journey. From Australia she sailed, on the American liner S.S. *Monterey*, to San Francisco, *en route* to Canada. Before leaving Sydney she had asked the Captain whether he thought she might learn to speak American on the voyage. 'No,' she explained ruefully on arrival in San Francisco, 'she hadn't *quite* learned to speak the language.'[8]

Her first glimpse of San Francisco, on 24 August 1959, delighted her. 'What a perfectly marvellous city!'[9] she exclaimed. Far from wanting to rest before taking that evening's train to Seattle and on to Vancouver, she insisted on a full tour of the bay region of the city.

Princess Alice spent almost two months in Canada, crossing the country by train and staying with friends in several major Canadian cities. She even managed a two-day fishing stay at Echo Lodge near Kamloops in British Columbia, where she and Lord Athlone had so often spent such happy holidays. Her luck on this occasion, she says frankly, was 'indifferent'.[10] In Ottawa the Princess was the guest at Rideau Hall of the newly-installed Governor-General and Mrs Georges Vanier. It was thirteen years since the Princess had last lived in the house: 'I find it difficult not to feel that I'm mistress here,'[11] she admitted. She felt, she said, so much at home. To the Governor-General, Princess Alice was 'the youngest middle-aged woman' he had ever known. She was also the easiest of guests. All she wanted, she said, was 'nice small meals with half-a-dozen real pals where we can have a good talk'.[12] One day, during her stay in Ottawa, an old man walked up to her in the street and gave her a hearty greeting. 'I haven't seen you in such a long time,' he said. The Princess was deeply touched. 'He was a stranger to me,' she says, 'but I appreciated the welcome *so* much.'[13]

In Montreal, where she was the guest of friends, the Princess spoke of her continuing interest in the Princess Alice Foundation Fund for youth leadership training which had been established with the farewell gift of money made to her by the women of Canada in 1946.

'So few young people will take responsibility today,' she complained. 'They're too busy. It's hard to find younger women to head groups such as the Girl Guides. The older people have to carry on. Clubs need youth leadership.' It is better, she claimed, to have 'good children than a washing machine'. More emphasis should be placed on religious training and discipline in the home and less on material acquisitions. 'Young people today have so much freedom, but they don't know how to use it. With good home training they will not go off the rails. They're sensible creatures, really wiser than preceding generations. They'll find a level as time goes on.'[14]

After a ten-day stay in Quebec, Princess Alice sailed back to England on 13 October 1959 in the *Empress of England.** She had been away for nine months. But this was not, by any means, the end of that year's travelling. Within a couple of weeks of her

---

* Four years later, in September 1963, Princess Alice again visited Ottawa to present regimental colours to the Princess Louise Dragoon Guards, of which she was an honorary colonel.

arrival home, she was in Cyprus on a private visit to the Governor, Sir Hugh Foot. And a few weeks after that, in January 1960, she set sail in the banana boat, *Camito,* for the West Indies.

'If we keep busy,' Princess Alice had said in Ottawa to her longstanding friend, the 74-year-old Senator Cairine Wilson, 'we'll be all right.' There was no doubt that she was keeping busy.

2

But Jamaica, during these years, remained Princess Alice's first love. For the fifteen years following Lord Athlone's death, the Princess continued to pay her annual visit to the West Indies. By the 1960s she had acquired a new travelling companion. This was her lady-in-waiting and friend, Miss Joan Lascelles. Joan Lascelles's brother, Capt. J.N.P. Lascelles, had been on the Athlones' staff in South Africa and ever since then she had done what she called 'odd jobs'[15] for the Princess. Now they became more closely associated. A good few years younger than Princess Alice, Joan Lascelles had a great deal of the Princess's own robust, enquiring and gregarious nature. Equally energetic, and equally oblivious of the hazards and discomforts of travel, yet exercising exactly the necessary degree of public unobtrusiveness, Joan Lascelles made the perfect royal companion. For something like fifteen years these two spirited women journeyed together.

Each January, sharing a small cabin on a banana boat[†] and accompanied by a single maid, Princess Alice and her companion sailed to Jamaica. On arrival they were met by the Governor. They would spend a fortnight or so at King's House, where the Princess would busy herself with her various duties as Chancellor of the University College of the West Indies. From 1957 until 1962 the Governor of Jamaica was Sir Kenneth Blackburne, and he and his wife quickly discovered, he says, 'that Princess Alice was the easiest of guests. Despite, or perhaps because of, her previous experience as wife of the Governor-General of South Africa and later Canada, she understood our problems and fitted admirably into our more simple way of life. Adored by all the domestic staff whose names and family circumstances she knew and remembered each year, thoughtful for the mundane commitments and worries of my wife and myself, and always ready to fall in with our plans, she was the perfect guest.'

She was also an extremely amusing one. The Princess's fund of funny stories was apparently inexhaustible. On one occasion, when Lord Mountbatten happened to be staying at King's House, the two of them delighted their hosts at the dinner table by

---

[†] An apocryphal story has it that, as Princess Alice lived deeper and deeper into her eighties, arrangements were made for a special coffin to be carried back in the refrigerated section of the banana boat in the event of her death. Year after year went by; the coffin remained empty; and the Princess stopped visiting Jamaica.

capping each other's funny stories; 'each one,' says Sir Kenneth, 'better than the last.'

During her first visit to the Blackburnes, Princess Alice was accompanied, not by Joan Lascelles, but by her sister-in-law, the Duchess of Coburg. By now the widowed Duchess of Coburg was much more happily placed than she had been during those dark days just after the war. Short, plump and speaking broken English at 'considerable length and speed', the Duchess shared Princess Alice's 'immense sense of fun'.[16] Some of the Duchess's humour, however, was unconscious. On one occasion, she came in from the beautiful grounds of King's House to compliment Sir Kenneth on the good manners of his gardeners. 'I found four of them sitting in a summer house playing cards,' she reported, 'and they got to their feet and bowed, and asked me to join them.'[17]

Sir Kenneth's only, and admittedly good-natured, complaint was the universal one: Princess Alice's inexhaustible energy. 'I was regularly made to walk into the hills above Kingston, where she used to outstrip both the Army Commander and myself as we sweated up the little forest paths.'[18] On her first visit to the Blackburnes, she 'insisted on climbing St Catherine's Peak . . . an expedition which I only managed once in five years. Accompanied by the Duchess of Coburg and an aide-de-camp she set off early one morning, returning in time for luncheon with two exhausted companions, but herself quite unruffled and full of the views which she had seen.'[19]

Politically, far-reaching changes were taking place in the West Indies during the years that Princess Alice was Chancellor. Sir Kenneth Blackburne's predecessor, Sir Hugh Foot, had presided over the changes towards internal self-government and Sir Kenneth Blackburne was responsible for guiding Jamaica to full internal self-government and independence in 1962, becoming the first Governor-General of an independent Jamaica.

Although Princess Alice would have been in full accord with the British Government's determination to grant eventual independence to its various dependencies, she might, with her naturally conservative views, have found this loosening of the British reins somewhat precipitate. A dinner guest at King's House, during Sir Hugh Foot's governorship, once found himself involved in a discussion on universal adult suffrage. His was the usual colonist's viewpoint; Sir Hugh's was more enlightened. Princess Alice listened intently to Sir Hugh Foot's arguments in favour of adult suffrage and, when he had finished, she 'stunned the assembled company' by exclaiming, 'Foot! I have never heard such balderdash in my life!'[20]

But these were her private views. In public the Princess's attitudes were always above reproach. Sir Kenneth Blackburne had nothing but praise for the skill and impartiality with which she handled university affairs during this period of political transition. With Jamaican independence in 1962, the University of the West Indies was granted its own Charter and not only was Princess Alice invited to remain on as Chancellor but she had the title of 'Chancellor Emeritus' conferred on her 'in recognition of her outstanding service to the institution and to the region'.[21]

As Chancellor, says Sir Kenneth, 'Princess Alice had to deal with representatives of all the then fourteen British Colonial Governments which existed in the West Indies. Six of the members of the Council were leading politicians who, like some of their colleagues nominated from educational sources, could at times express "extremist" views. The fact that she held this office for twenty-one years – eight years after the major territories of Barbados, Guyana, Jamaica and Trinidad had attained independence – is a striking tribute to the affection in which she was held by the people of the West Indies and to her powers of leadership."[22]

Princess Alice never revealed the slightest trace of colour prejudice. On the contrary, she befriended whomever she liked, regardless of their colour or social position. On one occasion, the Princess fell and broke her arm while on her afternoon walk on the north coast, and was taken to St Ann's Bay Hospital. After the fracture had been reduced under general anaesthesia – and as the hospital had no private rooms – she was admitted to a general ward where she lay among the other islanders. 'She showed no sign of prejudice at any time,' says a local doctor. 'I visited her on two or three occasions after her discharge to ensure satisfactory progress. A most genteel, soft-spoken, charming and gracious lady.'[23]

Jamaica's first black Governor-General, Sir Clifford Campbell, the Princess liked enormously. With a grace conspicuously lacking in some of the wives of Jamaica's white community, she would greet him – as the representative of the British monarch – with a deep curtsey. The only complaint she had about him was his longwindedness when making a speech. So, when seated beside him at some function, she would simply tug at his coat and whisper. 'Sit down.' 'He obeyed,' says one resident, 'and never minded.'[24]

At university graduation balls, the Princess danced quite happily with the students. On one occasion she found herself dancing with a young Jamaican who, being somewhat in awe of his illustrious partner, was handling her with exceptional reverence. 'Now wheel me, young man,' commanded Princess Alice, '*wheel* me.' And wheel her, with 'all the West Indian twirls and twists' the young man promptly proceeded to do.

This informality, this readiness to join in the fun, always endeared the Chancellor to the staff and students. Once, when the Princess was presiding over the formal opening of the first Hall of Residence for women, a black Labrador bitch belonging to the Vice-Principal, Philip Sherlock, joined the company on the dais. Princess Alice was very fond of dogs (years before in South Africa, in the course of a meeting of the National Council for Child Welfare, a dog had wandered into the hall and the Princess, taking a cushion from her chair, had put it on the floor for the dog to lie on) but this particular dog was definitely not welcome. She was on heat and had escaped from custody. Trailing a pack of slavering and lustfully prancing male dogs, she circled the Princess's chair before being hauled away by a red-faced Clerk of Works.

'Whose dog was that?' asked the highly-amused Princess.

Philip Sherlock kept cravenly silent. But his ten-year-old son was less reticent.

'That's my dog,' he piped up, 'and I'm mighty proud of her.'

'It was a long time,' remembers Sir Philip Sherlock, 'before Her Royal Highness allowed me to forget that.'[25]

As a member of the British royal family Princess Alice was in a position to involve her royal relations in the affairs of the University with much more ease than might otherwise have been possible. In 1952 she was instrumental in the presentation to the University of a gift of 335 books from Queen Mary's library at Marlborough House. Queen Elizabeth II and the Duke of Edinburgh paid visits to the campus and in 1965 the Princess conferred an honorary degree on Queen Elizabeth the Queen Mother.

The coming together of these two remarkable women ensured that the occasion was a blend of charm and humour. The speaker that year was the distinguished American politician, Adlai Stevenson. Having conferred the degrees with her usual grace and dignity, Princess Alice – quite forgetting that Adlai Stevenson had still not delivered his speech – started to make a firm announcement to the effect that 'The purpose for which we came together has been accomplished . . .' when an anguished colleague hissed, 'Ma'am, Ma'am, you have to call on Mr Stevenson.'

Instead of making the expected apology, Princess Alice simply covered her face with her programme and rocked with laughter. Gradually the entire audience, including Adlai Stevenson, joined in. After three or four hilarious minutes, the Princess called on her guest to speak.

Adlai Stevenson's opening remark caused another round of laughter. 'Ma'am,' he said, 'after your gallant effort to *save* me from all this . . . .'

Prompted, perhaps, by Princess Alice's unwitting attempt to do away with his speech altogether, Adlai Stevenson had the good sense to cut it short. 'My heart,' admits the Queen Mother, 'rather sank at the sight of his great wadge of notes'.[28] Her heart was correspondingly lifted when, very skilfully, the speaker dispensed with the greater part of them.

At the end of the ceremony, the Queen Mother spoke to Adlai Stevenson. 'Well, Mr Stevenson,' she said, with that characteristic tilt of the head and sparkle in the eye, 'we were together at Oxford six weeks ago, and now we meet here. Where shall it be next?'

Adlai Stevenson was equal to the occasion. 'You name the place, Ma'am,' he said gallantly, 'and I'll be there.'[27]

3

Her various annual university commitments over, Princess Alice would set off on her holiday on Jamaica's north coast. This remained her chief joy. Most often she took a house or stayed with friends in the parish of St Ann, the 'garden parish' of Jamaica. She felt that she 'belonged' there; she was, she would say, 'a parishioner.'[28] 'Where can I bathe?'[29] would be her first question on arriving at some new spot. Even in her eighties she was to be found swimming in the warm, translucent sea. On market days she would visit Brown's Town, showing every interest in the pedlars and their wares. No matter how hot the day or informal the occasion, she always looked immaculate.

'The day we encountered her darting about the market in St Ann's Bay,' remembered one resident, 'she was dressed in a practical manner to contend with the humid heat – large straw hat, sleeveless cotton dress, bare legs and sandals and a simple strand of pearls, but she maintained an indefinable air of regalness.'[30]

Her vitality, and her willingness to carry out any public duty asked of her, were inexhaustible. On one day, for instance, she opened an agricultural fair in Trelawny parish and toured the exhibition stands.

She then went on to a supermarket in St Ann's Bay where the Jamaican police corporal, who had been detailed to accompany her, had 'difficulty in keeping up with her as she moved rapidly about the store buying gifts for a children's party'.[31] That afternoon she took her usual long walk; and that evening, as fresh and lively and entertaining as ever, she attended a formal function. She was eighty-five at the time.

For all her celebrated charm of manner, the Princess was anything but a royal automaton. With the passing years, her comments became increasingly trenchant. 'I do not understand what these paintings are all about,' she once exclaimed at a display of children's art in a Jamaican school. 'People tell me that the children are expressing their own ideas. I sometimes wonder if they have any ideas to express.'[32]

Princess Alice never missed Sunday church service. The congregation of some humble and impoverished village church would always be delighted and flattered to have this small, soignée figure sitting in its midst. But she was not always recognised. 'On one occasion,' notes one observer, 'she decided to go to a somewhat bigger church in a town a little way inland. She was duly received by the rector and the church committee and ushered into a pew fairly near the front. The rest of the pew was empty.

'A late-comer, knowing nothing of the distinguished stranger, entered by the west door and slowly made her way forward, looking for an empty seat in the unusually crowded church. Seeing a nearly empty pew she approached and said audibly, "Move up, Missus."

'The Princess smilingly complied.'[33]

At the annual evening service of commemoration in the University Chapel the Princess always read the first lesson. This practice was not without its hazards. She had once just started to read in her 'firm, strong voice'[34] when there was a power failure. While there was a frantic scrabbling about in the pitch darkness to produce an emergency light, Princess Alice's voice continued imperturbably on; she knew the lesson by heart. A recording of the service subsequently proved that she had remained quite calm, confident and fluent throughout the upheaval.

Princess Alice was fond of telling her own church story. 'At Mattins one Sunday,' she would say, 'a lady with newly-washed hair was having great trouble to keep it from falling down. As she knelt, she re-sited one hairpin after another in a fruitless attempt to secure the whole. Finally, while the rest of the congregation was still kneeling, she sat up, gathered up every hair she could find, and pinned it as securely as possible.

'Then she heard an agonised whisper from behind. "Madam, you're pinning up my beard with your hair."'[35]

Taken together, such vignettes reveal that it was for her humour and stamina, almost as much as for her remarkable record as Chancellor, that Princess Alice became such a legend in Jamaica.

4

For well over fifty years, from the time that Princess Alice's mother, the Duchess of Albany, had first moved into Kensington Palace from Claremont, the Princess had been closely associated with the Royal Borough of Kensington. Since 1946 Kensington Palace had been her only home. By now, she was a familiar and well-loved figure in the Borough. She was often to be seen waiting for a bus or doing some shopping or, on a Sunday morning, attending service in St Mary Abbot Church in the High Street. Sometimes, in the early evening, quite alone, she might drop in on Sir Shuldham Redfern, who had been Lord Athlone's Private Secretary in Canada, at his home in nearby Sheffield Terrace, to discuss her notes for a speech. Unrecognised, she would go walking in Kensington Gardens or Hyde Park.

For years Princess Alice bought flowers at Mrs Ada Shakespeare's stall, quite content to wait her turn in the queue. Once, on looking in her bag, the Princess discovered that she had come out without any money. 'That's all right, Princess,' shrugged Mrs Shakespeare. 'Pay me some other time.'[36] When the flower-seller's stall was once threatened with removal, Princess Alice personally accompanied her to the Town Hall to get the matter settled.

In the years following the Second World War, the character of the Borough of Kensington began undergoing considerable changes. Princess Alice deeply regretted these changes. Day by day, in a frenzy of knocking down and rebuilding, the Borough seemed to be losing its identity; the last remains of its Georgian and Victorian personality were disappearing; its atmosphere was becoming that of any other bustling, commercial district.

When the Kensington Society was formed in 1953 Princess Alice, already the patron of so many societies, unhesitatingly agreed to become its patron. The objects of the Kensington Society were 'to preserve and improve the amenities of Kensington by stimulating interest in its history and records, by protecting its buildings of beauty and historic interest, by preserving its open spaces from disfigurement and encroachment and by encouraging good architecture in its future development'.[37]

As enthusiastically as any other member, Princess Alice associated herself with the work of the society, in both its preservation and planning capacities. 'I am outraged by So-and-so,' she would write to the Secretary, 'please keep me in touch.' With unflagging interest she attended the Society's functions – the general meetings, the sales of work, the lectures, the exhibitions and the social gatherings. Her only regret was that her royal status prevented her from playing an even more active part.

On 19 September 1978, when she was ninety-five, Princess Alice was to plant a tree on Kensington Square to mark the twenty-fifth anniversary of the founding of the Society. 'She really *planted* that tree,' claims the Secretary, 'not just a little symbolic shovelling of earth.'[38]*

On 3 October 1961, Princess Alice was extremely gratified to receive the freedom of the Royal Borough of Kensington and Chelsea. She was only the third person to be so honoured. The two previous Honorary Freemen were her aunt, Princess Louise, Duchess of Argyll, and Sir Winston Churchill. At a public ceremony, she accepted an ornate Georgian silver cup from the Mayor of Kensington.†

Even now, in her late eighties, the Princess continued with her official duties. Among her various other posts, she was Commandant-in-Chief, Women's Transport Service (FANY); President of the National Children's Adoption Association; President of the King Edward VII District Nursing Association; President of the Royal School of Needlework; President of the Royal Victoria League. And, of course, she was still President of the Duchess of Albany's creation – the Deptford Fund. The Princess never missed the Fund's Christmas luncheon, at which she always made a speech. Once, while in Deptford, she kept Queen Juliana of the Netherlands waiting at Kensington Palace while she drank tea and ate chocolate cake at the Darby and Joan Club. 'I can

---

* After the Princess's death, the Kensington Society launched an appeal for funds for the planting of an avenue of weeping beech trees in Kensington Gardens in memory of the Princess. The response, says the Secretary, was 'tremendous'.

† Princess Alice was also made an Honorary Freeman of the City of London.

have tea with Queen Juliana any day,' she is reported to have said, 'but not with these dear old ladies.'[39]

Her audiences were always delighted, and sometimes even astonished, by her sense of humour. She once told a group of student nurses, to whom she was presenting certificates, a story about a tough paratrooper with a dislocated shoulder who yelled with pain when the doctor began pushing back the joint.

'Be quiet,' commanded a nurse. 'There's a dear little woman in the room above who has just had a baby and she didn't make half as much fuss.'

'Yeah,' said the paratrooper, 'but you just try pushing it back.'[40]

After a moment of 'stunned silence' the assembled nurses roared with laughter.

It was during these years that the Princess established her routine of visiting her old friend, King Gustaf VI Adolf of Sweden each summer. The King's second wife, the spirited Queen Louise, died in 1965 and, as the years went by, so the King of Sweden and Princess Alice, almost exactly the same age, felt drawn together. Both utterly natural, both interested in gardening and the arts, both relics of a very different world yet forward-looking and interested in contemporary life, the couple had a great deal in common. An added attraction for Princess Alice on these Swedish holidays was the presence of her niece, the widowed Crown Princess Sibylla and her children. Princess Sibylla's daughter, Princess Margaretha, was said to be Princess Alice's favourite grand-niece.

In August 'when her staff were on holiday', Princess Alice would stay with the Duke and Duchess of Gloucester at their country home, Barnwell Manor in Northamptonshire. So many years had passed since, as a lonely boy at Eton, Prince Henry had gratefully come to tea with his Uncle Alge and Aunt Alice in the Henry III Tower at Windsor Castle. The Princess's close association with the Duchess of Gloucester had started in South Africa, when the then Lady Alice Montagu-Douglas-Scott had gone out for the wedding of her sister to a member of the Athlones' staff.

On these August holidays at Barnwell it was Princess Alice's undimmed vitality, vivacity and sense of fun that most impressed the Duchess of Gloucester. That, and her unfailing kindness. 'When my son was killed,' said the Duchess of Gloucester, referring to the death of the 30-year-old Prince William of Gloucester in a flying accident in 1972, 'the Princess was wonderfully sympathetic.'[41] Princess Alice knew what it was like to lose a son.

By now Princess Alice's grandchildren were all married. In 1957 her eldest granddaughter Anne married David Liddell Grainger; in 1960 her grandson Richard married Marcia Kendrew; in 1965 her granddaughter Elizabeth married Peter Wise. Each wedding was a full-scale royal occasion, with the Queen's permission being officially sought and granted, and the ceremony attended by members of the British and various continental royal families.

When a new generation of children began to arrive, the Princess was delighted to be able to refer to herself as 'a proud great-grandmother'.*

Strangely, with the years, Princess Alice's informality and adaptability seemed to increase. Instead of becoming more conventional, more circumspect, more set in her ways, she seemed to become less so. Except in matters of dress and manners, the free and easiness of modern life bothered her not at all; on the contrary, she welcomed it. Never anything less than regal, she was never stodgy or strait-laced. Guests arriving to stay at Kensington Palace were always astonished to find that their hostess would take them up to their rooms herself and even inspect the bathroom, to make sure that all their needs were met. 'Everything was so informal that it was difficult to realise,' writes one visitor, 'that one was staying in Kensington Palace as a guest of a member of the royal family.'[43]

'She even gave us a spare key to her front door in case we should be out late any night!'[44] says another guest.

The list of precise yet breezily worded instructions issued by the efficient Miss Mary Goldie reassured even the most apprehensive of guests. It also gave some indication of the hostess's busy life. *'Tonight, Wednesday:'* runs a typical example, 'I think H.R.H.

---

* The Princess was able to see her great-granddaughter, Richard Abel Smith's daughter Katherine, in her wedding dress on her marriage to the Hon. Hubert Beaumont on 16 October 1980.

is taking you out to dinner as it is the cook's day off! It will be just ordinary dress. *Thursday:* H.R.H. opens a Fair at 11 a.m. Luncheon Party here. Sir Robert and Lady Arundel (he is Governor of Barbados) the only guests, apart from Lady May. In the evening you will be going to a Concert at the Festival Hall with H.R.H. and Mrs Mure (lady-in-waiting). This will be evening dress. H.R.H. has to leave the Concert at the interval to go to Buckingham Palace but you and Mrs Mure will remain until the end of the Concert. *Friday:* H.R.H. attends a film in connection with a Midwives' Conference, of the operation on the Siamese twins here last year. She then tours the exhibition connected with this Conference and has luncheon with Sir William Gilliatt and Sir Cecil Wakeley, both noted surgeons. H.R.H. has asked that you be included in the arrangements and Mrs Mure will also be going.'[45]

Away from home, Princess Alice was even more informal. Invited to spend a weekend with friends she would arrive, quite alone, without even a maid, and insist on unpacking her own suitcase. 'On the first occasion,' writes one of her hosts, 'we found to our horror that she had made up her own bed – saying, when we protested, that she knew that we had no resident staff.'[46]

But, of course, Princess Alice could fit just as easily into the grandest of settings. Meeting her, for the first time, at a weekend house party at Wilton, the home of the Earls of Pembroke, Cecil Beaton was immediately struck by her air of assurance. 'Unlike most royalty . . .' he writes, 'she has a directness that is healthy, and her shyness is well under control.' After croquet under the great cedars of Lebanon, the party gathered in the library for a drink before changing for dinner. 'Princess Alice talked on her "Topic A" which was Queen Victoria,' says Beaton. Always articulate and amusing, the Princess regaled the company with stories about her grandmother: how intimidating she could be, yet how good-humoured and easily amused. The Queen 'was often making a hat,' reports Beaton, plaiting straw together, and the Princess Alice was furious at having to wear this hat which she considered hideous.'[47]

With the passing years, Princess Alice's memories, not only of Queen Victoria but of her girlhood and early life, became more and more valuable. 'Her memory,' says Princess Alice, Duchess of Gloucester, 'was really wonderful.'[48] Nor, by the mid-1960s, were there many of her royal contemporaries still alive. The death, in July 1966, of the Infanta Beatrice of Spain* meant that, besides Princess Alice, there were now only two surviving grandchildren of Queen Victoria: Lady Patricia Ramsay and Queen Ena of Spain. So for Princess Alice not to have recorded her always vivid memories would have been a great pity.

It was her old friend, Sir Bede Clifford, who first suggested, and finally persuaded, Princess Alice to

---

* The youngest daughter of Prince Alfred, Duke of Edinburgh (afterwards Duke of Coburg), always known as Baby Bee, who married the Infante Alfonso of Spain.

write her autobiography. With his active collaboration and with the help and encouragement of her secretary, Miss Mary Goldie, Princess Alice set about her task. Gradually, by studying the letters of her father, Prince Leopold, by rereading her own and Lord Athlone's letters to various members of the family, by checking books, notes, speeches, official papers and written accounts, and finally, by drawing on her own recollections, Princess Alice wrote down the story of her long and colourful life.

She enjoyed the undertaking immensely. One of Sir Bede Clifford's daughters remembered seeing 'Daddy and H.R.H. giggling away together like schoolchildren while deciding what could be written and what couldn't'. They were both greatly amused when Sir Bede pointed out that the opening of the Princess's book – 'I, Alice . . .' – echoed the opening of the monumental work of the Greek historian, 'I, Herodotus . . .' To the Princess's fear that 'posterity would not take her history as seriously as it had taken that of Herodotus' Sir Bede replied that as neither she nor he 'would be around to find out' it really did not matter.[49]

Titled *For my Grandchildren: Some Reminiscences of Her Royal Highness Princess Alice Countess of Athlone,* the book was published in the autumn of 1966 by that publisher of so many royal memoirs, Evans Brothers. Not only was the book dedicated to the Princess's grandchildren and great-grandchildren, but it was addressed to them throughout. 'Now that I am over eighty years of age,' ran its introductory sentence, 'I have decided to give you, my grandchildren and great-grandchildren, an account of some of the personalities, interesting and otherwise, who have played a part in my long life.'[50]

This approach ensured that the tone of the book remained informal, chatty, intimate. World figures are referred to by their family names: King Edward VII is Uncle Bertie; King George V is Uncle George or even George; Queen Mary is Aunt May; King George VI is Bertie; Queen Elizabeth II is Lillibet; Lord Athlone is Grandpa; Sir Henry Abel Smith is Daddy; Lady May Abel Smith is Mummy. The book, for all its sketchiness, confusion and lack of balance, is extraordinarily interesting: the author's personality is imprinted on every page – her modesty, her unpretentiousness, her frankness, her humour, her zest, her honesty and her unquenchable spirit. A great deal has been left unsaid or taken for granted but what has been put down forms an invaluable record of an exceptional life.

'I am now eighty-two,' read the last lines *of For my Grandchildren,* 'and it is time to end this story of my life, of which I wanted to give you a slight picture for remembrance. I cannot look forward to a long road now, but no one who trusts in God need fear any surprise, even death.'[51]

Thirteen years later, when the book (already reprinted before publication) had its second edition, she was still alive.

5

By the opening of the 1970s Princess Alice had decided that her 21 – year-long Chancellorship of the University of the West Indies should end. For one thing she was in her late eighties and could not really hope to continue her duties much longer. For another, her association with the University had become somewhat less happy. With the rise of the Black Power movement and the spread of militancy among the students, her position as Chancellor came to be resented by a vocal minority. On one occasion her appearance was actually greeted by a noisy demonstration. 'Sensitive always to the mood of the moment and in step with the demands of changing times,' runs one university tribute to its Chancellor, 'Her Royal Highness indicated her desire to retire to make way for a younger and abler Chancellor to deal with all the plans and projects for university development to be formulated in the future.'[52] In 1970 the Princess announced that she would resign just as soon as her successor was chosen.

So on 13 January 1971 Princess Alice set out on what was assumed would be her final voyage by banana boat to Jamaica. At the end of the month she carried out her last official duty by conferring degrees on over two hundred students. For the majority of the staff and students, the occasion was suffused with sadness. It was almost impossible to imagine anyone else being able to bring an equal lustre to the role of

Chancellor. 'By her own example, by the depth of her own commitment', reads one appreciation, 'Princess Alice inspired others to even greater efforts in the name of the University.'[53] In many ways, Princess Alice's Chancellorship of the University of the West Indies was the supreme achievement of her life.

'What did H.R.H. mean to us?' mused Sir Philip Sherlock in later years. 'A revelation of the greatness of character and of that wisdom which is knowledge transformed by humanity into something warm and precious; a sense of responsibility, and a devotion to duty that was as natural as breathing, so much so that one took it for granted; a quick interest in ideas and in people; and a strength of will without any effort at domination.'[54]

Certain sections of the Press did their best, of course, to attribute the Princess's resignation solely to the growing anti-British, anti-White feeling among the students. Her experiences, they said, had embittered her; she would now turn her back on the West Indies forever. But they were soon proved wrong. Within two years Princess Alice was back on the banana boat, headed for Jamaica. To surprised reporters who telephoned Kensington Palace to find out how the Princess could possibly forgive and forget, Mary Goldie had a deflating answer.

'She could hardly wait to get back,' she said.[55]

CHAPTER EIGHTEEN

1

On 25 February 1973, Princess Alice turned ninety. She was in Jamaica at the time, but three months later the occasion was marked by a lavish party given by Sir Henry and Lady May Abel Smith at the Turf Club, Carlton House Terrace. The invitations requested 'Tiaras if possible'; and tiaras there were in profusion. Among the forty or so royal guests gathered under the chandeliers in the club's dining-room were three queens (Queen Elizabeth II, Queen Elizabeth the Queen Mother and Queen Juliana of the Netherlands), the Grand Duchess of Luxembourg, and a galaxy of princes and princesses from various royal houses of Europe. With a small, delicately fashioned tiara on her silver hair, Princess Alice looked more like a woman in her early seventies than a nonagenarian. Slim, chic and vivacious, she moved with the sureness and vigour of a woman half her age. Highly social and always quite ready to be the centre of attention, Princess Alice enjoyed her ninetieth birthday enormously.

The main reason for Princess Alice's enduring youthfulness was her excellent health. Indeed, her refusal to acknowledge ill-health was in considerable measure due to the fact that she seldom suffered from it. 'She had an iron constitution,' says one of her close associates.[1]

'I have extraordinarily good health,' she once announced. 'We have always been outdoor people, and I go for a walk every day. I'd die if I didn't.'[2] She had very little patience with people who 'gave in' as she put it, to advancing age. 'Look at So-and-so,' she would say, when she herself was deep into her nineties, 'she's only eighty-three and she's just letting herself go. She looks quite decrepit.'[3]

The Princess was extremely conscious of her good figure, especially of her slim waist. She had a way of smoothing her hands over it as she sat down. 'Look at me, flat as a plank,' she would say, proudly patting, as a friend has put it, 'her little tummy'.[4] To another friend who complimented her, at the age of ninety-five, on 'her beautiful dress and young figure', the Princess's honest-to-goodness reply was 'that the latter was due to a special bra that she wore'.[5] As for her celebrated beauty, the passing years had somehow ennobled her features. With her aquiline profile and her high cheekbones, she looked more patrician than she had ever done. 'She had that marvellous little nose', said the Queen Mother, indicating a small, sharply-arched nose.[6]

But however much the Princess might try to ignore them, there were two or three indications that she was indeed ageing. One was that she was beginning to shrink, to become slightly stooped. Unless she made a conscious effort to straighten her previously ramrod back, she had a somewhat hunched appearance. She also suffered from what she airily dismissed as 'a touch of rheumatism'[7] in one of her legs and, more and more as the years went by, was obliged to use a stick when she walked. Typically, she had the stick disguised as a parasol. But her most apparent affliction was her gradually increasing deafness. At ninety, her hearing was not too seriously affected but as she moved deeper and deeper into the nineties, so did her affliction worsen. Eventually, even a hearing aid could do little to alleviate her deafness. But certainly, until she was ninety-five or six, she could follow most conversations and she always remained an animated, humorous and interesting conversationalist.

If anyone had imagined that Princess Alice's ninetieth birthday-party would mark the start of a more retiring, more sedentary way of life, they would soon have been proved wrong. Although her Jamaica trip, earlier that year, was to prove to be her last visit to the West Indies, the indomitable Princess had already embarked on a new series of journeys.

Africa, she once told a reporter, was her favourite continent, 'It is so varied, so original; there is more strangeness.'[8] So in January 1972 Princess Alice had visited Africa once more. With her lady-in-waiting,

Miss Joan Lascelles, she had set sail in S.S. *Oranje* for Cape Town. It was to be the first of the half-dozen voyages that she was to make to South Africa in the years ahead.

2

Politically, the choice of South Africa as a regular holiday place had been a difficult one to make. Since Princess Alice's last visits, with Lord Athlone,* the political situation had altered considerably in South Africa. In those days the country had been a generally highly regarded member of the British Commonwealth; now it was looked upon as an outcast among the world's nations. Since the coming to power of the National Party in 1948, the doctrine of racial discrimination, or *apartheid,* had become more and more thoroughly entrenched. This, in turn, had led to South Africa's withdrawal from the multiracial British Commonwealth. In 1961 South Africa had become a republic and the century-and-a-half-long link with the British monarchy had been severed. A president had replaced Queen Elizabeth II as the South African Head of State. No member of the British royal family had paid an official visit to South Africa since the triumphant tour of King George VI, Queen Elizabeth and their two daughters in 1947.

---

* The Athlones had visited South Africa in 1953 as well as in 1948.

During the previous two decades, Princess Alice had often toyed with the idea of returning to South Africa, but the thought that the Queen, or the British Government, might disapprove of her action had prevented her from doing so. By now, however, she had decided – with, quite possibly, the imperiousness of old age – that there could really be no harm in her, an elderly and relatively unimportant member of the royal family, paying a strictly private visit to South Africa. She was looking for somewhere different from Jamaica; she wanted an annual holiday in the sun; she was anxious to go to a country where English was spoken; she wanted a place that she knew well, where she was well known, where she would feel at home and where she had friends. South Africa was the obvious choice. As she so often said, South Africa was where she had spent the happiest years of her life.

There was never any doubt as to the sort of welcome Princess Alice would get in South Africa. Many a monarchist heart beat loyal and true among the English-speaking section of the community and even the largely republican Afrikaner element were flattered by the idea of a member of the British royal family choosing the country for a holiday. Hostesses vied with each other to entertain the Princess to the most elegant luncheon parties or to drop the deepest curtsies.

During Princess Alice's first return journey, in 1972, she toured the entire country. The trip was not without its share of disasters. One by one the ageing friends with whom she was to stay in Cape Town, Johannesburg and Durban fell ill before her arrival. This meant several last-minute changes or adaptations of plan. Her stay in Durban was so trouble-fraught as to be almost hilarious. The Johannesburg-based son of her 87-year-old Durban hostess had had the forethought to fly two young women down to Durban to help his mother entertain the Princess and her lady-in-waiting. One of these young women, Mrs Julia Ludwig, has the most vivid memories of the episode.

Julia and her companion arrived in Durban a day before the Princess in order, or so ran her optimistic instructions, 'to get in some food and do a few flowers'. What they discovered on reaching their destination was a musty, derelict old house, some of whose rooms had not been opened for fourteen years, a Zulu manservant old enough to have been a flag-bearer in the Boer War and whose old-fashioned methods included the cleaning of brass with parsley, and the mistress of the house in bed with a septic leg. Princess Alice and Miss Lascelles were expected to share a double room without its own bathroom.

The best that the girls could do in one day was to get the Princess's room as clean and tidy as possible and to brighten up the rest of the house with flowers. Having convinced a sceptical station-master that it was indeed a princess whom they had to meet at the station the following day, they were allowed to drive the car onto the platform and to be given the protection of a policeman.

Interestingly enough, when the train drew in the girls had no difficulty in recognising the Princess. 'Princess Alice did look just like "royalty",' remembers the admiring Julia, 'and how she managed to achieve it on that ghastly train, I don't know, but Prudence and I were perfectly spellbound as she looked beautiful, with every hair in place and like a piece of Dresden china.'

With the hostess upstairs in bed, it was left to Julia – a London-trained Cordon Bleu cook – to entertain the royal guest. 'We tried to organise lunches,' she sighs, 'but found that most of H.R.H.'s original friends were either dead or senile.' The Princess was especially anxious to visit King's House – Durban's Government House where she had so often spent the South African winter months – but this too was a disappointment: no one had been notified and it was shrouded in dust sheets.

But Princess Alice sailed through it all with the greatest good humour. She never complained; she never seemed put out. 'I was amazed,' says Julia, 'at her agility and her memory. . . she reminisced a great deal and I was pleased that she remembered my grandfather, Justice Matthews, who was Judge President of Natal at the time of her stay there. She told us stories of her life at Kensington Palace and some lively memories of her Grandma Victoria. She really was a wonderful person who put us both totally at ease, and really didn't need a Cordon Bleu cook for her needs.'

Princess Alice had arranged to travel from Durban back to Cape Town by coach, a tiring journey lasting several days. The South African Government offered to provide her with a chauffeur-driven car, and the two young women begged her to take advantage of the offer, but the Princess was adamant: 'she had made up her mind and we could not budge her.'[9] So fourteen pieces of luggage were loaded onto the coach and the Princess and Joan Lascelles set out on their 1,500-mile journey back.

They broke their journey in the charming little town of George where they stayed at the 'humble home' of Brigadier and Mrs Pieter de Waal; the Brigadier had been an aide de camp to the Athlones during the 1920s. 'Her greatest joy,' remembers her hostess, 'was walking in the country and having picnics.'[10]

After this first visit, Princess Alice's journeys to South Africa became part of her annual routine. Each January she would set sail from Southampton, spend some eight weeks in South Africa and return to Kensington Palace early in April. When the regular passenger lines ceased operating between Britain and South Africa (in any case, the cost of the passage was becoming prohibitive for the far-from-wealthy Princess Alice) she and Joan Lascelles would fly out. No, the Princess once protested when the airline authorities offered her a seat in the first class: she had paid for tourist class and tourist class she would travel. All the inconveniences of long-distance flying – the delays, the queuing, the cramped conditions, the diversions, the unscheduled stop-overs – Princess Alice would take in her stride. On one flight to South Africa, when she was in her ninety-fourth year, her plane was diverted to Zurich and, at dead of a winter's night, she and Joan Lascelles, having carried their own luggage, were obliged to wait for several hours until the flight could be resumed. The journey, from London to Cape Town, with yet another delay at Nairobi, lasted for something like twenty-four hours. The Princess considered it all highly amusing.

Princess Alice spent the greater part of her South African holidays in Cape Town; in Vergenoeg,* the home of Mr and Mrs Gardner Williams. The large Cape-Dutch-styled house stands, quite isolated, on the beach at Muizenburg. The Gardner Williams had first played host to the Princess in their Johannesburg home when her intended hostess had fallen ill. Princess Alice had spent three weeks with them on that occasion. Now, on her subsequent visits, the Gardner Williams made their seaside home available to her.

The Princess loved the house — 'my beloved Vergenoeg' she would call it – as it allowed her to walk for miles along the white beach beside the pounding surf. From Vergenoeg she would go and spend a week or so with other friends, such as Miss

---

* Literally 'Far Enough'.

Kathleen Murray on her apple farm at Elgin, Mrs Joy Van der Byl on her farm Fairfield near Caledon or Mrs Joyce Newton Thompson who now lived in Gwelo Goodman's old home in Cape Town. Another friend from the old Government House days was Stella, Lady Bailey, who had been Stella Chiappini.

Princess Alice lived a highly social life, entertaining and being entertained. But she was just as happy in more informal surroundings: walking, picnicking, visiting the famous Botanical Gardens at Kirstenbosch. She had friends in every walk of life: she would visit the State President and Mrs Diederich in her old home, Westbrooke; she would take tea with old ladies in bedsittingrooms in residential hotels. She loved meeting new people. Hostesses would scrabble round in an effort to find someone fresh and interesting to present to the Princess.

In no time, with the sense of royal obligation which was second nature to her, the Princess was carrying out public duties. She revisited as many as possible of the institutions with which she had once been officially associated. Each year she would go to the Princess Christian Home to have tea with the residents. She would even inspect the bathrooms, approving of the fact that there were bars on the baths to help the old ladies get in and out. One year the Princess was shown a photograph of herself taken on a previous visit: she was highly amused when Joan Lascelles exclaimed, 'Oh, Ma'am, isn't it a good thing you are not wearing the same dress today!'[11]

When she presented the Queen's Plate at a race meeting she caused considerable embarrassment by announcing that, 'When my late husband and I were in Pretoria we sometimes went racing in Johannesburg and they seemed to have some *very* strange results. Have they improved?'[12] On visiting the Priory of St John in Johannesburg, which had its headquarters in the Dairymples' old home, Glensheil, where she had so often stayed in the 1920s, the Princess stared out of the windows of her old suite and remarked dictatorially, 'The trees need cutting back . . . they have become too thick.'[13]

As always, her memory astonished her listeners. On arriving at St George's Cathedral in Cape Town one Sunday morning, she turned to the Precentor and asked, 'Does Mr Pitt still assist with the services?' On being told that 'Pop' Pitt, who was by now a very old man, did indeed still assist at the services, the Princess said, 'It is forty years since we were here and I would very much like to meet him again.'" And after the service the astonished Mr Pitt was delighted to be greeted like an old friend by the Princess.

No church service was ever too long for her. When the Bishop of George was to be consecrated in the Cathedral in Cape Town, it was thought that the Princess might like to attend the consecration service. But as the service was to last for over two hours, it was doubted whether she would accept the invitation. 'Well,' said Joan Lascelles on being telephoned about it, 'today she has been complaining that nobody asks her out any more as they all think she is now too old, so I shall ask her, if you would just wait a moment.'[15] The Princess was delighted: she had never before attended the consecration of a bishop.

And not only did the 95-year-old Princess sit through the service but she afterwards joined the cheese and wine party in the Cathedral gardens before going on to a luncheon engagement.

'Walking down from the church one evening,' remembers the Rector of the little Holy Trinity Church near Muizenberg, 'her lady-in-waiting said to me, "I suppose the Princess will want to go to the Three Hours' Service on Good Friday." Princess Alice was preceding us down the steps, her little body bent over, but she obviously overheard us and turned round to say, "What was that? Of course we are coming to the Three Hour Service – always been to the Three Hour Service." She duly came and sat at the front of the church for the full three hours and then came across to the neo-Georgian Rectory for tea and hot cross buns.'[16]

It was with considerable regret that the Princess said goodbye, each March or April, to the sunshine, scenery and hospitality of the Cape Peninsula. 'See you next year,' she would call out cheerfully, 'if I'm still alive!'[17]

3

Just as South Africa had replaced Jamaica in Princess Alice's annual itinerary so, in these years, did Austria replace Sweden as the place where she spent her summer holidays. The Princess's old friend, King Gustaf VI Adolf, with whom she had spent so many happy hours gardening at Sofiero, died at the age of ninety on 15 September 1973. His daughter-in-law, Princess Alice's niece Princess Sibylla, had died the year before, at the age of sixty-four. This meant that the grandson of Princess Alice's late brother Charlie, the Duke of Coburg, was now King Carl XVI Gustaf of Sweden. It also meant that the Princess's previously close ties with Sweden had somewhat slackened.

Fortunately, it was at about this time that the Princess's American friends, Dr and Mrs Matthew Mellon, acquired a house overlooking Kitzbühel in the Austrian Tyrol, and it was with them that she spent a month or so each summer from then on.

Dr Matthew Mellon was a member of the immensely wealthy Mellon family (the bulk of whose fortune came from Gulf Oil) and he and his wife had first met Princess Alice at a polo match in Jamaica in the late 1950s. After the Mellons had moved into a house which they had built above Runaway Bay, Jamaica, they would often entertain the Princess to luncheon or dinner. The Mellons, in turn, were entertained at Kensington Palace.

In 1976, accompanied by Miss Joan Lascelles and her Austrian maid, Princess Alice spent the first of several summer holidays with the Mellons at Haus Mellon near Kitzbühel. These holidays brought her, after an interval of over sixty years, back into a world which she had known so well as a young woman. The Duke of Coburg had owned a castle at Hinterris in the Austrian Tyrol; in those halcyon days before the First World War, as the Prince and Princess Alexander of Teck, the Athlones had often gone chamois hunting here. Her mother, the Duchess of Albany, had died and was buried at Hinterris.

Haus Mellon was a large, baroque-style, white-painted house, luxuriously furnished and boasting every amenity. The Mellons, the Princess would say, were 'perfect hosts'.[18] Having had a late breakfast, Princess Alice would sit in the sunshine beside the swimming-pool reading the *Frankfürter Zeitung*. Her German remained excellent; in fact, the Mellons had first noticed the Princess, sitting apart from the other spectators at that polo match in Jamaica, 'talking fluent German' to her companion, the Duchess of Coburg.* The paper read, the Princess would resume work on her tapestry. She belonged to a generation that never wasted time. ('Princess Alice is the only woman I have ever known,' a lady-in-waiting once confessed, 'who continues to knit while walking up a Balmoral mountain.'[19])

Although the Mellons were always careful to keep the simply curious or the socially ambitious at arm's length, there were usually guests for luncheon. Once, at such a luncheon party, some of the Princess's fellow

---

* Mr William Nash, Superintendent of Windsor Castle, remembers the Princess's extraordinary rapid translation of everything he was saying into German, for the benefit of a group of relations whom she was showing over the castle.

guests, anxious to impress, were disagreeing on the provenance of the china off which they were eating. Princess Alice simply put on her glasses, turned over her plate and announced firmly, 'Nymphenburg.'

In the afternoons there would be walks or drives through the spectacular mountain scenery to various view sights or points of interest. Princess Alice loved these outings. She was always fascinated by the hang-gliders sailing, so apparently effortlessly, in the wide blue sky above. Occasionally, the party would stop for tea in some small, picturesque village. If the weather were too bad for an outing they would take tea in one of the small living-rooms of Haus Mellon.

Before dinner, she would take a short nap and then, having changed, would join the others in the library for a glass of whisky. After dinner, over coffee in front of a blazing fire, Princess Alice would hold the Mellons enthralled with her great fund of stories and anecdotes.

'It was not only a great honour to have been a friend of this sweet and very interesting woman,' says Dr Matthew Mellon, 'but one of the great pleasures of our life.'[20]

4

As the 1970s progressed, so was there an extraordinary revival of public interest in Princess Alice. The deaths, of Queen Ena of Spain in 1969 and of Lady Patricia Ramsay in 1974, meant that Princess Alice was the only surviving grandchild of Queen Victoria. And although there were still members of the royal family living who had been born during the reign of Queen Victoria, there were none who had been as old as eighteen at the time of the Queen's death. With that excellent memory and her gift of expression, Princess Alice was proving invaluable, not only to members of the family, but to historians.

The Princess had always been interested in writers and now she would happily speak to any serious writer engaged on research into the various royal houses of Europe during the nineteenth and twentieth centuries. Her information was always colourful, useful and to the point; her opinions frank, trenchant and amusing. She never rambled boringly on, as so many old people are apt to do, about extraneous matters. It was fascinating to realise that the world-famous figures under discussion were simply relations to her; and that world-famous events had been part of everyday family talk.

The politically enlightened and cruelly misunderstood Empress Frederick, battling vainly against the reactionary militarism of Bismarck's Germany, had been Princess Alice's 'bossy'[21] Aunt Vicky. The last, tragic Empress of All the Russias, murdered by the Bolsheviks, had been her shy cousin Alicky whom the Duchess of Albany, with Princess Alice by her side, had had to chaperone when she was being courted by the future Tsar Nicholas II. The showy, vainglorious, neurotic Kaiser Wilhelm II had often partnered her at tennis.

About all these personalities Princess Alice would speak with a refreshing candour. She once described that theatrical, maverick, self-regarding nineteenth-century Spanish princess, the Infant Eulalia, as 'a lady for whom the truth never had much significance. Perhaps I am prejudiced, as my mother, a very straitlaced character, had a very poor opinion of the lady. Eulalia had a queer start in life as the daughter of Queen Isabella of Spain, but as [her nephew] King Alfonso XIII told me with glee, her papa was one of the Queen's bodyguards. . . .'[22]

'I know you think I look like a movie star,' Princess Alice's vain and always dramatically dressed cousin, Queen Marie of Romania once said to her, 'but that's how my people want me to look.'[23]

She remembered once sharing a bath with her cousin's – the Empress Alexandra's – youngest daughter, Grand Duchess Anastasia and noting that she had 'hammer' toes. As Anna Anderson, the woman who later claimed to be the Tsar's daughter, did not have hammer toes, she could not possibly be the real Grand Duchess Anastasia, maintained Princess Alice.

Only in the intimacy of her family circle, though, would Princess Alice ever discuss the present generation of the royal family. But one thing was always apparent: her unfeigned admiration for Queen Elizabeth II. Princess Alice had nothing but praise for the dedication, professionalism and grace with which her grand-niece carried out her duties. She recognised in Queen Elizabeth II her own attitude towards the monarchy: that it was something to be cherished, defended and served to the utmost of one's abilities.

'Royalty is not,' the Princess once wrote, 'comparable with the pampered lot of the queen bee. It was, and is, an arduous profession whose members are seldom granted an opportunity of opting in or out of their pre-destined fate; they have to endure a rigorous training and abide a strict programme. Their lives are dedicated from childhood to the service of nations. Their daily tasks, for months ahead, are prescribed and set out in a diary of engagements from which only severe illness can excuse them. None but those trained from youth to such an ordeal can sustain it with amiability and composure. The royal motto – *Ich Dien* – is no empty phrase. It means just what it says – I serve.'[24]

And everything that Princess Alice did, even to her insistence on never looking anything other than immaculate, was designed to serve the cause of monarchy. It was her *raison d'etre*. In its service she was once said to hold the record for royal engagements, having carried out over twenty thousand. Even at the age of ninety-four she put on her uniform as Commandant-in-Chief of the 'FANYs' and inspected the parade marking the seventieth anniversary of the founding of the corps.*

---

* 'Three successive corps commanders have every reason to be grateful for her help and advice. Forty-seven years of enthusiasm, encouragement and support in so many ways, but above all, always laughter.' (Mrs S. Y. Parkinson in *The Times,* 15 January 1981.)

504

It was this reverence for the institution of monarchy which made Princess Alice so conscious of the niceties of royal protocol. After the Queen's Birthday Parade in 1972 she refused to appear on the balcony with the other members of the royal family on the grounds that she was still in mourning for the Duke of Windsor, who had died on 28 May that year. If King Edward VIII had failed in his royal obligations, she was not going to be guilty of doing so.

And at the wedding of Queen Elizabeth II's only daughter, Princess Anne, to Captain Mark Phillips on 14 November 1973 Princess Alice refused to ride to Westminster Abbey in the Irish State Coach. Her rank, in relationship to the bride, she protested, did not give her the right to ride in the Irish State Coach. She went instead by car.

In 1977, eighty years after driving in Queen Victoria's Diamond Jubilee procession, Princess Alice drove in Queen Elizabeth II's Silver Jubilee procession. And in that same year she appeared, for the first time, on television in the BBC's film *Royal Heritage*. An additional film devoted exclusively to Princess Alice and entitled *Victorian Memory* was made from the material gathered for *Royal Heritage*. Millions of viewers, who had until then known her chiefly as a well-dressed little old lady appearing, year after year, in group photographs of royal weddings and christenings, were charmed by her liveliness, her grace and her impishness. For the first time, perhaps, the general public became conscious of the fact that this doyenne of the royal family was more than just another ageing princess; that she was a woman of considerable verve and great good humour.

On 15 July 1977 Princess Alice passed an important milestone in her life. On that day she set a record by living longer than any previous member of the British royal family. Until then the longest-lived member had been Lord Athlone's Aunt Augusta – the Grand Duchess of Mecklenburg-Strelitz, who had been born Princess Augusta of Cambridge, a granddaughter of King George III. Over sixty-five years had passed since Lord Athlone and Princess Alice, as the young Prince and Princess Alexander of Teck, had travelled to Neu Strelitz to visit the redoubtable old Grand Duchess. She had died in 1916, at the age of 94 years 139 days.

Typically, Princess Alice had been quite unaware of the fact that by living 94 years 140 days she had broken any record. When the news was given to her by a member of her household, she was 'both surprised and amused'.[25] The thought, she said, had never occurred to her. No less typically, the Princess was carrying out an official duty that day. That evening she took the salute and made a speech at the Royal Tournament.

Photographs taken by Lord Snowdon for her ninety-fifth birthday, on 25 February 1978, again brought her to the attention of a wide public. Reproductions appeared in newspapers and magazines throughout the world. Wearing a floor-length dress and seated in a throne-like chair, Princess Alice looks assured, interesting, unmistakably royal. On the table beside her was a framed photograph of her grandmother, Queen Victoria.

At the end of October 1979, Princess Alice passed another milestone. By having lived for 96 years 248 days she had outlived one of the two longest-lived continental royals – Princess Anna of Montenegro.* There remained only Princess Alicia de Borbon, a great-great-granddaughter of King Carlos IV of Spain, who had died in 1975 at the age of 98 years 206 days. If Princess Alice were to live until 18 September 1981, she would have lived longer than any person born into a European royal family.

The wonder of it all was not that Princess Alice should have reached this great age, but that she should have reached it while retaining so much of her broadmindedness, her adaptability, her puckishness, her curiosity, her adventurousness and her zest. It was not only her age that was remarkable; she was a remarkable person.

5

Even in extreme old age Princess Alice not only kept up old friendships but was always ready to embark on new ones. Letters, in her large, looped handwriting,

---

* Princess Anna of Montenegro died on 22 April 1971.

went all over the world, and there were few days on which she was not welcoming visitors, often from distant countries, to tea or a meal at Kensington Palace.

To call on Princess Alice during these last years of her life was always a pleasurable and interesting experience. The visitor would give his name to the policeman in the little wooden guard-house near the main entrance to Kensington Palace. Another policeman, standing under the central archway, would direct him or her to the door of the Clock House. Kensington Palace accommodates several other members of the royal family: Princess Margaret and her children; the Duke and Duchess of Gloucester and their family; Princess Alice, Duchess of Gloucester; Prince and Princess Michael of Kent and their family. The air within the great paved courtyard of the Palace is hushed; the white-framed windows in the red-brick walls look blank, impersonal. Only occasionally, on the arrival or departure of one or other of the resident members of the royal family is there a short burst of activity.

The large, black-painted door of the Clock House would be opened by Princess Alice's butler. Apart from her secretary, the indispensable Miss Mary Goldie, the Princess employed a staff of seven: the butler, a lady's maid, a housemaid, a cook, two daily cleaners and a kitchen help. By royal standards it was a very modest household. But then Princess Alice had never been wealthy. She received no direct grant from Parliament. By the terms of the Civil List Act of

1975, Queen Elizabeth II accepted personal responsibility for the payment of the official expenses of the Duke of Gloucester, the Duke of Kent, Princess Alexandra and Princess Alice, Countess of Athlone. Payment is made from the Consolidated Fund, which is financed, indirectly, by the income from the various royal estates. In the financial year 1978/79 these combined payments came to £165,500. Of this sum, Princess Alice's allowance to cover her official expenses was £6,500. Each year she received an increase to keep pace with inflation. The Princess was known to grumble about the meagreness of the allowance granted to fringe members of the royal family. She always expressed gratitude to the Queen, who generously augmented the grant laid down by Parliament.

The atmosphere within the Clock House was dignified without being solemn. Everywhere there was the gleam of highly polished floors and furniture, the feel of soft carpets underfoot, the scent of freshly arranged flowers, the soft glow of indirect lighting, the shimmer of gold leaf. In the entrance hall hung the large double portrait of Princess Alice and the Earl of Athlone presented to them on their Golden Wedding. Beside it stood white marble busts of the Princess's parents, the Duke and Duchess of Albany.

In Lord Athlone's study, where the Princess sometimes received visitors, was a large desk, two or three comfortable chairs, a small table with its clutter of silver-framed family photographs, including one of Lord Athlone's mother, the plump and ebullient Duchess of Teck. In the panelled inner hallway hung Laszlo's spirited painting of the young Princess Alice; on the other walls were more formal studies of a uniformed Lord Athlone and a regal Queen Mary.

The dining-room was a beautiful room, all blue and white. The Princess's collection of Delft pieces lined the white-painted display shelves. The curtains at the long windows were in a complementary blue and white design; the carpet was dark blue, and the dining-table could seat twelve. Upstairs, the drawing-room was a large double room with views across Palace Green to the trees in Kensington Palace Gardens. The sofas and chairs had loose covers in blue or grey; on the floor were Persian carpets; on the walls hung Gwelo Goodman's paintings ('bought for a song,'[28] the Princess would say) of South African scenes. There were flowers everywhere: in vases, in bowls and in elaborate pot-plant arrangements. And, of course, there were the framed photographs of the kings, queens, princes and princesses who were part of Princess Alice's internationally spread family.

Beside the drawing-room was the Princess's private sitting-room-cum-study. This was a small, business-like room, furnished with two desks, cabinets and bookcases. Here again were numerous family photographs but of a more informal, more intimate kind. There was one particularly striking one, unframed, of the Queen in a headscarf and Princess Alice in a slouch hat, taken at the Windsor Horse Show.

More bookcases, reaching from floor to ceiling, lined the area leading to the secretary's office and the Green Corridor. With its pale green walls, its gilded, pale-green upholstered chairs and its windows overlooking yet another of the palace courtyards, the Green Corridor was a light, cheerful, comfortable room where the Princess sometimes breakfasted or took tea. Leading off it was her bedroom and a guest suite. There were more guest bedrooms upstairs.

The first impression of Princess Alice, in the second half of her nineties, was of smallness and delicacy. She looked very thin, very hunched, very brittle. When she walked, she used a stick. The second impression was of bandbox elegance. Her silver hair was simply drawn back from her fine-boned, still porcelain-like features. Her dress would be of some pale, silky fabric. She looked cool, handsome, flawlessly groomed. At night, at a formal dinner party, in long evening dress and sparkling jewels, she looked as exquisite and delicate as an ornament.

But these fragile looks belied her personality. People meeting her for the first time and expecting to be faced with nothing more than a historical curiosity, were always amazed by her verve. 'She entered the room bent almost double over her stick,' writes one observer, meeting her at the home of a mutual friend, 'but that apparent frailty was deceptive. "I have had such a busy morning's shopping," she announced. "Is that Dubonnet I see?" The restorative was succeeded by an egg dish, roast lamb and two helpings of *Fraises des bois.* [27]

Her conversation, accompanied by 'the vivacious gestures of her generation'[28] was a delight. She was alert, animated, full of talk. She laughed easily; she had a fund of funny stories and a quick wit. On one occasion, while she was pouring tea at her dining-room table (she liked to do this herself), she knocked over a cup. A quick-thinking guest slipped a plate under the tablecloth to protect the surface of the table from the hot tea.

'It's a trick my mother taught me,' explained the guest.

'Ah,' countered Princess Alice. 'Now I'll show you a trick *my* mother taught me.' With that she poured the spilt tea from her saucer back into her cup.

Her appetite was good. 'Sheer greed,' she would say, helping herself to another slice of cake or another spoonful of pudding. 'Please smoke, if you wish,' she would always remember to say at the appropriate time.[29]

With age, her views became increasingly conservative, forthright, dogmatic. Her daily paper was the *Telegraph.* For no apparent good reason, the Princess was scathing about television. Yet she was very interested in the filming of her appearance in *Royal Heritage.* 'Of course I saw it,' she would afterwards say. 'I don't know why people keep asking me if I saw it. Wouldn't *you* have seen it if you'd been in it?'[30]

Tolerant about so many things, Princess Alice deplored the current sloppiness of dress; or what she called 'young people in those strange clothes and with all that hair'.[31] When she attended a ball at Buckingham Palace in honour of Princess Anne's forthcoming marriage, she was appalled by some of the clothes. 'What a fright some of them looked,'[32] she commented.

Unwittingly, her increasing imperiousness could even extend to her relations with Queen Elizabeth II. On one occasion, as the Queen was taking her leave after visiting her great-aunt, Princess Alice – in the presence of others – rapped out an instruction. 'Turn off that heater when you go out,'[33] she commanded. Smilingly, the Queen obeyed.

By the end of the 1970s, that incredible energy had begun slowing down. In 1978 the Princess had a fall, hurt her shoulder and was obliged to spend a few days in hospital. Although she recovered from the accident, it seemed to mark the beginning of a gradual deterioration in her health. There might have been nothing wrong with her medically but she was at last beginning to feel the weight of her years. She began spending more time in bed. Having read late into the night, she would sleep late in the mornings. Yet, says one of her close associates, the Princess still 'looked lovely'.[34] She was still interested in things; she was just as anxious to be amused and diverted. Only her deafness prevented her from seeing as

513

many people as she would have liked. This sometimes made her, she used to sigh, 'frightfully bored'.[35]

The Princess was regularly visited by other members of the royal family: among them the Queen, Queen Elizabeth the Queen Mother, and her neighbours Princess Margaret and Princess Alice, Duchess of Gloucester. Occasionally some continental relation – a German prince or a Dutch or Swedish princess – would come in to see her. Princess (formerly Queen) Juliana of the Netherlands called whenever she was in London. Her lady-in-waiting, Miss Joan Lascelles, came every day. And of course, her daughter and son-in-law, Lady May and Sir Henry Abel Smith, and their children and grandchildren, were often in the house. Even towards the end, when she was bedridden, Princess Alice would keep her visitors waiting, says the Queen Mother, while she 'put a little powder on her face and had her hair attended to'.[36]

Gradually, with each passing month, the Princess weakened. If she could not walk, she once said, she would die. By the end of 1980 she could no longer walk and she was undoubtedly dying. Watched over by the faithful Miss Goldie and with day and night nurses in constant attendance, she lived out her last days; fading away, as she once said of her husband, 'as a candle burns itself out'.[37]

6

514

Princess Alice died, peacefully in her sleep, on the morning of Saturday, 3 January 1981. She would have turned ninety-eight the following month. Queen Elizabeth II is said to have heard the news 'with great sadness' and Dr Robert Runcie, the Archbishop of Canterbury, preaching to the royal family at Sandringham parish church the following day, gave thanks for her 'long and full life'. Princess Alice had carried from childhood, he said, 'the values and standards of a devout Christian.'[38]

The funeral service was held on 8 January 1981 in St George's Chapel, Windsor. It was a quiet, private service attended not only by Queen Elizabeth II and other members of the British royal family but by a number of those continental royalties to whom the Princess had been just as closely related: among them were King Olav of Norway, King Carl Gustaf of Sweden, Princess Juliana of the Netherlands and Princess Alice's nephew, Prince Friedrich of Saxe-Coburg and Gotha. To represent those countries to which the Princess had given so much service were the South African Ambassador, the Canadian High Commissioner and the High Commissioner for Jamaica. Also present among her family, friends and associates were the six nurses who had tended her during her last days. The service was conducted by the Dean of Windsor, the Right Reverend Michael Mann.

St George's Chapel had been the scene of so many events, sad and joyful, in Princess Alice's story:

the marriage of her parents, the funeral of her father, her own marriage, the funerals of her son, Viscount Trematon, and of her husband, the Earl of Athlone. Now in a coffin draped with the royal standard and carried on the shoulders of a party of crimson-jacketed Life Guards, Princess Alice left St George's Chapel for the last time. Her coffin was followed down the steps by Lady May and Sir Henry Abel Smith. She was buried, beside her husband and her son, at the royal burial ground at Frogmore.

7

All in all, Princess Alice had led a remarkable life. Spanning almost a century, it had carried her through some of the most revolutionary changes in the history of the world. 'The things that have happened in the eight hundred years that separated the people of the (Norman) Conquest from the mid-Victorian era,' she once wrote, 'were trifling compared with those which have occurred during the past hundred years.'[39] Raised in a world of candlelight, gaslight, horse-drawn carriages and even the occasional sailing ship, Princess Alice lived into an age of atomic power, space travel and of men landing on the moon. Forbidden to wear make-up, to be seen in public without a chaperone, to ride on the upper deck of a bus lest she show an ankle on descending the stairs, she witnessed all the turmoil of female emancipation.

Born during the premiership of Gladstone, she saw the advent of Britain's first woman prime minister.

As a young woman, Princess Alice had been part of the last great flowering of European monarchy. Growing to maturity at a time when kings and emperors appeared to command the destinies of the world, she saw the fall of most of these once-proud royal houses – in Germany, Russia, Austria, Spain, Portugal, Italy, Romania, Bulgaria, Yugoslavia, Albania and Greece. Born into a world of rank and class and privilege, she experienced the birth of the Welfare State. When she was a girl, Britain was the mightiest nation on earth and her grandmother had reigned over the greatest Empire that the world has ever known. At the time of her death her grand-niece was one of a mere handful of monarchs and Britain had lost most of its wealth and its power.

But Princess Alice's longevity was far from being her only claim to fame. She had been more than just the doyenne of the royal family, a magnificent relic from another age. Questing and independent, she was very much a personality in her own right. But more significant than this had been Princess Alice's contribution to public life. For over ninety years, from the time that she first 'christened' a fire-engine at Esher, the Princess had dedicated herself to the service of the monarchy, the country and the Commonwealth. She had carried out official duties in every continent; she had served, beside the Earl of Athlone, in two of the most sensitive imperial posts;

she had been Chancellor of the University of the West Indies throughout years of political tension and transition.

Yet she seems never to have put a foot wrong. Her career, both public and private, had been, for all its colourfulness, remarkably free from criticism. Princess Alice had always been greatly respected, greatly admired and greatly loved.

The reason is that never for a moment did Princess Alice forget that she was a representative of the Crown. Even when most relaxed, she remained conscious of her royal status and obligations.

'I always maintain,' claims a member of Lord Athlone's Canadian staff, 'that if there had been no such thing as the hereditary right of succession, and one had been obliged to choose someone with all the necessary qualities as a queen, one would have chosen Princess Alice. She would have made a wonderful queen.'[40]

As it was, she made a wonderful princess.

APPENDIXES

NOTES ON SOURCES

Abbreviations

(Full details of both published and unpublished sources will be found in the Bibliography)

FMG   Alice, H.R.H. Princess: *For my Grandchildren.*

QVJ   Victoria, Queen: *The Journals of Queen Victoria,*

MKR   Pickersgill, J. W. (4 vols) *The Mackenzie King Record.*

KB   Blackburne, Sir Kenneth: *Some Happy Recollections of H.R.H Princess Alice, Countess of Athlone.*

CHAPTER ONE

1 QVJ, 19 March 1883 (Longford: *Victoria R.I.,* p. 447)

2 FMG, p. 9.

3 *Ibid*

4 QVJ, 19 March 1883 (Longford, *Victoria R.I.,* p. 447)

5 Victoria, Queen: *Advice to a grand-daughter, p.* 45

6 Woodham-Smith: *Queen Victoria, p.* 328

7 Marie Louise: *Memories,* p. 20

8 QVJ, 26 March 1883 (Royal Archives)

9 Knightly: *Journals,* p. 361

10 *Ibid*

11 Longford: *Victoria R.I., p.* 461

12 QVJ, 22 April 1853 (Longford: *Victoria R.I., p.* 234)

13 Woodham-Smith: *Queen Victoria,* p. 328

14 Victoria, Queen: *Further Letters,* p. 37

15 Woodham-Smith: *Queen Victoria,* p. 413

16 Victoria, Queen: *Darling Child,* p. 79

17 *Ibid,* p. 116

18 Ponsonby, Arthur: *Henry Ponsonby,* p. 89

19 *Ibid,* p. 90

20 Victoria, Queen: *Darling Child,* p. 233

21 *Ibid,* p. 289

22 Longford: Victoria R.I., p. 461

23 FMG, p. 21

24 *Ibid*

25 *Ibid, p.* 27

26 Ibid, p. 22

27 Ponsonby, Arthur: *Henry Ponsonby,* p. 89

28 *Ibid*

29 Longford: *Victoria R.I.,* p. 461

30 FMG, pp. 19, 20

31 Warwick: *Life's Ebb and Flow,* p. 32

32 FMG, p. 38

33 *Ibid,* p. 15

34 Anon: *Life of the Duke of Albany,* p. 14

35 Victoria, Queen: *Letters,* 26 June 1879, p. 28

36 Ware: *Life and Speeches,* p. 27

37 Warwick: *Life's Ebb and Flow,* p. 32

38 *Ibid,* p. 34

39 Victoria of Prussia: *Queen Victoria at Windsor and Balmoral,* p. 22

40 Ibid

41 Longford: *Victoria R.I.*, p. 447

42 *Ibid*

43 QVJ, 18 Nov. 1881 *(Letters,* p. 249)

44 *The Graphic,* 26 Nov. 1881, p. 530

45 FMG, p. 41

46 Wilhelmina, Queen: *Lonely but not Alone,* p. 26

47 FMG, p. 42

48 Sewell: *Personal Letters of King Edward VII,* p. 60

49 Victoria, Queen: *Advice to a Granddaughter,* p. 29

50 QVJ, 7 April 1882 *(Letters,* p. 269)

51 FMG, pp. 43, 44

52 *The Graphic,* 6 May 1882, p. 21

53 *Illustrated London News,* 6 May 1882, p. 439

54 QVJ, 27 April 1882 *(Letters,* p. 270)

CHAPTER TWO

I *Illustrated London News,* 6 May 1882, p. 439

2 Monckton Milnes: *H.R.H.*
   Prince Leopold, p. 12

3 Ponsonby, Arthur: *Henry Ponsonby,* p. 257

4 Victoria, Queen: *Advice to a Granddaughter,* p. 39

5 Ponsonby, Arthur: *Henry Ponsonby,* p. 90

6 QVJ, 25 Feb. 1883 (Royal Archives)

7 FMG, p. 10

8 Anon: *Prince Leopold,* p. 10

9 Cooper: *The Story of Claremont,* p. 53

10 FMG, pp. 46, 47

11 *Ibid,* p. 50

12 QVJ, 21 Feb. 1884 *(Letters,* p. 478)

13 *The Graphic,* 5 April 1884, p. 31

14 QVJ, 28 March 1884 *(Letters,* p. 478)

15 *Ibid,* p. 490

16 *Ibid,* 29 March 1884 *(Letters,* p. 493)

17 Victoria, Queen: *Advice to a Granddaughter,* p. 68

18 *Ibid,* p. 71

CHAPTER THREE

1 Arthur Ponson by: Henry Pon*sonby,* p. 257

2 FMG, p. 1

3 Conversation with Princess Alice

4 *Ibid*

5 FMG, p. 66

6 Carroll: *Diaries,* p. 488

7 *Guardian,* 30 Nov. 1960

8 FMG, p. 62

9 *Ibid*

10 Byng: *Up the Stream of Time,* pp. 24, 25

11 FMG, p. 4

12 *Ibid,* p. 63

13 *Ibid,* p. 64

14 *The Times,* 18 Nov. 1908

15 *Ibid*

16 FMG, p. 98

17 *Ibid,* p. 65

18 Victoria, Queen: *Advice to a Granddaughter,* p. 29

19 *Ibid*

20 FMG, p. 66

21 *Ibid,* p. 65

22 *Ibid*

23 Pope-Hennessy: *Queen Mary,* p. 196

24 FMG, p. 68

25 Marie of Romania: *The Story* of *My Life,* Vol I, p. 2026 FMG, p. 68

27 Marie of Romania: *The Story of my Life,* Vol I, p. 19

28 *Ibid,* p. 20

29 *Ibid*

30 FMG, p. 69

31 *Ibid*

32 Victoria of Prussia: *Queen Victoria at Windsor and Balmoral,* p. 39

33 Victoria, Queen: Advice to a Granddaughter, p. 80

34 Ibid, p. 95

35 FMG, p. 291

36 Pope-Hennessy: *Queen Mary,* p. 206

37 Victoria of Prussia: *Queen Victoria at Windsor and Balmoral,* p. 56

38 Mallet: *Life with Queen Victoria,* p. 13

39 FMG, p. 71

40 *Ibid,* p. 291

41 Pope-Hennessy: *Queen Mary,* p. 285

42 FMG, p. 71

43 *Ibid*

44 Carey: *The Empress Eugenie in Exile,* p. 210

45 FMG, p. 6

46 *Ibid,* p. 71

47 *Ibid,* p. 76

48 *Ibid,* p. 78

49 Ibid, p. 72

50 *Ibid,* p. 77

51 *Ibid,* p. 78

52 *Ibid,* p. 117

53 Conv. with Princess Alice

54 *Ibid*

55 BBC Interview with Princess Alice

56 FMG, p. 76

57 Wilhelm II: *My Early Life,* p. 65

CHAPTER FOUR

1 Pope-Hennessy: *Queen Mary,* p. 154

2 *Ibid,* p. 178

3 FMG, p. 41

4 *Ibid,* p. 123

5 Marie of Romania: *The Story of my Life,* Vol I, p. 43

6 Victoria, Queen: *Advice to a Granddaughter,* p. 79

7 FMG, p. 80

8 *Ibid,* p. 74

9 Wilhelmina, Queen: *Lonely but not Alone,* p. 26

10 FMG, p. 80

11 Ibid, p. 81

12 Wilhelmina, Queen: *Lonely but not Alone,* p. 44

13 *Ibid,* p. 27

14 QVJ, 2 May 1895 (*Letters,* p. 499)

15 Mallet: *Life with Queen Victoria,* p. 92

16 FMG, p. 76

17 Maxwell: *Sixty Years a Queen,* p. 206

18 *Ibid,* p. 204

19 *Ibid,* p. 208

20 FMG, p. 75

21 Pope-Hennessy: *Queen Mary,* p. 335

22 FMG, p. 75

23 *Ibid*

24 *Ibid,* p. 4

25 Longford: Victoria R.I., p. 447

26 FMG, p. 5

27 Pope-Hennessy: *Queen Mary,* p. 76

28 *Ibid,* p. 77

29 Marie Louise: My *Memories,* p. 43

30 FMG, p. 39

CHAPTER FIVE

1 Hyde: Mexican Empire, p. 115

2 Pope-Hennessy: Queen Mary, p. 301

3 Marie of Romania: *The Story of my Life,* Vol I, p. 184

4 FMG, p. 85

5 *Ibid,* p. 89

6 Victoria, Queen: Advice to a Granddaughter, p. 170

7 FMG, p. 86

8 Marie of Romania: *The Story of my Life,* Vol I, p. 156

9 *Ibid,* p. 199

10 Aston: The Duke of Connaught, p. 219

11 Victoria, Queen: *Advice to a Granddaughter,* p. 144

12 QVJ, 23 June 1899 *(Letters,* p. 384)

13 FMG, p. 84

14 *Ibid*

15 *Ibid, p.* 88

16 Marie of Romania: *The Story of my Life,* Vol I, p. 156

17 FMG, p. 90

18 Victoria, Queen: *Letters,* 9 April 1900, p. 384

19 Disraeli: *Letters,* Vol II, p. 177

20 Hamilton: *Vanished World,* p. 369

21 FMG, p. 92

22 *Ibid,* p. 100

23 *Ibid,* pp. 152, 153

24 *Ibid,* p. 99

25 Pless: *Daisy, Princess of Pless,* p. 285

26 FMG, p. 91

27 Hamilton: *Vanished World,* p. 335

28 FMG, p. 96

29 *Ibid,* p. 95

30 *Ibid*

31 Hamilton: *Vanished World,* p. 336

32 FMG, p. 97

33 *Ibid,* p. 98

34 Wilhelmina, Queen: *Lonely but not Alone,* p. 65

35 Marie of Romania: *The Story of my Life,* Vol I, p. 197

36 FMG, p. 95

37 *Ibid,* p. 98

38 *The Times,* 18 Nov. 1908

39 FMG, p. 38

40 *Ibid,* p. 101

41 *Ibid,* p. 103

CHAPTER SIX

1 FMG, p. I

2 *The Graphic,* 13 Feb. 1904, p. 209

3 FMG, p. 7

4 *Ibid, p.* 124

5 *Ottawa Citizen,* 2 July 1966

6 Anon: *Some Letters,* p. 140

7 FMG, p. 6

8 Ibid, p. 115

9 *Ibid,* p. 109

10 Marie Louise: *My Memories,* p. 19

11 FMG, p. 112

12 Kennedy: *My dear Duchess,* p. 116

13 Pope-Hennessy: Queen Mary, p. 45

14 *Ibid*

15 Cooke: *Princess Mary Adelaide,* Vol II, p. 68

16 Sara: *Earl of Athlone,* p. 31

17 Pope-Hennessy: *Queen Mary,* p. 60

18 Cooke: *Princess Mary Adelaide,* Vol II, p. 91

19 Pope-Hennessy: *Queen Mary,* p. 67

20 *Ibid,* p. 76

21 *Ibid,* p. 144

22 *Ibid*

23 Sara: *Earl of Athlone,* p. 42

24 *Ibid,* p. 44

25 Cooke: *Princess Mary Adelaide,* Vol II, p. 287

26 FMG, p. 115

27 Pope-Hennessy: *Queen Mary,* p. 304

28 *Ibid,* p. 320

29 *The Graphic*, 13 Feb. 1904, p. 208

30 *Ibid*

31 Pope-Hennessy: *Queen Mary*, p. 338

32 *Ibid*

33 *Ibid*, p. 347

34 *Ibid*

35 *Ibid*, p. 367

36 FMG, p. 115

37 Ponsonby, Frederick: *Recollections*, p. 202

38 Cust: *King Edward VII*, p. 170

39 *The Graphic*, 20 Feb. 1904, p. 195

40 *Ibid*

CHAPTER SEVEN

1 FMG, p. 102

2 *Ibid*, p. 121

3 *Ibid*, p. 116

4 Marie Louise: *My Memories*, p. 165

5 FMG, p. 143

6 *Ibid*

7 *Ibid*, p. 122

8 *Ibid*, p. 3

9 *Ibid*, p. 127

10 Ibid, p. 86

11 Pope-Hennessy: *Queen Mary*, p. 38

12 *Ibid*, p. 91

13 *Ibid*, p. 101

14 Erbach-Schönberg: *Reminiscences*, p. 308

15 *Ibid*, pp. 314, 315

16 *Ibid*

17 Pope-Hennessy: *Queen Mary,* p. 406

18 FMG, p. 127

19 Pope-Hennessy: *Queen Mary,* p. 38

20 Dubourg: *Royal Haemophilia,* p. 12

21 *The Times,* 4 Nov. 1908

22 *Ibid*

23 FMG, p. 129

24 Ibid, p. 126

25 *Ibid,* p. 124

26 Pope-Hennessy: *Queen Mary,* p. 378

27 FMG, p. 129

28 Marie of Romania: *The Story of my Life,* Vol II, p. 211

29 FMG, p. 90

30 *Ibid,* p. 143

31 Dugdale: *Maurice de Bunsen,* p. 130

32 FMG, p. 138

33 Dugdale: *Maurice de Bunsen,* p. 130

34 FMG, p. 134

35 *Ibid,* p. 142

36 Hubbard: *Rideau Hall,* p. 6

37 *The Times,* 8 May 1914

CHAPTER EIGHT

1 FMG, p. 149

2 Ibid, p. 151

3 Ibid, p. 105

4 The Times, 29 March 1919

5 FMG, p. 155

6 Ibid, p. 151

7 The Times, 18 April 1928

8 Letter in possession of Hugo Vickers

9 FMG, p. 159

10 *Ibid*

11 *Ibid,* p. 161

12 Cammaerts: *Albert King of the Belgians,* pp. 229, 230

13 *London Gazette,* 9 Nov. 1917

14 FMG, p. 160

15 FMG, p. 162

16 *The Argus,* Cape Town, 21 Jan. 1924

CHAPTER NINE

1 Conv. with Princess Alice

2 FMG, p. 121

3 Conv. with Princess Alice

4 FMG, p. 120

5 Conv. with Sir Shuldham Redfern

6 FMG, p. 165

7 Conv. with Lady May Abel Smith

8 FMG, p. 165

9 *Ibid,* p. 39

10 *The Times,* 4 Sept. 1922

11 FMG, p. 165

12 *Ibid,* p. 39

13 *Ibid,* p. 166

14 *Cape Times,* 18 Dec. 1923

15 *Ibid*

16 FMG, p. 168

17 FMG, p. 169

CHAPTER TEN

1 Marquard: History of South Africa, p. 232

2 Kruger: Age of the Generals, p. 115

3 FMG, p. 171

4 *Argus,* 31 Aug. 1929

5 FMG, p. 171

6 *Ibid*

7 Conv. with Princess Alice, Duchess of Gloucester

8 FMG, p. 170

9 Schoeman: Bloemfontein, p. 218

10 FMG, p. 175

11 *Ibid,* p. 176

12 *Ibid,* p. 170

13 *Ibid,* p. 174

14 *Ibid,* p. 170

15 Conv. with Princess Alice

16 FMG, p. 173

17 *Ibid*

18 Lacour-Gayet: South Africa, p. 267

19 Mrs Eva Taylor to the author

20 Eeman: *Diplomatic Bag,* p. 109

21 *Argus,* 7 Nov. 1930

22 Lady Bailey to the author

23 Mrs C. Wintringham White to the author

24 Mrs Marcia Dalrymple to the author

25 Mr R.C. Molk to the author

26 Mrs Grace Doyle to the author

27 Conv. with Princess Alice

28 FMG, p. 182

29 *Cape Times,* 12 Dec. 1930

30 S.A. National Council for Child Welfare Memorandum, p. 3

31 *Cape Times,* 12 Dec. 1930

32 *Ibid*

33 Letter from Princess Alice to the author

34 FMG, p. 105

35 Conv. with Princess Alice, Duchess of Gloucester

36 Conv. with Queen Elizabeth The Queen Mother

37 FMG, p. 180

38 *Ibid*

39 Adcock, *The Prince of Wales's African Book,* p. 23

40 *Ibid*

41 *Ibid*

42 FMG, p. 180

CHAPTER ELEVEN

1 FMG, p. 174

2 Harris: Pioneer, Soldier and Politician, p. 243

3 Conv. with Mrs Marga Diederichs, wife of South African State President.

4 Harris: Pioneer, Soldier and Politician, p. 243

5 Lacour-Gayet: *South Africa,* p. 270

6 FMG, p. 178

7 *Ibid,* p. 187

8 Ibid, p. 184

9 Ibid, p. 177

10 Perham: *African Apprenticeship*, p. 159

11 FMG, p. 170

12 *Argus*, 14 Jan. 1926

13 *The Times*, 15 Nov. 1927

14 *Ibid*

15 Perham: *African Apprenticeship*, p. 171

16 *Argus*, 17 Jan. 1928

17 FMG, p. 184

18 *Ibid*, p. 188

19 Conv. with Lady May Abel Smith

20 Mrs Jean Watkins to the author

21 Mrs J. A. Blackmore to the author

22 Schapera: *Golden Days in Namaqualand* (excerpt from ms sent by Mrs M. Faiman)

23 FMG, p. 181

24 Wolhuter: *H.R.H. Princess Alice*

25 *Ibid*

26 FMG, p. 185

27 *Ibid*, p. 188

28 *Ibid*, p. 183

29 Lady Bailey to the author

30 *Ibid*

31 Mrs Emé de Villiers to the author

32 *The Times*, 17 April 1928

33 *Ibid*

34 *Ibid*

35 *Ibid*

36 FMG, p. 186

37 *Ibid*

38 *Ibid*

39 *Ibid*, p. 185

40 *Ibid*, p. 186

41 Letter from Princess Alice to Mrs İ. de Waal, 25 June 1977

42 *Cape Times*, 21 April 1928

43 *Ibid*

44 FMG, p. 187

45 *Ibid*

46 Nicolson: *King George V*, p. 554

47 FMG, p. 187

48 *Ibid*, p. 175

49 Sara: *The Earl of Athlone*, p. 218

50 *Argus*, 9 Feb. 1929

51 Lady Bailey to the author

52 *Argus*, 6 Nov. 1930

53 *Ibid*

54 *Cape Times*, 6 Nov. 1930

55 Argus, 6 Nov. 1930

56 Sara: *The Earl of Athlone*, p. 221

57 *Ibid*, p. 222

CHAPTER TWELVE

1 FMG, p. 188

2 Mrs C. Wintringham White to the author

3 FMG, p. 198

4 *Ibid*, p. 188

5 *Ibid*, p. 200

6 *Ibid,* p. 202

7 *Ibid*

8 Mellon: Princess Alice

9 FMG, p. 203

10 *Ibid,* pp. 206–9

11 *Ibid,* p. 209

12 *Sunday Graphic,* 25 Nov. 1953

13 Baden-Powell: *Window on my Heart,* p. 140

14 FMG, p. 211

15 *Ibid,* pp. 212–14

16 *Ibid,* pp. 218–21

17 Airlie: *Thatched with Gold,* p. 194

18 Frankland: *Henry, Duke of Gloucester,* p. 124

19 FMG, p. 222

20 *Ibid,* p. 223

CHAPTER THIRTEEN

1 FMG, p. 243

2 Viktoria Luise: The Kaiser's Daughter, pp. 171–8

3 Donaldson: *Edward VIII,* p. 198

4 FMG, p. 223

5 Viktoria Luise: The Kaiser's Daughter, p. 188

6 Donaldson: Edward VIII, p. 199

7 *Ibid*

8 Letter from Princess Alice to Dr van Rensburg, 15 April 1957

9 FMG, p. 223

10 Airlie: *Thatched with Gold,* p. 199

11 FMG, p. 223

12 Killearn, *Diaries,* p. 96

13 Conv. with Princess Alice

14 Conv. with Sir Shuldham Redfern

15 *The Times,* 8 Jan. 1937

16 FMG, p. 224

17 *Ibid,* p. 104

18 *Ibid,* p. 242

19 *Ibid,* p. 230

20 *Ibid,* p. 233

21 *Ibid,* p. 227

22 *Ibid,* p. 239

23 Quoted in Thompson: *Gwelo Goodman,* p. 118

24 FMG, p. 245

25 *Ibid,* p. 246

26 Sara: *The Earl of Athlone,* p. 247

27 FMG, p. 246

28 Cowan: *Canada's Governors-General,* p. 184

29 FMG, p. 247

30 *Ibid,* p. 249

CHAPTER FOURTEEN

1 FMG, p. 249

2 *Canadian Home Journal,* June 1940

3 *The Citizen,* Ottawa, 22 June 1940

4 Hubbard: Rideau Hall, p. 184

5 Ibid, p. 221

6 Ibid, p. 135

7 FMG, p. 250

8 *Ibid*

9 Hubbard: *Rideau Hall,* p. 163

10 *Ibid*

11 Conv. with Sir Shuldham Redfern

12 McNaught: *History of Canada,* p. 94

13 *Ibid,* p. 235

14 Hubbard: *Rideau Hall,* p. 159

15 Pearson: *Through Diplomacy,* p. 87

16 MKR, Vol 1, p. 146

17 FMG, p. 262

18 MKR, Vol 1, p. 146

19 *Ibid,* Vol 2, p. 415

20 FMG, p. 255

21 *Ibid,* p. 262

22 Conv. with Sir Shuldham Redfern

23 MKR, Vol 2, p. 414

24 Conv. with Lord Harewood

25 Cowan: *Canada's Governors-General,* pp. 191, 192

26 Massey: *What's Past is Prologue,* p. 330

27 Conv. with Sir Shuldham Redfern

28 Massey: *What's Past is Prologue,* p. 330

29 FMG, p. 251

30 *Ibid,* p. 252

31 Conv. with Sir Shuldham Redfern

32 *The Citizen,* 2 July 1966

33 Hubbard: *Rideau Hall,* p. 168

34 Conv. with Lord Harewood

35 Mr Neville Ussher to the author

36 Conv. with Lord Harewood

37 FMG, p. 251

38 Wilhelmina, Queen: *Lonely but not Alone,* p. 156

39 *Ibid*

40 FMG, p. 250

41 Wilhelmina, Queen: *Lonely but not Alone,* p. 184

42 FMG, p. 251

43 *Montreal Gazette,* 17 Jan. 1957

44 Mr Neville Ussher to the author

45 Cowan: *Canada's Governors-General,* pp 191, 192

46 Conv. with Sir Shuldham Redfern

47 *Ibid*

48 Hubbard: Rideau Hall, p. 202

49 *Echoes,* Autumn, 1945

50 MacDonald: *Titans and Others,* pp. 115, 116

51 Hubbard: *Rideau Hall,* p. 201

52 Hardwicke: *Victorian in Orbit,* p. 206

53 Mrs B. Evans to the author

54 FMG, p. 254

55 *Ibid,* p. 265

56 *Ibid*

57 Hubbard: *Rideau Hall,* p. 203

58 Wilhelmina, Queen: *Lonely but not Alone,* p. 187

59 FMG, p. 260

60 *Ibid,* p. 261

61 MKR, Vol I, p. 694

62 Conv. with Queen Elizabeth The Queen Mother

63 FMG, p. 255

64 *Ibid,* p. 253

65 *Ibid,* p. 263

CHAPTER FIFTEEN

1 FMG, p. 259

2 *Ibid,* p. 263

3 *Ibid,* p. 260

4 *Ibid,* p. 242

5 *Ibid,* p. 260

6 Ibid, p. 259

7 Ibid, p. 268

8 Conv. with Sir Shuldham Redfern

9 Mr Neville Ussher to the author

10 Mrs F. Dickson to the author

11 MKR, Vol I, p. 530

12 Conv. with Sir Shuldham Redfern

13 Mr R. Campbell Ross to the author

14 Conv. with Princess Alice, Duchess of Gloucester

15 FMG, p. 268

16 Conv. with Sir Shuldham Redfern

17 MKR, Vol I, p. 528

18 FMG, p. 267

19 MKR, Vol 2, p. 60

20 *Ibid,* pp. 87, 88

21 FMG, p. 261

22 Hutchison: *Mr Prime Minister,* p. 202

23 FMG, p. 254

24 Pearson: *Through diplomacy,* p. 224

25 *Ibid*

26 *Ibid,* p. 225

27 *Ibid,* p. 224

28 Mrs F Dickson to the author

29 FMG, p. 269
30 *Ibid*, p. 273
31 Mrs N. Lundy to the author
32 Mr Neville Ussher to the author
33 FMG, pp. 269, 270
34 *Echoes*, Autumn, 1945
35 *The Citizen*, 15 March 1946
36 *Ibid*
37 *Ibid*, 18 March 1946
38 FMG, p. 270
39 *The Citizen*, 18 March 1946

CHAPTER SIXTEEN

1 FMG, p. 274
2 Conv. with Sir Shuldham Redfern
3 FMG, p. 274
4 Ibid, p. 275
5 Conv. with Sir Shuldham Redfern
6 FMG, p. 273
7 Conv. with Miss Mary Goldie
8 FMG, p. 274
9 The Chancellor's Address 1952, U.C.W.I.
10 FMG, p. 275
11 *Ibid*, p. 281
12 Alexandra, Queen: *For a King's Love*, p. 163
13 *Ibid*
14 FMG, p. 282
15 *The Times*, 21 Jan. 1957 (Lord Beveridge)
16 FMG, p. 277

17 *Smuts Papers:* Letter to M.C. Gillet, p. 176

18 FMG, p. 278

19 Mrs Z. Pearce to the author

20 Mrs J. Digby to the author

21 FMG, p. 280

22 *Ibid*

23 *Ibid,* p. 279

24 *Ibid,* p. 281

25 *The Times,* 5 Aug. 1949

26 FMG, p. 1

27 *Ibid,* p. 283

28 *Ibid*

29 Huggins: *Too much to tell,* pp. 158, 159

30 *The Christmas Herald,* Kingston, Jamaica, Dec. 1950

31 Blackburne: *Lasting Legacy,* p. 171

32 KB, p. 4

33 Harold J. Ashwell to the author

34 *Daily Cleaner,* Kingston, 6 Jan. 1981

35 *The Advocate News,* Barbados, 6 Feb. 1969 (H. Phillips)

36 Sir Philip Sherlock to the author

37 *Ibid*

38 *Ibid*

39 FMG, p. 284

40 *Ibid*

41 Huggins: *Too much to Tell,* pp. 158, 159

42 Conv. with Mrs V. Heyliger

43 FMG, p. 284

44 Conv. with Mrs V. Heyliger

45 Harold J Ashwell to the author

46 Conv. with Mrs V. Heyliger

47 Chancellor's Address 1952

48 FMG, p. 284

49 *Ibid,* p. 285

50 *Ibid,* p. 104

51 *Evening Standard,* 21 Jan. 1955

52 Information given to the author

53 Conv. with Miss Mary Goldie

54 FMG, p. 293

55 Letter from Princess Alice to Gen. P. de Waal, 18 April 1954

56 *Ibid*

57 FMG, pp. 285, 293

58 Conv. with Queen Elizabeth The Queen Mother

59 Letter to Gen. P. de Waal

60 FMG, p. 293

61 *Ibid*

62 *Ibid*

63 Princess Alice to Mrs W. Forrest

CHAPTER SEVENTEEN

1 A.S.J. Fisher: *An Anthology of Prayers* (information supplied by Mrs M. Houghton)

2 FMG, p 292

3 *Evening Standard,* 1 April 1962

4 *Ibid,* 14 April 1962

5 *Sunday Express,* 25 April 1965

6 Mrs E Machanick to the author

7 FMG, p. 293

8 *Montreal Star,* 24 Aug. 1959

9 *Ibid*

10 *Ibid,* 28 Sept. 1959

11 *Ibid,* 24 Sept. 1959

12 Speaight, *Vanier,* p. 384

13 *Montreal Star,* 28 Sept. 1959

14 *Ibid,* 24 Sept. 1959

15 Conv. with Miss Joan Lascelles

16 KB, pp. 1–4

17 Blackburne: *Lasting Legacy,* p. 168

18 *Ibid*

19 KB, p. 3

20 H.J. Ashwell to the author

21 *Daily Gleaner,* 5 Jan. 1981

22 KB, p. 4

23 W.W. Wilson to the author

24 Mrs May Todd to the author

25 Sir Philip Sherlock to the author

26 Conv. with Queen Elizabeth The Queen Mother

27 Sir Philip Sherlock to the author

28 Mrs H. D. Tucker to the author

29 *Daily Telegraph,* 19 March 1964

30 Mrs J. Mackenzie-Elliot to the author

31 *Ibid*

32 Miss D Parsons to the author

33 *Ibid*

34 Mr D.W.F. Jellyman to the author

35 Miss D. Parsons to the author

36 *Evening Standard,* 8 Dec. 1956

37 Kensington Society, Annual Report

38 Conv. with Mrs G. Christiansen

39 *New York Times,* 25 Jan. 1978

40 *Daily Mirror,* 16 Oct. 1953

41 Conv.with Princess Alice, Duchess of Gloucester

42 FMG, p. 292

43 KB. p. 2

44 Mrs M. Williams to the author

45 Supplied by Mrs I. de Waal

46 KB, p. 2

47 Beaton: *Self Portrait with Friends,* p. 389

48 Conv. with Princess Alice, Duchess of Gloucester

49 Mrs A. Maddin to the author

50 FMG, p. 1

51 *Ibid,* p. 294

52 *Daily Gleaner,* 5 Jan. 1981

53 *Ibid*

54 Sir Philip Sherlock to the author

55 *Evening Standard,* 23 Feb. 1973

CHAPTER EIGHTEEN

1 Conv. with Miss Mary Goldie

2 *The Times,* 15 July 1977

3 Conv. with Princess Alice

4 Lady Bailey to the author

5 Mrs C Wintringham White to the author

6 Conv. with Queen Elizabeth The Queen Mother

7 Conv. with Princess Alice

8 *Montreal Star,* 24 Sept. 1959

9 Mrs Julia Ludwig to the author

10 Mrs I. de Waal to the author

11 Mrs Ailsa Stephens to the author

12 Mr R. Caradoc Davies to the author

13 Mrs M. Dalrymple to the author

14 William Manning, Bishop of George, to the author

15 *Ibid*

16 The Rev G.F. Davies to the author

17 Conv. with Princess Alice

18 *Ibid*

19 *Sunday Telegraph,* 4 Jan. 1981 (Kenneth Rose)

20 Mellon: *Princess Alice*

21 Conv. with Princess Alice

22 Letter from Princess Alice to the author

23 *Ibid*

24 FMG, p. 7

25 *Evening Standard,* 15 July 1977

26 Conv. with Princess Alice

27 *Sunday Telegraph,* 4 Jan. 1981 (Kenneth Rose)

28 *Ibid*

29 Conv. with Princess Alice

30 *Ibid*

31 *The Times,* 15 July 1977

32 Conv. with Miss Kathleen Murray

33 Conv. with Sir Shuldham Redfern

34 Conv. with Miss Joan Lascelles

35 *Ibid*

36 Conv. with Queen Elizabeth
   The Queen Mother

37 FMG, p. 285

38 *The Times,* 5 Jan. 1981

39 FMG, p. 2

40 Conv. with Sir Shuldham Redfern

SELECT BIBLIOGRAPHY

Adcock, St J. *The Prince of Wales's African Book.* Hodder & Stoughton, London, 1925.

Airlie, Mabel, Countess of. *Thatched with Gold.* Hutchinson, London, 1962.

Albert I, King of the Belgians. *The War Diaries of Albert I.* (ed. R. Van Overstraeten). William Kimber, London, 1954.

Alexandra of Yugoslavia, Queen. For A King's Love. Odhams Press, London, 1956.

Alice, H.R.H. Princess. *For My Grandchildren.* Evans Brothers, London, 1966.

Anon. *The Life of the Duke of Albany.* Crown Publishing Co., London, 1884.

Anon. *Some Letters from a Man of No Importance.* Cape, London, 1928.

Asquith, Margot. *Places and Persons.* Thornton Butterworth, London, 1925.

—— *More Memories.* Cassell, London, 1933.

Aston, Sir George. *H.R.H. The Duke of Connaught and Strathearn.* Harrap, London, 1929.

Baden-Powell, Olave. *Window on my Heart.* Hodder & Stoughton, London, 1973.

Balfour, Michael. *The Kaiser and His Times.* Cresset Press, London, 1964.

Beaton, Cecil. *Self Portrait with Friends.* (ed. Richard Buckle). Weidenfeld & Nicolson, London, 1979.

Bennett, Daphne. *Queen Victoria's Children.* Gollancz, London, 1980.

Bierme, Maria. *La Famille Royale de Belgique, 1900–1930.* Libraire Albert Deuit, Brussels, 1930.

Blackburne, Sir Kenneth. *Lasting Legacy.* Johnson, London, 1976.

Bullock, Rev. Charles (ed.) *Talks with the People by Men of Mark: H.R.H. Prince Leopold, Duke of Albany.* Home Words Publishing Office, London, 1882.

Byng of Vimy, Viscountess. *Up the Stream of Time.* Methuen, Toronto, 1945.

Cammaerts, Emile. *Albert, King of the Belgians.* Nicolson & Watson, London, 1935.

Carey, Agnes. *The Empress Eugénie in Exile.* Eveleigh Nash, London, 1922.

Carroll, Lewis. *Diaries.* 2 vols. Cassell, London, 1953.

Clifford, Sir Bede. *Proconsul.* Evans Brothers, London, 1964.

Collier, Joy. *Portrait of Cape Town.* Longman, Cape Town, 1961.

Cooke, C. Kinloch. *A Memoir of Princess Mary Adelaide, Duchess of Teck.* John Murray, London, 1900.

Cooper, Phyllis M. *The Story of Claremont.* West Brothers, London, 1956.

Cowan, John. *Canada's Governors-General.* York Publishing Co., Toronto, 1965.

Cust, Sir Lionel. *King Edward VII and his Court.* John Murray, London, 1930.

Disraeli, Benjamin. *Letters of Disraeli to Lady Bradford and Lady Chesterfield.* 2 vols. Ernest Benn, London, 1929.

Donaldson, Frances. *Edward VIII.* Weidenfeld & Nicolson, London, 1974.

Dubourg, Alain-Yves. *Royal Haemophilia.* Abbottempo Book 2. Abbott Universal Ltd., Amsterdam, 1967.

Dugdale, E.T.S. *Maurice de Bunsen.* John Murray, London. 1934.

Eeman, Harold. *Diplomatic Bag.* Robert Hale, London, 1980.

Epton, Nina. *Victoria and her Daughters.* Weidenfeld & Nicolson, London, 1971.

Erbach-Schonberg, Princess Marie zu. *Reminiscences.* Allen &Unwin, London, 1925.

Ernst II, Duke of Saxe-Coburg-Gotha. *Memoirs.*4 vols. Remington & Co., London, 1888–90.

Erskine, Mrs Steuart. *Twenty-nine Years: The Reign of King Alfonso XIII of Spain.* Hutchinson, London, 1931.

Fischer, Henry W. *The Private Lives of William II and His Consort.* Heinemann, London, 1905.

Fjellman, Margit. *Louise Mountbatten, Queen of Sweden.* Allen & Unwin, London, 1968.

Frankland, Noble. *Prince Henry, Duke of Gloucester.* Weidenfeld & Nicolson, London, 1980.

Galet, Emile Joseph. *Albert, King of the Belgians, in the Great War.* Putnams, New York, 1934.

Gore, John. *King George V.* John Murray, London, 1941.

Graham, Evelyn. *The Queen of Spain.* Hutchinson, London, 1929.

Graham, Evelyn. *The Life Story of King Alphonso XIII.* Herbert Jenkins, London, 1930.

Graham, Gerald S. *A Concise History of Canada.* Thames & Hudson, London, 1968.

Gutsche, Thelma. *No Ordinary Woman.* Howard Timmins, Cape Town, 1966.

Hamilton, Lord Frederic. *The Vanished World of Yesterday.* Hodder & Stoughton, London, 1950.

Hamilton, Gerald. *Blood Royal.* Anthony Gibb & Phillips, London, 1964.

Hardwicke, Sir Cedric. *A Victorian in Orbit.* Methuen, London, 1961.

Harris, Col. Sir David. *Pioneer, Soldier and Politician.* Central News Agency, Cape Town, 1931.

Hibbert, Christopher. *The Court of St James.* Weidenfeld & Nicolson, London, 1979.

Hough, Richard. *Louis and Victoria.* Hutchinson, London, 1974.

Howard, Philip. *The British Monarchy.* Hamish Hamilton, London, 1977.

Hubbard, R.H. *Rideau Hall.* McGill-Queens University Press, Montreal, 1977.

Huggins, Molly. *Too Much to Tell.* Heinemann, London, 1967.

Hutchison, Bruce. *Mr Prime Minister.* Longman, Canada, 1964.

Hyde, H. Montgomery. *Mexican Empire.* Macmillan, London, 1946.

Kennedy, A.L. *My Dear Duchess: Social and Political Letters to the Duchess of Manchester 1858–1869.* John Murray, London, 1956.

Killearn, Lord. *The Killearn Diaries.* Sidgwick & Jackson, London, 1972.

Knightly, Lady. *Journals.* John Murray, London, 1915.

Kruger, D.W. *The Age of the Generals.* Dagbreek, Johannesburg, 1958.

Lacour-Gayet, Robert. *A History of South Africa.* Cassell, London, 1970.

Longford, Elizabeth. *Victoria R.I.* Weidenfeld & Nicolson, London, 1964.

Louise, Princess of Schleswig-Holstein. *Behind the Scenes at the Prussian Court.* John Murray, London, 1934.

Lucas, Netley (pseud. Evelyn Graham). *Albert the Brave, King of the Belgians.* Hutchinson, London, 1934.

Lucas, Reginald. *Prince Francis of Teck.* A.L. Humphreys, London, 1910

MacDonald, Rt Hon Malcolm. *Titans and Others.* Collins, London, 1972.

McNaught, Kenneth. *The Pelican History of Canada.* Allen Lane, London, 1978.

Magnus, Philip. *King Edward the Seventh.* John Murray, London, 1964.

Mallet, Marie. *Life with Queen Victoria: Marie Mallet's Letters from the Court 1887–1901.* John Murray, London, 1968.

Marie Louise, Princess. *My Memories of Six Reigns.* Evans Brothers, London, 1956.

Marie of Romania, Queen. *The Story of My Life.* 3 vols. Cassell, London, 1934–5.

Marquard, Leo. *The Story of South Africa.* Faber, London, 1955.

Massey, Vincent. *What's Past is Prologue.* Macmillan, London, 1963.

Maxwell, Sir Herbert. *Sixty Years A Queen.* Eyre & Spottiswoode, London, 1897.

Milnes, Richard Monckton. *H.R.H. Prince Leopold, Duke of Albany. In Memoriam.* Miscellanies of the Philobiblon Society, vol. XV. C. Whittington, London, 1877–84.

Monet, Jacques. *The Canadian Crown.* Clarke, Irwin & Co., Toronto, 1979.

Nicolson, Harold. *King George V.* Constable, London, 1952.

Owen, Sidney Cunliffe. *Elisabeth, Queen of the Belgians.* Herbert Jenkins, London, 1954.

Paget, Lady Walburga. *Embassies of Other Days.* 2 vols. Hutchinson, London, 1923.

Paton, Alan. *Apartheid and the Archbishop.* David Philip, Cape Town, 1973

Pearson, Lester B. *Through Diplomacy to Politics.* Gollancz, London, 1973.

Perham, Margery. *African Apprenticeship.* Faber, London, 1974.

Pickersgill, J.W. *The Mackenzie King Record.* 4 vols. University of Toronto Press, 1960–70.

Pless, Daisy, Princess of. *Daisy, Princess of Pless.* John Murray, London, 1928.

Ponsonby, Arthur. *Henry Ponsonby: His Life and Letters.* Macmillan, London, 1942.

Ponsonby, Sir Frederick. *Recollections of three Reigns.* Eyre & Spottiswoode, London, 1951.

Pope-Hennessy, James. *Queen Mary.* Allen & Unwin, London, 1959.

Sara, M.E. *The Rt Hon the Earl of Athlone.* Stanley Paul, London, 1941.

Schoeman, K. *Bloemfontein.* Human & Rousseau, Cape Town, 1950.

Sewell, Lt-Col. J.P.C. *Personal Letters of King Edward VII.* Hutchinson, London, 1931.

Sharp, Ann. *Lewis Carroll: A Biography.* Dent, London, 1979.

Shirer, William L. *The Rise and Fall of the Third Reich.* Simon & Schuster, New York, 1960.

Sinclair, Andrew. *The Last of the Best.* Weidenfeld & Nicolson, London, 1967.

Smuts, Field-Marshal J. C. (ed. W.K. Hancock & Jean Van der Poel.) 7 vols. *Selections from the Smuts Papers.* Cambridge University Press, 1966–73.

Speaight, Robert. *Vanier.* Collins & Harvill Press, London, 1970.

Story, Norah. *The Oxford Companion to Canadian History and Literature.* Oxford University Press, 1967.

Thompson, Joyce Newton. *Gwelo Goodman, South African Artist.* Howard Timmins, Cape Town, 1951.

Troeller, Gary. *The Birth of Saudi Arabia.* Frank Cass, London, 1976.

Victoria, German Empress. (ed. A. Gould-Lee). *The Empress Frederick writes to Sophie.* Faber, London, 1955.

Victoria of Prussia, Princess. *My Memoirs.* Eveleigh Nash, London, 1929.

—— (ed. J. Pope-Hennessy). *Queen Victoria at Windsor and Balmoral.* Allen & Unwin, London, 1956.

Victoria, Queen. *The Letters of Queen Victoria: A selection from Her Majesty's Correspondence and Journal between the years 1886–1901.* John Murray, London, 1930.

—— (ed. Hector Bolitho). *Further Letters of Queen Victoria: From the*

Archives of the House of Brandenburg-Prussia. Thornton Butterworth, London, 1938.

—— (ed. Richard Hough). *Advice to a Granddaughter.* Heinemann, London, 1975.

—— (ed. Roger Fulford). *Darling Child: Private Correspondence of Queen Victoria and the Crown Princess of Prussia 1871–1878.* Evans Brothers, London, 1976.

Viktoria Luise, Princess of Prussia. The Kaiser's Daughter. W.H. Allen, London, 1977.

Ware, J. Redding (ed.). Life and Speeches of His Royal Highness Prince Leopold. Diprose & Bateman, London, 1884.

Warwick, Frances, Countess of. *Life's Ebb and Flow.* Hutchinson, London, 1929.

Wilhelm II, Emperor of Germany. *My Memoirs 1878–1918.* Cassell, London, 1922.

—— *My Early Life.* Methuen, London, 1926.

Wilhelmina, H.R.H Princess (trans. John Peereboom). *Lonely But Not Alone.* Hutchinson, London, 1960.

Woodham-Smith, Cecil. *Queen Victoria.* Hamish Hamilton, London, 1972.

NEWSPAPERS, MAGAZINES AND REFERENCE BOOKS

Daily Mirror; Daily Telegraph; Evening Standard; The Graphic; The Guardian; Household Brigade Magazine; Illustrated London News; London Gazette; London Figaro; The Observer; Sunday Express; Sunday Graphic; Sunday Telegraph; Sunday Times; The Times; Whitehall Review; Canadian Home Journal; The Citizen, Ottawa; *Montreal Gazette; Montreal Star; Vancouver Daily Province; The Argus, Cape* Town; *Cape Times,* Cape Town; *The Star,* Johannesburg; *Advocate News,* Jamaica; *Christmas Herald,* Jamaica; *Daily Gleaner,* Kingston, Jamaica; *Burke's Royal Families of the World.*

UNPUBLISHED SOURCES

Alice, H.R.H. Princess. Chancellor's Address 1952 (University of the West Indies)

Blackburne, Sir Kenneth. *Some happy recollections of H.R.H. Princess Alice, Countess of Athlone*

Dalrymple, Marcia. *H.R.H. Princess Alice, Countess of Athlone*

Dowling, Eska. *Memorandum on H.R.H. Princess Alice, first President of the S.A. National Council for Child Welfare*

Ludwig, Julia. *H.R.H. Princess Alice visits Durban*

Mellon, Dr Matthew. *The Princess Alice*

Schapera, Abe. *Golden Days in Namaqualand*

Sherlock, Sir Philip. *H.R.H. Princess Alice and the University of the West Indies*

Victoria, Queen. *The Journals of Queen Victoria* (Royal Archives)

Wolhuter, S.G. *H.R.H. Princess Alice*

20504382R00331

Made in the USA
Middletown, DE
28 May 2015